To Roy and Fiona

Michael 19th October
2012

The *Journey's End* Battalion

9th East Surrey in the Great War

Michael Lucas

Pen & Sword
MILITARY

First published in Great Britain in 2012 by
PEN & SWORD MILITARY
An imprint of
Pen & Sword Books Ltd
47 Church Street
Barnsley
South Yorkshire
S70 2AS

ISBN 978-1-84884-503-9

Typeset by Concept, Huddersfield, West Yorkshire.
Printed and bound in England by CPI Group (UK) Ltd, Croydon, CR0 4YY.

Pen & Sword Books Ltd incorporates the imprints of Pen & Sword Aviation,
Pen & Sword Family History, Pen & Sword Maritime, Pen & Sword Military,
Pen & Sword Discovery, Wharncliffe Local History, Wharncliffe True Crime,
Wharncliffe Transport, Pen & Sword Select, Pen & Sword Military Classics,
Leo Cooper, The Praetorian Press, Remember When, Seaforth Publishing and
Frontline Publishing.

For a complete list of Pen & Sword titles please contact
PEN & SWORD BOOKS LIMITED
47 Church Street, Barnsley, South Yorkshire, S70 2AS, England
E-mail: enquiries@pen-and-sword.co.uk
Website: www.pen-and-sword.co.uk

Contents

Preface vii
Author's Note ix
Acknowledgements xi

Part I. From Sussex to the Somme, August 1914–September 1916 . . 1
1. Call to Arms, August 1914–August 1915 3
2. Loos, September 1915 10
3. Recovery, October 1915–March 1916 25
4. Wulverghem, March–July 1916 39
5. Somme-Guillemont and Delville Wood, August–September 1916 48

Part II. Through Attrition to Final Victory, September 1916–
  November 1918 69
6. Return to Loos, September–December 1916 71
7. A Hard Winter, January–April 1917 81
8. Messines and Pilckem Ridge, April–September 1917 99
9. Before the Storm, September 1917–February 1918 112
10. *Kaiserschlacht*, March 1918 120
11. Holding the Line, April–September 1918 143
12. Advance to Victory, October–11 November 1918 151

Part III. Reflections 161
13. 9th Battalion East Surrey Regiment in Review 163
14. After the Armistice 172
15. R.C. Sherriff's *Journey's End* 181
16. The Last of the 'Gallants' 187

Appendix I: Roll of Honour 190
Appendix II: 9/East Surrey Fatalities by Month 211
Appendix III: Awards and Decorations 212
Appendix IV: Officers Serving Abroad with 9/East Surrey, 1915–1918 216
Appendix V: 24th Division Orders of Battle, 1915–1918 225

Appendix VI: Orders for a Raid, 24/25 July 1918 226
Notes 228
Bibliography 238
Index 242

Preface

When I started to research 9th Battalion East Surrey Regiment in 2005, I was unaware of its link to R.C. Sherriff and his famous play *Journey's End*. My mother had started my particular interest in this unit by telling me of a long-dead great uncle who had served with it, as a private soldier, for three years on the Western Front.

Finding out that Sherriff had also served with this battalion, I sought out his autobiography *No Leading Lady*. I was very surprised and disappointed, however, to find that although this says much about the writing of *Journey's End*, it only begins with his life after the First World War. I was already researching in the regimental archives at Surrey History Centre, so it was a happy coincidence when I found that it also held the voluminous unpublished letters and papers of R.C. Sherriff. I gradually uncovered exactly what had happened to him and possible reasons for his later reticence. Along the way, I found that a number of statements made, over the years, by others about Sherriff are wrong, whether relating to his family, his period of front-line service or his wounds.

This book is not intended to be simply a day by day narrative history of the battalion. Such a one appeared, in brief, very soon after the First World War, as part of a wider *History of the East Surrey Regiment*. It was written by H.W. Pearse and H.S. Sloman, two senior regular officers, neither of whom had served with the battalion. They relied heavily on the battalion's war diary, supplemented with input from some survivors. As a consequence, whilst their book has its strengths, there is a lack of context for the modern reader and controversial matters are avoided. A number of sources for the battalion's history were also not available to the original authors then, even if they had wished to use them. These include, in particular, Sherriff's letters and other writings, and the diaries of Sergeant Billman and Captain Pirie, along with those of men serving in other units of 24th Division; and surviving Army personnel records.

What I have aimed to provide is a battalion history that considers the context of events; makes the widest possible use of available sources; and attempts to examine some of the issues that Pearse and Sloman felt it unnecessary to address, or chose to avoid addressing, or did not have the space to include. I have endeavoured to give particular attention not only to the 'big events' in the history of the battalion; but also to the time that Sherriff was serving with it, for most of which Pearse and Sloman pass over only briefly. At the same time, I have tried to convey something of the experience of serving with this unit, both in and out of the front line. I have also sought to determine how the battalion changed over time, in terms of its make-up, its leadership and its effectiveness.

Sherriff was profoundly influenced by his time with the battalion, with which he saw all his front-line service. I have endeavoured to clarify his experiences and his reactions to them. Many of the characters and situations in *Journey's End* can be directly linked to these experiences and I have considered these in a separate chapter. Sherriff should not, however, be assumed to be either a typical soldier of the time, nor even a typical officer.

Through my son Andrew this book aims to break new ground in British First World War unit histories by considering, wherever possible, the perspective of the German units facing 9/East Surrey. Inspired by the work of Jack Sheldon, Andrew has, with much industry, identified these units and translated German material, principally from regimental histories. In a number of cases this has made it possible to give accounts of the same incidents from both sides of no-man's-land.

No writer can be free of the attitudes and prejudices of their own time, but I have tried to avoid imposing those of the present on 1914 to 1918. The past truly is 'a foreign country', where things were done differently and for reasons that seemed to make good sense at the time. It is easy to be appalled by the sufferings of the battalion at the hands of plans made by higher authority, most especially at Loos. Warfare is, however, never easy. At that time it was particularly difficult, as British commanders were pushed into premature offensives against the most powerful and professional army of that era, in order to support Britain's allies. Those commanders, their allies and their enemies were also struggling to learn how to wage a new kind of warfare on the Western Front, with innovative and ever more deadly weapons, but essentially primitive battlefield communications. As these pages will show, the mistakes, failures and hardships were not all on one side.

I have tried to bear in mind two different audiences, in particular. There are those with a particular interest in the First World War, who may be interested in a history of a 'Kitchener' battalion from south-east England, when modern histories generally relate to regulars, 'Pals' units from northern England or predominantly middle-class London Territorial units. There are others who may be drawn to the book simply because of their interest in *Journey's End*. I hope that there is not too much explanation of some matters for one audience, and too little for the other.

Michael Lucas
Birchington
February 2012

Author's Note

British Army Unit Nomenclature and Abbreviations

Infantry regiments had titles that were usually territorially related to their recruitment area (sometimes with additional honorific titles), rather than numbers, and battalions were numbered within the regiment. However, regimental seniority, which was extensively used, from seniority within brigades to the filing of records, was based on the old regimental numbers used up to 1881 (e.g. The East Surrey Regiment was thirty-first in seniority). I have used the basic title, in an abbreviated form, and battalion number to identify units, e.g. 8/R West Kent for the 8th Battalion Queen's Own (Royal West Kent Regiment). The separate rifle companies within a battalion were given letters, normally A, B, C, D.

Infantry brigades and divisions (except the Guards) were given Arabic numbers – originally brigades were numbered consecutively through the divisions. In this book British brigades are denoted by cardinal numbers, e.g. 72 Brigade. Cavalry regiments retained numbers and their brigades and divisions were numbered separately from the infantry.

German Army Unit Nomenclature and Abbreviations

This requires more explanation, as the system is more complex and less familiar to most readers.

Units could have a number, a territorial title and an honorific title, although not all had. For example, Infantry Regiment 105 was also the 6th Royal Saxon Infantry Regiment and had the honorific title *König Wilhelm von Württemberg*. Units had numbers to denote their seniority within the Prussian Army, within their branch of service. The only groups outside this were the Prussian Guard and the semi-autonomous Bavarian Army, which had their own numbering. (Units of the semi-autonomous Saxon and Wurttemberg armies were included in the Prussian sequence. This meant that, for example, Saxon units with a history dating back more than 200 years had higher numbers than much younger units of Prussian origin.)

Within the infantry, with the exceptions referred to, all were numbered within a single sequence, running from 1 to 182 for the 'active' regiments' extent in peacetime. The new 'active' regiments formed in wartime were numbered from 183 upwards and almost always lacked any special titles. Reserve (and *Landwehr*) regiments, however, were numbered separately. In the infantry, they received either the same number as an existing 'active' regiment from the same corps district, or else an entirely new number not duplicated in the 'active' sequence.

To keep things simple, the abbreviated title, only, is used, based on the German Army's abbreviated forms:

FR – fusilier regiment;
FAR – field artillery regiment;
Fs AR – foot (i.e. heavy) artillery regiment;
GR – grenadier regiment;
IR – infantry regiment;
JägB – jäger battalion;
JägR – jäger regiment;
LGR – life (guard) grenadier regiment;
RJägB – reserve jäger battalion;
RIR – reserve infantry regiment;
SR – Schützen (rifle) regiment.

Within the infantry regiment, of three battalions, each battalion was denoted by a Roman numeral. The four rifle companies in each were given Arabic numerals that ran in a common sequence, e.g. 5 Company was always in II Battalion. Machine-gun companies (MGK) were numbered separately, with the number corresponding to its parent battalion.

As for higher formations, to differentiate clearly between British and German divisions (and again the Germans numbered their Prussian Guard, Bavarian, Jäger, Naval, Reserve, Ersatz and Landwehr divisions separately from the regular infantry divisions), I have given the British ordinal numbers and the Germans cardinal. Thus, e.g. 24th Division is British and 123 Division is German. I have retained Roman cardinal numbers for the corps of both armies, as there is less likelihood of confusion.

N.B. The above conventions are not always followed in original maps copied for this book and quotations from original sources.

Place Names in France and Belgium

For place names in these two countries I have followed the spellings familiar to the British Army in 1914–1918. Whilst there has been little change in French place names, many places in Belgian Flanders are now known by their Flemish language names.

Spelling, Grammar, Abbreviations and Punctuation in Original Sources

These have not been altered, where quoted, to fit in with the rest of the text, even if incorrect by the standards of the time. Where it has been necessary to insert additional words – in place of illegible ones or otherwise to make sense – these have been placed within square brackets. Only where errors in the original text appear particularly gross have I put *sic* in square brackets.

Acknowledgements

My greatest debt is to my wife, Ann, for her love and patience. Much of this book was written during, and whilst recovering from, serious ill-health, and I owe much to the NHS staff of East Kent. I am indebted to my son, Andrew, in particular for assistance in identifying, locating and translating numerous German sources, and for advice on all matters pertaining to the Kaiser's army. All the translations from German are Andrew's, with some assistance from Diana Zachau, except for those from books published in English. Andrew has also provided assistance with illustrations. Ann, amongst much other help, produced the diagram for Appendix II.

I am very grateful to Jon Cooksey, editor of *Stand To!*, the journal of the Western Front Association, for publishing my articles on 9/East Surrey and officer records in that publication and for introducing me to my publisher. Much of the material that first appeared in those articles has been updated and reworked with Jon's agreement for this book. My editor, Rupert Harding of Pen & Sword, has been very encouraging and helpful in seeing the book through to publication. Thanks are also due to my subeditor Alison Miles.

I have been grateful, over many visits, for help from the staff of a number of archives and libraries, notably the Imperial War Museum, Kent Libraries, Surrey History Centre (SHC) (especially Di Stiff) and The National Archives.

I am particularly grateful to the family of Captain G.S. Pirie, for so generously giving me a copy of his diary; and Jürgen Schmieschek for providing much German material. For information and/or photographs relating to particular individuals I am indebted to: Dr David Brooke on 'Syd' Hannan, Keith Perry on H.V.M. de la Fontaine, David Seymour on George Rivers, Felicity Williams on Godfrey Warre-Dymond, and Terry Woodbury on Charles Woodbury. For general information I am grateful to Ian Chatfield of the Queen's Royal Surrey Regiment Museum, Ron Clifton, Taff Gillingham and Dr Eric Webb and to Paul Reed for a photograph.

For permission to quote extensively from copyright published material, to quote from unpublished copyright material and/or reproduce copyright material I am grateful to the following: the family of the late A.J. Abraham for his memoir held in the Imperial War Museum (IWM); the Brotherton Library, University of Leeds for Peter Liddle's interview of Major General L.C. Thomas; Philippa Anne Clegg for the papers of Major T.H. Westmacott held at IWM; Jon Cooksey for extensive quotation from 'Jimmy Carpenter's War Diary', published in *Stand To!*; Curtis

Brown Group Ltd London on behalf of the estate of R.C. Sherriff, Kingston Grammar School and the Scout Association for unpublished letters and papers held at SHC, *Journey's End*, the novel, published 1930, 'My Diary' in the *Journal of the East Surrey Regiment*, published 1936–1939, *No Leading Lady*, published 1968, 'The English Public Schools in the Great War' in G. Panichas's *Promise of Greatness: The War of 1914–1918*, published 1968; the Trustees of IWM for photographs from its collection, the diaries of F.W. Billman and the oral history recording of C.F. Miller; Kingston Grammar School, additionally, for photographs from R.C. Sherriff's collection held at SHC; Nigel Lillywhite for the papers of his father, Colonel G. Lillywhite, OBE, TD, held at IWM; the Queen's Royal Surrey Regiment Museum and Surrey History Centre for the regiment's newsletter and papers and photographs from the regimental collection held in the care of SHC; the family of Captain G.S. Pirie for his writings and photographs; Jürgen Schmieschek for photographs from his collection; Timothy d'Arch Smith for Gilbert Frankau's *Peter Jackson, Cigar Merchant*, published 1947; The National Archives (UK) for numerous official documents in its care; Rupert Tower for the memoir by his grandfather, Lieutenant Colonel K.F.B. Tower, MC, held at IWM; Felicity Williams for the letter from Captain G.W. Warre-Dymond in the Sherriff papers at SHC.

Wherever I have used information provided by families, I hope they will consider I have treated their ancestor fairly.

Despite my best endeavours, I have not managed to trace all copyright holders. I apologise to them. If they will contact me through my publishers, I shall be delighted to ensure appropriate acknowledgement in any future edition of this book.

The maps and illustrations in the text are taken from the following sources:

Anon. *The History of the Eighth Battalion The Queen's Own Royal West Kent Regiment 1914–19* (London and Aylesbury, 1921): p. 230; F. Behrmann, *Die Osterschlacht bei Arras 1917, 1. Teil: Zwischen Lens und Scarpe* (Oldenburg and Berlin, 1929): pp. 87, 91; Sir J.E. Edmonds, *History of the Great War Military Operations France and Belgium: 1915 Volume II The Battles of Festubert, Aubers Ridge and Loos* (London, 1928): pp. 16, 18; Sir J.E. Edmonds, *History of the Great War Military Operations France and Belgium: 1916 Volume I Sir Douglas Haig's command to the 1st July: Battle of the Somme* (London, 1932): p. 41; Sir J.E. Edmonds, *History of the Great War Military Operations France and Belgium: 1917 Volume II 7th June–10th November: Messines and Third Ypres (Passchendaele)* (London, 1948): p. 105; Sir J.E. Edmonds, *History of the Great War Military Operations France and Belgium: 1918 Volume I The German March offensive and its preliminaries* (London, 1935, with accompanying appendices volume and map case): pp. 124, 129, 131, 134, 136, 138; E. Gruson, *Das Königlich Preussische 4. Thüringische Infanterie-Regiment Nr. 72 im Weltkrieg* (Oldenburg, 1930): p. 76; A. Huttmann and W. Krueger, *Das Infanterie Regiment von Lutzow (1. Rhein.) Nr. 25 im Weltkrieg 1914–18* (Berlin, 1929): p. 153; Captain W. Miles, *The History of the Great War Military Operations France and Belgium 1916 Volume II 2nd July 1916 to the end of the Battle of the Somme* (London, 1938): pp. 60, 62; L. Orgeldinger, *Das Württembergische Reserve-Infanterie-Regiment Nr. 246* (Stuttgart, 1931): p. 34; K. Otto, *Das Kgl. Sächs. Feldartillerie-Regiment Nr. 246* (Dresden, 1928): p. 30; H.W. Pearse and H.S. Sloman, *History of the East Surrey Regiment*, Vol. II (London, 1924): pp. 27, 55; Surrey History Centre: p. 116 (ref. ESR 19/1/5), p. 173 (ref. ESR 19/1/6).

Part I
From Sussex to the Somme,
August 1914–September 1916

Chapter 1

Call to Arms,
August 1914–August 1915

With the assassination of the Austrian Archduke Franz Ferdinand and his wife on 28 June 1914 and Austria-Hungary's declaration of war on Serbia, the great powers of Europe mobilised in succession. Germany's violation of Belgian neutrality, to assist its attack on France, led directly to a British ultimatum. When this expired, at 11.00pm on 4 August, Britain was at war.

Whilst war with Germany was by no means unexpected, particularly with the recent naval arms race, British governments had done little to prepare the country, or its army, for war with a first-class power on the European Continent. Although the British Army, reformed in the light of hard lessons from the Boer War, was now well trained and equipped and also fully prepared to launch an expeditionary force, it could not compare in size with the armies of the great Continental powers. The German Army had a peacetime strength of 700,000. On mobilisation it could be quickly expanded with trained and equipped reserves to 3,800,000 men. By comparison, the British regular Army was only around 250,000 strong. Moreover, much of the Army was serving abroad in Imperial garrisons. Its reserves were modest at around 210,000. Beyond these stood only the Territorial Army at around 270,000 strong, which was committed to home defence. Whilst some had argued conscription was essential, this was seen as politically unacceptable to public opinion.

Many, even amongst military professionals, expected the war to be a short one, like Prussia's brief and decisive campaigns of 1866 against Austria and 1870–1871 against France. Britain's new Secretary for War, Lord Kitchener, did not agree. He believed the war would be a long one and would require Britain to raise, equip and train numbers many times larger than its regular Army. Immediately he asked Parliament to authorise an additional 500,000 men for the Army. With much of the regular Army already committed in France, Kitchener appealed for 100,000 volunteers. Within two weeks the target number was reached, providing the First Kitchener Army, or K1, and further appeals followed, allowing the raising of further Kitchener Armies. Men enlisted from a variety of motives, including patriotism, a sense of adventure, social pressure and economic hardship.

Rather than use the Territorial Army as an instrument for expansion, Kitchener relied principally on raising 'service battalions', directly linked to regular regiments. He seems to have distrusted the Territorials, run by local associations.

Moreover, Territorials were raised for home defence, with no obligation to serve abroad. Men in Kitchener's new units were to serve for three years or the duration of the war and be liable for service anywhere.

The East Surrey Regiment was one of sixty-eight regiments of infantry of the line, which were vastly expanded to provide a mass army. The regiment had been created like most others in 1881, with the amalgamation of existing regiments (in this case the 31st and 70th) and linked to a specific county, to encourage local recruitment. With its proximity to the capital, however, the regiment was also able to draw many recruits from London.

Like other regiments, the East Surrey had a rich vein of tradition, over more than 200 years of campaigning, which was inculcated into its recruits. The 31st had distinguished itself at Dettingen in 1743 against the French. There King George II had mistaken it for the Buffs, one of the oldest and most distinguished of regiments, and gave it the nickname of 'The Young Buffs'. It shared Surrey with the Queen's Royal Regiment, the most venerable of English regiments of the line, so that both regiments liked to refer to its rival as 'the other Surrey regiment'.

At the outbreak of war, the East Surrey Regiment had six battalions: 1st and 2nd were regular, 3rd was the Reserve, 4th Extra Reserve and 5th and 6th Territorials. The regimental depot was at Kingston upon Thames. During the course of the war, each Territorial battalion raised two more. In addition, eight service or reserve battalions were raised. Of these eighteen battalions, nine saw active service overseas.

Big recruitment meetings were held in Surrey and London, as elsewhere, and prominent local citizens and officers of the regiment appealed for recruits. Initially, recruits were clothed and equipped at the depot, but their numbers soon outran accommodation and uniforms and equipment, as the government had not made contingency arrangements before the war. Soon recruits had to be sent on to the battalions, within 24 hours, with neither uniforms nor equipment.

9th Battalion, East Surrey Regiment (9/East Surrey) was created as part of Kitchener's Third Army, at Shoreham, Sussex, in September 1914. Major R.H. Baldwin, recently returned from duty in West Africa, was given command. By 19 September, the unit was over 1,000 strong. The ranks held many old soldiers, but 300 were soon drawn off to reinforce 1/East Surrey, which had suffered heavy losses serving with the British Expeditionary Force (BEF).

R.C. Sherriff, who served with the battalion from October 1916, described the men of the original unit as a 'mixed crowd' and 'East End dock labourers, navvies, lawyers, coalmen, shopmen, hawkers, police, burglars – I don't think there was a trade in London went unrepresented.'[1] Although many had left the battalion by the time he joined, Sherriff's description seems apt.

Looking at the first 100 of the unit's other ranks (ORs) fatalities, and assuming these were typical of the original battalion, it is possible, using Anon., *Soldiers Died in the Great War 1914–19 Part 36 The East Surrey Regiment* (London, 1920), to arrive at statistical conclusions as to likely place of residence, although not occupation. Where, as in most cases, no place of residence is shown, I have relied on place of enlistment. Place of birth can be misleading in view of the considerable migration into London at the time. The results are:

Surrey	53%
London	29%
Middlesex	10%
Midlands	3%
South Central	2%
North	1%
East Anglia	1%
Kent	1%
Total	100%

'London' at this time means the County of London – a much smaller area than the later Greater London. Surrey and Middlesex included much of what is now considered suburban London.

Gilbert Frankau, later to achieve some eminence as a novelist, wrote in fictionalised form about his experiences as an officer in the battalion, in *Peter Jackson, Cigar Merchant* and, very briefly, in his autobiography, *Self Portrait*. The regimental journal says his 'Peter Jackson records so much of the Battalion's experiences during the early days of its career.'[2] Thus, his fiction has credibility as an account of the battalion's early history. He emphasises that the men of the battalion were overwhelmingly Londoners of one kind or another.

Taking all this evidence together, it would be fair to describe the 9/East Surrey ORs in 1914–1915, as largely from Greater London and predominantly working class. If not born in London, they had moved there, or worked there. Sherriff, again in 1916, saw them as 'a tough regiment'.[3] A recruit in 1917 was taken aback by his experiences at the regiment's depot at Kingston, with rough characters, terrible food and no cutlery provided. He managed to move to the London Rifle Brigade, a middle-class Territorial unit in which he was very happy. Unlike the East Surrey, it had 'all clerks and people in the drapery trade' and 'No rough characters whatsoever'.[4]

Traditionally, British Army officers came almost exclusively from the aristocracy and upper middle classes. Many came from service families. Pre-war, pay for junior officers was generally insufficient, so some private income was necessary. Except for quartermasters and riding masters, traditionally promoted from NCOs, only 2 per cent of officers were promoted from the ranks.

By late 1914, there was a desperate shortage of officers trained in and experienced in modern warfare. The great majority of regular officers were with the BEF, with many becoming casualties. Very few were left for Kitchener's Third Army. Where were the officers required to come from? A number of officers were brought out of retirement. Unfortunately, many had been long retired or had served only with the Territorials, and/or its predecessor, the Militia, and were unkindly called 'dugouts'. As for the junior officers, it was considered in April

1915 that these required adequate military knowledge; a public-school education or the equivalent; and normally to be aged no more than 27.[5] The obvious answer to the Army was to appoint to temporary commissions those who had been to public schools and with Officer Training Corps (OTC) experience. The Army did not expect to teach leadership or motivation and the public-school virtues of patriotism, self-sacrifice and athleticism were seen as those required for officers. Besides public school and OTC men, there was also a preference for men who had served abroad in responsible positions, whether civilian or military. Either way, those appointed would then have to learn the necessary skills as they went along, as there was, at first, no formal training for temporary officers.

Let us consider the results for 9/East Surrey for September 1915, using the official *Army List* and surviving War Office files for some individual officers in The National Archives (TNA). Both the commanding officer (CO), Sanders, and his second in command, Major Welch, were former Militia officers, who had retired in 1910 and 1905 respectively. Captain Fenwick, a barrister, appears to have no previous military experience beyond cadets at Harrow and a brief period in the ranks of the Artists' Rifles from August 1914. Captain Barnett was a mining engineer who had served three years in the Cape Mounted Rifles in the Boer War, before enlisting in the ranks in September 1914. Lieutenant Birt was the managing director of a shipping company, but his only military experience seems to have been gained with Harrow OTC. Lieutenant Elverson had had two years in Cambridge University's OTC. Second Lieutenant Whiteman, a clerk, had been in the OTC at St Paul's School and had served in the ranks of the Surrey Yeomanry since 1911. By the time the battalion reached the Front, possibly the only one of its officers who had been trained as a regular was the Adjutant, Captain O'Connor. (Major Bretell, formerly of 1/East Surrey, left 9/East Surrey, on promotion, in mid-September 1915.) O'Connor, the son of a doctor, had attended Sandhurst and been commissioned in the East Surrey Regiment in 1910. He had, however, resigned for financial reasons after eighteen months, and had since endeavoured to make a living as a tea planter and then as a Sub Inspector in the Fiji Police.[6] Even at this early date, it should be noted that the *Army List* is not an accurate list of officers serving with the battalion. For example, Second Lieutenant Tetley is included in it for July 1915, but did not join the battalion, from 10/East Surrey, until October.

The battalion's Adjutant from September 1914 to June 1915 had been Captain Saville-Farr, who seems to been a divisive character, but one who had the confidence of Baldwin the CO. A civilian engineer and signals specialist, he had served during the Boxer Rebellion in China and later in the Militia. Gilbert Frankau, in *Peter Jackson, Cigar Merchant*, has his adjutant character, 'Locksley-Jones', a thoroughly obnoxious man. Amongst other faults, he abuses his position to advance the promotion of friends at the expense of others. Eventually, with regard to Saville-Farr, Frankau 'Intimated to our colonel that one of us must go, because I would not obey the order of a Territorial, who had refused to volunteer for active service.' Matters were only resolved by Frankau obtaining a transfer to the Royal Field Artillery (RFA) of 24th Division in early 1915. Frankau wrote that with one solitary exception all the soldier characters in his novel were composites and purely fictitious. The solitary exception 'died before he could bring his threatened libel case'.[7] Saville-Farr never served on the Western Front, but in Africa from 1916. Frankau's novel appeared in 1919 and Saville-Farr died three or four years later.[8]

Within the Third Kitchener Army, 9/East Surrey was allocated to 24th Division, Each division had an establishment of around 18,000 men. There were twelve infantry battalions, divided between three brigades. Various changes were made during the course of the war, but the 1914 battalion establishment was 1,007, including 30 officers. Each battalion had 4 companies, each 227 strong, including 6 officers. Each company was divided into 4 platoons, each of 4 sections. Battalion HQ included the CO and his staff, signallers, the medical officer and his men, horse transport drivers and pioneers. There was also a machine-gun section with two Vickers guns. In addition to its infantry, each division had its own artillery, engineers, supply column and field ambulances. A pioneer infantry battalion was added in 1915. German divisions were of broadly similar strength, in men, artillery and machine guns. However, in 1914, a German division had its 12 battalions in 2 brigades each of 2 regiments.

The infantry of 24th Division were almost all from south-east England and East Anglia. 9/East Surrey was in 72 Brigade with 8th Queen's (Royal West Surrey) (8/Queen's), 8th Buffs (East Kent) (8/Buffs) and 8th Queen's Own (Royal West Kent) (8/R West Kent). They were commanded by Brigadier General B.R. Mitford, formerly of the Buffs. Born in 1863, he had much active service experience in the Sudan and South Africa. He had retired as a Brigadier General in 1910. Major General Sir John Ramsay, a retired Indian Army officer, aged 57, commanded the division. Ramsay had had a worthy career fighting the Afghans, tribesmen and the Chinese.

The early days of the battalion, in autumn 1914, were clearly chaotic, with experienced officers and NCOs in short supply and enormous shortages of almost everything needed to clothe, equip and arm the unit. Although there were sufficient tents and cooking pots, there were insufficient blankets. Even after an appeal to local civilians, there were only enough for one per man. The camp lay on the Downs above Shoreham and the weather, initially good, turned cold and frosty at night. As for the training, Private Jimmy Carpenter of 8/Buffs recalled drill, lectures, physical training and route marches.[9]

With no uniforms, initially the men had to wear their civilian clothes. Private Fred Billman, a Norfolk-born gardener, who had enlisted on 15 September, wrote eight days later 'Shall try and get up to London one of these weekends when we get our uniform.'[10] A letter from a neighbouring battalion, published in November, refers to the East Surrey men in scarlet uniforms (presumably old full dress or undress jackets). It is not clear if there were enough for all.[11] Be that as it may, in a Christmas 1914 photograph Billman is wearing what appears to be the emergency blue-serge uniform, with side cap, widely distributed to Kitchener units.[12] It was very unpopular with the men, who considered it unmilitary: 'our convict garb', as Carpenter called it.[13]

Rain turned the Shoreham campsite into a bog. Carpenter described it as 'a quagmire of flowing mud. We had mud for meals, and we slept in it. It flowed round and inside our tents and we were soon in a very muddy state. It was over our ankles, so that we could do very few parades, and spent our time in having lectures and playing cards.'[14] Frankau pays tribute to the endurance of the troops then and later:

> Men of the people: uneducated, unwashed, foulmouthed; our 'proletariat', product of shop and board school, of mill and mine, of farm and factory: those men who came voluntarily from all the earth, waving no flags, moved only by that dumb, blind British spirit which has made and unmade kings since the beginning of time – how shall one write of these?
>
> They had, in those early days, few leaders and less equipment. They trained, grotesquely, with blocks of rough wood hewn to the semblance of a rifle. They were herded ... together, in leaking tents with never a floorboard between their one blanket and the mud below. They were flung out into our towns in suits of sloppy blue ... They had scarcely any leave. Their wives and children starved because their separation allowances were not paid. Their own food was cooked, weather permitting, in shallow trenches on the bare ground ...
>
> And when the sodden camps chosen for them stood two feet deep in greasy slime, when neither their single blankets nor their single suits could be dried ...
>
> Till gradually that first fine enthusiasm which made them trainable even by the untrained, oozed from their souls – even as the mud oozed up from the ground on which they slept – till all the keenness evaporated; leaving nothing save the dour, stark spirit of Great Britain to carry them on ...
>
> And as, in mud and muddle and incompetence, these early volunteers began their soldiering; so in blood and incompetence and disaster, most of them ended it. Yet though they grumbled, they never weakened; though the song died on their lips and the jest from their eyes, neither their hearts nor their limbs flinched from the tasks appointed.[15]

At the end of November, the battalion moved into billets at Worthing. The men were kindly received by the local people. Indeed, at least one soldier found romance. Private 'Teddy' Cutt, who had enlisted in September 1914, aged 18, was billeted at Broadwater, near Worthing with the Dabbs family. Nellie, their school-teacher daughter, and 'Teddy' became sweethearts.[16]

Training proceeded over the winter, to the extent that equipment shortages allowed. 8/R West Kent recorded that initially they had only a few imitation rifles, then six 'Drill purpose only' rifles per company. A full issue of such 'weapons' was made to that battalion in December, and miniature rifle ranges were used for musketry training over the winter.[17] Frankau mentions the use of old Lee–Metford rifles at this time in his novel.[18]

At the beginning of April the brigade moved to Redhill and Reigate in Surrey to build trenches as part of the outer defences of London. Colonel Baldwin moved to 7/East Surrey and Major Sanders, the second in command, a retired Militia officer, took over command.

On 19 April the battalion returned to Shoreham, where the whole division was concentrated. It was accommodated in newly built, but incomplete huts on its old campsite, before moving to Blackdown Camp, near Aldershot in June. Here, it seems, the brigade received its service rifles at last and as much training as possible was devoted to their use.

After an inspection of the division by Lord Kitchener, the main body of the battalion embarked from Folkestone for Boulogne on 31 August 1915, whilst the transport had travelled via Southampton to Le Havre. A French private soldier was allocated to the battalion as interpreter. The unit then entrained for Montreuil and stayed billeted in farm buildings and houses for around a fortnight at Humbert, 18 miles north-east. With the novelty of active service, routine orders were diligently copied down in the battalion war diary,[19] as was the death of a draught horse from over-eating. Amongst these orders was one that 'All cameras in possession of Officers and men to be returned at once to England. After 30th inst. anyone found in possession of a camera to be put into arrest & report to be made to GHQ.' Sadly, therefore, photographs of the battalion on service are few. (The Germans, in contrast, took a more relaxed attitude to private cameras.)

There seem to have been some disciplinary problems, as the war diary records, including, worryingly, with some senior NCOs. A Company Quartermaster Sergeant (CQMS) was tried on 13 September, for neglect of duty before leaving Britain and reduced in rank. A reminder had to be issued on 16 September against sale of spirits to NCOs and men and a warning that those caught selling or imbibing would be punished severely. Just four days earlier, Sergeant Pugh of the battalion had been assaulted by a sergeant and six men of the Buffs who accused him of stopping their drinking. On the other hand, on 16 September, an East Surrey private was remanded for a court martial with being absent from parade, drunk, striking an NCO and resisting escort. A sergeant was similarly remanded the following day for being absent on the night of 15/16 and drunk. This was followed on 18 September by the ex-CQMS going absent!

During further training, including entrenching, shooting and gas precautions, small parties of officers and NCOs were sent to various specialist schools. They were also sent to the Front to gain an appreciation of conditions there that almost all lacked. Captain Birt found the Front 'tremendous fun'[20] after the boredom of the rear areas: boredom that was, perhaps, only briefly relieved by a report, noted in the war diary for 9 September, of two suspected spies 'driving around in [a] car endeavouring to obtain information from troops', to be arrested on sight. However, the battalion was soon to have all too much experience of the Front.

Chapter 2

Loos,
September 1915

With 24th Division, 9/East Surrey was fated to see its first experience of war in the biggest battle fought up to that date by the British Army.

Lord Kitchener's original plan was to build up the strength of the British Army so that it would be ready to strike the decisive blow in 1916 or 1917. This, though, required the French and Russian armies to bear the main weight of the conflict in the meantime. Unfortunately, the situation in mid-1915 did not allow this. Both these armies had already suffered huge losses. The French, however, with a large part of their country, including much of their industrial base, occupied by the Germans, were understandably not prepared to stand on the defensive. On the Eastern Front, the Central Powers, following the failure of the Schlieffen Plan on the Western Front in 1914, were making a major effort to knock out Russia. The British-led attack on the Dardanelles, in part to assist Russia, had proved a major disappointment.

In these circumstances, Britain came under heavy pressure to assist its allies, by joining a major offensive on the Western Front. However, the BEF was ill prepared for this. Whilst its numbers had grown considerably, it was seriously short of artillery, especially heavy guns, and shells. As for infantry weapons, there were few light machine guns as yet and the grenades in use were much inferior to those of the Germans. Apart from material deficiencies, commanders were struggling with the new challenges of taking the offensive in trench warfare. With the enormous expansion of the Army and huge casualties amongst the regulars in 1914, there was also a serious shortage of trained and experienced officers in the newer units, especially, and of staff officers most of all.

In spite of these difficulties, Sir John French, commanding the BEF, and Sir Douglas Haig, commanding his First Army, were mindful of the need to put pressure on the Germans and were not opposed to offensive action. Both were, however, unhappy with the proposals from the French Commander in Chief, Joffre, as to how the British might assist. Joffre planned offensives in Artois and Champagne at either end of the huge salient occupied by the Germans. If successful, these could force the Germans to evacuate a large area, or risk being cut off. Joffre wanted the British to join with the French Artois offensive, by attacking near Lens, at Loos. Haig saw this as most unsuitable ground for an attack, being broken up by coal mines, pitheads (*fosses* and *puits*), mining villages and slag heaps (*crassiers*) and in generally flat and open land, dominated by the German artillery.

Nevertheless, the French were insistent on the need for British support for their offensive; the Gallipoli campaign had become a bloody stalemate; and it was feared that Russia could collapse. In these circumstances, Kitchener concluded, 'We must act with all energy and do our utmost to help the French in their offensive even though by doing so we suffer very heavy losses indeed.'[1] The Cabinet agreed, on 20 August 1915, to support the French offensive over reinforcing Gallipoli. As Kitchener saw it, 'We must make war as we must; not as we should like.'[2]

With Britain committed to an attack at Loos, Sir John French left the planning very much to Haig. Sir Douglas threw himself into organising an ambitious attack. He thought a new weapon for the British Army, poison gas (used against it by the Germans earlier in 1915), could make up for his weakness in artillery.

Haig's plans assumed the wholesale commitment of his own First Army, so where were the reserves to come from to exploit the expected breakthrough? There were three infantry divisions uncommitted to either of the two British armies in France – 21st, 24th and the Guards, in XI Corps under General Haking, a notably aggressive commander. Haig's plans assumed that these would be under his control for the battle. Sir John French, however, was reluctant, for whatever reason, to release them. He only agreed, a week before the battle was due to commence, to move them forward, but still under his control.

Be that as it may, the 21st and 24th Divisions, both raw 'New Army' units, were sent towards Loos, followed by the Guards. In the two New Army divisions 4 out of 6 brigade commanders were re-employed retired officers and of 26 battalion commanders all but 1 were re-employed retired officers, some from the Territorials or Militia. Almost all the officers were newly commissioned, and there were few old soldiers in the ranks. These divisions were keen, but very lacking in experience. But according to Colonel Stewart, chief staff officer to 24th Division, General Haking's views, as stated before the battle, were that 'Not having been previously engaged in this way, they would go into action for the first time full of esprit and élan and being ignorant of the effects of fire and the intensity of it, would go forward irresistibly and do great things.'[3]

This is all ominously reminiscent of the German attacks at Ypres in 1914, where several divisions of inexperienced troops, their numbers made up with war volunteers and often led by elderly officers, suffered terrible losses when thrown against the long-service regulars of the BEF, in particular.

After just three weeks in France, spent well behind the Front, 9/East Surrey set out for Loos early on 21 September, 30 officers and 901 ORs strong.[4] After a series of marches in hot weather, then heavy rain, the battalion rested on 24 September at Berguette. At 6.00pm the troops received their last solid meal for 60 hours.[5] The brigade then set off for Béthune taking 7 hours. Breakfast, planned for 4.30am, failed to arrive, through a staff officer's mistake. Each division, with its artillery and transport, required 15 miles of road and the march had been very considerably prolonged by severe congestion on the few available roads immediately behind this part of the Front. There had been inadequate planning by the First Army staff, to get reinforcements forward through all the other traffic. The men had but a short rest and all had arrived 'wet through'. Private Fred Billman of 9/East Surrey recalled, 'Now we were absolutely tired and hungry, and even the thunder of the guns could not keep us awake.'[6]

The Battle of Loos commenced early on 25 September. Initial reports were encouraging. At 7am, Haig requested Sir John French to move XI Corps forward. After a further prompt, French, at 9.30am, ordered that 21st and 24th Divisions should move forward to First Army's trenches 'as soon as the situation requires and permits' (not 'immediately') and come under Haig on arrival there. Haking then ordered 21st and 24th Divisions to move up – about 2 miles to Mazingarbe/Vermelles, about 1½ miles behind the British start line. French kept the Guards Division under his own command.

9/East Surrey had turned out of billets at 7.00am (Billman says 9.00am) and was then kept waiting in readiness until 11.15am, when it set off marching to Vermelles. Billman wrote, 'We were still very tired and stiff with our heavy marching, but the excitement of going into action kept us going.' The troops were again delayed by congestion. Billman also refers to the numbers of wounded they encountered. Mitford remembered, years later, 'Some of them were pitiable cases ... They must have been rather a shock to new troops who had never seen a wounded man before'.[7]

On the basis of optimistic reports received earlier, Haig ordered Haking, at 2.35pm, to detach one brigade from each division to shore up the line elsewhere and push on with the remainder, as far as the Heute Deule Canal crossings. However, there was delay in getting the orders through and then in getting the men forward, so a less ambitious advance was substituted – to the Hulluch–Lens road, unless moonlight allowed a further move forward. In the early evening, before receipt of these orders, 72 Brigade advanced under shellfire, sustaining light casualties, crossing the German trenches captured in the morning. Later, soon after midnight, as scouts reported that Hulluch was occupied by the Germans, the brigadier ordered a halt. Billman remarked, 'Shells began to drop around, and it was pitch dark and raining, not a very comfortable experience for troops quite new to war.' 9/East Surrey dug in about half a mile south-west of the outskirts of Hulluch. So far, the battalion had suffered only Second Lieutenant Johnson and two men wounded. It was difficult to establish positions with adequate maps, guides and signposting all lacking. Moreover, 'The only landmark guiding light was the burning "pylons" of Loos and even they at times were obscured by the mist.'[8] The battalion continued entrenching until near dawn, with only the men's entrenching tools to dig in the hard chalky soil. A short retirement to a captured German trench was then ordered, as it was apparent that the newly dug trench was not deep enough to protect the men. Rain in the night was 'very welcome', Billman recalled, 'as we were awfully thirsty and we spread our waterproof sheets out to get a few drops together. Several of us even sucked the water out of our hats.' An attempt to bring up rations was frustrated by enemy shellfire, the trenches being visible to the Germans.

Haig believed that there had been some real successes on the first day. On the right, the German first line of defence and the village of Loos had been seized from 117 Division, which had taken heavy losses, although the British left attack had been unsuccessful. It was important to exploit any opportunity to breakthrough the second German position, whilst there was still time. However, the attacking divisions had sustained heavy casualties and were all but exhausted. Haig had been obliged to realise there had been insufficient time to use the reserve on 25 September. That evening he ordered that 21st and 24th Divisions should be ready to advance the following morning. However, both had been much reduced in strength by detachments to shore up the line and, far from being rested, had spent much of the night crossing the battlefield and in entrenching.

Earlier on 25 September, it seemed there could have been a real opportunity for a British breakthrough. Many Germans as well as British believed this, with the Germans having nothing behind the dominant position of Hill 70, but only a single battalion from Infantry Regiment (IR) 182 detached from 123 Division and a scratch force of cavalry, divisional *Pioniere* (engineers) and armed rear-area personnel holding the crucial Lens defences. (When attacked by the French in the afternoon, to the south, 123 Division, with all its reserves committed, had grave difficulty in holding them off.)

Three companies of I/IR 26, from 7 Division, to the left of 117 Division, which were hurried forward to fill a gap, were told that morning,

> The enemy has attacked and taken Loos. There are no other [friendly] troops in front of us over a 5km breadth, and the field artillery is lost. How far the enemy has broken through we know not; ahead of us there are started [i.e. incomplete] positions. The battalion will advance, until it meets the enemy, and hold no matter what.[9]

7.7cm guns from Field Artillery Regiment (FAR) 75, of 8 Division (which was initially in Army Reserve at Douai) were sent forward, with great urgency, through Pont à Vendin, under British artillery fire, and had to push their way through retreating transport. One battery was directed to the western edge of the Bois des Dames, around 900m behind the line held by I/IR 26, the men of which greeted the gunners with enthusiasm, knowing they had now at least some immediate support.[10]

By the following day opportunity for a British breakthrough had been lost, as the Germans had brought up numerous reinforcements and strengthened their positions. East of Hulluch, I/IR 26 had found only the strongpoint and barbed wire defences complete, and a single inadequate trench line. But it had been given ample time to deepen the trench, and had suffered little whilst doing so from British artillery fire. Moreover, on the morning of 26 September, the Germans had recaptured Bois Hugo in advance of their second line, from 21st Division, and had held on to the summit of Hill 70, giving them observation over much of the British lines. But Lieutenant Colonel Stewart of 24th Division recalled later, 'The idea given was that the Germans had been heavily defeated and were retiring everywhere. There was no idea of meeting organised resistance.'[11]

Haig's plan for 26 September was for attacks to secure Hill 70 on the right and Cité St Elie and Hulluch on the left. With their flanks thus protected, 21st and 24th divisions were to seize the German second line and advance to the canal beyond.

At dawn on 26 September, Brigadier General Mitford sent Major Kay to divisional HQ to request orders At 9.45am Kay returned with verbal orders to commence an attack, at 11.00am, the written orders not having been received. 24th Division was to capture the German second defensive system running south from *Puits No.13bis* (a small coal mine and strongpoint which the Germans called *Stutzpunkt* III) to *Stutzpunkt* IV, another German strongpoint. This line, which had completely open fields in front, could not be readily observed from the British positions, because of the lie of the land. Whilst there was some dead ground to begin with, attackers would soon advance into a salient and be exposed to enfilade fire from Hulluch village on their left and Chalkpit Wood and Bois Hugo on their right, in advance of the German trench line, unless these positions were neutralised first.

With detachments having been made, 24th Division's attack was to be limited to 72 Brigade, reinforced to seven battalions with two battalions from 71 Brigade and the divisional pioneer battalion. The attack was to take place in conjunction with one on the left by 1st Division dealing with Hulluch and one by 21st Division on the right, which was supposed to be already holding Bois Hugo. The confirmatory written order was only received many hours later, at nightfall.

> Following are arrangements for attack. 1st Division attacks HULLUCH at 11a.m., 72nd Bde to attack objective H. twenty D. three nine exclusive of redoubt in H.20.D.to to H.14.c8.5. 21st Div will attack on your right the redoubt in H.20.D inclusive. The attack will be preceded by an artillery bombardment. The attack will cross the LENS–LA BASSEE road at eleven a.m. acknowledge. 24th Division 7.10 a.m.[12]

The German 117 Division, which had originally held the Loos Front and had been very badly battered in the previous day's fighting, had by now been substantially reinforced. Although IV *Armeekorps* had its three divisions (7, 117 and 123) fully committed in trying to hold off both the British and French attacks, 8 Division was rushed up from the general reserve. By the morning of 26 September, one battalion of IR 157 (117 Division) was holding Hulluch; between Hulluch and *Stutzpunkt* IV was one battalion of IR 26 (7 Division); and three battalions from IR 153 (8 Division), from the little Duchy of Saxe-Altenburg, were stationed around Bois Hugo (where this regiment had suffered heavy losses the previous night). Elements of the Saxon Reserve Infantry Regiment (RIR) 106 and IR 178, from 123 Division were also present here. Other troops were on their left in Cité St Auguste. In the early afternoon three companies of reinforcements, from IR 165 of 7 Division, arrived to support IR 153.

As for the German artillery, 117 Division had lost most of its field artillery the day before. However, some abandoned guns were retrieved and heavier artillery was available, along with some field artillery reinforcements from 8 Division. One of the latter's batteries (of FAR 75), as previously mentioned, was already positioned behind I/IR 26. The artillery available to the Germans on 26 September was to prove quite sufficient.

The German position to be attacked now had not been bombarded properly earlier in the battle .The support now given by the British artillery was badly organised and its effect very modest. An artillery brigade allocated to support 72 Brigade had been unable to find it in the dark and had had to fall back to Le Rutoire.[13] The field guns supposed to support the attack were found, when the early morning mist lifted, to be all too exposed to German fire. 7th battery of Saxon Foot Artillery Regiment (Fs. AR) 19, armed with 15cm howitzers, claimed that, on 26 September, it shot up two British batteries 'moving in the open' with 'precision fire, gun by gun and ammunition wagon by ammunition wagon'. Unlike its sister batteries, which, fighting the French, took serious casualties from counter battery fire, no mention is made of such being suffered at British hands.[14]

Mitford, after a quick conference with his battalion commanders, divided his units into three lines of two battalions each, with the pioneers in reserve. 9/East Surrey was placed on the right of the leading line, with C and D companies in front and A and B in support. On the left flank, through a misunderstanding, the only support that would be provided from 1st Division was an advance by 2nd Welch (2/Welch).

Mitford's attack went in promptly, at 11.00am, with the leading line around a mile from the objective. As Billman saw it, 'The boys did not hesitate, and in the lovely bright sunlight ... they mounted the parapet, and started off to the attack.' Mitford recalled, 'I went through most of the trenches where the men were under cover: though no one in the Brigade had had any sleep, the men were bright and keen, and delighted at the idea of coming to close touch with the enemy, to make up for the toil and discomforts of the preceding days.'[15]

Observers were impressed by the steady advance, Major Johnson of 15th Durham Light Infantry, 21st Division, observing from the right remarked, 'We watched through field glasses, as if on manoeuvres, wave upon wave of battalions in extended order move at right angles across our front about a mile away. Starting near the northern end of Loos we followed their progress intently and critically until we lost sight of them behind the wood, or folds in the ground. The scene was fascinating and exciting as we could not see what happened. There was no sign of battle; no noise, no bursting shells, no enemy in sight, just like an Aldershot field day with troops in wonderful alignment for the most part. Very critically, we scanned the long lines, and wondered what their objective could be. It was an imposing sight.'[16]

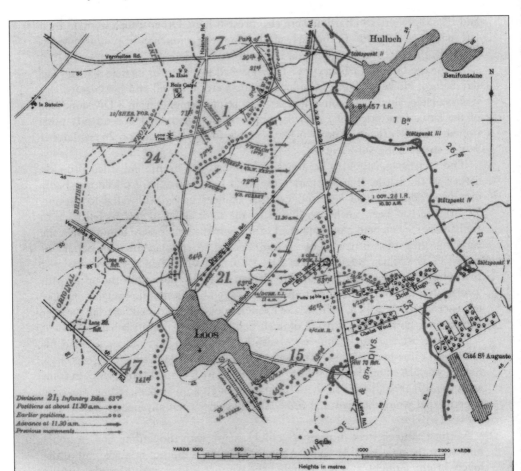

Figure 1. 24th Division begins to advance at Loos, but 21st Division is already in difficulties, 26 September 1915.

The regimental staff of IR 157, placed in area command, had, optimistically, ordered forward at 10.00am German time (1 hour in advance of British time), a company from I/IR 26 to occupy the line of the Lens–La Bassée highway. This company went forward but with 72 Brigade advancing, found itself facing annihilation. The Germans fled, leaving casualties.

At first, German fire was comparatively light, but as the Hulluch–Lens road was reached, and the advancing British became more exposed, heavy fire was encountered, from artillery, machine guns and rifles. Enfilade fire came in from houses in Hulluch and a trench on the left of the advance. Snipers in trees along the road sought particularly to shoot officers, whose uniforms and equipment marked them out from their men.[17] Casualties were heavy, but the brigade continued to advance steadily up the gentle, open slope leading to the objective.

2/Welch, on the left of 24th Division, sought to suppress fire from the Hulluch direction, with only limited success.

Trying to keep touch with the 21st Division to the right, as ordered, 9/East Surrey inclined somewhat to the right, and 8/Buffs was moved up to fill the gap. 11/Essex from the third line was ordered to assist by attacking the Germans flanking the brigade on the left. As it advanced, 9/East Surrey saw 63 Brigade of 21st Division falling back on the right, but its own resolute advance helped steady that brigade. But when 9/East Surrey advanced along the north edge of Chalk Pit Wood, captured earlier by IR 153 and companies of IR 178 and RIR 106, it came under a terrible enfilade fire, which retarded the advance somewhat. As it advanced further, nonetheless, it came under flank fire from more of IR 153 and Saxons in Bois Hugo, which was supposed to have been held by 21st Division. On the brigade's other flank, two half batteries of field guns concealed in Hulluch enfiladed the advancing lines. 21st Division, which had already suffered heavily trying to capture Hill 70 on the far right and hold on to Bois Hugo, was in no position to be of much assistance.

As the troops neared the German position they topped the rise and could see ahead a formidable barbed-wire entanglement in front of the German trench. Shortly before noon, the brigade, in spite of severe losses, with supporting battalions moved up, reached this wire in front of its objective, the German trench line. The wire was a considerable obstacle. It was reported to be 4ft high, many feet deep, well staked and quite undamaged by artillery fire. Desperate attempts were made to break through, with few wire cutters available, but without success. Meanwhile, some shells from their own artillery fell amongst the British. The Germans threw grenades at the struggling men, who could not make an effective response with their own grenades, which were few and of poor quality. The only shelter for the men to fire at the German trenches was the long grass. The brigade was quite unsupported, as the intended attacks by the divisions either side had failed, leaving it fully open to enfilade fire from both flanks.

9/East Surrey, enfiladed from Bois Hugo, which was also heavily wired[18] and endeavouring to follow its orders to maintain touch with 21st Division on the right, had its right flank thrown back, and intermingled with elements of that division. As to how far it was from the German main wire, Mitford[19] suggests the battalion's left only got within 200 yards from the Germans. Captain Fenwick, however, said he fell 20 or 30 yards short of the wire, another wounded man reported lying within 6 yards of it and other survivors explicitly stated that they had reached the wire. Lance Corporal Stanbury, from Swansea, later wrote to Lieutenant Elverson's family, 'We all advanced like heroes, and we got to the wires outside the German trenches. We were firing for a time then an order was passed along the line to retire ... It was a hell on earth, what with our guns, and the German guns, and machine guns that enfiladed us, also the snipers fire and the rifle fire from the German trenches'.[20]

The German IR 153 faced attack from both 9/ESR and elements of 21st Division.

The threat on the right flank of the 1st Battalion had still not been repelled. The reserves charged with the defence of the flank – 9 and 10 Companies, as well as parts of the Regimental *Pionier* Company (which had been committed by *Zugs* and *Gruppen* [roughly platoons and squads] meanwhile in various places) and the MG-*Zug* under *Feldwebel* Peter – had a very heavy task to fulfil. Over a rise in the ground opposite dense columns approach, the commanders in the lead on horseback – a picture from peacetime manoeuvres. Right into these columns spit our fire and shrapnel . . . the enemy formations flutter apart and hurry forward into the hollow . . . where Peter's machine guns take them in the flank . . . the whole British battalion was wiped out . . . About 1pm 5 Company IR 165 arrives and must likewise be committed immediately on the right flank. Around 2pm 6 and 8 Companies IR 165 appear, just at the right time to throw back the British who are already around

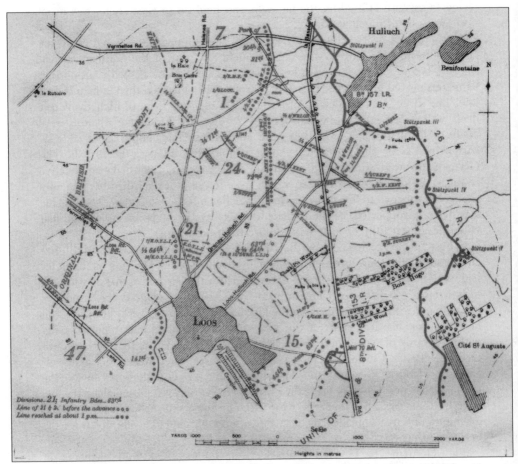

Figure 2. 24th Division attacks into a sack, facing fire on three sides, at Loos, 26 September 1915.

the wood to the east. In the course of the afternoon the British renewed their professionally conducted attacks against the right flank five times, until their strength flagged.[21]

To the right of IR 153, was I/IR 26. Watching the attack was Dr Bertling, the battalion's medical officer, with the battalion staff on the left flank, south of *Stutzpunkt* IV. He recalled 'The Englishmen attacked in whole hosts and with real guts. Our men shot standing upright as rapidly as they could pull the triggers. No Englishman got through the wire. The attack[ers] flooded backwards. Along the front where they had attacked lay numerous dead and wounded.'[22]

With shattering losses, 9/East Surrey now retired, with 8/Buffs from its own brigade and with the 21st Division, as that fell back on the right. Soon afterwards, faced by an impossible obstacle, seeing the retreat on their right, with very many officers down, and having suffered enormous casualties, someone called 'Retire' and the main body of the brigade, too, began to fall back to its starting point. Some stayed behind, sniping at the Germans. The retirement was arrested at the original starting line, the trenches were manned and the men continued under enemy shellfire, suffering further casualties. The Germans decided they were not strong enough to mount a counterattack, but made a limited advance to no further than the Hulluch–Lens road, taking prisoners.

Haking spoke to a number of the survivors whose view was, he reported, 'We did not understand what it was like. We will do all right next time.'[23] Billman recorded,

At night we were relieved by the Guards. [The Guards attacked east from Loos on 27 and 28 September, suffering heavy losses, without success.] We were absolutely done up and staggered back to a field, still well under shellfire, and there came the sad part of calling the roll. After the excitement of the fight wears down, it's heartrending to hear name after name of one's pals called out, and no answer to it. Many and many a brave deed was done that day, and a fine battalion of men had been badly smashed. The fight was still raging but I slept on the grass as soundly as ever I've slept at home ... By daylight we could see only too well how we had suffered.

The total for 72 Brigade's 4 battalions, alone, was 75 officers and 1,979 ORs[24] out of about 3,600. Of these, 9/East Surrey lost 16 officers and 438 ORs killed, wounded and missing.[25] Amongst the officers, Major Welch, Captains Barnett, Collinson and Dealtry, Lieutenants Campbell and Elverson and Second Lieutenants Bate, Coutts and Murray were killed, or mortally wounded, some dying in enemy hands. Captains Fenwick and Birt survived as prisoners of war (POWs), although Birt died within a few months. Five more officers were wounded, but escaped capture. One of these, Captain O'Connor, the adjutant, was awarded the MC 'for conspicuous gallantry and devotion to duty ... although wounded, he continued to advance ... until overcome by weakness caused by his wounds'.[26] As for the men, more than 150 had been killed outright on the day, or died of wounds by the end of the month. Some more, doubtless, succumbed to their wounds later.

Very many wounded had to be left behind in the withdrawal. The Germans sent out medical orderlies to attend them and allowed a number who could walk to return to the British lines. When men from the 24th Division went out the following morning to retrieve the wounded, as far as they could, they reported that many had been removed by the Germans. Dr Bertling and his medical orderlies from IR 26 had gone forward as soon as the end of 72 Brigade's attack, but had withdrawn when they came under machine-gun fire.

> Henceforward the wounded Englishmen were gradually brought in over the following nights. A few individuals lay like this for five days outside, but all were remarkably lively, especially when given a cigarette. An English major even asked for beer whilst his wounds were being dressed. We had meanwhile settled ourselves so firmly in our positions that none of the attacks got as far as our wire. Only the acute shortage of water discomforted us. We cleaned our bloody hands as best as we could in the wet grass.[27]

I/IR 26 was finally relieved on 29 September.

A number of those from the 9/East Surrey who survived as POWs were interviewed following repatriation.[28] Lance Corporal David Ballantyne, from Wimbledon, was wounded in the arm and the lung by shrapnel.

> I was unconscious for the whole of the day. A German soldier came round to collect all the 'jack knives'. Then another German came along and gave me water. I told him I was hungry and he went away and returned with some Peters milk chocolate. I was unable to eat it owing to having no moisture in my mouth. I laid four days on the ground. I can only remember having drink once, but I have seen other German soldiers give drink to others from water bottles. A German officer came to me, I believe on the second morning, and gave me first aid.

Private Morrissey of Paddington had been badly wounded in the foot. 'I was lying out about six days and then the Germans picked me up. They were very good to me.' Lance Corporal Herbert Marten, from Sutton, had been shot in the thigh. He reported that he,

> lay on field about 6 yards from German's barbed wire from 12 noon on 26th to between 3 and 4pm on 28th when some Germans came out of their trenches. One man kicked informant and asked if he could walk, but as he was unable to do so, he was left until dusk when a German Red Cross man picked him up and carried to a cart, in which he was brought to Lens Cathedral where he had first dressing, a basin of coffee and basin of soup.

It is not surprising that the Germans found their medical facilities overwhelmed in dealing not only with their own substantial casualties, but also those of the British left within reach of the German lines. Some men, however, were picked up much sooner than others. Private Henry Dorsett from the Minories had two bullet wounds – above the right elbow and in the back. He 'was wounded during the advance about 11a.m. Lay on the ground for about five hours. Had just started to try to return to lines when about 40 of the enemy came out from a wood on the flank [Bois Hugo] and captured me ... Was taken to a house at Lens, where wounds were dressed'.

Private Brauer had been wounded in the left arm by shrapnel. 'We were lying down in muddy road trying to hide ourselves'. However, he was captured that same day. One man who was using a rifle as a crutch was shot by the Germans. Brauer and his score of companions had their wounds dressed and were then made to 'march for 14 hours without food or drink'. Brauer recalled only one of these men was unwounded, having been captured tending a wounded man.

All of the men quoted above were amongst those agreed later by the Germans for repatriation to Britain because of the severity of their wounds, including, as they did, a number of amputees. One man who remained in captivity to the end was Captain Fenwick, 'I was hit by a machine-gun bullet just past the Hulluch–Lens road which partially disabled me. After about 5 minutes I followed up the regiment but was again hit. Owing to my wounds I was unable to move.'[29]

As for the dead, these lay so thickly that the Germans called it the Loos Field of Corpses (*Leichenfeld von Loos*). Few of them were ever identified to have a known grave. Nearly all, therefore, are simply recorded on the Loos Memorial to the Missing. Amongst the names are those of Edgar and Percy Fletcher, aged 19 and 21 respectively. Sons of George and Alice Fletcher of South Tottenham, they had enlisted together, with consecutive serial numbers, and had died together.

Many men of the battalion were missing, fate uncertain. Their families went through long periods of anguish, not knowing whether their loved ones were alive or dead. Private William Ainge was a general labourer, aged 41, living in Kensington, who had joined up in April 1915 and was 'missing' after Loos. He and his wife, Florence, already had seven children, and Florence was pregnant with an eighth. He was still 'missing' the following June, when his wife was granted 33 shillings a week for herself and eight children.[30] He is commemorated on the Loos Memorial to the Missing. Private 'Teddy' Cutt, too, was missing at Loos. His sweetheart, Nellie, frantically sought news of him from the War Office, the Red Cross, the Salvation Army, surviving members of his battalion and even the King of Spain, who tried to mediate in such cases. Rumours that Cutt had been taken prisoner were never substantiated, and, a year after his disappearance, the War Office concluded he was dead. Poor Nellie had a breakdown, remained devoted to her lost love and never married. She treasured a lock of Teddy's hair to the end of her long life.[31]

Amongst the officers, Major Howard Welch, almost 60 years old, was reported missing believed killed. (Colonel Romer, killed leading 8/Buffs at Loos was even older at 64.) Earlier in the advance, under shellfire, Welch, a keen sportsman, had a hare pass just in front of him, and could not resist a 'View holloa'![32] Private Marshallsay stated, some weeks later,

> I passed this officer, when I was retiring and he was badly hit in the head and I think in the hip too ... I even got him up on his feet but I could not move him. He was so heavy ... He was an exceedingly popular officer and I should have liked to have saved him, but I was quite helpless to move him.

In his letter quoted above, Lance Corporal Stanbury also described encountering Major Welch, badly wounded, close to the German wire, where Elverson and he had dressed the Major's wounds. Private Budd, who had been taken prisoner, reported seeing the Major alive in October, as a prisoner, in hospital. But there was no report from the Germans that he had been captured. It was some months later, and only after a photograph had been supplied to them, that they could confirm that the 'Major Wegh' they had reported dying of wounds in October 1915 was Major Welch.[33]

In the case of Lieutenant Elverson, also reported wounded and missing at Loos, with no positive news the War Office concluded, in May 1916, that he, too, must have been killed. His family, however, remained hopeful that he could still be alive. They sent the War Office a collection of statements from survivors who had seen him wounded, but alive, on the field. Three years later, writing to solicitors, the War Office advised that even then a formal death certificate could not be issued, but it was constrained to conclude that Elverson was dead.[34]

Loos meant the loss of their lives, or crippling wounds, for many men. For others it saw their reputations destroyed. There was an unpleasant rush to shift blame. Sir John French unwisely tried to conceal his share of responsibility for the debacle around the use of the reserve. He implied that he had handed over command of 21st and 24th Divisions at 9.30am on 25 September, with the inference that any delay in them being deployed on the battlefield was the fault of others. This, on top of his ill health and erratic behaviour, led to his removal and his replacement by Sir Douglas Haig, who was much more successful in escaping censure over his conduct of the battle. A little lower down the chain of command, Major General Ramsay, feeling well out of his depth, sought to resign command of 24th Division the morning after the battle.

As for 9/East Surrey, its CO, Lieutenant Colonel Sanders (the only battalion commander in the brigade who was not a casualty), was obliged to resign by Mitford, his CO. The brigadier wrote on 30 September,

> Since the arrival of the Division in France, the 9th Battn. East Surrey Regt. has fallen considerably behind the other Battns. of the 72nd Infantry Brigade, both with regard to discipline and training, which in my opinion is due to lack of supervision and indifference on the part of the officer commanding. It is therefore considered essential in the interests of this Battalion that a change should be made in the command.

The unhappy Sanders wrote to the War Office on 24 October suggesting that he was being removed on grounds of age (he was 52) rather than competence and emphasising that the battalion's battlefield performance seemed to suggest there was not much wrong with it. He begged alternative employment in the rear, but was ignored.[35]

As for the 21st and 24th Divisions, their reputations were blasted in their very first action. Haking and Haig blamed their late arrival on their poor march discipline and inexperience, as well as their late release by General Headquarters (GHQ). The two generals preferred to ignore the shortcomings of their own staff work, including poor road-traffic management and lack of provision of adequate maps and guides. They also criticised the two divisions' performance on the battle-field. Some accused the two divisions of 'bolting'. 2/Welch, on the left, recorded seeing 'a wild panic'. A German history refers to the survivors of the British assault having 'flooded back in unholy disorder'.[36] As far as 24th Division, at least, was concerned, this criticism does not seem to have been fair. It seems more likely that the men, as a whole, retired, in no particular formation, but carrying their weapons, because they could not break through. According to Robert Graves, serving well to the left in 2nd Division, 'They flocked back, not in panic, but stupidly, like a crowd returning from a cup final, with shrapnel bursting above them.'[37]

Major General Capper, who succeeded Ramsay in command of the division, considered, 'The conditions before the men were engaged were very trying indeed, that when called upon to act, both officers and men advanced gallantly and did their best, and that the best trained troops in the whole of the British or any other army would have found it difficult to succeed where the infantry of the 24th Division failed.' He also judged, 'I have no personal knowledge of the facts but I am con-fident that the unofficial reports alluded to in GHQ's letter are entirely unwarranted and cast a most undeserved slur on the conduct of the infantry of the division.'[38] Mitford, addressing his brigade on 3 October, praised his men, 'You were an example in steadiness and determination to carry out your task, not only to the New Armies, but also to seasoned troops, who could not have done better than you.'[39]

Nevertheless, received opinion in the rest of the Army was, as heard in October, by Captain Westmacott, of the Indian Cavalry, 'We had two fresh divisions ..., waiting with busses [*sic*] and cars to rush them up, but John French said they must march on their flat feet, and when they got to Loos they were deadbeat. When told to advance, they bolted as soon as they came under fire, and only the Guards' Division saved the situation.'[40] R.C. Sherriff, who served with the battalion from 1916–1917, encountered similar prejudice, '"The 24th? Oh yes, you mean the Division that ran away at Loos." You hear this expression everywhere.'[41]

It took a long time for 24th Division to live down this ignominy and the injustice of it was much resented by the survivors. Colonel Stewart wrote to the Official Historian after the war, to put the record straight and put the principal blame on XI Corps and its commander, Haking,

I was proud and cherished the 24th Div. and its name was blackened in dispatches, to my idea absolutely wrongly ... I think it is only fair and right that now the official history of the war is being written that as far as I am able, I should do what I can to ensure justice being done to so many gallant officers and men who fell in their duty then and later.[42]

Indeed, whatever the balance of blame should be between the various senior officers, it is difficult to see how any other troops could have done any better, with no effective artillery support and being required to attack frontally a well-defended and all but impenetrable barrier of barbed wire.

Ironically, it was their enemies who were more generous to the men of the 24th Division, than their own side. It is believed that 9/East Surrey's nickname 'The Gallants' came from a remark made by German officers after the battle on the battalion's performance.

Unfortunately, despite the sacrifices made, Loos was of very little benefit to the Allied cause. The French offensives had, similarly, suffered heavy losses for minor gains, although German losses had not been light. Loos had come too late to be of any assistance to the Russians. Whilst some lessons from the battle were learned by the British Army, conclusions were also drawn and applied by the Germans, who realised their defences would have to be a good deal stronger and in greater depth in future. Therefore, heavy British losses for little gain would again be seen the following summer at the beginning of the Somme campaign, when once more an inadequately prepared BEF had to enter into a premature offensive to support its allies.

Chapter 3

Recovery,
October 1915–March 1916

Following its bloody initiation at Loos, 24th Division's losses needed to be made good and other perceived deficiencies addressed. It had then to take its place in the trenches, to hold the line over the winter period when active operations were likely to be reduced.

As for 9/East Surrey, drafts were received from its parent regiment to fill the depleted ranks. Around 500 men arrived between 30 September and 16 October, almost all from 10th Battalion. This had been formed at Dover in October 1914, as part of Kitchener's Fourth New Army, initially with an overflow of men from 3rd Battalion. Of the remainder who joined, 'about 95 per cent came from the London district, principally South London, Croydon and Richmond'.[1] In April 1915, the infantry battalions of Fourth and Fifth New Armies had been converted to 'Reserve Battalions' – no longer to be deployed as units, but instead to furnish drafts of reinforcements to the older battalions.

Amongst those now joining the battalion were such as Lance Corporal Richard Cattell, an Oxfordshire gamekeeper, aged 24, Private 'Syd' Hannan, not yet 16, Private Frederick Ivey, a Cobham, Surrey, blacksmith, aged 20, Private John Kirk, a London paperhanger, aged 22, Private Frederick Plested a shoemaker from Chesham, Buckinghamshire, aged 21, Corporal Walter Summers a 'cinematograph producer', aged around 20, and Private Charles Woodbury, aged 24, from Cobham and shortly due to inherit a substantial fortune.

The removal of Lieutenant Colonel Sanders has already been discussed. He left the battalion on 15 October and his replacement, Lieutenant Colonel H.V.M. de la Fontaine, arrived four days later. Aged 42, de la Fontaine was a regular officer of the East Surrey Regiment with over twenty years' service. Son of an Indian Army colonel, he had served with distinction in the Boer War, passed through Staff College and was a major by 1911. He had served early in the present war as a staff officer, but wanted a field command. De la Fontaine was both popular and highly regarded, not only within his unit but also outside it. He took practical steps for the welfare of his men, never hesitated to put himself in danger and always made sure that his officers and NCOs understood thoroughly what was required of them for a particular operation.[2] He was just the man to lead the battalion's recovery from Loos.

As for 24th Division, Major General Ramsay's resignation had been accepted. His replacement, Major General J.E. Capper, succeeded him on 3 October. Capper, aged 54, was the son of a Bengal civil servant. A Royal Engineers (RE) officer, he had served in India and South Africa, before commanding the Army's Balloon School. He was promoted Major General in 1915, serving as Chief Engineer to Third Army. His brother, Major General 'Tommy' Capper, had distinguished himself at Ypres and been killed at Loos. His own son, John, was to die on the Somme in 1916. Capper was an energetic commander who liked to see things for himself, including the front line. He was also a great promoter of 'blood and hatred' towards the Germans.

Replacing senior officers seen to have failed was considered insufficient on its own. The authorities decided that 24th Division would be one of the divisions that would exchange an infantry brigade with a regular division. Accordingly, on 11 October, 24th Division exchanged its 71 Brigade for 17 Brigade, of four regular battalions, with 6th Division. Battalions were moved around between the three brigades, 17, 72 and 73 so that each had at least one regular unit. Thus, 72 Brigade gave up 8/Buffs, in exchange for 1st North Staffordshire.

Whilst mixing New Army and regular units made sense in terms of spreading experience, the timing was unfortunate. It would have been much better done before 24th Division had been thrown into a full-scale battle. Moreover, following Loos, it was seen as adding stiffening to a failed division. However, Kitchener had been firmly opposed to breaking up his New Army divisions. It was explained to 2nd Leinster (2/Leinster), a regular battalion, by its CO, as recorded by one of his officers, Second Lieutenant Hitchcock, that it was 'being sent into 24th Division as a backbone ... although we were joining a new brigade to teach them how to soldier, we must not overdo the "old soldier"'.[3]

Whilst Hitchcock makes no criticism of the New Army battalions of 24th Division, the varying reactions of some regulars were recorded by the future Lord Moran, then serving as Medical Officer to 1st Royal Fusiliers (1/R Fusiliers), under Lieutenant Colonel Price, in 17 Brigade, which now included as well as the regular 1/R Fusiliers and 3/Rifle Brigade, the 'Kitchener' 8/Buffs and 12/R Fusiliers.

Some in 1/R Fusiliers were upset by their CO volunteering to keep his own battalion in the line until the relieving Kitchener battalion was adequately familiar with the trenches to be taken over. Moran recalled one officer saying, 'I don't know what to make of these people. We left a division where nothing mattered but the good name of the Regiment and we found a mob.' Moran said that in the view of some, 'These damned people will never be any use to anyone.' But most, he noted, kept their views to themselves. 'There is hardly any criticism of the 24th Division and the men just take things as they come ... though ... they don't think much of amateur soldiers'.[4]

Whilst all this change was taking place, 24th Division was transferred to the Ypres Salient, which had seen very heavy fighting in late 1914 and early 1915. The Germans sought to drive the Allies from this last corner of Belgium and had

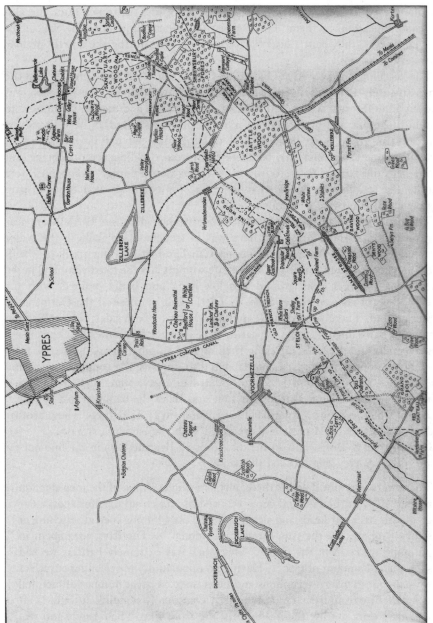

Figure 3. A general map of south and east Ypres.

captured the higher ground to the east in late 1914 and early 1915, although the Allies still hung on to the ruins of Ypres itself. Much of the Salient lay under the direct view of German artillery observers – not just the trench lines, but also the communications to them. Thus, whilst the Allies clung on to the Salient for four long years, they paid a heavy price in lives, even during the quieter periods between offensives.

The battalion was housed at Ouderdem Camp, south-west of Ypres. Whilst the ranks so sorely depleted at Loos had been filled with drafts, the battalion was wanting in both organisation and training, with officers and men as yet unused to working together and a shortage of trained specialists. Matters were, however, gradually improved with both general training and the particular training of machine gunners, signallers and bombers. For instance, Billman records being sent to the machine-gun school at Wisques for Lewis gun training.[5] Companies were sent to the trenches, attached to other units, for two days at a time, to gain experience of front-line conditions.

The battalion began its first regular tour of trench duty, on 19 October, near Voormezelle due south of Ypres. This was in trenches U24–U26 in the sector between the Bluff on the Ypres–Comines Canal and St Eloi, for six days – with two companies in front, a third in immediate support and the fourth and HQ in the Spoil Bank dugouts. The ground was low-lying and badly drained, with the trenches poorly constructed and closely overlooked by those of the Germans on higher ground. There was extensive mining activity by both sides, close to St Eloi. The Spoil Bank dugouts, near the canal, were damp and rat infested. The enemy was generally quiet except for some shelling and sniping. Working parties from the infantry, under RE supervision, laboured to improve the communication and fire trenches. Regulars from 1/North Staffordshire gave some night-time wiring tuition in no-man's-land. During this tour and relief the battalion lost two dead and eight wounded. The former included Lieutenant H.T. Barnett, whose brother had, on 1 October, died of wounds received with the battalion at Loos.

Carpenter of 8/Buffs, now in the division's 17 Brigade, was in the line not far from 9/East Surrey. He recalled this time,

> There were very few dugouts there, just a few holes. Most of the men slept on the fire step. In the rain and snow we used to crouch up together, cover our greatcoats over our heads and sleep, wakened only for our spell at watching or sentry – or in case the rum ration came along ... The days were spent in pumping water from the trench. This work was extremely hard as we had such a small amount of rest ... Having no opportunity for cleaning ourselves we soon got in a very verminous and filthy state. A great number of men fell sick suffering from trench foot, caused by continually standing in water ... It was hard work getting the dead out of the front line. Their hands and feet were tied up, a groundsheet wrapped around their head (if it was still on) and then by means of a rope half a dozen of us used to drag them through the mud.

We did eight days in the front line and four in reserve which was almost as bad, except that one could get hot tea in reserve. Men in reserve had to attend to the various fatigues, such as rations, etc ...

The task of a ration party is no sinecure. At St Eloi we had to trudge through mud and water, loaded with sacks of coke, bread, tins of bully beef and boxes of biscuits. For the greater part the journey [was] under machine gun fire and occasionally shrapnel to help us along – especially when a star shell revealed to the ever watchful enemy the party at work ...[6]

On being relieved on 25 October, the battalion marched to Reninghelst, where it had to camp in tents, in what even the normally restrained History calls a 'quagmire'.[7] On 27 October, the battalion fielded around 170 survivors of Loos for an inspection of men from 24th Division by the King. 'Rest' in Reninghelst is described as consisting of 'continual fatigues' and in appalling conditions, by Second Lieutenant Hitchcock.[8]

9/East Surrey returned to the same trenches on 30 October for another six-day tour. Incessant rain wrecked trenches and dugouts, and constant labour was required to repair the defences. On 2 November, Captain Hitchcock, with 2/Leinster in 73 Brigade, to the right of 9/East Surrey, by St Eloi, recorded 'one continuous nightmare of mud'.[9] Luckily, the German infantrymen opposite were in much the same state and chose to abstain from hostile acts and instead 'live and let live', walking on top of their trenches to escape the flooding. The German artillery, however, continued to fire. The Germans even greeted Hitchcock on 4 November with 'Good morning' on his rounds of his posts.[10] The regular 2/Leinster had no problem, under the prevailing conditions, in joining in with 'live and let live'. The Germans facing 9/East Surrey were not recorded as quite that relaxed, but were described in the war diary for 3 November, when the brigadier visited, as 'so quiet that they waved their arms and showed bottles over the parapet'.[11] It is possible, however, that neither the war diary nor the History would wish to record the battalion's participation in 'live and let live'. Alternatively, it would seem that the Germans facing 9/East Surrey were not in as bad a state as their comrades opposite 2/Leinster. The end of the tour gave little relief, with the campsite deep in mud, even worse than before.

Facing 24th Division at this time was the German 123 Division. This Saxon unit had been at Loos and one battalion from each of its IR 178 and RIR 106 had fought against the attack on 26 September. It had then been engaged with the British Guards Division on the following day, and also with the French at Souchez, before RIR 106 was thrown into an ill-judged counterattack at Loos. After all this 123 Division had been seriously depleted, although not as badly hit as 24th Division, and was similarly engaged in incorporating reinforcements and training them, whilst holding the line in a relatively quiet sector. RIR 106 was facing 9/East Surrey and others, holding the line between St Eloi and the canal, with two battalions in line and one in reserve. Each battalion served six days in the line and then three at 'rest', although like the British this included working parties.

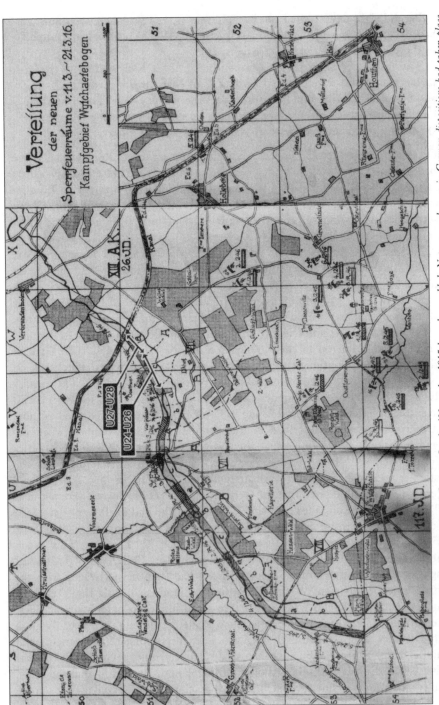

Figure 4. St Eloi, early 1916. Positions of 9/E Surrey, October/November 1915 have been added. Note some changes in German dispositions had taken place since then.

The Germans were troubled by British heavy artillery directed from observers on Mount Kemmel. However, before the heavy rain at the end of October and into November, the Germans had considered their defences here generally satisfactory, with thick barbed wire, and the front line behind revetted with fascines, providing good cover, with 'countless' steel sniper plates and periscopes and many machine guns in the front line.

> Since July [when infantry of 123 Division had briefly held the line] substantial progress had been made ... About 100–200 metres behind the front line (1A Line) there was now a second line (1B Line) with numerous communication trenches leading forwards. Immediately in front of the Damstrasse there was an intermediate position, and further back behind this strong points under construction.

As well as the divisional artillery, there was support available from some basic smoothbore mortars, rather than the proper rifled *minenwerfer*. The heavy rain, however, raised the water table and played havoc with the German defences: 'the water parties ... had to remain at their posts nigh-on continuously to achieve the necessary drainage of the torrential rain; whilst doing so they inevitably suffered losses from the relentless enemy artillery fire'.[12]

9/East Surrey returned to the line on 9 November, but in trenches U27 and 28, right up by the canal bank, with the reserve company and HQ in the Canal Bank dugouts. De la Fontaine with two other officers, walking to the trenches on 10/11 November, encountered an 8/R West Kent fatigue party filling sandbags in the open. He ordered them to take cover, just before the German artillery opened fire, and had to take cover himself, standing up to his waist in water. Even so, there were a number of casualties. Conditions in the trenches remained very bad, as the divisional commander saw for himself when he visited the line on 13 November. However, the enemy was fairly quiet, so the only casualties for this tour were three wounded.

As for the German artillery, the history of FAR 246, supporting the German infantry in this sector, records for 11 November, for instance, firing seventy-seven rounds, including on British troops marching at the canal crossing by the lock, and on several occasions that day on men digging, including '50 digging Englishmen at Osthoek'. This was where 9/East Surrey was holding the line supported by fatigue parties from the 8/R West Kent, and could be the incident described above from the British side. However, this artillery unit was also finding the weather trying. On 12 November, it was noted, 'Due to the continuous downpour the gun pits, the dugouts for the gun crew and the communication trenches, which were clad with neither boards nor fascines, to a large extent collapsed. The munitions lockers consisted merely of holes in the ground, in which the ammunition was also partly submerged in water.'[13]

After the hardships of the previous month, battling with the weather conditions more than with the Germans, it was with general relief that 24th Division was ordered, on 19 November, to rest. The battalion marched, on 25 November reaching Tournehem, near St Omer, where it was billeted in houses and barns. Sir Herbert Plumer, Second Army commander, looked in to see if the battalion was comfortably settled in.

The battalion was fortunate to spend a month at Tournehem, largely devoted to training. In addition, a recreation room was established, along with a piano and baths were arranged at the local brewery. Besides training, both general and specialist, football matches, cross-country runs, boxing and shooting competitions were organised. The war diary also recorded that Major General Capper lectured the battalion on the causes of the war and 'the spirit we should adopt against the Hun'. The Royal West Kents recalled the general's 'well known doctrine of hatred of the Hun as displayed by blood on the bayonet'.[14]

Whilst the battalion at rest was spared combat casualties, there was always the possibility of losses from other causes. Second Lieutenant Britts and Lance Sergeant Childs had been killed on 6 November in a grenade-school accident.

Training was not simply confined to the battalion. There were arrangements to try and share latest and best practice within the BEF. For instance, the brigade war diary shows reports on raids carried out were circulated to spread experience. Officers of the different arms were also brought together. Major Hamilton of the division's artillery recorded attending a course in January, which included infantry officers, too. Indeed, he got on well with an unnamed captain from 9/East Surrey, 'We exchanged experiences about Loos. Apparently it was even a worse muddle than I ever realised'. As for the course,

> We had two lectures to-day – in the morning on Aeroplane Co-operation with Artillery, which was quite interesting, and in the afternoon on Guns in support of Infantry. This course is not really for the purpose of teaching us anything, but to promote discussions and get ideas from Battery commanders. It is also very useful, as it enables artillery and infantry officers to exchange views in a peaceful atmosphere, and to get some insight into each other's needs and difficulties.

Four months later Hamilton, himself, lectured on 'Artillery in Trench Warfare' at the Divisional School, to a mixed group of junior officers and sergeants.[15]

On 13 December, 9/East Surrey had received a new medical officer, Captain George Pirie, a South African, aged 27, who had already distinguished himself at Gallipoli, where he had been wounded. Pirie became devoted to the battalion and maintained a detailed diary from March 1916.

Christmas was a holiday and celebrated with seasonal fare. On 5/6 January the battalion had to leave. Relations with the inhabitants of Tournehem had been excellent and letters were received from the mayor and parish priest regretting the battalion's departure.

The year 1915 had been one of disasters for the Allies: offensives on the Western Front had achieved little at heavy cost, whilst Russia had been put under heavy pressure on the Eastern Front. The Allied attempt, through the Dardanelles, to knock Turkey out of the war and succour Russia, had been an expensive failure.

Whilst Italy had joined the Allies, Bulgaria had joined the Central Powers and Serbia had been overrun. In danger of losing the war, the Allies aimed to fight back in 1916 with simultaneous offensives on all major fronts, at a time to be agreed, in the spring.

In early January 24th Division moved to the Hooge sector of Ypres, which had become notorious during bitter fighting, especially the previous summer, which had included the use of mines and flamethrowers. On hearing the news of the move, Hamilton remarked on its reputation as 'the worst spot in the whole line!'.[16] Hooge, by the Menin Road, dominated the lower ground to the west. A relatively small area had been repeatedly fought over, and was full of human remains. A British counterattack had recovered ground in August, which the Germans were keen to recapture, when conditions allowed. At this time, however, quite apart from the ground conditions at Hooge, artillery ammunition was to be husbanded to maximise resources for the great attack on the French at Verdun, to commence in February, which would pre-empt the Allied offensives. However, the Germans did recover the ground from the Canadians in June 1916, after 24th Division had moved on. Although Hooge may have been quieter when 24th Division was there than at other times, it was still considerably more active than St Eloi, with enemy sniping and machine-gunning, and with the lines so close together in places, occasional grenade throwing, as well as frequent shelling.

After reaching camp near Poperinghe, 9/East Surrey took over trenches C.4 to C.7 at Hooge, for six days, from 7 January with two companies in front, one in dugouts and the Culvert as immediate support and the fourth and HQ in the Halfway House dugouts. Two of the trenches were full of water and with a low parapet, whilst another trench, by the ruins of Hooge Chateau stables, was only 20 yards from the enemy.

Each man was now issued with gumboots – previously there had been a serious shortage. Everything required in the trenches had to be carried for about 2,000 yards from 'Hell Fire Corner', which was as far as the transport could reach. A total of 6 men were killed and 5 wounded, in the 6 days. When the brigade was relieved at least the battalion found itself at the excellent Camp 'A', 2 miles south-west of Poperinghe.

The Germans holding the Hooge sector were from IR 121 of 26 Division. This Württemberg division was a highly professional one with a formidable combat record, but no experience of trench warfare. It had only recently arrived from the Balkan Front.

9/East Surrey, by comparison, was still generally inexperienced and recovering from its terrible initiation at Loos. Second Lieutenant Richard Marchant, a former dispenser commissioned in November 1915, aged 26, after a year's service in the RAMC, and with 9/East Surrey since December, wrote to his mother on 25 January,

> I shall certainly be home if they do not decide to make the big advance that is the whole trouble, if they do all leave will be stopped throughout the B. Army

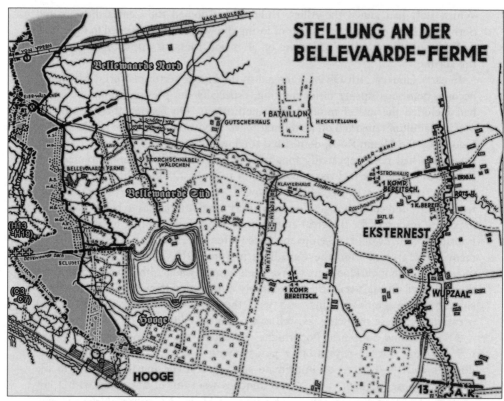

Figure 5. Bellewaarde/Hooge, January 1916. No-man's-land is in grey. British sector boundaries are shown as +++. German sector names added. The Menin Road is bottom left. Eierwäldchen is Railway Wood.

and Mr. Fritz will wish himself in Berlin. I am in the front line of a certain famous battleground. Dead bodies buried in the trenches itself, and I have two platoons to command . . . Shall I tell you the name the East Surreys have earned out here it will amuse Dear old Dad.

> Mein Gott, mein Gott what a bl . . . dy fine lot
> What . . . use are we
> We cannot march we cannot fight what b . . . use are we
> But when we enter Berlin Town the Kaiser he will say
> Hock Hock Hock what a bl . . . y fine [lot] are the 9th E.S.

Well Mother Darling if I do not get leave and I might run in to a bullet I have a good sum at the bank, which as I said before I have made a will with all my possessions are to be given to my beloved Mother.[17]

The battalion's next six-day tour in the line began on 26 January in trenches H.13 to 17 and H.19, north of the Hooge ones and to the east of 'Y' Wood. Some of these were in a very bad state and the Germans were active, with 5 Surrey men being killed, 4 wounded and 1 believed wounded and captured. Here the battalion was facing initially, around Bellewaarde Farm, Württembergers of RIR 246 of 54 Reserve Division. This, unusually, was a mixed Württemberg/Saxon division, which had taken a terrible beating in its first action at First Ypres in autumn 1914. This unit was relieved late on 27 January by the Mecklenburgers of RIR 214 temporarily detached from 46 Reserve Division. However, before the relief took place, men of RIR 246 came into close and violent contact with 9/East Surrey.

According to the German regimental history,

> In this period in the trenches, the infantry activity extended mainly to patrols. Every night the area in front of our positions was alive with German scouts. We held undisputed dominion over no-man's-land. Should the Englishman dare approach our line, he would pay dearly for it. Thus on 27 January 1916 at about 5.00 am, an English patrol penetrated our wire immediately south of the *Knorzersappe*. When 10 Company opened fire and hurled hand grenades at them, they withdrew hurriedly. However, at the same time a German patrol was near the English trenches. They were just on their way back when the Englishmen fell right into their hands. The German patrol (*Vizefeldwebel* Zimmer, *Unteroffizier* Steidle, *Ersatzreservist* Staehle and *Musketier* Gustav Deininger) put paid to the English with revolver shots and hand grenades, killing three of them. They got 'home' safe and sound, bringing with them two of the English dead together with caps and shoulder straps. The Englishmen belonged to the East Surrey Regiment. All those who had taken part in the patrol were decorated with the Iron Cross 2nd Class.[18]

These casualties were Second Lieutenant Marchant and Sergeant Leonard Masters, who had been on patrol with a private, who survived. It was a very dark night, Marchant confused the German lines with his own and the party was fired on. According to the private, Marchant, slightly wounded, refused to leave his seriously wounded sergeant, sending the private for assistance, who then lost his way. Marchant's death was only established when the Germans returned his effects five months later.[19]

To make matters worse, another officer, Second Lieutenant Handford, was killed by machine-gun fire, again on patrol, probably the following night. Lieutenant Vaughan went out with an NCO to recover the body, but could not find it in the dark. Again, the incident appears to be covered in German sources. The Saxon Reserve Jäger Battalion 26 from 54 Reserve Division was holding the sector facing Railway Wood. It recorded,

> It was on the Kaiser's birthday [27th January] that R.Jäg.B. 26 left the heavily contested *Ypernstellung*, the blood-soaked scene of its glorious deeds, behind them. II/212, a Hanseatic unit (45 RD, XXII RK) arrived on time and conducted the relief without casualties. Nevertheless the relief proceeded anything but smoothly for them. The new troops, who must surely have known their business from their former front on the Yser, had great difficulty

negotiating the swampy tangle of trenches. In their uniquely Hanseatic manner, they paid little attention to the enemy whilst doing so, and made a great deal of noise! The enemy evidently noticed and so something appeared, which during the entirety of the previous month had not once been in evidence: an enemy patrol at the wire!

By chance, in the glow of a flare cartridge an enemy officer was spotted a few metres in front of the trenches, who, half-upright and astonished, seemed to be seeking [the source of] the noise of the relief. Immediately several men were to hand [from both units?], among them Jäger Lehnert. The enemy was chased away with well-aimed shots, leaving their patrol leader lying dead behind them.[20]

Relieving RIR 246 in the adjoining Bellewaarde Farm sector the newly arriving Mecklenburgers, of RIR 214, who only stayed until 2 February, remembered,

The positions were in good condition, the trenches generally around two metres deep, floored with duckboards and reinforced at the sides with strong hurdles. The hardness of the ground was quite pleasingly apparent, something we had missed most terribly at Bixschoote. Opposite us were Englishmen, who were extraordinarily active, so that each individual had to stay tensely on the alert. The gas alarm was repeatedly sounded. All day long the artillery was active, and the use of [heavy calibre] flat-trajectory guns by the enemy made itself especially and uncomfortably apparent. During the night vigorous rifle and machine-gun fire was prevalent; patrols went out from both sides into no man's land, clashed here and there and fought it out with hand grenades. Men of 8 Company managed to bring the corpse of a member of an English patrol (an officer) back into our positions.[21]

When not in the front line, 9/East Surrey had to take its turn in Brigade Support at Zillebeke/Belgian Chateau.

Amongst the officer replacements arriving that month was Second Lieutenant Charles 'Nobby' Clark. Having enlisted in 1896 aged 17, he had served with the East Surrey Regiment in the Boer War. Regimental Sergeant Major (R.S.M.) by April 1914, he had been commissioned in January 1916. He took over as Adjutant on 31 January. Clark was to gain a great reputation with 9/East Surrey.

The battalion returned, on 3 February, to the Hooge trenches, which were in an even worse state than before, following German bombardment. Much of the front line was now a series of water-filled shell holes, and bringing up supplies was even more difficult and dangerous. For the rest of the month and into March the battalion served in this sector. It was lucky to miss the explosion of German mines under its former sector on 14 February, which caused considerable casualties amongst 9/R Sussex. It was 17 Brigade, rather than 72 Brigade, that was in the Hooge trenches in the middle of February, when the Germans unleashed a ferocious bombardment over several days, accompanied by mine detonations and infantry attacks, with the apparent intention of seizing them. The Germans then attempted to fraternise with the East Surrey men on 21 February with shouts of 'Tommy' and 'friend'. They were, however, rebuffed, with snipers killing a German waving his hat. The Württembergers on the Western Front were not known for fraternisation, but had been used to it with the Russians.

On 1 March, by the stables (called by the Germans the *Preussenhaus*) where the lines were closest, Germans threw several grenades at the battalion's No. 2 bombing post, but these fell short. The East Surrey men retaliated with fifteen of their own. The enemy replied with more grenades 2 hours later, which invited a vigorous retaliation in kind, which seems to have discouraged further action. The battalion's war diary was pleased to note, 'At daybreak it was seen that our bombs had done considerable damage to the enemy's new work, sandbags being torn and timber scattered about.'

A British bombardment on 2 March led to German retaliation with trench mortars and artillery. 'C' company bore the brunt with seven men killed, another ten wounded and others buried and severely shaken. Second Lieutenant Tetley and Privates Jewson and O'Connell distinguished themselves by rescuing the wounded and buried and reorganising the defences under heavy artillery and trench mortar fire. The war diary was gratified to note that 'Several NCOs and men behaved remarkably well and worked at once in repairing parapets and establishing new posts when the old ones had been blown in or destroyed. This work was done in most cases by private soldiers acting on their own initiative.'

When not in the front line, the battalion was obliged to provide working parties, for the front line and creating a reserve line, often under fire. Private Bob Lambert noted in his diary for 4 March 'Awful weather. Snowing. Fritz bombards camp. No damage. Leaving Chateau for Rest Camp. Fritz gives us a hot time before we go. Shells all around. Raining old iron but nobody hurt or damage done.'[22]

On 21 March, the Division exchanged sectors with the Canadians, moving a few miles south to the Wulverghem sector, opposite Messines Ridge. As Wulverghem was then a quiet sector, this seemed a good deal. On 18 March, Captain Pirie, the Medical Officer, had resumed the diary he had kept at Gallipoli. 'It's good-bye to Wipers tomorrow and we shall be glad to see the last of the Menin Gate, Lille Gate, the cellars, etc.'[23]

During its time at Ypres in the six months from October 1915 to March 1916, the battalion appears to have lost four officers dead from enemy action which fell within this period. It also lost twenty-seven ORs killed and eighteen died of wounds according to Anon., *Soldiers Died in the Great War 1914–19 Part 36 The East Surrey Regiment* (London, 1920). There is some imprecision as the war diary does not, as it was to later, unusually, include a monthly list of casualties, by name, rank and number. Let us assume, however, that half the ORs 'died of wounds' had been hit at Loos in September. This would leave 4 officers and 36 men killed in 6 months by enemy action – on average less than 1 officer and just 6 men killed per month. These were mercifully light casualties, not only after Loos, but compared with the battalion's average for the whole of its stay on the Western Front – 1 or 2 officers and 20 men killed per month. As for the number of wounded, including officers known to have survived their wounds, there were, according to the war diary, around sixty during October 1915 to March 1916 inclusive. Some of the ORs in this number may have succumbed to their wounds, and so be included in the killed total above.

The History sums up matters, with its usual understatement,

The two and a half months spent in the neighbourhood of Hooge had been fairly trying, but far preferable to the time spent in the trenches near St Eloi. The most unpleasant feature had again been the weather. In trenches perpetually full of water, which occasionally turned into ice, the greatest care was necessary to prevent the men's feet from becoming frostbitten. But the camps in the rear were much more comfortable than that at Reninghelst. The Battalion, moreover, was fairly fortunate in not suffering greater casualties than it did.[24]

Chapter 4

Wulverghem, March–July 1916

By the time of the battalion's move to the Wulverghem sector, the pace of the war had quickened. The Allies had planned a series of co-ordinated offensives for 1916. However, the Germans had struck first – at Verdun. The French believed they must hold Verdun, whatever the cost. The intense fighting there dominated the first half of 1916, sucking in huge resources of men and munitions, as the Germans and French fought to destroy each other.

The Wulverghem sector was a pleasant contrast to Hooge. It lay in rolling countryside, between Kemmel Hill on the British side and Messines Ridge on the German side. It was reputed to be a quiet sector and unlike around Ypres, there was 'dead' ground, out of direct observation by the Germans. Many buildings behind the lines were not, as yet, devastated. 'Estaminets and small shops were open in and around Wulverghem, less than three quarters of a mile from the front line, and farmers were working in the fields just as close.'[1]

The defensive scheme detailed in 72 Brigade's war diary describes the front-line trenches running roughly NNW/SSE as,

> For the most part on the crest of a spur running S.S.E. from the main KEMMEL – WYTSCHAETE Ridge. In rear of the front line trenches the ground slopes down to the STUIVERBECK, a stream about 3 feet wide.
>
> This slope, a large portion of which is not visible from the enemy lines is covered by fire from Machine Gun emplacements and Strong Points. ZIG ZAG double apron wire connects these points and is so placed as to be enfiladed.[2]

Looking back the Royal West Kents were not so impressed. 'There was only one line of trenches on our front, and, as was the custom in those days, every firebay had a section of men in it. About 400 yards behind the line were absurd Strong Points built overground of sandbags. Each was held by a platoon.'[3]

After a pleasant few days rest at Mont des Cats, 9/East Surrey joined in relieving the Canadians on 26 March. It was initially in Brigade Reserve at Tea, Aircraft and Kandahar Farms, but next day took over front-line trenches D2, 4, 5, 6 and E1, astride the Wulverghem to Wytschaete road, about a mile north-east of the former. Three companies held the front line, whilst the fourth was in dugouts at RE Farm. Unlike those previously experienced, these trenches were almost all in good condition and dry. The Germans could, however, be close by. Hamilton describes them as 'on the right a long way apart, over a hundred yards; but on our left they are only separated by some thirty yards'.[4]

The new sector soon belied its reputation as a quiet one. Hamilton had been told they were coming to 'a land of milk and honey' and was therefore surprised to be greeted on arrival at the battery he was taking over from by three German shells.[5] The Canadians believed they had faced Saxons, known for lack of aggression unless provoked, and that they had just been replaced by Prussians. In fact, 117 Division, Silesian Prussians, had been opposite, temporarily reinforced by the Saxon RIR 242. 117 Division had been very badly hit in previous fighting. It had suffered well over 5,000 'out of action' against the French in May 1915, and then a further 6,500 at Loos in September where it took the brunt of the British attack and lost most of its artillery. After these terrible experiences it had arrived at Messines in October and had since been busy training up replacements. It would, therefore, be disinclined to be aggressive. In mid-March, however, it was replaced by the largely Pomeranian 45 Reserve Division, elements of which 24th Division had previously encountered near Hooge. Pomerania traditionally provided the toughest troops in the old Prussian Army. According to the old German saying, 'The Pomeranian will march till he dies, the Brandenburger until he drops, the Saxon until he is tired, and the Rhinelander as long as he feels inclined.'[6] RIR 212 from Hamburg/Altona, was directly facing 9/East Surrey. RIR 209, from Stettin, held the adjoining sector on the right, including Spanbroekmolen.

A further circumstance to destroy the sector's tranquillity was that the British artillery was now better supplied with ammunition and its attacks on the Germans were followed by retaliation in kind. In the trenches, the Germans sent over rifle grenades and small 'aerial torpedoes'. (These latter were probably *granatenwerfer* projectiles, 2-kilogram pineapple-shaped missiles launched from a small spigot mortar.) 9/East Surrey responded with rifle grenades, aiming to give three for one, as well as 3.7in mortar bombs from the brigade mortars. By night, enemy snipers and machine guns were very active. The battalion mounted night patrols to keep a close eye on the enemy. This first 6-day tour cost 5 dead, including Second Lieutenant Schooling, and 10 wounded. New officers felt under pressure to demonstrate their courage. Schooling died only three days after he joined the battalion. He was mortally wounded in the stomach whilst strengthening a parapet, although repeatedly warned of the danger by an NCO.[7]

Pirie, from his dressing station at Elbow Farm, on 2 April, noted 'a swine of a sniper who shoots at us along the road between here and H.Q., and he is some shot as he has picked off ten Canadians at 1,200 yds. He shoots down our valley from a place on the ridge called Span Broukmolen, hence he is called Mr. S.B. Moulen, and don't we hate him!'[8] (This sniper nearly managed to shoot Hamilton on a visit to the trenches in May.)

Yet, on the other side of the line, 45 Reserve Division was by no means happy with its positions. It was occupying the southern half of the 'Wytschaete Salient', and thereby open to some flanking fire. Moreover, just as the British felt them-

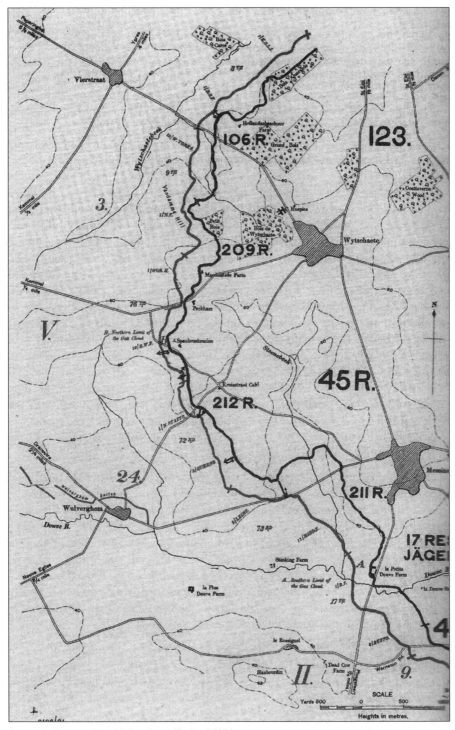

Figure 6. Gas attack at Wulverghem, 30 April 1916.

selves exposed to German artillery observers on Messines Ridge and the other high ground to the east, so the Germans felt themselves similarly naked to observers on Kemmel Hill – '*Der Kemmel sieht alles*' ('The Kemmel sees all'). On the other hand, the lie of the land was such that the Germans could not see immediately behind the British line. Coming from Zonnebeke, RIR 212 was thoroughly dissatisfied with the defences it took over. The trenches were narrow and shallow, making movement difficult and potentially dangerous. The parados, duckboards and wire obstacles were 'without exception, in a wretched condition'. Moreover, at one point no-man's-land was only 30–40yd wide. Behind the line, the approach road from Messines and the communication trenches were under enemy observation in several places so could only be negotiated safely by small groups or at night. However, the most serious deficiency was seen as the lack of dugouts, which were inadequate in number and too flimsy to withstand a direct hit even from light shells. The battalion battle HQ was too small and the second- and third-line positions rudimentary. 'All in all, the positions gave the impression of definite neglect, possibly deriving from very frequent changes of trench garrison.'[9] The regiment was obliged to put a great deal of effort into improving its defences and making good damage from British trench mortars, in particular. Whilst 45 Reserve Division was increasing its complement of mortars, the crews were ordered to refrain from unnecessary provocation, until the infantry had sufficient shell-proof dugouts. Another enemy was the rat. So numerous were they that the troops were permitted to keep dogs in the trenches. At this same time, bad weather, relentless British action and heavy labouring work meant a heavy sick list.

9/East Surrey moved into Divisional Reserve at Dranoutre on 2 April. The village with its shops, estaminets, canteen and YMCA tent was popular with the men, but daily working parties had to be furnished for the front line, under fire.

Around this time, many ORs got leave, after nine months or so abroad. Leave later seems to have been less generous. Billman got his in mid-April,

> Oh what a feeling! No one but the Tommy knows what it is. After ten months of war & all its horrors, I was getting leave to go home ... for seven clear days ... best of all it was going to be a surprise, as I did not know, till it was time to start for the station, so I could not let anyone at home know I was coming ... [After a short break in London, it was home to Norfolk]. I arrived there at about 8pm, meeting my mother on the way, as she was just taking a quiet stroll, & what a surprise for her! It was not long before I was sitting down to a good meal & the kettle was singing just the same as it used to do before this awful war commenced ... I could hardly believe that forty eight hours previous I was in the firing line in Flanders. A little later I was off to bed, a real bed, & how I slept.[10]

Lambert, also abroad since 31 August 1915, got his leave in May. Woodbury, out since early October, managed to get his in late March, to see his heavily pregnant wife and 2-year-old son.

Further tours of duty in the front line and then Brigade Reserve followed for the battalion. Fred Billman recorded how death could arrive so suddenly and unexpectedly,

> The next day was Good Friday, & although Fridays are generally reckoned to be unlucky, my luck must have been in this time, as I had a very narrow escape from death, by a shrapnel shell bursting over me, whilst talking to three other chaps in the trench. One of them was killed outright, & the other two very badly wounded, & I was left standing there, untouched. It was the only shell that came over that part of the line that day ... Such a thing as that is not reported in the papers, but it is such that makes the long casualty list in the papers each day, while the official news says 'All quiet on the Western Front'.

On 24 April there was an intense bombardment of the battalion's D5 and D6 trenches. The shelling extended to the rear areas. Pirie recorded,

> One fine incident ... The wire was cut between H.Q. & B. Coy, so signaller Joe Gibbs went out in lee of his dug-out and began to signal the message by flags. He was blown down once by a shell but got up again and began again when he was wounded by a shell bursting in front of him.

The British responded the following day with 20 minutes of artillery, trench mortars and rifle grenades. Unfortunately, as Pirie wrote,

> A most sad incident occurred. Lieut. W.S. Howell, our bombing officer was killed, sad to say by a piece of our own shell which must have blown back. We are all most cut up about it. To think that poor old Gladys, as we used to call him, has crossed the bar; this is a sad war! Well, he was a hot tempered, but brave man, always looked after his men well and did his work well, and a great loss to us as a friend. It's been a gorgeous spring day, birds singing, heard the cuckoo to-day for the first time this spring. Oh, it sounded so peaceful! The trees are coming into leaf rapidly too and soon the country will be smiling but it's been a sad day with Howell being called away.

Pirie recorded Howell's funeral three days later,

> He was given full military honours. It was most sad. I had a lump in my throat. The saddest part of all was when the firing party filed away and his bombers who had acted as the choir marched off. Watmore, Howell's servant walked up to the grave, paused and saluted and I thought I saw tears in his eyes. What a ghastly waste of life this war is and what sadness it brings to thousands.

During April, the second battalion of Pionier Regiment 36, gas-warfare specialists, began preparations for a major gas attack at Wulverghem. Known unaffectionately by other German troops as the *Stinkpioniere*, they demanded carrying parties for their monstrous iron cylinders from the infantry, whilst adding to their dangers. For instance, ten soldiers of RIR 209 were hospitalised when a British shell punctured a cylinder on 14 April. Nevertheless, large numbers of cylinders were emplaced, ready for a favourable wind. (In introducing gas warfare to the Western Front in 1915, the Germans had taken too little account of the prevailing wind being westerly.)

The German plan was to launch a large raid under cover of gas, demolishing dugouts and mine entrances. (The German infantry were rightly concerned about British mining operations, although their own experts came, mistakenly, to discount them in this sector because of the geology. They would cause appalling German losses at Messines, Spanbroekmolen, etc. a year later.) From RIR 209 there would be two parties of sixty men each, accompanied by a few combat engineers, from the divisional *Pioniere*, with explosive charges. On their left, RIR 212 was to provide two similar parties, all volunteers. Further south, RIR 210 would also participate. On 20 April, there was a massed divisional *minenwerfer* bombardment, which seemed to cause considerable damage, although British retaliation punctured another gas cylinder, lightly gassing five Germans. The sight of the escaping gas also gave a warning to the British of German intentions. Wind conditions were finally judged suitable on 29 April and the gas was released at 1.40am the following night, with vigorous rifle and machine-gun fire as on previous nights, to cover the noise of the gas. The release was along the line facing two of 24th Division's brigades and one of the adjoining 3rd Division's. The British, however, were not deceived. Very lights revealed the gas cloud and heavy fire was opened on the German lines, but, nevertheless, the raiders attacked. RIR 209's parties were repulsed, losing seven dead and thirteen wounded, besides an officer gassed and casualties to its trench garrison. The regiment subsequently reckoned, correctly, that the operation had been betrayed to the British by deserters (on both 26 and 29 April). RIR 212 did rather better, entering the British trenches, leaving a charge in a mineshaft and bringing away prisoners, but at the cost of nearly sixty casualties.

A working party of fifty men from 9/East Surrey had assisted 1/North Staffordshire in driving the raiders back. Fred Billman was there,

We knew the wind was in the enemy's favour, so of course we were prepared for him to loose off gas at any minute. It came over at a quarter to one on the Sunday morning … & at the first horrible sound of gongs and hooters, we adjusted our gas helmets over our heads & got ourselves into some formation as we knew there would almost certainly be an infantry attack. As soon as the waves of gas came rolling towards us … the enemy's gunners fed up a tremendous barrage of shells & shrapnel at the back of our front line, to stop any help coming to us. But the party I was with & myself escaped unhurt, how we don't know, as it seemed impossible to live amid such shelling. The enemy succeeded in getting a few men into one part of the trench, but was quickly ejected by our bombers, & after an hour & a half all was as quiet as death.

Total casualties for 24th Division had been more than 500, including well over 300 from gas. The gas had arrived quickly and many men had not heard the gas alarms, which were drowned out by the noise of heavy gunfire. Those who heard the alarms found difficulty in shooting wearing the clumsy gas helmets and that the gas tended to jam their weapons.[11] (Chlorine produces a green patina on exposed metalwork.)

May saw the usual rotation between front-line and Reserve duty. Lewis guns were used on promising targets and the battalion's snipers were active. In Reserve, whenever the demand for working parties allowed, as many men as possible were trained in the Lewis gun, grenade throwing, wiring, etc. Shelling destroyed or damaged the farms being used as battalion HQ, the regimental first-aid post, etc. However, newly arrived, at a quiet time, Second Lieutenant Geoffery Lillywhite, who spent his first day in the trenches on 29 May, wrote home,

> I am surprised to find how quiet it is. Except for sniping there is nothing doing. The Gunners have quite got the upper hand. We have been straffing [*sic*] gently all day, but as soon as Fritz got really annoyed he sent a few over here. Then you should have heard how our guns tore him to bits. He soon packed up.[12]

On 2 June Lillywhite wrote,

> I have been walking round the country just behind the lines, and it is strange to see the country people here cultivating their fields among the shell holes. Cows and chickens run about and do not seem to mind the crashing of the guns and shells.
>
> There are only a few houses still untouched so I don't know where the people live.
>
> I am now getting quite an expert in recognising the sounds made by ours and their shells, and also what kind they are.
>
> They have all got the most queer names – Crumps, Whizz-bangs, Turnips, Silent Sues, Creeping Jimmies, Pip-Squeeks, etc.
>
> There are the greatest old rats up in the trenches that you ever saw. Some are as big as small cats, and they are so tame that they won't run away but just toddle along in front of you just out of reach ...
>
> You should hear us in the dug-out not fifty yards from the Hun roaring out the latest music on a gramophone. Fritz must be able to hear it, so I wonder what he thinks. Nobody would think there was a war on to see the way the chaps carry on.

After the 30 April attack, the Germans had replaced the empty gas cylinders and their infantry had then to live with them for many weeks, awaiting favourable conditions. At 1.20am on 17 June they tried again, but the attack was something of a fiasco. The gas was slow to reach 24th Division's lines and the British opened fire with all they had. The raiders from RIR 209 and RIR 212 wisely decided not to attack and, indeed, the gas blew back into the German lines. The two German regiments had nearly sixty casualties. Again, a working party from 9/East Surrey, of 250 men, was on hand to repulse a gas attack. 24th Division's casualties, however, were not insignificant. The gas protection worn by the infantry, the 'PH helmet', as worn at Loos, had proved ineffective against heavy concentrations of gas, as well as severely restricting vision. However, after what seemed to the Germans a second debacle, the unpopular *Stinkpioniere* took themselves and their hated cylinders elsewhere, whilst the German infantry braced themselves for a British gas attack.

The morale of RIR 212 was somewhat depressed by the continued dominance of enemy artillery observation, enfilade fire and the 'constantly active' enemy infantry of 72 Brigade opposite. From 2–10 June fifty-one casualties were incurred. The division even reported being bombarded by an armoured train.[13]

On 23 June there was a heavy German bombardment – Lillywhite was told it was the worst the battalion had been through. After a morning shelling, Pirie recorded,

> Then about 8 pm. the real strafe began. It was wet and misty and they sent over Minnies [mortar bombs, the largest as big as a small dustbin, shot from a *minenwerfer*] and H.E. [high-explosive shells, as opposed to shrapnel] on our front line, also on R.E. Farm. It was absolute inferno and the ground fair rattled. This went on till about 10 o'clock and then the whole night through every now and again they would send over Minnies. These beastly Minnies bashed our parapets badly and buried a lot of men who came down very shaken with shell shock, some raving mad and had to be lashed to the stretcher. It was pitiful to see them. We had remarkably few wounded almost all shell shock. One very sad incident was Lt. Youngman, M. Cross being killed while digging out buried men. He had got two out of three unearthed when he was shot through the head. His death was met in a manner typical of him, absolutely fearless he was.

Sergeant Walter Summers gained a reputation for audacity. On the night of 27 June he led a patrol right up to the enemy parapet, shot the German who challenged him and got his patrol back. For this and his conspicuous gallantry on several previous occasions, he was awarded the Distinguished Conduct Medal (DCM).

On the night of 28/29 June, under cover of artillery fire and gas and smoke, 8/Queen's mounted a very successful raid on the Germans, in conjunction with ones by the Canadians and Buffs. RIR 212 had seventy-seven casualties. The Germans responded with artillery, causing 9/East Surrey sixteen casualties.

On the following night, a discharge of gas by the brigade on the right again led to German retaliation, just when the battalion was being relieved by 1/North Staffordshire, causing numerous casualties in both units. Lambert recorded an 'Exciting journey from the trenches. Shells and shrapnel all around'.[14] 9/East Surrey had twenty-two wounded.

On 30 June, the division was relieved by 20th Division and moved to Locre, near Bailleul.

Although the casualties suffered by the Battalion during this period amounted to nearly 200 killed and wounded, it was considered this sector compared in many ways favourably with the St. Eloi and Hooge sectors. The trenches were well constructed and well drained. The Battalion transport, under Lieut. Whiteman, though it had many narrow escapes, always succeeded in taking the rations as far as the reserve company at 'R.E.' Farm. The village of Dranoutre . . . was much liked. On the other hand, the perpetual shelling and bombardments on the part of the enemy, their employment of '*minenwerfers*', of aerial torpedoes, of every kind of trench mortar and gas, rendered the casualties of the Division and of the Battalion particularly heavy. Another great disadvantage of the sector was that so many working parties had to be furnished, that there was little rest and hardly any opportunity for training newly arrived officers, NCOs and men.[15]

From Locre, for some days, whilst 'at rest', the battalion provided large working parties for cable burying – to protect communications from interruption from German shellfire.

On 8 July the battalion marched through Neuve Eglise and took over, with two companies, Winter Trench and Trenches 134 and 135, opposite La Petite Douve Farm, south of Messines and north of Ploegsteert Wood. HQ and the remaining companies were at Red Lodge, under the steep slope of Hill 63. In addition, four days later, the battalion took over Trenches 136 to 138, with one company, whilst HQ and the reserve company moved to Stinking Farm and Douve Dugouts. This was a quiet sector and the opposing lines at their nearest 200 yards apart. It was not that the enemy were by nature passive: RIR 211 from the same Pomeranian division as at Wulverghem held the line down to the Douve. However, neither side expected to gain much from belligerence. There were some exchanges of artillery and mortar fire and Lewis guns were used to disperse working parties and other enemy groups. The battalion's own casualties were limited to two dead and two wounded over ten days in these trenches. On 19 July the battalion moved, by bus, into a brief rest and then training, including bayonet fighting.

Meanwhile, the Somme offensive had opened on 1 July and there were rumours that the division would join it. These rumours soon proved all too correct. Pirie, however, was positive, writing on 22 July, 'Last night we heard we are going South to the Somme on Monday. I'm glad and quite looking forward to it. I just hope the Regt. does well but I hate to think of the casualties.' and the following day, 'I just hope I manage to do my part properly and not be a funk.'

Chapter 5

Somme-Guillemont and Delville Wood, August–September 1916

The great Battle of the Somme had commenced on 1 July, whilst 24th Division was in Flanders. Like Loos, but on a much larger scale, it was a battle that the British had been obliged to fight, not from choice, but to support their allies. By the beginning of 1916, the BEF had expanded to thirty-eight infantry and five cavalry divisions. Nevertheless, Haig would have preferred to build up its size further before a major offensive, and for such an offensive to be in Flanders, which was of considerable strategic importance to the British. The French, however, wanted a combined attack, and on the Somme. But the German assault on Verdun, beginning in February, drew off much of the French Army's strength that could otherwise have been devoted to the Somme. Moreover, the French were put under such pressure at Verdun, that they, in turn, pressed the British ever harder to commence the Somme offensive and force the Germans to divert resources from attacking Verdun.

The Somme offensive, now largely a British operation with the French taking a subsidiary role on the southern flank, had begun with disaster. On 1 July the British Army had sustained its heaviest casualties ever on a single day: nearly 60,000 dead, wounded and missing. German casualties were far lower and Allied advances made were relatively modest. Where ground had been captured, this was largely in the south and much of it by the French. Too much faith had been placed in an inflexible artillery barrage and the infantry tactics used were often unsophisticated, leading to massive losses from German machine guns, in particular. However, the German High Command realised it had miscalculated the weight of the Somme offensive and started to suspend offensive action at Verdun and send reinforcements towards the Somme. As for its Austrian ally, this was reeling under the pressure of a great Russian offensive, and a further attack by Italy. To make matters worse, Rumania, encouraged by Austria's weakness, looked likely to attack her.

The Allies continued their attacks on the Somme and the Germans counterattacked, both almost regardless of cost. On 14 July, with concentrated artillery support, on a narrow front, the British were able to capture much of the German Second Position. Delville Wood was seized by the British on 27 July, after a devastating bombardment, but the Germans refused to give up, responding with heavy shelling and counterattacks.

By early August, Haig recognised that limited attacks, with adequate preparation, were the only way forward. However, this prescription to his commanders, as given on 3 August, was not consistently followed and he, at times, displayed impatience with progress. A large number of piecemeal attacks, not by any means always adequately prepared or resourced, were launched over the following weeks, to gain better positions for a more general attack. According to Prior and Wilson, from 15 July to 14 September, i.e. between two major, and relatively successful, offensives, the British on the Somme suffered perhaps 82,000 casualties, whilst capturing less ground than on 1 July, although the proportion of casualties inflicted on the Germans compared with 1 July must have been much greater.[1]

At the end of July, 9/East Surrey had set out for the Somme. It reached the Sandpits, near Méaulte, just south of Albert, late on 1 August. Billman recalled the approach march, 'The heat was intense and the dust nearly choked us.'[2] Pirie had to send some men to hospital with heatstroke. Training continued and officers and men were given the opportunity to see captured German defences near Fricourt.

The division's training for offensive action at the end of July had been intensive. GHQ had issued 'Training of Divisions for Offensive Action' in early May, setting out much good practice, but had been obliged to recognise 'that officers and troops generally do not now possess that military knowledge arising from a long and high state of training which enables them to act promptly on sound lines in unexpected situations. They have become accustomed to deliberate action based on precise detailed orders.' It therefore emphasised the need for clear understanding in all ranks as to what might need to be done in different situations.[3] For Hitchcock with 2/Leinster,

> The important item was practising for the new barrage system of shell-fire. We were taught how to advance when the barrage lifted; to make matters more realistic, the Battalion drummers beat a roll to represent shell-fire.
>
> We advanced at walking pace, the men carrying their rifles at the high port. The Battalion attacked in waves of platoons on a two company frontage; each wave had its special role, and was followed by a party called the 'Moppers-up'. The moppers-up were responsible for clearing up all captured trenches, destroying all dug-outs and killing or capturing all spare Huns! At the beginning of the offensive some Divisions had bitter experience when capturing several lines without these 'Moppers-up'. There were several instances of Germans in the front lines scuttling into their deep dug-outs allowing the British to advance on to their second objective, and then coming to the surface again with machine-guns to pour a withering fire into the backs of the attackers.[4]

General Capper followed up the tactical training by addressing his men. 'He impressed on us the necessity to send back information as to our position in battle and that we must dig in properly to consolidate.'[5]

As for weapons, the infantry had lost their Vickers guns and gunners to brigade machine-gun companies, but by now should have had sixteen Lewis guns per

battalion instead. Surviving Battalion Orders for 3 August list the company Lewis
gun teams. Each consists of an officer and fifteen ORs. It may be that there were
only two guns available then, per company. The sections were relatively large to
manage the ammunition supply. In 'D' Company's section was Corporal Fred
Billman.[6] Hitchcock was dismissive of the Lewis, 'a very shoddy affair after the
Vickers'.[7] However, the Lewis guns were frequently crucial in the fighting to
come, especially as the standard of musketry in the New Armies could never com-
pete with that of the pre-war regulars. There was now also a plentiful supply of an
effective grenade, the Mills. As for immediate fire support, each infantry brigade
now had both Vickers machine-gun and trench-mortar units. An officer and a
number of men from each battalion were recorded as transferred to these latter
units in April 1916 in the brigade war diary.[8]

The artillery had grown enormously in numbers and power since Loos,
although still handicapped by often poor quality ammunition and a lack of
flexibility. Attempts were being made to improve liaison between infantry and
artillery, in the absence of hand-portable wireless equipment. These included
fairly primitive and not always successful means for artillery co-operation aeroplanes to follow the infantry's progress on the ground.

By this time, a system of battle patches had been introduced to 24th Division, as
with many others, to assist identification in battle, without making this too obvious
to the enemy. 24th Division's sign was a white diamond, surrounded by four white
triangles, all on a red ground. 9/East Surrey was distinguished by a green cross
on the shoulder, surmounted by a diamond-blue for 'A' Company, green for 'B',
red for 'C' and yellow for 'D'. Specialists had further badges, like a three-legged
badge for runners and streamers worn from the shoulder strap for 'moppers up'.
At least the longer serving of the battalion's officers, unusually, were distinguished
by black, white and red ribbons on the rear collars of their jackets and greatcoats,
having arrived in France wearing them.[9]

The battalion's officers were a properly coherent and professional group by this
time. They had had relatively few casualties since Loos (eight killed and more
wounded, but most of the latter had returned), although there would have been the
usual turnover from sickness and some transfers to other units. (See Chapter 13.)

Lieutenant Colonel de la Fontaine was an effective leader and one who was
known to care for his men, and never hesitated to share their dangers. 'Syd'
Hannan recalled, many years later,

> He was very popular with all. The following incident concerning the Col. is
> true and caused me to both admire and respect him. As a company bomber I
> was relieved of a lot of firestep duties with the exception of stand-to at dawn,
> when all were on duty. We had to go out and act as listening patrols to cover
> the wire, etc. These were usually two man affairs for about 1 hour at a time.
> We had a sergeant ... as mad as a March Hare when sober, but a real menace
> when the rum was in him – we never liked going on any of his patrols. This
> particular night, another private and myself were preparing to go out when he

said 'hold it, an officer is coming with you.' This officer turned out to be the CO, De la Fontaine. We had no rifle, just Mills bombs and a club studded with barbed wire and nails driven in. He had just a revolver and the inevitable cane. He did not take over, gave no orders but told us to carry on normally. He asked questions, we answered and after about half an hour he came in – us with him ... As soon as the Col thanked us and left, the sergeant sent us back out again to finish our shift. We found out that this was not an isolated case. He had done the same on the other Company fronts, but little things like that cause you to both admire and respect a person.[10]

De la Fontaine was also conscious that those under heavy stress needed a break, even if they did not recognise it themselves. In June 1916, he secretly arranged with the brigadier for Pirie to be sent off to a rest station for a week. Pirie recorded, 'I didn't want to go, but he insisted.'[11] The officers of the battalion had much more expertise than their predecessors who had attacked at Loos. Those who had survived that battle now had considerable experience of trench warfare. They had been joined by others, a number of whom had combat experience in the ranks. Looking at the officers' origins, most had associations with Surrey or London. Socially, they were still predominantly upper middle class in background with public school, and sometimes university education, too. However, some officers were lower middle-class men who had been to grammar schools and had generally served in the ranks before being commissioned.

By now, the *Army List* is seriously adrift as to who was serving in the field with the battalion. The July 1916 edition includes, for instance, half a dozen officers killed at Loos and a POW. It is only some months later that the war diary commences listing officers serving with the battalion, although this includes some on secondment to other units in the BEF. However, various officers are mentioned in the war diary or by Pirie. Taking some of the captains, substantive or otherwise, for instance, O'Connor was a Loos survivor and had served briefly as a regular officer pre-war. John Lyndhurst Vaughan, aged only 20, had served in Harrow's OTC and had applied successfully for a commission straight from school in August 1914, being described by his school as 'a boy of exceptional grit and drive'. His father was a retired colonel. His elder brother, a captain in the Seaforths, had been killed at Loos. Charles Hilton, aged 25, was a produce broker, who had joined the ranks of the TA in 1912. He had served from March 1915 in France, as a sergeant in the Civil Service Rifles, a middle-class Territorial unit. A total of 170 men left that year for officer training and Hilton was one, being commissioned in December 1915.

As for the subalterns, whilst Clark, the adjutant, was a regular long-service former senior NCO in the regiment, this was very unusual. Charles Cuthbert, aged 24, had served four years in the Royal Scots TF and then two months with the London Scottish in the BEF before being commissioned. Henry Schofield, aged 22, had served in Manchester University OTC, whilst Henry Spurling, aged 20, had been in the OTC at Oundle School. Gerald Tetley, aged 29, was a barrister who had enlisted in the ranks of the Royal Fusiliers in September 1914, before being commissioned. George Rivers and James Picton had both been commissioned after enlisting in the Inns of Court OTC in autumn 1914. Geoffery Lillywhite had attended a grammar school, rather than a public school, and had been a War Office clerk before being commissioned. Most unusually, Lawrence Hadenham, killed in July 1916, was a former waiter and the son of a gardener and domestic servant. After four months as a sergeant at the Front with 8/East Surrey, he had been commissioned in November 1915.[12] Pirie had paid tribute to him in his diary as 'a good friend and a very fine soldier'.

Officer training, until February 1916, with the formation of Officer Cadet Battalions, had been somewhat haphazard. Before January 1915 there had been no real system for non-regular officers. From after that time, however, ranker candidates, recommended by their COs, were given a short course of four weeks with such as the Inns of Court, Artists' Rifles and university OTCs.[13]

From Pirie's diary, the officers seem to have been generally dedicated, cheerful and supportive. They enjoyed eating together in the trenches, or out of the line, ending with a sing-song. There was some occasional light-hearted boisterous behaviour. Pirie recorded on 16 June, 'We had a great rag at C. Coy's billet last night. I went to D Coy. after dinner and we then all went to C. Coy and dragged "Buggie" Picton out of bed and Cuthbert doused him with tomato sauce.!!!'

It is somewhat difficult to judge officer/man relations, but with the fine example set by de la Fontaine, Hannan's remarks and references in Pirie's diary, it would seem reasonable to expect these were generally good. Lillywhite was surprised to find soon after his arrival that the men were doing their work in Reserve, singing.[14] On the positive side, the officers seem to have regarded their men with paternal affection. On the downside, they seem to have been pleasantly surprised when they showed initiative. On the matter of discipline, there seems to be no further mention of the sort of problems that the battalion had experienced around its arrival in France, including with senior NCOs. There was only one case of a man from the battalion being sentenced to death. This was Private W. Hill, who was convicted of insubordination and disobedience on 3 June 1916. His sentence was, however, commuted to five years' penal servitude.[15] There are occasional references to the sort of disciplinary problems that any unit had in the few surviving Battalion Orders for 1916, or the 'Burnt Records' of individuals.[16]

Regarding discipline, Sidney Rogerson, who was an officer with a regular battalion of the West Yorkshire Regiment, later wrote,

It had always seemed absurd to me to try and adhere rigidly to the conventional formalities of discipline in the trenches where officers lived cheek by jowl with their men, shared the same dangers, the same dug-outs, and sometimes the same mess-tins … I believed … that the best way to get the best out of the British soldier was for an officer to show that he was the friend of his men, and to treat them as friends. This naturally involved a relaxation of pre-war codes of behaviour, but it did not mean that an officer should rub shoulders with his men at every opportunity, or allow them to become familiar with him ... He had consequently to steer a delicate course between treating those under him as equals in humanity if inferiors in status, and losing their respect by becoming too much one of them ... He had, in short, to discriminate between the men who would appreciate his interest and those who would be foolish enough to try and impose upon his good nature.[17]

It seems likely a similar attitude was taken by officers in 9/East Surrey.

Pirie was a dedicated front-line medic and the attitude of the Medical Officer (MO) could be very important for morale. Pirie expected to tour the trenches and be on hand where most required, regardless of his personal safety. Not all MOs were like this. He noted on meeting his Canadian predecessor on 26 March, 'I wanted to go up and have a look at the trenches but the Doctor ... said "He didn't hold with going up to the trenches."' Lodge Patch, MO of 8/Queen's from 1915 to 1919, was unsympathetic to his men for most of his service. He only had some change of heart after witnessing their sufferings in the Great Retreat of March 1918.[18] One of his men, Private Abraham, called him 'Iodine Dick' and criticised him for his superficial examinations and lack of compassion.[19] Pirie, however, frequently expresses admiration for the men in his diary – individually and collectively. He clearly recommended a number of his men for medals. He was also prepared to move men out who were no longer fit for trench warfare. On 29 April he noted, 'A man Budgeon, who had an old wound, I had to go up before the A.D.M.S. to get him off trench warfare and managed to get him marked "permanent base."' Around the same time he sent away an officer, Wills, a survivor of Loos he noted, with 'nerves'.

As for chaplains, it was often a standing joke that these liked to keep well away from danger. Chaplain Poole, shared with 8/R West Kent, was not one of these. Pirie noted on 10 September 'We often see him in the trenches.' Indeed, he was later decorated for bravery.

All in all, the battalion, compared with what it had been before Loos, was now a well-trained and led unit, containing a good number of experienced soldiers. It had, however, no experience of attacking since Loos.

24th Division was part of XIV Corps, with the French on its right. The division was to relieve 6th Division opposite Guillemont. This village was a very strong position with open approaches and had a most determined garrison. It had numerous tunnels and dugouts, which gave the occupants good cover and also enabled them to sally forth and take attackers in the rear. Guillemont had been repeatedly attacked without success. On 10 August, the Battalion took over reserve trenches near Maricourt. From there, the battalion provided men to dig an advanced trench – Lamb Trench. This was first frustrated by a bombardment and then hindered by continual sniping.

Late on 13 August, 'A' and 'B' companies took over front-line trenches near Arrow Head Copse, whilst 'C' and 'D' under Captain Vaughan rehearsed an attack to be made later on the enemy strongpoint opposite, near the end of a sunken section of road. This was intended to assist with the major attack on Guillemont, in conjunction with the French, which was to take place two days later.

Billman described what he saw,

All around was ruin and desolation. In front of us lay the remains of the once pretty village of Guillemont, and between us and the Germans were hundreds of dead bodies of both our troops and the enemy's. Being hot weather the stench alone was something to put up with, as there had been no time to bury the dead. I am not detailing any of the scenes I witnessed at this time, they are too bad for words, but enough to say that we get hardened to all such things.

On 16 August, the attack proceeded. 3rd Division was to attack on the right, whilst 'C' and 'D' companies of 9/East Surrey were to seize the strongpoint and part of the sunken road behind. These positions were very strong and had been unsuccessfully attacked previously. Lieutenant Colonel de la Fontaine recognised the difficulty and requested that the undamaged German strongpoint, of concrete and iron rails, should be destroyed first by 9.2in howitzers. All that was provided, however, was some shelling by a 6in gun, with little benefit. As for the barrage to be provided to cover the advance, this was restricted through fear of hitting 3rd Division's men, and both failed to prevent the Germans firing and interfered with the British advance.

'C' and 'D' companies were to attack in three waves, the first two from Lamb Trench, each around eighty strong. An officer and fifteen men were also to advance, maintaining touch with 3rd Division. The half-hour bombardment commenced at 5.10pm, causing some East Surrey casualties by firing short. At 5.40pm 3rd Division units attacked, but were soon mown down by machine-gun fire and forced to retire. This soon left the two East Surrey companies, attacking 2 minutes later, alone. Almost immediately, the attackers were met by intense rifle fire ahead and machine-gun fire from both flanks. As they approached the sunken road they met a shower of grenades. Very few got into the enemy position and they were immediately overwhelmed. With the first two waves destroyed, Captain Hilton saw the position was hopeless and ordered the third wave to retire. An advance by about thirty Germans was, however, broken up by a Lewis gun.

Billman afterwards described the day and the all but unbearable waiting for the advance.

At last the morning of the 16th of August dawned, the day planned for our attack. Many were the anxious words that passed between us, as to whether we should succeed or not, and whether we should come out of the day safely ... At about 3pm we took our places in an advanced line, from where we were going over and our guns got at it harder than ever. No one on earth but one who has experienced it knows what it is to wait for time, at a time like this. It is impossible to hear one speak, and of course all are wondering how it will go with them ... Visions of home and dear ones will present themselves at such

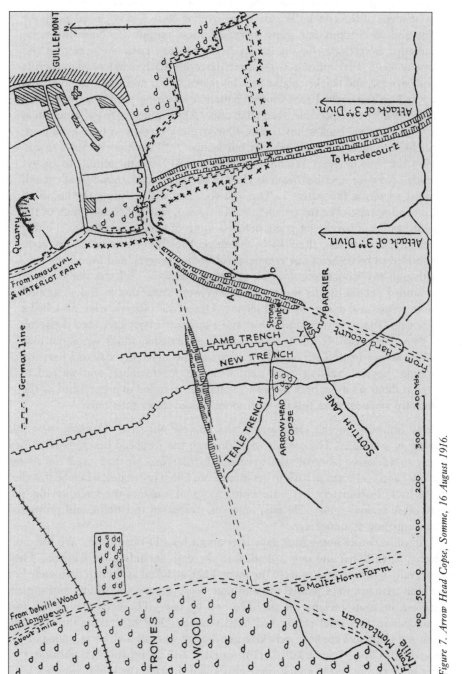

Figure 7. Arrow Head Copse, Somme, 16 August 1916.

times and all are wishing the time up, so that the strain is taken off by the excitement of the attack. 'We are going over at 20 to 6' was passed along the line and at 5.10pm our guns increased their output ... Now the noise exceeded everything, for the enemy began to drop great shells around and among us ... 'Five minutes to go' came the order. Each man looked to his rifle and bayonet, and cracked a joke with his mates. 'Four minutes to go.' I looked up and on our right I saw another battalion attacking ... I was very much fascinated by the spectacle, then all at once 'Three minutes to go' came along and brought me back to my senses. Our artillery seemed to have gone mad. Shells screamed and whistled over our heads ... 'Two more minutes to go.' How the time dragged. Would it never come? At last 'One minute to go, get ready'. Now for it, either death or glory or perhaps a nice wound good enough to get us across the water ... 'Out you go.', and with a spring the heroes of England sprang over the parapet ... However, I was not to see much of the sport, as I had barely got going before a lump of shrapnel or shrapnel bullet put me out of action, altho' I was able to get back into the trench. I was soon attended to by some of our regimental stretcher bearers, and found out that, although my wound was painful, it was not serious ... I was not the only wounded person by any means. Now they were streaming in and all around were groans and dying and dead men ... One of our officers, who was killed a few days later, was very kind to me, and a sergeant-major gave me a cigarette. I know I was awfully thirsty, but couldn't get a drink, and it was about four hours before I could get out of the trenches and make my way to a dressing station. Several walking cases went with me, I remember, and we had to tramp about six miles back before we could get attended to properly, as all the forward stations were full up with more serious cases than ours.

Also wounded in the same attack was 16-year-old 'Syd' Hannan, who was serving as a bomber. His pal was shot through the forehead beside him as they began to advance. Hannan was wounded further on. He had used up all his grenades and was turning back to get more from fallen comrades, when he was shot in the back. Fortunately, his entrenching tool took some of the force, saving him from more serious injury. He was, however, evacuated to Britain, and prevented from returning as under age.[20]

Lillywhite wrote home four days later about his ('D') company, 'We lost four officers, three killed and one wounded, in the coy., including the Captain. They were really splendid and so were the men. They attacked as though on parade but the Hun trenches were packed full and some were coming up behind, and snipers were out in front picking off the men one by one.' The casualties of the two companies in this brief action had been terrible. Of 9 officers in the attack 6, including Captain Vaughan, were killed or died of wounds and 1 was wounded. Of around 240 ORs, 31 were killed, 116 wounded and 29 missing. In addition, two more officers, not in the attack, were also killed. During the night, searches were made to recover the wounded. The following morning, the battalion was relieved.

General Capper reviewed the survivors of 'C' and 'D' companies and made a sympathetic speech.

Pirie had found 16 August 'worse than Hell'. After naming the officers who were casualties, he wrote in his diary,

> The saddest part of all was Corp. Halliday was mortally wounded in the abdomen whilst getting away the second last stretcher case; that finished me off, I wept then. He's an awful loss to me. I don't know what I shall do without him. I am so sad at losing all those officers as we were just like a big family.

Numerous families would have received notification of the death of a loved one in this action and letters of condolence. Second Lieutenant Frank Ball was amongst the dead. A bank clerk, aged 21, he had enlisted in the Public Schools Battalion in October 1914. He was commissioned in the East Surrey Regiment in May 1915, serving with 9th Battalion from March 1916. De la Fontaine wrote to his father, 'He was shot by a rifle bullet and his death was instantaneous. I can't tell you how much we all regret his loss. He was a very popular officer and liked by everyone. All officers here have asked me to convey to you and your family their feelings of deepest sympathy with you in your sad loss.' The chaplain also wrote to the family.[21] With no known grave, Ball is commemorated on the Thiepval Memorial. As for Captain Vaughan, his father painted a picture, 'The Spirit of the Regiment', as a memorial to his son, perhaps inspired by a poem of the time. The painting shows men of 9/East Surrey attacking, followed by their predecessors in Napoleonic period uniform.[22]

Lillywhite, writing home on 17 August, after earlier optimism, was feeling bitter

> I should hope the people are satisfied with what is being done out here. I would give anything for the wretched shysters to see a fine battalion go into action & then see it crawl out a few days later a shattered wreck, nothing but a handful of men. But these little handfuls are very proud because they say the same as the Gurkha said 'If only a very few come back they will know we have been fighting.' The Hun realises that in spite of his terrific efforts we are every day snatching a fresh little piece of his ground. The result is so insignificant on the map but the cost is heavy. It makes one realise what a hopelessly impossible task it would be to storm the whole line and drive them bodily back.

Lillywhite believed his battalion had been facing the Prussian Guard. In fact, the opposing units were drawn from the Württemberg 27 Division. This was a very tough formation, still four infantry regiments strong, and holding this sector since 31 July. The Württemberg divisions maintained their reputation with Allied Intelligence even in late 1918. Within 27 Division was Grenadier Regiment (GR) 123, whose soldiers wore *litzen* (lace) on their jackets, as did the Prussian Guard. It seems they fought 9/East Surrey on 16 August.

After a brief rest, GR 123 had returned to the front line, under heavy fire, on the night of 15/16 August. They had also endured a 'viciously effective' shelling that morning causing forty-three casualties. On their left was IR 120 holding Guillemont itself.

> The external appearance of the battle zone differed in no respect from that of the preceding one. The desolate field of craters in front seemed struck from the same stamp; in many places, due to levelling by artillery fire continuous trenches no longer existed, and at most only individual men or in the very best case a single squad lay within the sight of their platoon commander. There were no communication trenches, and during the day traffic [i.e. movement between front and rear] was only possible by moving in bounds and making use of the shell craters. From Combles an open footpath marked with a white band led to the KTK [*Kampf-Truppen-Kommandeur* – in this context battalion front-line HQ]; it lay literally all day long under an English blocking barrage, and anyone who ever – even once, under cover of night – ran for his life, through the mad hail of shot and shell, from the heights south of Leuze Wood down the slope to the KTK, would never forget their passage through this hell on earth. No approach march was ever as dreaded as this, and no party ever made the crossing without casualties, stragglers and men losing their way. The difficulties involved are clearly apparent from the fact alone, that a message from 9 Company in the front line on the evening of the 16th took 7½ hours to reach the KTK. As upon the area between the lines, so also upon the front line the barrage persisted unrelentingly for hours at a time, and every kind of material aid – of which a great abundance lay at the disposal of the enemy – was employed to wear down the Germans.

After this, the infantry attacks came almost as a relief.

> The 16th August had already torn cruel holes in [the ranks of] the fighting troops, and in powerless rage the brave [men] had seen one or another of their comrades torn away. But they did not despair and, when at 6.20 in the evening [German time], the English moved their infantry forward for the assault in many dense waves, some elements even in section columns, they found an unshaken garrison, who had prepared a bloody welcome for them with rifles and machine guns, supported by those of IRs 120 and 127. Isolated enemy detachments had the courage to advance towards our positions at a slow walking pace, and eyewitnesses report that it gave one the impression that the enemy had reckoned with no opposition whatsoever. The counter fire at a range of a few hundred metres hit the front rows with such dreadful effect that they were cut down, and the rest were driven back with clearly visible heavy losses. A renewed assault with meagre forces at 7.30 achieved no better result, and another at 10 o'clock in the evening was no more successful in shaking the troops, who were confident of victory. Only by the company on the left, where a 50–60m wide gap had been blasted, did a small English party

succeed in breaking through and establishing themselves in the sunken road. Our own losses were heavy, mainly on the right flank, where at the southern edge of Guillemont the barrage was at its most intense. 9 Company alone, after 24 hours in action, already reported 20 dead and 38 wounded, and nearby and behind them amongst 12 Company, who had reinforced them in front too early, it was not much different. There were shortages of ammunition, hand grenades, dressings, flare- and signal-cartridges and of food, not to mention water. The wounded lay scattered about, wretched and moaning, and clung despairingly to the last hope, that the stretcher-bearers had been urgently sent for. Dreadful hours: even the toughest lifted their gaze toward the eternal heavens, and the twinkling stars were never more enigmatic than in the night which fell over such a battlefield.'[23]

On 18 August 9/East Surrey, as part of 72 Brigade, was in support, when its division's 17 and 73 Brigades attacked Guillemont, after a 36-hour bombardment. There were mixed results, with 3/Rifle Brigade doing particularly well, advancing close behind the barrage and then keeping touch with the artillery. But the western outskirts of the village, only, including the station, were captured. Major General Capper observed the attack from an observation balloon.[24] On 21 August, the battalion moved with 8/Queen's to the new front line, sustaining a number of casualties to shelling, including Hilton and Lillywhite wounded. (Lillywhite had multiple wounds from shell fragments, which became infected, and did not return to the battalion.) A further attack on Guillemont by the division that day had very little success. The village did not finally fall – to 20th Division, assisted by 16th Division – until 3 September.

On 22 August the division's relief commenced and some days were spent in billets, with two in training. Hitchcock, however, with 2/Leinster was still in the line, from where 9/East Surrey had attacked on 16 August, not being relieved until 26 August. The opposing Germans, astride the sunken road, full of dead, were now Hanoverians from FR 73, 111 Division, and included Ernst Jünger, who later described his experiences in the classic *The Storm of Steel*.

At rest, Moran, with the division's 1/Royal Fusiliers, noted rumours on the morning of 29 August of a return to the fighting. 'It seems that a division is dipped twice into the Somme, with perhaps a week's rest and quiet sandwiched between. The second time it is kept in until it has no further fighting value.'[25]

The rumours proved all too true. On 30 August, in rain and mud, 72 Brigade took over positions in Delville Wood. 9/East Surrey went into reserve trenches at Montauban, prior to a move to the wood. After weeks of fighting, the wood and its surroundings resembled a wrecked abattoir. The abiding memory of the once-attractive landscape for Second Lieutenant Martin in 1/North Staffordshire was of the approach to the wood.

The most dreadful picture in my Somme gallery is a landscape – a wide upland slope, uniformly drab, dirty white, chalk mixed with decaying vegetation, not a tree stump or a bush left, just desolation, with a track named

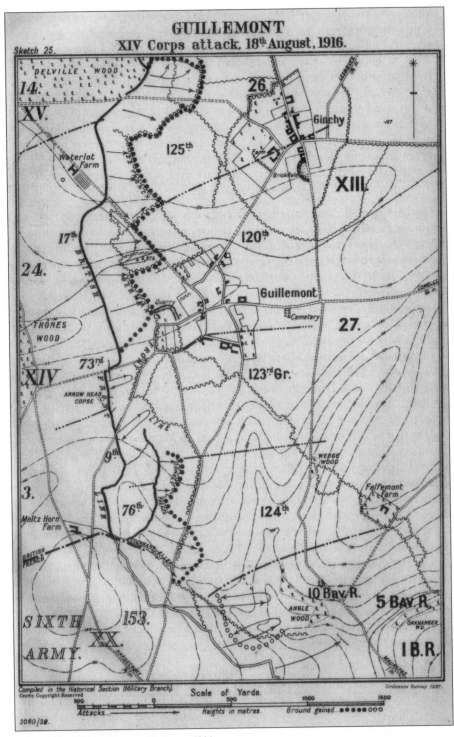

Figure 8. Guillemont, Somme, 18 August 1916.

Crucifix Alley for men to walk round or through shell holes to the larger desolation of Delville Wood. The whole blasted slope clotted to the very edges with dead bodies, too many to bury, and too costly, the area being under constant fire from artillery, This awful display of dead men looked like a set piece, as though some celestial undertaker had spaced the corpses evenly for interment and then been interrupted. Several times I picked my way through this cemetery of the unburied. A landscape picture my memory turns up in horror.[26]

In August, 9/East Surrey had lost 9 officers and 53 ORs, killed or died of wounds, 6 officers and 175 ORs wounded and 29 ORs missing. The fighting strength on 31 August was only around 325 all ranks.[27] The division had lost around 3,500 all ranks.

The Official History summed up August as,

a period of bitter fighting when hardly any ground was gained and the struggle became, more than ever, a grim test of endurance. There was little to encourage or inspire the troops of all arms who fought on the Somme in August: subjected to heavy losses, great hardships, and tremendous physical and moral strain, they had only their own dogged spirit to maintain them.[28]

Unfortunately, the opening days of September were no better. On 1 September, the battalion, during an enemy bombardment, took over front-line trenches along the eastern edge of Delville Wood. By this time, there was little of the wood left. Hitchcock says the wood 'provided no cover whatsoever. There was no undergrowth left, and all the paths through the wood were taped to the square foot by the enemy artillery.'[29] A German officer, of IR 88, 56 Division, seeing it on 31 August, recalled, 'the wretched remains, of the shattered Delville Wood ... we could see enemy trenches criss-crossing the so-called wood, which was so thin that we were able to see the ruins of the village of Longueval behind it'.[30] There had been an attack on the wood that day, as part of the German policy of counterattacking whenever and wherever possible. It had made relatively little progress at heavy cost and what ground had been gained was recaptured by 3/Rifle Brigade and 8/Buffs on 1 September.

56 Division, largely Hessian, was a formidable formation that had fought earlier at Verdun. It had taken over the line at Ginchy and Delville Wood on 24 August and then taken part in the attack on the wood on 31 August. It had had some success then, but had sustained heavy casualties from British infantry and artillery. It was thus forced to contract its front, with 4 Bavarian Division on the right taking up the slack. 56 Division had IR 118 on its right, FR 35 on its left and IR 88 as a reserve.

The Brandenburgers of FR 35 recorded on 1 September,

Thirsty, hungry and ground down, officers and men lay together in mud-filled craters amongst dead comrades who could not be carried back. We were

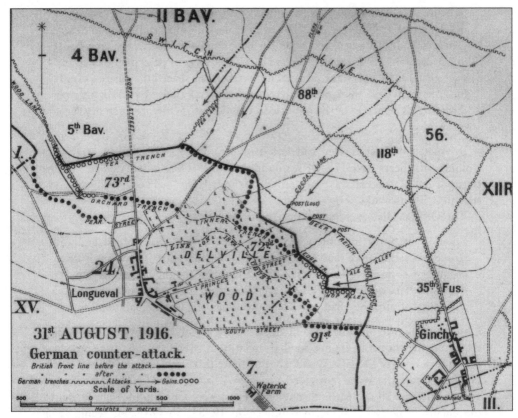

Figure 9. Delville Wood, Somme, 31 August 1916.

obliged to be satisfied if the dead could be given a hasty shallow burial where they fell. However, the fallen who lay between the trenches, and often also further to the rear, remained unburied. As a result, the stench of corpses was virtually overwhelming and thousands upon thousands of flies put the troops off their food despite their hunger.[31]

9/East Surrey spent 2 September deepening the trenches and using Lewis guns, with effect, on the enemy in Ale Alley. As a result, ten Germans from IR 118, opposite, surrendered.

As for the night of 2/3 September, FR 35 facing 9/East Surrey, recorded

Throughout the night the enemy artillery fire thundered on, accompanied by a constant heavy rain. Contact with the front line was scarcely possible even under cover of darkness. The brave carrying parties with the food and ammunition got forwards only with unspeakable difficulty ... Since there was no barbed wire in front (and it was impossible to set any up) and since continuous trench lines were lacking and the dark night blurred the boundaries between friend and foe, the bearers ran the risk of ending up, with their heavy loads, amongst the enemy.[32]

On 3 September, 7th Division, on the right of 24th Division was to attack Ginchy, half a mile south-east of 9/East Surrey. Germans in Ale Alley and Hop Alley could enfilade units advancing on Ginchy. The battalion was ordered to assist by attacking, at noon, Ale Alley from the north-west, whilst a bombing party from the brigade on the right would attack from the south. The battalion was also to capture Beer Trench, which was then lightly held. However, the neighbouring brigade declared a change of plan, so that their bombers would attack Hop Alley instead. Captain Ingrams and Second Lieutenant Tetley led around forty men attacking Ale Alley at noon, with a second attack 40 minutes later. Unfortunately, the attack by the brigade on the right did not progress and the Surrey men failed to break into the two Alleys. Captain Ingrams was killed and Lieutenant Colonel de la Fontaine was very severely wounded leading an attack. An officer and three men crawled forward to a shell hole and sniped at Germans, who they reported to be holding Ale and Hop Alleys in strength. Part of Beer Trench was, however, seized and thirty Germans advancing towards it were badly hit by Lewis gun fire. The war diary complained of the support given to the battalion's attack. 'Our own artillery did not assist us very much. Our heavy guns were throwing shells into our trench instead of ALE ALLEY. Our stokes guns failed to fire anywhere near the enemy trench and the T.M. firing smoke bombs stopped firing much too soon.'[33]

FR 35, facing 9/East Surrey, but with its left extending to Ginchy, had come under heavy fire from early on.

From 6.00am the enemy artillery fire increased in strength to a truly infernal din; the heavy calibre [shells] made the earth shake. The bad weather turned out to be a real stroke of fortune, as the muddy ground swallowed up many of the shells as 'duds.' ... At 1.00 pm [German time] there ensued an infantry attack along the entire length of the front. The advanced trenches of 1 and 2 [companies] FR 35 at Delville Wood were first covered with mortar bombs and rifle grenades, whilst enemy aircraft masked the proceedings in front from rearward observation with smoke bombs. The machine guns with the 1 and 2 Companies, well emplaced to give flanking fire, were buried and their crews put out of action. The Fusiliers in the protruding cornerstone of the position at Delville Wood thus saw they could only rely on themselves when the assault was launched. Nevertheless ... they stood unshaken against over-whelmingly superior force ... Finally the constantly renewed assault flagged, and with bloodied heads the English withdrew.[34]

In answer to red flares from the German infantry by Delville Wood, and the attack on Ginchy, IR 88 recalled 'Our artillery opened up the most violent defensive barrage and well paced fire for effect with heavy calibres.'[35] 9/East Surrey suffered severely from the terrible bombardment, which lasted many hours. Major Ottley, sent from the Royal Fusiliers, to take command of the battalion, was killed, as was most of a party from 8/Buffs, sent to reinforce the battalion. As a result of the day's fighting, the battalion was reduced to 9 officers and 100–150 ORs, under command of Lieutenant Clark, the adjutant. During the evening, two companies of 1/North Staffordshire moved up in support. The German bombardment continued. On 4 September, about ninety men of the battalion were left holding on in the wood. The war diary recorded,

> Strong petition received from the 4 remaining officers urging instant relief on account of the exhaustive [*sic*] state of the men. Lt. C.A. Clark (Adjutant) sent a message asking that they try and stick it until it was our time for relief. A message in reply was received saying they would stick it to the last for the sake of the Regiment, and thanking Adjutant for his encouraging message.

What was left of the battalion remained, holding part of the front line, until 5 September, when the division was relieved. In those first 5 days of September the battalion had lost 4 officers and 42 ORs killed or died of wounds, 10 officers and 112 ORs wounded and 25 ORs missing. Captain Pirie wrote on 12 September, to Second Lieutenant Denny, wounded on 16 August,

> Up we went again & oh H . . ., it was H . . . much worse than the previous events, your attack was nil to it. I have never seen such shelling. We were on the edge of a wood & of course had our line taped. We were up when the village was taken, your old objective is no more now. It was a very successful day. The OC was shot through both lungs leading a bombing show & we all thought at first he would die, but his grit & determination has pulled him through, & he is doing very well indeed. He was magnificent the way he led those tired men they were irresistible. Poor Parker Ingrams was killed well forward in the attack. He was OC B Coy. Monro was also wounded knee and arm & is home now. Gold slightly wounded, Castle badly. Urban, Haines, & Major Ottley our 2/command killed by direct hits of shells . . . only Clarke & I survive who have been up each time & I don't know how we did you can expect to see Clarke an M. Cross winner for leading a bombing party to the line through H . . . s own barrage. He was great. Tetley rejoined us the day of the attack was only ½ hr up when over he went and survived. He was magnificent. Sgt. Summers still exists – marvellous. He's up for decoration again.[36]

In his diary, Pirie had written on 6 September about the Delville Wood ordeal,

> Those four days and five nights were the most trying I have ever spent, very little sleep and very heavy shelling. I don't know how anyone got out alive. The wood was so heavily shelled by day and night that all wounded were stored in Hun dugouts all day till between 5 and 8a.m. and 5 and 8p.m, during which periods the shelling seemed to die down and so allow the cases to be got out to my aid post then they were carried from me by R.A.M.C. bearers to a dressing station . . . My regt. bearers did very fine work, especially Mead, Trish, Oyston and Hardiker, they were fearless and worked like slaves.

Amongst the many who died in Delville Wood, was Private William Coxhill. His wife, struggling to bring up two young children, wrote in March 1917,

> I must say I was very much surprised at not receiving more of his belongings as I know he had many more photos and two prayer books and watch that were given to him before he left for France, also that he must have had money on him, as his last letter written to me two days before his death said he would be sending me some the first opportunity.
>
> I am disappointed at not receiving all his belongings as they would have been treasured by my two little sons when they are old enough to understand how their father died.[37]

The Germans opposite, in 56 Division, had also had a terrible experience. The commander of 10 Company, IR 88 had felt obliged to write to his battalion commander on 5 September,

> The company has now spent nearly twelve days in the line (the seven hour stop over in Rocquiny does not count as rest) and during this time the men have had no rest at night and hot food only on occasional days. The men are so weakened as a result that they can no longer be used as fighting troops. The state of morale is such that if the relief promised for yesterday does not take place tonight I cannot be responsible for the consequences.

This was sent on to higher authority with the battalion commander's endorsement.

Like the 9/East Surrey, however, they somehow held on, until relieved late the following day and after having to take part in a counterattack.[38] 56 Division's 3 infantry regiments, alone, had around 3,200 casualties, including nearly 1,100 dead or missing from 25 August to 8 September. Ginchy finally fell on 9 September.

Within 24th Division, it would seem that the regulars still had an edge. Before the Somme fighting, they had suffered comparatively few casualties for some time, so should have had a greater proportion of veterans and their particular *esprit de corps*. They seem to have done well in the Somme fighting. Nevertheless, a number of the division's eight Kitchener battalions also had some successes. Moran says that by the Somme, most of the division's Kitchener battalions that had suffered so severely at Loos had recovered.

> But two battalions never got over that battle – probably their officers were to blame. Six months before the Somme that was common knowledge, but General Capper, whose energy had done much for the Division could not bring himself to acknowledge that he had failed with these battalions. When in the Somme fighting they crumpled up leaving the units on their flanks in the air, the Division paid in full the price of his failure to cut losses.[39]

Although he does not name them, the most obvious candidate for Moran's criticism was 13/Middlesex, although this unit had suffered less heavily than other battalions in the division at Loos. The Middlesex battalion had been very badly hit on 18 August and broke up when taken by surprise in Delville Wood on 31 August by Bavarian IR 5. German Intelligence reported after interviewing a number of POWs, 'there exists no longer any cohesion … about two thirds of the men have reached the battalion over the last few days as various batches of replacements'.[40] Moran refers later, critically, to the 8/Buffs, without naming it, with regard to a raid in January 1917, when it lost fifty prisoners in a German raid and the CO was sacked. It seems to have done well enough on the Somme, though. He refers to 9/Sussex as 'yokels', with 'men who do not seem to think at all', but also says 'The strength of the yokel soldier lay in his obstinate refusal to recognise danger when it was all around him.'[41] This battalion had made a good defence against the German attack at Hooge in February 1916 and did well repulsing the German attack at Delville Wood. However, Hitchcock who was with 2/Leinster in support of the 13/Middlesex and 9/Sussex, was not impressed with the orders given him by the Sussex commander, which cost the lives of twelve of his platoon. But Hitchcock generously commends the initiative shown by another Kitchener battalion, 8/Queen's, during this same German attack, in advancing 50 yards from their trench to a line of shell holes, which much reduced their bombardment casualties. He also records that it was 3/Rifle Brigade (regular) and 8/Buffs (Kitchener) which recovered the ground lost by the collapse of the 13/Middlesex, which he confirms had been filled up with young and inexperienced men after heavy losses.[42] In January 1918 it was 8/Buffs and 12/Royal Fusiliers which were disbanded from 24th Division.

72 Brigade has a 'Narrative of Operations August 16th–20th 1916' in its war diary. In referring to the disastrous East Surrey attack on 16 August at Arrow Head Copse, it makes no criticism of the battalion, but infers a good deal of unhappiness with the plan and the artillery support, in particular. As for Delville Wood, the battalion did not give way, but was nearly annihilated by artillery fire.

The battalion's contribution was recognised by numerous decorations. A DSO went to de la Fontaine, and MCs to Clark and Lieutenant Gold, who had taken command in turn after the more senior officers had fallen. As for the men, a DCM went to Lance Corporal Webb, a stretcher bearer, and there were thirteen Military Medals (MMs).

24th Division had had a frustrating time on the Somme. Like other divisions at this time, it had been used up in a series of piecemeal actions and had seen little success. It had acquired useful experience, but at a terrible cost in casualties. All too often, the veterans had filled the casualty lists, to be replaced by raw new-comers. Although progress had often been slow and uneven, the British Army did, however, learn important lessons from the Somme fighting, particularly around combined arms operations. Unfortunately for 24th Division, these were most obviously applied after its departure from this front. They would be taken into account for the offensives of the following year.

As for the German Army, it could not face another Somme. Even at the expense of giving up conquered territory, something previously considered unthinkable, it realised it must fight defensively in the West in 1917, and from new fortified positions, well behind the Somme front line. For 27 Division, which had fought so hard defending Guillemont,

A culminating point was reached which was never again approached. What we experienced surpassed all previous conception. The enemy's fire never ceased for an hour. It fell night and day on the front line and tore fearful gaps in the ranks of the defenders. It fell on the approaches to the front line and made all movement towards the front hell. It fell on the rearward trenches and battery positions and smashed men and material in a manner never seen before or since. It repeatedly reached even the resting battalions behind the front and occasioned there terrible losses. Our artillery was powerless against it ... In the Somme fighting of 1916 there was a spirit of heroism which was never again found in the division, however conspicuous its fighting power remained until the end of the war.[43]

Ernst Jünger, who had been fortunate to be wounded and evacuated before the fall of Guillemont, put it in even more dramatic language,

It was the days at Guillemont that first made me aware of the overwhelming effects of the war of material. We had to adapt ourselves to an entirely new phase of war ... There was a zone of a kilometre behind the front line where explosives held absolute sway ... a battle was no longer an episode that spent itself in blood and fire; it was a condition of things that dug itself in remorselessly week after week and even month after month. What was a man's life in this wilderness whose vapour was laden with the stench of thousands upon thousands of decaying bodies? Death lay in ambush for each one in every shell-hole, merciless, and making one merciless in turn. Chivalry here took a final farewell. It had to yield to the heightened intensity of war, just as all fine and personal feeling has to yield when machinery gets the upper hand ... The names of the tiniest Picardy hamlets are memorials of heroic battles to which the history of the world can find no parallel. There it was that the dust first drank the blood of our trained and disciplined youth. Those fine qualities which had raised the German race to greatness leapt up once more in dazzling flame and then slowly went out in a sea of mud and blood.[44]

Part II
Through Attrition to Final Victory, September 1916–November 1918

Chapter 6

Return to Loos,
September–December 1916

The battalion had come out of the Somme, wrecked. Lieutenant Colonel H.S. Tew, East Surrey Regiment took command of the remnants from Lieutenant Clark. There were just 10 officers and around 200 men, with few NCOs. Tew was a regular who had served as Major with 1/East Surrey at Mons. Pirie found him 'very quiet and dry, but nice'.[1] In order to recover, 9/East Surrey was soon moved to Francières for the Abbeville training area, where it remained until 24 September. It received drafts which soon made up its numbers to 40 officers and about 700 men. The first priority was to ensure the new men were properly trained and integrated. With so few experienced officers, initially Tew and Clark had to do much of the training themselves. Billman, recovered from his wound, rejoined at this time. He was shocked,

> to find the remnants of what, a few weeks before, was a smart and strong battalion. The battles on the Somme had thinned the ranks awfully . . . Just a few of my old pals remained, and I was soon listening to the accounts of some terrible times they had after I was wounded. However, the good name of the regiment had been upheld, although at such a price, and there was satisfaction that the Boche was getting a good hiding.[2]

As well as training there were opportunities for recreation. Pirie relished the peaceful countryside after the Somme. For 12 September he recorded, 'This afternoon the Division had a horse show for all the transport units in it. It was a fine turn out. Then there was some flat racing. The divisional band turned out and tea and drinks in a marquee, so really one might have been at an agricultural show at home.'

The Somme survivors were also given leave – 140 men and 4 officers were sent to the seaside for 3 days. Pirie and his friend Hilton, however, set off for two days in Paris, visiting various tourist sites including the *Folies-Bergère* for a revue. '(We didn't understand much of the show but the music was very pretty) . . . One would scarcely say a war was on, as the Restaurants are as good as ever and theatres, etc all going, only the girls aren't as brightly dressed as in peace time.'

With 24th Division taking over a sector facing Vimy Ridge, the battalion moved, by stages, to Estrée-Cauchie (called 'Extra-Cushy' by the troops). This was

10 miles north-west of Arras. There it remained, in Brigade Support, for the rest of the month and continued training.

On 1 October, three more new subalterns joined the battalion: Louis Abrams, Percy High and Bob Sherriff. Sherriff was later to write *Journey's End*, the most famous play on the First World War, based on his experiences with 9/East Surrey. As an 18-year-old insurance clerk he had sought a commission in August 1914. But his grammar school (which did not have an OTC) was not on the approved list and he was rejected. He enlisted in the Artists' Rifles in November 1915 and was commissioned in the East Surrey Regiment in September 1916.

Sherriff wrote much about his service. 'I had written long letters home: my mother and father had kept them all, and when I got back I had collected them together and written them up as a continuous narrative.'[3] Sherriff later used this narrative, which, however, covered only the early days of his service when everything was a novelty, to write a series of articles, 'My Diary'. They appeared in six episodes in the regimental journal from 1936–1939, and were brought to a premature end by the Second World War. They covered his journey to the Front and his first ten days with the battalion. Sherriff explained to the editor of the journal that the worked up narrative did not run after Christmas 1916. He had resisted previous suggestions to publish the 'Diary', because of the personal nature of some of it. For the articles he had left out long descriptions of fellow officers and had changed the names of the 8/Queen's officers mentioned.[4] Many letters, but not the narrative, are held at Surrey History Centre.[5]

In 1968 Sherriff published his autobiography, *No Leading Lady*, and also contributed an essay to a collection commemorating the fiftieth anniversary of the Armistice. The autobiography has much to say about his writing *Journey's End*, but only begins after the war. The essay, 'The English Public Schools in the War', told of Sherriff's original failure to secure a commission, which he took to be simply because he hadn't been to a public school, but then generously, and unfashionably, paid tribute to the contribution of the public schoolboy as officer. It also described his last days at the Front and being wounded.

Sherriff in 'My Diary' recalled his arrival and what the battalion had suffered on the Somme. 'So we found them at Estree-Cauchie, still exhausted, but slowly recovering and ready to begin again.'[6]

Sherriff goes on to give vivid portraits of the leading officers. Of 'Nobby Clark', then adjutant,

> a great soldier who knew very detail of his work (and everyone else's too.) He was very popular and commanded the respect of officers and men without distinction. I think this was because his rigid training as a regular soldier had never robbed him of his sense of humour and his understanding of civilians in temporary uniform . . . On parade he was the personification of the Old Army. In the Mess Room he would talk with the most junior subaltern as if they were fellow members of a village cricket team.[7]

Sherriff also recalls two of the company commanders – Hilton of 'C' (in which Sherriff saw all his service with the battalion) and Tetley of 'D'. 'I never knew whether I really liked Hilton or not – he was a bluff, good natured man; a magnificent soldier who understood and did all in his power to lighten the burden of his men. Yet he had the most relentless sarcasm for people he disliked; he was quick to note little peculiarities of voice or manner and unmercifully mimic them. But he was the best and easily the most senior Company Commander.' As for Tetley,

> He was, I think, the most unsoldierlike man I ever saw in the Army ... the greatest object of amusement to the men and at the same time the greatest object of affection and admiration. In the line he was a marvel: naturally highly strung and nervous, he was always with his men should there be any danger ... He would go around the line with a cheery word and a joke with every man – then he would go down into his dugout and fly into a furious rage because a drop of water from the roof had trickled down his neck.[8]

Tew, the CO, was 'a stout, stolid man' who drummed their responsibilities into the new officers. 'He lay bare the cold, uncoloured truth of war; he spoke of the qualities that a young officer should possess and the duties that he should understand. A cold dread came over me "Am I an efficient officer?" "Do I know enough?" "Will I be sent back to England as an awful example of incompetence?"'[9] With Sherriff feeling lonely and inadequate, he was pleased to receive a welcome from the other officers.

On 2 October 9/East Surrey went into Divisional Reserve near Souchez, close to Vimy Ridge. The French had fought particularly bitter engagements here a year previously, as part of the joint offensive in which the British had fought the Battle of Loos. The battalion provided 400-strong working parties for the front support line. The Germans still held commanding positions on Vimy Ridge. Sherriff found himself in a strange 'Alice in Wonderland' world. As for the men of 'C' Company, when he first saw them, 'They looked the biggest set of ruffians I had ever set eyes on. Anyone seeing them without knowing who they were might have thought that Ali Baba's Forty Thieves and the Pirate Crew from "Treasure Island" had amalgamated to do some deed of super villainy.'[10] He described his first, exhausting march with them through the communication trenches and the desolate scenery of a blasted wilderness 'dreary beyond belief'.

Whilst in Reserve, the men were kept busy with labouring. Billman wrote of this time,

> In the daytime, parties of men were busy improving our own particular trench and dugouts, and at night, parties were sent up further forward, on one or the other of the hundreds of jobs that fall to the lot of an infantryman. When there's fighting to be done, the infantry are in the thick of it; when not fighting they are kept from getting lazy by plenty of strenuous work. For all,

this, with the hardships thrown in, the man of the front line trenches gets paid the lowest wage.

The higher pay went to engineers, as skilled artisans, which caused much resentment amongst the infantry.

For his first night in the front line, Sherriff was attached to 8/Queen's, doing the rounds with the company commander. This included a visit to Ersatz Crater, in no-man's-land, 'a secluded little hell on earth' with the Germans holding the opposite side. Taking in the strange new sights and sounds he mused,

> Many others like me were spending their first night in the line; standing about awkwardly like children in a strange room – fingering their new revolver holsters and remembering the time – not so far distant – when they last wore weapons as pirates or brigands defending a summer-house in a garden.
>
> Along this line that looked so beautiful and impressive with the lights hovering over it – along this line men were dying at the rate of twenty an hour – sometimes less – often more.[11]

Later that same night, the Germans seized a couple of prisoners for identification at Ersatz Crater, leaving one of their own men dead.

Sherriff's 'My Diary' comes to a sudden end with the battalion taking over the front line the next day, 10 October. There, the battalion was facing RIR 101 of the Saxon 23 Reserve Division, which had arrived on 23 August. The Saxons had suffered heavy losses against the French on the Somme's southern sector and had the same task of rebuilding shattered units as 24th Division. They were inclined to 'live and let live', but 2/Leinster would have none of that, sending over salvoes of rifle grenades and on 25 September letting Saxons who tried to fraternise with one of their posts get close before opening fire.[12] In the face of this aggression and a raid on 7 October, the Saxons felt obliged to respond. It was the Division's *Sturmkompanie* which raided Ersatz Crater on 9/10 October.

The Surrey battalion incurred sixteen casualties during the week following, with frequent exchanges of artillery and especially trench-mortar fire between the two sides, as well as sniping and machine-gun fire. On 12 October, Pirie recorded that the Germans were by no means necessarily dominating the mortar exchanges,

> This afternoon there was a proper trench mortar strafe. It began at 2p.m., we, with Stokes Mortars, toffee apples, so called as it consists of a 60lb shell on the end of a three foot steel stick, and with our raw huge '¼ to 10 gun' (so called as it's a trench mortar with a 9.45 bore and it throws a huge shell 194 lbs weight and makes a 14 feet deep hole). Fritz replied with Minnies but we soon shut him up, because for every one he sent over he got at least four back. You can follow the flight of all these shells in the air, all the strafing seems to be done by mortars here, very few shells.

Sherriff mentioned to his father on 14 October that Hilton had sent him into no-man's-land with a corporal, to inspect wire 'to gain confidence'.

Tew was badly injured whilst riding on 17 October and T.H.S. Swanton, also of the East Surrey Regiment, took over as CO. Swanton, aged 28, was another pre-war regular officer. He had joined 1/East Surrey in France, as a lieutenant, in May 1915. According to Pirie, writing four weeks later, Swanton had soon made himself generally unpopular.

The battalion's stay facing Vimy Ridge was short. Pirie was sorry to leave 'a nice piece of the line, good dugouts and such like'. After another week at Estrée-Cauchie, the battalion moved to Noeux-les-Mines. This was part of the move north of 24th Division to the Hulluch-Loos sector, where it had come to grief almost exactly a year previously. (General Mitford had held a function for the survivors on 1 October.)

Hitchcock of 2/Leinster looked out from higher ground over the new sector,

> One could liken the Loos Salient to half a plate, with the enemy trenches looking down into ours from its outer edge. Hulluch on the extreme left, then the shambles of Loos and its Tower Bridge, now reduced to a wreckage of twisted iron girders, and the Loos Crassier shooting out towards the Boche lines, where Hart's and Harrison's craters lay midway in no-man's-land. The trenches then curved down across Hill 70, coming to an abrupt turn at the famous Triangle to straighten themselves out towards the Double Crassier – huge mammoths of waste slag and charcoal, which started at the top of Hill 70 to run for some 1000 yards through German and British lines – on the extreme right and neck of the Salient.[13]

9/East Surrey was in Brigade Support from 25 October and took over the front-line trenches in the left sub-sector on 31 October, with three companies and one in local reserve. Until 10 February it was to hold these trenches alternately with 8/Queen's, for six days at a time. When not holding them, it was either in Brigade Support about a mile west of Hulluch, or in Brigade Reserve at Philosophe, a ruined mining village near Vermelles. Pirie, seeing it for the first time, was not impressed, 'a wretched looking country, flat and nothing but dirty coal mining villages with crowds of huge slag heaps and chimney stacks'. As for the front line, which Pirie was visiting every morning when the battalion held it, 'It's in a wretched state, mud galore and parapets all falling in. It will take months of work to repair it.' Tower, the new Brigade Major who arrived in December, recalled, 'The Hulluch sector of the line was a horrible place. Our front line hardly existed being continually smashed in with minenwerfer.'[14]

The Loos sector was indeed notorious for German trench mortars. Along with mortar and artillery activity, the infantry joined in with rifle grenades, machine guns and sniping. At night patrols checked the wire and no-man's-land. A couple of attempts to capture an enemy sentry at a sap head in mid-November were unsuccessful. Pirie described the first attempt. He and his orderly were on hand in case of casualties,

> There was no luck in the raid last night. Thomas, Sgt. Summers, DCM, L/Cpl. Husk (Taffy), Pte. Brunt, a red headed fellow and six others went out,

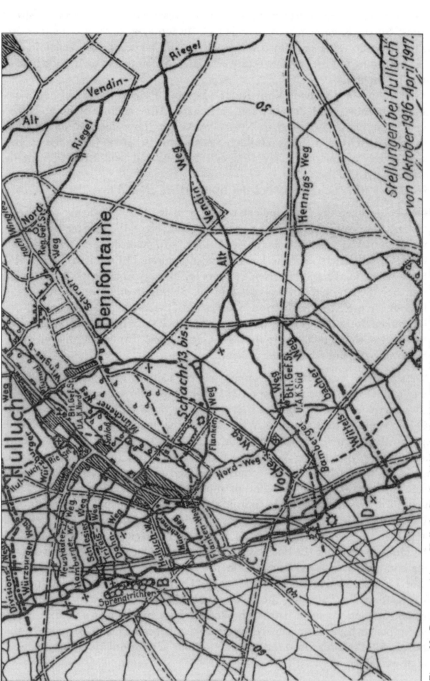

Figure 10. German positions, Hulluch, October 1916–April 1917. The thick black line is the German front line.

crawled right past the Hun wire and lay in waiting for three hours to catch the Hun but he never came along so they had to come in as it was fearfully cold and the moon would soon be up. We were in the front line trench and about frozen but they must have been frozen meat, lying out in No Man's Land!!

Opposing the British here was 8 Division, which was rated First Class by Allied Intelligence as late as August 1918. It was recruited from Prussian Saxony and the Thuringian states. It had fought in the battles at Loos in September to October 1915 and stayed there until July 1916. It had then endured two bloody tours on the Somme. In need of a rest on a quiet front, it was sent back to Loos in early October. Opposite 72 Brigade and 9/East Surrey was 8 Division's IR 72. This held its sector, which included the ruins of Hulluch, Benifontaine and *Puits* 13, with two battalions in line and the third in reserve. Each of these served twelve days in the line and six in 'rest' (with working parties included). The distance between the hostile front lines was mostly around 120–150 metres, but in a few places only 50 metres. A large cluster of mine craters, a little west of Hulluch, made it possible for enemy raiders to get dangerously close. To make matters worse, IR 72 found the trenches in a seriously dilapidated state. This was partly due to heavy rain and an overflowing stream, but mostly to a recent massive British mortar barrage. The Germans were obliged to undertake immediate repairs to make the sector defensible, although flooding continued. IR 72 was seriously overstretched with meagre reinforcements received to replace its heavy Somme losses and to defend 2.4km of front. As a result, great reliance had to be placed on advance posts and night patrols to guard against enemy incursions. Just as the British complained of *minenwerfer* missiles, IR 72 found the numerous and destructive British mortar bombs, in particular, hard to endure.[15]

On the British side of the lines, as usual, Brigade Support meant supplying extensive working and carrying parties for the front line and 'resting' did not always seem that. Lambert expressed his disgust on 9 November, 'Resting, or supposed to be resting. Nothing but parades and drills all day.'[16] Captain Hitchcock, with 2/Leinster, echoed Lambert's dissatisfaction on 14 November. 'The word "Rest" in this new sector was a "camouflage" name. This "Rest" proved a continual fatigue. Every night, even the first night of rest, when we had only returned from the front line in the morning, my whole Company was split up on various fatigues to and from the trenches.'[17]

Private Robert Lambert, formerly a stretcher bearer and now a machine-gunner was killed on 15 November, aged 33. Corporal Skinner of the Signals Section wrote a letter of condolence,

The gun that Bob was a team member of was getting too much of a nuisance for the Germans, who decided to put it out at all costs, three nights running they came with bombs creeping as near as possible and then throwing bombs but without avail, they next decided to shell it and started with whiz-bangs, this was also of no use so on this particular morning they put into force their trump card shelling with 9.2s a very long shell, they started firing and searching the ground and 'Old Bob' and this team were told that they had better shift, but this didn't agree with them so they stayed on and at last the Huns got a shell right on top of the gun killing Bob and his chum instantly. There was no pain felt by him and he was taken down to the Military Cemetery and as the Battalion was coming out of the trenches the same day, he was buried with full Military honours, all the old boys attending and the Signal Section, with whom Bob was a general favourite en masse. Bob or 'Old Bob' as he was known was a 'man' what more can I say, he done [*sic*] his duty like a man and died like one.[18]

The battalion war diary records 26 casualties in November, including a spate of accidental injuries – 2 sergeants accidentally wounded and 2 more men with accidentally self-inflicted wounds, all on different days. It also recorded a suicide. No explanation is given in the war diary and Pirie does not mention these in his diary. He does, however, record the strain on the men's bodies on 18 November after a spell in the front line, 'worn out with work and the cold. We have had three cases of Trench Foot ... but luckily only slight ones, so we kept them in a dugout for twenty-four hours when they were quite O.K. again'.

Full details of one of the accidental injuries survive in the 'Burnt Records' of one of the victims, Sergeant William Foot, demonstrating how seriously the Army took suspicious injuries. During 'Stand to', Foot had slipped and putting out his hand to save himself from falling had wounded his hand severely on Corporal Maxwell's fixed bayonet. Statements were obtained from witnesses and the incident reported on to Brigade and Division, with all concurring it was an accident.[19]

Second Lieutenant Grant had taken over writing the war diary from Clark that autumn, which seems to have a less restrained style as a result. On 20 December, for example,

Our Howitzers (4.5) happily were able to gain several direct hits on the 'Minnie' located yesterday. It has 'ceased from troubling' but there are others. Enemy darts [probably *granatenwerfer* bombs] troublesome & many rounds of Stokes [light mortar shells] needed to quiet them. Our Snipers had a splendid target in a Hun getting over a broken trench: they took full advantage.[20]

On the other side, IR 72 recorded as many as 400 British mortar bombs falling, daily, in one of its sectors around this time. These caused considerable damage, but relatively few casualties.

Neither side was inclined to reduce aggression over the season of goodwill and Christmas saw both tragedy and celebration. On Christmas Eve the battalion came out of the line into Brigade Support. Unfortunately, as Billman recorded, four men were

blown to pieces on their way out of the trenches ... it was so very sad, just before Xmas and only that morning those men had received letters wishing them a Happy Christmas. By noon, the remainder of us were passing through

Vermelles as our billets [were] about a mile away. The mud had pretty well dried on us, and we did look some objects, but with a cigarette on, & many jokes flying about, we at last reached Philosophe and started to tidy up a bit, so as to lose no time the next day. Xmas Day arrived, and we made the most of it, enjoying a real good dinner, and attending a fine concert at night in the recreation room. The day soon passed, with many pleasant memories of happier Xmas's, and sincere wishes that the next would be spent in peace and quietness in our dear old Blighty.

Pirie wrote on Christmas Day, 'All the officers subscribed towards the men's dinners and they had Pork or Beef and plum puddings, oranges and beer so they didn't do so badly. This evening there is to be a concert given by B & D Coys. And after it all the officers are to dine together.' The following day he added,

The concert last night was a huge success, especially the Trio Hilton, Tetley and Lindsay when they sung a parody on 'Another little drink won't do us any harm.' Half way through the concert there was an interval when beer and sandwiches were handed round to the men. Our Xmas dinner was a huge success – twenty-six officers sat down together and Lt. Mase provided an excellent dinner and most wonderful programmes were painted (water colours) by Pte. Cole, one of our men. The dinner party finally dispersed at 12.30, Clark having been in great form. A & C Coys held their concert this evening.

On the other side of no-man's-land, there were celebrations, too. The Kaiser's peace proposals had been published on 12 December and many Germans hoped fervently that the Allies would now agree to end the war.

Sherriff had not been serving with the battalion since late October and the move to Loos. He had been loaned, with a number of men, to the RE tunnelling companies, which required additional labour. He was presumably chosen by Hilton or Clark as one of the least experienced officers, who could be more easily spared.

Sherriff was writing frequent letters home, including to his mother. On 5 November 'I am still with the R.E. party . . . Compared with the arduous work in the line this is a rest . . . I am not miserable at present, dear, trust me to let you know when I am miserable.' Six days later he was happy to be with the working party 'for the duration of the war. There is so much more freedom than when you are with the Battalion.' But by 12 November 'When I spent that first 8 days in the trenches I never got the feeling of fear so much as I sometimes do now – but let's hope I shall soon get over it and I grow used to it.' On 14 November,

I don't know why it is but some men seem to stroll about the trenches when they are shelling just as though nothing was happening, they must be made very differently to me for it makes me tremble and breathe hard . . . After a fortnight's absolute quiet you can imagine it has come as rather a shock to find we are well under fire when [the Germans] want to make us so.

Two days later Sherriff wrote,

> I am always on the lookout for some branch of the service that would not be such a stress as the infantry work is … anything in preference to that waiting and waiting that characterises the infantryman's work – there can be nothing more arduous than that – I would far sooner be one of the miners picking away all the time they are on duty than to do the work of an infantryman.

At this time he expressed a preference for both flying and tunnelling to infantry work, which he found dull, monotonous and lacking in intellectual challenge, although on 20 November he was 'afraid that my applying for the transfer [to the REs] may annoy the Commanding Officer so that he will bring me back to my Company'. A week later, 'I would rather spend it [Christmas] with the REs than the battalion.' He was in trouble with his battalion over the appearance of his men who were 'all the worst, because they want to get rid of them from the Battalion' and after a later incident expected to be relieved because of it. In spite of further similar criticism from Swanton, Sherriff spent Christmas with the REs, and was only returned to duty with the battalion on 29 December. Swanton told him he was too short of officers to agree to his transfer to the REs and Sherriff decided to make the best of it.

9/East Surrey had sustained nineteen casualties in December. The New Year was to bring greater challenges for both Sherriff and the battalion.

Chapter 7

A Hard Winter,
January–April 1917

After heavy losses at Verdun and the Somme, Germany's plans for 1917, under its new military leaders, Hindenburg as Chief of the General Staff and Ludendorff as First Quartermaster-General, did not include an offensive on the Western Front. Instead, there would be a planned withdrawal to a new line behind the Somme Front – the Hindenburg Line. This would offer stronger positions on a shorter line, allowing a greater density of defenders. As for offensive action against the Allies, it was expected that an unrestricted submarine campaign from 1 February would bring the greatest pressure on them, especially Britain.

On the Allied side, there were also changes of top leadership. Lloyd George had become British Prime Minister in December. He was horrified by the losses of the BEF, did not believe that the war could only be won or lost on the Western Front and wanted to divert resources to other fronts. He did not have confidence in Haig, but did not feel able to replace him. As for France, in December 1916, General Nivelle replaced Joffre as commander in chief. Nivelle won over Lloyd George with his plan for a grand spring offensive on the Chemin des Dames. Haig was required to support him with an offensive at Arras. Only if Nivelle's plan failed would the British then attack on Haig's chosen front – Ypres. Before these various plans for the Western Front could be implemented, the troops had first to endure the coldest winter for many years.

New Year's Day at Loos was greeted by a heavy German bombardment. As the battalion war diary recorded,

> A very active day. At 7.30 a.m. the enemy started shelling our area with whizzbangs, 4.2s & 5.9s. Front line, supports, reserve line NINTH & TENTH AVENUES all received attention. Bn. H.Q. received some gas shells as well. This activity eased up somewhat at 1.30p.m. As well as shelling, the enemy also heavily minnied the front and support lines of the left and centre Coys and slightly the right. The left Coy suffered severely. Our T.M's were apparently out of action. 12 noon – 1.30p.m. our artillery had a shoot, shelling enemy T.M. emplacements with 9.2s & the enemy front and support lines with 6 inch howitzers. In spite of this however from 2.45p.m.–3.30p.m. enemy sent over Minnies and whizzbangs all along the line. In the evening the enemy cooled down & the night was quiet.[1]

A total of six men had been killed and four wounded.

Going around the trenches on 2 January, Pirie noted, 'The top of Hay Alley is knee deep in mud and water and in all the trenches are in a bad state ... Six days in such a piece of the line is far too long a period both from a mental and physical point of view.' The following day, Pirie recorded dealing with five wounded and added, 'To-day has been one worry after another over cases of threatened trench foot and amongst them are three cases of trench foot ... I marvel there hasn't been dozens of cases'.[2]

However, the weather was now turning exceptionally cold.

From the beginning of January until a day or two before we left this sector, on February 12, the weather was very cold. There was some snow at the beginning of this long period, and the frost held so consistently that it was lying on the ground for over five weeks. All this time it was perfectly dry, and the trenches were in a far better state than at any other time during the winter.[3]

On 5 January, Pirie was advised a replacement MO, Lieutenant Hartley, was arriving. He wrote,

I have now been just short of thirteen months with this Regiment ... and have sort of grown to be one of them and am most downhearted about leaving them for I'll miss Hilton, Tetley, Whiteman and Clark badly, still I need a change badly as I'm warworn and nervy so it's for the Regiment's good to get someone fresh and full of energy.

He later added that he could not work with Swanton as CO. He had arranged a transfer to 74th Field Ambulance, one of three with 24th Division. Swanton was lucky not to join the casualty list when a 'minnie' exploded near him and his orderly, burying the latter up to his waist.

In spite of the bitter cold, there was also now an extensive programme of raids. There had been raids around Loos in late 1916, but the tempo increased in January. According to Hitchcock,

Raids consisted of a brief attack with some special object on a section of the opposing trench ... The characteristics of these operations, the preparation of a passage through our wire and the enemy's wire, the crossing of the ground unseen, the penetration of the enemy's line, the hand-to-hand fighting in the darkness, and the uncertainty as to the strength of the opposing forces – gave peculiar scope to gallantry, dash, and quickness of decision by the troops engaged.

The object of these expeditions can be described as fourfold:

I   To gain prisoners and, therefore, to obtain information by identification.
II To inflict loss and lower the opponent's morale, a form of terrorism, and to kill as many of the enemy as possible, before beating a retreat; also to destroy his dug-outs and mine-shafts.
III To get junior regimental officers accustomed to handling men in the open and give them scope for using their initiative.

IV To blood all ranks into the offensive spirit and quicken their wits after months of stagnant trench warfare.

Hitchcock adds that raids became unpopular when the men in the trenches began to feel that sometimes these risky enterprises arose from rivalry between higher formations, rather than military necessity.[4]

It would be wrong to think that only the British high command wanted raids. Their German counterparts were of the same opinion. Indeed, at this time and place, it seems the Germans took the initiative. 2/Leinster had repulsed a raid on 4 December. IR 72 had then attempted a major raid on 12/13 December. This, however, was a fiasco. An accidental grenade explosion helped lose surprise and the Germans were bloodily repulsed, suffering twenty-eight casualties. But this was followed by a very successful attack on 8/Buffs on 5 January. A large raiding party caught the Buffs quite unawares. Around fifty men, including some tunnellers, were captured. To add to the humiliation, General Capper personally investigated the front line, after a German radio report boasted of the exploit. Peering across no-man's-land, he saw a large notice, in English, 'SAY What about those 50 rations?'[5] The regular CO of the Buffs took full responsibility and was removed.[6]

Unsurprisingly, 24th Division which had done relatively little raiding up until then, launched a series of raids. 8/Queen's raided successfully on 9 January. According to IR 72, they wounded a man, took a prisoner and blew in a dugout in sub sector 'B', which was in the vicinity of the mine craters. 2/Leinster launched its raid at 4.20pm on 10 January, using five officers and eighty men. It was a considerable success, seizing eight prisoners and killing many more Germans, for five fatalities and more wounded amongst the raiders. This was followed by further raids by different battalions from the division, and by the Germans, with mixed results. On 23 January, the Germans attempted to surprise men of 9/East Surrey in No. 2 Crater Post. But the garrison was alert and allowed the enemy to get close before opening rapid fire. The Germans fled leaving two dead and two wounded. A day later, there was a more serious raid on 7/Northamptonshire.

On 25 January 9/East Surrey carried out its first full-scale raid – against IR 72. This was carefully planned, and launched, exceptionally, in broad daylight. It aimed to identify the opposing formation; inflict losses on the enemy; and secure a sample of German ration bread. (It was the 'Turnip Winter' of severe food shortages in Germany).[7] The raiders were 3 officers, 50 ORs and 6 sappers with explosives. Second Lieutenant Davies was in overall charge. There were 4 fighting squads, each 7 strong, 2 each under Second Lieutenant Thomas (Battalion Bombing Officer) and Sergeant Summers. Two more squads, with sappers, were mopping up squads. The remaining two were blocking and connecting squads. The third officer was Second Lieutenant Lindsay. 'Nobby' Clark described the leaders, years later,

> Davies … a good steady fellow unemotional and reliable … Thomas
> (Tommy the Bomber) was one of the most courageous men I ever met. Never

happy unless he was in the thick of it. Would volunteer for any job against the enemy, no matter how dangerous. Would be most unhappy if left out of any stunt ... A splendid personality men would follow him anywhere – so cool, so calm and so inspiring. 2 Lt. Lindsay. A cheerful and charming young fellow. Full of freshness and laughter. Very efficient and very brave. Sergt. Summers an outstandingly brave fellow. He loved to crawl about No Man's Land and scare the enemy. He and Thomas together were the best combination in the Bn. in dealing with the Boche.[8]

Nearly sixty years later Thomas recalled the raid,

We said, and all the bombers agreed, that we wanted to do it in daylight because [of] the casualties by doing it at night. They were so alert, these Germans, that the casualties were very heavy and I thought, well, the time we are most relaxed is during the dinner hour in the midday and probably the Germans the same.

He recalled resistance from brigade, but that division said those undertaking the raid should have the final say. Whilst the battalion was at rest, the German trenches to be attacked were marked out and those men chosen for the raid practised repeatedly with them.[9]

Gaps in the enemy wire had been made for the raid by artillery and mortars. Patrols checked the progress with this nightly. The raiders attacked just after noon from a sap, under cover of artillery, mortar and Lewis gun fire. They quickly reached the enemy trench, catching the Germans completely by surprise. Whilst the Germans expected a raid, because of the wire cutting, they assumed it would be at night. There were two sentries encountered who had their hands in their pockets. A machine gun which killed two raiders was silenced by an 18pdr shell. After 10 minutes of the raiders taking prisoners, killing those resisting and throwing explosive charges into dugouts where the occupants refused to come out, withdrawal was ordered.

The raid was judged a great success. There were three prisoners taken and around a score of Germans were believed killed or wounded. A sample of ration bread had been obtained and also a gas helmet. Compared with other raids, the British losses were very light – three killed and four wounded. The Army Commander, General Horne, gave his congratulations, as proudly recorded in the battalion war diary, 'The conception, careful preparation, and soldier-like manner in which it was brought to a successful issue, reflects credit on the 72nd Infantry Brigade and the 9th East Surrey Regiment.' Thomas, Lindsay and Summers were amongst those subsequently decorated for the raid.

Unaware of the raid's objectives and unable accurately to assess British casualties, IR 72 gave its own account of the attack.

Although the companies were at their posts and laid down a vigorous fire ... several parties of the advancing enemy succeeded in breaking into the trenches at approximately the same place as on 9 January. After bitter close combat they were thrown out by 8 Company. Another party advanced southwards against sub-sector 'C' and attacked 4 Company. Here also the enemy did not get forward, but succeeded in seizing three men from the right flanking group after a melee. The whole raid played itself out in five to six minutes. The troops, particularly 8 Company, held firm in an exemplary manner and prevented the opposition from further exploiting their success. In any case the demolition charges which they had been obliged to leave behind in the trenches, allowed us to gather that they had planned to do more than they had achieved. Eight English dead were observed in front of the wire, which were then recovered by the enemy under cover of the smoke. Our losses amounted to two dead, three wounded and three missing.[10]

This was not the end of raiding for the month, with the 8/Buffs and 12/R Fusiliers launching a big operation with 240 men on 26 January, netting eighteen prisoners.

The relatively heavy casualties for 9/East Surrey in January totalled fifty-five, including two deliberately self-inflicted wounds. Raiding was continued in February by both sides, but less successfully. IR 72's raid on 10 February was a disaster, as was the British raid a day later.

Out of the line, 8/R West Kent remembered,

good times at Philosophe for six days in twenty-four. It was just a one-street miners' village, with the outer shells of most of the houses intact, but lacking such comforts as window-panes and furniture. Our first tour was far from comfortable, but we and the other battalions in the Brigade made improvements every time we were there, and when we left the sector it was a very satisfactory rest area. There were still some very dirty civilians about, mostly those connected with the mines, and some of them did quite a good trade selling odds and ends to the troops at a very large profit. Bethune was only a few miles away, and was very popular. Shops and estaminets were open there almost as in normal times, and divisional cinemas or concert parties often gave their shows in the town.[11]

After several months in the Loos salient, 24th Division was relieved on 12 February. 8/R West Kent recalled, 'We were really sorry to leave Hulluch. We had been in the area so long that we knew its advantages and disadvantages, and were able to make full use of the former and avoid the latter to a great extent.'[12]

Initially, from late December, Sherriff had been back with 9/East Surrey, undertaking duties as a company officer and was with Tetley during the New Year's Day bombardment. On 14 January, however, he wrote home, 'I am on a special Engineering job of draining trenches, etc', which he found 'quite interesting'. 'Our second in command put me in charge of the job because as I put in for an Engineering Commission I suppose he thought I understood a lot about it.'[13] However, from 24 January to 12 February, Sherriff was away from the battalion, sick with neuralgia[14] (severe nerve pain) that appeared to him, in the light of what he wrote at various times, to have been psychosomatic in origin. On 10 February he wrote home, 'Although I feel better for the rest I don't think my [?] have improved much; any noises worry me and I can't set my mind properly to anything – But I shall have to go back to the regiment I expect and see how I get on – the feelings may wear off later on.'

The division now moved to a training area at Allouagne, near Béthune. After two days' rest, the remainder of February was given over to training and some recreation. Billman acted as an instructor there for some weeks, enjoying the break from the dangers and discomfort of the front line. 'We made good friends with the villagers and quite improved our small knowledge of their language. In fact, we were treated well, and I shall always remember with pleasure my stay at Allouagne.'[15] Sherriff, back with the battalion, writing to his father on 19 February was pleased that he'd received 'A New Year's Present from my old Company Commander [Tetley] in the form of a letter case commemorating one new year's day when we had a pretty hot time for 12 hours in the line.' A total of thirteen casualties had arisen from enemy action in February and three more in a training accident.

24th Division returned to the Front a little south-west of Loos, at the Cité Calonne sector opposite Lens, where the lines had long been static, and immediately north of Vimy Ridge. On 2 March 9/East Surrey took over the right sub-section facing Liévin, from the Canadians. The battalion went into Divisional Reserve at Bully-Grenay on 8 March and Lieutenant Colonel de la Fontaine, recovered from his Somme wound, resumed command, with Swanton becoming second in command. Two days later, Mitford left the brigade, to take command of 42nd Division. Brigade Major Tower had found Mitford 'A very brave man but a difficult man to get on with', but worked well with his successor, Brigadier General W.F. Sweny.[16]

Pirie managed to get transferred back to the battalion on 14 March, and two days later he described a visit to the peculiar front line,

We started from Bn. H.Q. in York Street, then turned right into Hougomont Street, which runs on top of the ground behind the houses and along past the left of the two Mine Heads, and then got into Temple Street, which is a trench and very muddy and then turned left into Boyau Thomas which brought us into the Rt. Coy. support line which is behind a row of houses and is called Morgan Trench and the Coy. H.Q. which is in one of the cellars of the house. There I saw Tetley (Capt.) and his lot. Then we turned left into Boyau 214 which brought us into the Rt. Coy's front line which consists of houses and sandbags as parapets, a most extraordinary line. On the right of the line is another Mine-head and on the left a high railway embankment called the Burning Byng as it smokes all day long and gives off tarry fumes. The trench runs up the Byng along the top and down the other side. The stones in the trench on the Byng are quite hot and the men like that trench on cold nights. On top of the byng are a lot of railway trucks and an engine (now

Figure 11. Lens, immediately before the Battle of Arras, April 1917, annotated to show the Burning Byng and known German sectors. There is some uncertainty regarding sector boundaries and there was possibly another sector between Mecklenburg and Neustadt.

in a ruined condition), evidently abandoned there when the war zone reached this region. From the top of the byng you can get a good view of the surrounding country, nothing but coal mine-heads and model villages to be seen all around you ... As you go down the side of the Byng you pass Pit Prop Corner and then Mersey Tunnel which passes through the Burning Byng. This railway embankment also runs through the Hun lines and opposite the Rt. Coy. it is very hard to make out where the Hun line is as it's amongst houses also. After the Byng the front line runs straight to the left in open country and is about 300 yards from the Huns.

The battalion continued in this area, in the front line, or Brigade Support at Calonne (the area around the village square) and Maroc village, or Divisional Reserve at Bully-Grenay for the rest of March and into April.

Up to 25/26 March, 9/East Surrey faced the Silesian 11 Reserve Division at Liévin. This had been badly mauled at Verdun and then again, twice, on the Somme Many of the Silesians were miners and enjoyed good relations with the local people, who remembered German assistance in a mining disaster ten years before. However, they had little rest at Liévin, where they had been since November, as the Canadians opposite became increasingly aggressive. The Double Crassier, on the right, was hotly disputed. It was RIR 10, principally, in its *Neustadt* sector, to the left, facing 9/East Surrey. *Neustadt* sector comprised the semi-ruinous, built-up area of Liévin town and its suburbs. Opposite the 'Burning Byng', the German front line ran along the row of houses at the edge of Cité des Cornailles. The German view of the British position was dominated by the wrecked pit head of Fosse 2 from which the mine railway ran up and over the 'Burning Byng' embankment.

The German High Command was keen to implement lessons learned from the Somme. During February, infantry units from 11 Reserve Division were temporarily relieved by units from 79 Reserve Division, taken out of the line and re-trained and re-equipped in the rear at Douai. Picked assault squads were organised and trained in each company to spearhead immediate counterattacks. Each regiment, which had long possessed its own *Granatenwerfer* teams, now formed a full regimental *Minenwerfer-Kompanie* with twelve light (7.58cm) weapons operated by infantrymen; the divisional *Minenwerfer-Kompanie* would now consist of eight medium (17cm) and four heavy (25cm) weapons operated by *Pioniere*. RIR 10 records it also received 'light' machine guns for the first time, each rifle company being equipped with six MG08/15. What was less welcome was the order to dispense with deep dugouts in the first line, leaving splinter-proof 'funk holes' only, because of the danger of men being trapped in dugouts in the event of a sudden enemy attack.

At Liévin German artillery and trench mortars often fired, being especially concerned to hit the British trench mortar emplacements (many situated behind the 'Burning Byng'), which were causing them particular concern. The big British 'Flying Pig' mortar shells of 9.45in calibre must have been as unpleasant to the

Germans as the larger of the *minenwerfer* missiles were to the British. Snipers were also a particular danger.

The weather was bad, with snow which continued into April. It was fortunate for the men of 24th Division that the cellars of Calonne provided shelter, 'many of them were provided with stoves, fuel being plentiful in the shape of beams from ruined houses'.[17] Sherriff wrote a short story, probably whilst in France, entitled 'The cellars of the Cité Calonne'. It concludes with an affectionate account of a pleasant evening spent with brother officers.[18]

Sherriff was sent behind the lines to train recruits. On 18 March he had written home that he was on this pleasant duty, for about a fortnight,

> I got it first because I am now practically senior officer in the Company – it is extraordinary how quickly officers come and go – for instance there were about 11 in my company when I joined and since then 8 have gone – either transfers to other units or companies and we have new officers to take their place.

He was back with the battalion on 24 March, which returned to the line the following day. 9/East Surrey's total casualties for March were twenty-five.

On the other side of the lines, 56 Division, which 24th Division had previously encountered at Delville Wood, took over from 11 Reserve Division on the night of 25/26 March with the Hessians of IR 118 facing the 'Burning Byng'. The new arrivals welcomed the comfortable accommodation in cellars, but found the rear defences particularly neglected. To the veterans British artillery fire appeared weak at first, although they complained of British mortar activity and frequent machine-gun fire. However, British artillery fire became significantly heavier in early April, in the lead up to the British offensive .

Behind the Front, the 'resting' battalions were busy with tactical exercises which – although relatively realistic – seem to have been conducted in a surprisingly jolly atmosphere.

> 6 Company. [FR 35] was given the honour of preparing for a review of trench-fighting by the brigade commander. At the time sufficient allowance was still not being made for this type of combat in the training of recruits in the homeland. In trench-fighting everything depends on quickness. One must be over there, before the enemy's defensive barrage starts. A couple of hand grenades in the enemy trench, spring forward and roll up to left and right. Besides this there is the rolling up of saps with hand grenades, encircling of machine-gun nests, crawling, destruction of barbed-wire obstacles and so on. All of these were practiced – most especially in the training of the *Stoss-truppen*, each of which consisted of two squads of picked men.
>
> The review, which took place on 7th April before the regimental commander – the brigade commander having cancelled – was a very light-hearted affair. We had set up straw dummies in civilian suits in the enemy trenches and made a wooden machine-gun, which got terribly beaten up by hand

grenades. As preparation [the enemy position] was accurately shot up with live mortar rounds, then following behind the main frontal assault a working party lay down in artificial shell-holes [?] and established a communication trench. Everything went off well and a good deal of fun was had by participants and spectators alike. Accompanied by the regimental band 6 Company returned to the village.[19]

The Battle of Arras began on 9 April with great success, including the seizure of Vimy Ridge by the Canadians. 9/East Surrey greeted this by erecting a large board in no-man's-land with, in German, 'We have captured over 10,000 prisoners and 100 guns at Vimy. Will you surrender too?' 24th Division assisted the Canadian left on 12 April, by clearing Bois en Hache and the eastern end of the Lorette Spur, at considerable cost to 9/Royal Sussex and 2/Leinster.

With the commanding heights of Vimy Ridge lost, the Germans realised their withdrawal from much of the Lens salient was urgently required. A retreat between Loos and Gavrelle was ordered for the nights of 11/12 and 12/13 April. For 56 Division it would mean withdrawal to the line on the outskirts of Lens. Liévin and Cité St Pierre would have to be abandoned. During the first night the German infantry held the line, whilst other troops withdrew, along with the remaining inhabitants from Lens. An incident here showed the state that the Germans were reduced to.

Unfortunately the evacuation had a deeply shameful epilogue. Scarcely had the last citizen left his house, when several locations were plundered. Worst of all – it was at the food depot. The nourishment of the troops, although still much better than in the homeland, was now truly meagre and wretched. There was still a midday meal, though many men would rather have seen no more of the dried vegetables, affectionately nicknamed 'barbed wire'. However the cold foodstuffs – consisting of unidentifiable lard-substitute, unappetising preserved sausage, and otherwise of jam of every conceivable shade – were now provided only in homeopathic portions. The young soldier was never free of a faint feeling of hunger ... and now he seemed to be in the land of milk and honey! A large depot, which as throughout the occupied territory was administered for the civil population by a Spanish-American aid committee, concealed unsuspected treasures – and no longer belonged to anyone. So, charge at the bacon! They went at the lard barrels with the spade, flour sacks were lugged away, someone jealous sneakily cut into them with his knife. It came to fighting, which took on a serious character, before finally a pair of officers with pistols in their fists put an end to the chaos and organised an orderly transportation of the valuable goods. Provisioning vehicles from all of the formations in the surrounding area now took the wares to their respective units, where they were used to improve the rations. We rarely had such magnificent eating! Once again you could stand your spoon upright in it, and whoever went on leave could take a parcel home with him.[20]

On the second night, rearguards concealed the withdrawal with lavish use of signal flares and small-arms fire.

On 12 and 13 April numerous fires and explosions were noticed behind the German lines. It became apparent that the Germans intended to withdraw following their loss of Vimy Ridge. On 13 April, strong patrols were sent forward and found the enemy had abandoned his front line. The artillery endeavoured to harass the retreating Germans. The East Surrey companies advanced nearly to Liévin, capturing two trench mortars. With the civilian population gone, the

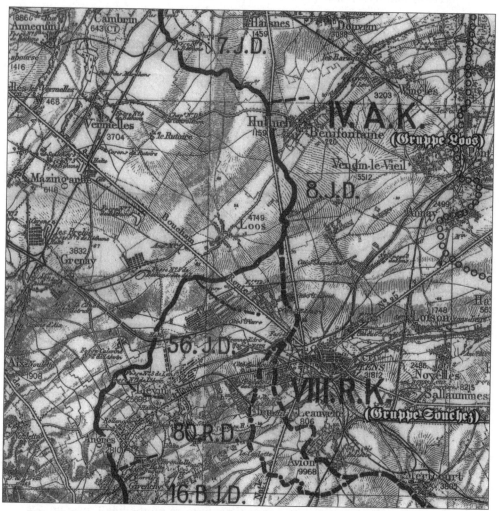

Figure 12. Lens, showing the German withdrawal after Arras, 1917. The dashed line indicates the front line after the German withdrawal as at midday 13 April. The dot-dash line shows their slightly improved line established by 30 April. German Gruppen *have been added.*

British could now bombard Lens heavily with gas shells. The city became an all-out war zone. By the end of the war it would be completely devastated.

On 16 April, Pirie with Lindsay was looking for a suitable location for Battalion HQ and a dressing station,

> We found splendid cellars on the eastern edge of Cite St. Pierre which had been the Hun Brigade Commander's place. The cellars all have tons of concrete on top and nothing on earth could come through. The Hun General's cellar is luxuriously got up, but they have hacked everything to pieces in their mess, chairs, tables and a piano are in ruins. He certainly didn't mean us to use it, but they must have retired very rapidly as they haven't blown up the cellars. The cellar where four of H.Q. officers sleep in was pulled to pieces too and the servants found a trap set, a wire attached to a bomb but luckily they spotted it and cut the wire.

The battalion took over the new front line on the night of 16/17 April, about 1,000yd from the outskirts of Lens. By then, the positions on both sides had hardened, with a reversion to conventional trench warfare The Germans now became more aggressive, with artillery fire registering onto new targets as well as sniping and raiding. An attempted raid on 17 April on a 'B' Company front-line post was repulsed. Cité St Pierre, in which were the support companies, was shelled for much of 17–19 April.

The division was relieved on 19 April and the battalion moved to Coyecques, south of St Omer. The rest of the month was spent in training. During April thirty-seven casualties had been sustained. Amongst these were two officers of Sherriff's company – Trenchard wounded on 12 April and Kiver killed on 17 April.

Meanwhile, Sherriff's personal crisis had been worsening. On 7 April, he wrote to his father about his neuralgia, 'I seem to always get this when I get near the guns but I am always hoping it will get better in time.' A week later he wrote, 'I absolutely could not bring myself to face the line again and I went to a Doctor and explained everything to him, he has given me a few days rest with the Transport.'

On 17 April Sherriff confided in his father,

> I received your letter yesterday advising me to see the Doctor about my trouble and I had already taken your advice by visiting him and explaining to him how my nerves were affected and how neuralgia troubled me.
>
>   Naturally Doctors are suspicious of these kind of cases as there are no doubt many who try this on ... He examined me and said there was no question as to my nervousness and asked if I could think of any reason for it – I told him I had always been rather highly strung ... he finished up by giving me some tablets to take & I have to call and see him this afternoon – I am absolutely in his hands – if he decides I am fit to go up the line I must go – but what I dread is that by going up I should make some serious mistake through lack of confidence ... When you first get out here you realise that

there is a certain strain to put up with – one gets to the line and is rather surprised at its quietness – shells are not flying over incessantly and in the period when I arrived there were none to spare on our front at all – they were being used in a more serious place.

You feel rather agreeably surprised – and then soon someone says 'look out! here's a Minnie' and you see what appears to be a shell making apparently slowly upwards, then turns and comes down with a swish and makes a terrific explosion ... This goes on day after day and then one day a man may be blown to pieces by a 'Minnie' ... and every time you walk past the shattered piece of trench you have the pleasure of seeing pieces of his anatomy hanging on bits of barbed wire, etc. – one day a man is sniped and you may see his bloodstained helmet carried away ... The more familiar you become with a sector of line the more you learn its danger spots and there are times when you pass certain places as fast as your legs will carry you.

It is when you get to this stage – which may take any length of time according to your state of nerves (and with some men apparently never comes) that the suspense of long hours of duty in the line tells upon you – and it is then that even when some way behind the line where shells only can reach you that you get a kind of instinct to pick up any sign of a recent shell burst ... I think nearly everyone gets to this stage soon or later and it is of course a question of their powers of being able to conceal their fear after that.

Sherriff's symptoms were approaching those of 'shellshock' or neurasthenia. A year earlier, Second Lieutenant Spofforth had been sent home sick from the battalion, after a trench had been blown in on him. His medical board found 'Following three months active service in France he developed symptoms of neurasthenia-emotionalism, depression, loss of confidence, over-reaction to stimuli, a constant feeling of horror, and clear visual pictures of experiences in the trenches.'[21]

With Sherriff on the verge of mental breakdown, it seems timely to consider the wider context. It should be borne in mind that men under officers who succumbed to stress in the front line could lose their own lives as a result.

Lord Moran wrote *The Anatomy of Courage* during the Second World War, when he was Winston Churchill's personal physician. However, many of his thoughts derived from his experience as MO with 1/R Fusiliers, 1914–1917, much of it in 24th Division. It seems appropriate, therefore, to consider some of his conclusions, even if, at times, these are perhaps coloured for literary effect.

There seemed to be four degrees of courage and four orders of men ... Men who did not feel fear; men who felt fear but did not show it; men who felt fear and showed it but did their job; men who felt fear, showed it and shirked ... few men spent their trench lives with their feet firmly planted on one rung of this ladder. They might have days without showing fear followed by days when their plight was plain to all ... At other times they were possessed by the fear that they would be found wanting and branded as cowards, when in the toil and bloody sweat of trying to conquer themselves they would end by doing their job without a sign of fear.[22]

However, Moran says elsewhere that an army should begin, through selection, 'by eliminating those who are incapable of fighting'.[23] But even so,

Courage is will-power, whereof no man has an unlimited stock; and when in war it is used up, he is finished. A man's courage is his capital and he is always spending. The call on the bank may be only the daily drain of the front line or it may be a sudden draft which threatens to close the account. His will is perhaps almost destroyed by intensive shelling ... or it is gradually used up by monotony, by exposure, by the loss of the support of stauncher spirits ... by physical exhaustion, by a wrong attitude to danger, to casualties, to war, to death itself.[24]

'Fear even when morbid is not cowardice ... What passes through his mind is his own affair ...'. Considering men who had survived a long time in the trenches and then decided they had enough, he wrote,

He had gazed upon the face of death too long until exhaustion had dried him up ... There was no dramatic failure in the line, no act of cowardice in the face of the enemy; only a subtle undermining of his will which led him to stay in England where illness or a wound had honourably taken him to seek out jobs where he might exist in safety ... All this may be indefensible but it is not cowardice.[25]

As for the 'weeding out' process, Moran recalls a fellow officer commenting on a draft of seventeen officers received by his battalion to replace Somme losses,

'I give the best of them two months.'
    Two months have gone and his verdict is in a fair way of proving true ... A few, and these the fortunate, were hit, happily before they showed signs of wear. And some went on leave and did not return, and some went sick, and some were discarded to trench mortars or in drafts to other Fusilier battalions.[26]

Officers and men in 9/East Surrey naturally faced the same challenges. Whilst there were some men like Thomas and Summers who seemed fearless and happy positively to seek out danger, most men screwed themselves up to do their duty, out of self respect and loyalty to their comrades, their regiment, their country.

As Moran observes, even men who had showed great bravery had their limits. Pirie distinguished himself as a courageous front-line medic both at Gallipoli and the Somme, but even he was 'finished off' and reduced to tears when, following the death of many friends, his corporal was mortally wounded with him at Delville Wood. Tetley had previously won the MC for digging men out during a bombardment, but as Pirie records, the one on New Year's Day 1917 had shaken him so much, that he had temporarily to hand over command of his company.

The Army was suspicious of those who developed psychiatric problems. It required a 'W3436 Report to be rendered in the case of Officers and other ranks, who, without any visible wound, become non-effective from physical conditions claimed or presumed to have originated from the effects of British or enemy weapons in action.' For example, that for Lieutenant Felix Seel of 9/East Surrey was completed by the battalion and the RAMC. It certified he had been subjected to exceptional exposure when leaving a deep dugout to go on duty, in November 1917, a 5.9in shell had burst near the entrance, causing him to fall down the steps. Although somewhat shaken up he had gone up the line for two days duty. However, he afterwards had difficulty functioning, was hospitalised and diagnosed as suffering from shellshock.[27]

Wise COs and MOs recognised excessive stress and gave men a rest when they needed it. De la Fontaine arranged for Pirie to have a break, although he hadn't asked for it. Men with long front-line service were seen as needing and deserving of a long break. It meant that some of them survived the war. Hilton, Sherriff's first company commander, had been in France since March 1915, first as an NCO with the Civil Service Rifles and then as an officer with 9/East Surrey. Wounded in the head and wrist on the Somme, he was back after eight days. He was sent to the REs for a rest, as his friend Pirie recorded, on 31 December 1916, because of his long service at the Front. Hilton was serving with the battalion at the Armistice, but his chances of making that had been considerably increased, no doubt, by a period as an instructor at Base in early 1917, and six months out as an instructor in Britain, ending in April 1918. Thus he missed the March 1918 *Kaiserschlacht*.

Some officers, as Moran observed, were simply not suited for front-line service. Early in the war they would not have undergone any testing selection procedure. Nor had they necessarily volunteered for the infantry, but that was where the great need was and so where they were sent. Some were moved on fairly quickly to more appropriate positions. Christopher Wishart had applied for a commission in Motor Transport. He became a physical training and bayonet fighting instructor and embarkation and billeting officer in France. He was then 'combed out' and sent to 9/East Surrey in July 1917. He was sick with muscle pain after two weeks. Nine days after returning to the battalion he was sent to assist the Town Major and on various administrative duties and did not return, although was still listed as serving with the battalion in its war diary.[28]

Second Lieutenant Louis Abrams who had arrived with Sheriff, however, was not so lucky. He was a customs officer in Trinidad. Thanks to a recommendation from the Colonial Office, and with only three months' service in the Trinidad Mounted Infantry, he gained admission to an officer cadet battalion. Commissioned into the East Surrey Regiment in September 1916, he was sent to France immediately. He saw some service at the Front, as well as having a couple of hospital admissions for physical complaints. Whilst at Base on the coast, he was responsible for transferring men to their units. He seems to have had some sort of breakdown and went Absent Without Leave (AWOL) at Boulogne in February

1917, as far as the Army was concerned, for two weeks. On reappearance he was arrested, court-martialled and cashiered. The War Office was not, however, vindictive, recognising that his medical condition may not have been fully considered. He was allowed to return to Trinidad and not be liable to conscription in Britain, as a cashiered officer normally was.[29] Apparently, no other officer suffered the indignity of being cashiered whilst serving with the battalion.

As for Moran's remarks about officer turnover, 9/East Surrey's war diary assists by listing officers 'serving with the battalion', monthly, from 31 December 1916. It is clear that officer turnover was fairly high, but except at times of heavy fighting was related to sickness or transfer to other units, rather than battle casualties. This issue is discussed at length in Chapter 13.

The position of ORs under the stress of front-line service was more difficult in a number of respects. Wounds and illness could give a man respite from the front line – often for lengthy periods, with no antibiotics. (In 1916, 57.5 per cent of wounded and 35 per cent of sick and injured were evacuated to Britain.)[30] Even a well-motivated man like Billman was hospitalised from sickness, including two months with pleurisy from December 1915. Men returning from hospital could find it difficult to get back to their own units, with their mates. After the terrible losses on the Somme, the Army wanted to send men to where they were needed most, regardless of regimental affiliations, and frequently did. Transfers within the Army, out of the infantry, were either because a man was no longer medically fit, or because, rarely, the Army could not do without his specialist skills for another corps. Private Charles Woodbury, after nine months at the Front and a 'Blighty wound', tried, unsuccessfully, to be transferred to the Motor Transport section of the ASC. More successful was Lance Corporal George Stanbury, a Swansea miner. After fighting at Loos he transferred to an RE tunnelling company in 1916 and survived the war. On the other hand, men who did not enlist in the infantry quite often found themselves transferred to it, to replace casualties, when manpower was short. Private Arthur Rochell, a Staffordshire farm servant, had enlisted in the ASC in March 1915. He was compulsorily transferred to 9/East Surrey in July 1917, although whether as a driver or in the line is unclear. He died of influenza in January 1919.[31]

Many, both officers and men, hoped for a 'Blighty wound' as an honourable means of escape from the Front. Some deliberately sought one. For the few truly desperate, there were self-inflicted wounds or desertion as possible ways out. There were some cases of the former in the battalion. Those judged to have inflicted such wounds would, however, face disciplinary action. Deserters from the Front could face the firing squad. No one from the battalion was so sentenced. However, in the 'Burnt Records' of individual men, there are cases of men overstaying leave and going AWOL, when due to return to France. One case encountered is of a man serving originally with 12/East Surrey. Enlisting in August 1915, he had soon proved to be a most unsatisfactory soldier. He had gone AWOL or been apprehended as a deserter whilst in Britain on several occasions. On one of these he was apprehended by the civilian police for stealing a violin!

On release from Wandsworth Prison, the Army sentenced him to six months. However, he was soon sent to 9/East Surrey instead. He was killed six months later.

Like the officers, some ORs, especially NCOs, like Fred Billman, were sent away on courses or given a break training recruits.

One would expect from Sherriff's mental state, as described by himself, that he would have had a complete breakdown and been sent away, permanently, from the battalion. This, however, was not what happened. His problems seem to have included not only difficulty in controlling his fear, but also lack of confidence in his own abilities as an officer. He felt he was temperamentally unsuited to the infantry and wanted to transfer to the tunnellers or the RFC – neither exactly free of danger. In the infantry he was deeply fearful that he would make a mistake. Young officers were repeatedly reminded that their misjudgements could cost their men their lives and Sherriff's regard for his men meant that he took this very seriously. The attractions of the RFC could include greater control over his own life and death and reduced responsibility for others.

It is unclear to what extent Sherriff's fears were noticed by his fellow officers. Years later, Sherriff was friendly with 'Nobby' Clark. Clark recalled Sherriff then as 'A steady unassuming young fellow of good presence. Carried a warm charm in his personality and had a certain calm, quiet air of distinction. Much respected by his men.'[32] Sherriff's papers also include a number of affectionate letters from brother officers, sent to him in Britain after his wounding, which will be quoted later.

There are a number of circumstances that may have assisted Sherriff's recovery from his crisis of mid-April. It must have helped that the battalion was away from the Front until mid-May. He wrote to his father on 25 April,

> We are coming out for a rest and I have come out with the others with a report from the Doctor whom I have been visiting, suggesting to our own Battalion's Doctor that my neuralgia should be 'looked into', the Doctor I had been visiting thought it may be due to the straining of the eye muscles – I don't care what it is if only someone can cure it for me. The trouble is it comes on for about an hour 2 or 3 times a day and while it is on it makes me feel absolutely knotted up – when it is over I feel quite fit again.

As Sherriff seems to have assumed before that his neuralgia was psychosomatic, this diagnosis must have been greatly reassuring.

It seems highly likely that his company commander, Godfrey Warre-Dymond, became a key influence. Born in 1890, educated at Marlborough and Cambridge, he had been commissioned in January 1915. He had arrived in France at the end of August 1916 and was with the battalion on 1 September. With 9/East Surrey having lost so many officers on the Somme, he was acting Officer Commanding (OC) of 'B' company from mid-September for two months. He was then acting OC of 'C' company, in which Sherriff served, from 10 March 1917, whilst Hilton was away at Base. When Hilton returned, Warre-Dymond kept 'C' and Hilton had to be second in command to Tetley in 'D'. Whilst Sherriff respected Hilton's various qualities, I have previously quoted his recollection of Hilton's relentless sarcasm. One suspects Sherriff had suffered from this and it would have done nothing for his confidence.

Sherriff's relations with Warre-Dymond were more positive. He clearly found him inspirational. His relationship with Warre-Dymond will be explored further in Chapter 15, in the context of *Journey's End*. For now I will quote Sherriff's later reflections,

> We had five different Company Commanders and twenty different officers while I was with the Company and my greatest pleasure to look back on is that I remained with 'C' Company all the time I was on Active Service. Every day I became bound more surely to 'C' Company, and every day I loved and esteemed it more.
>
> I came to the Company when it numbered fifty men: old, battered men who had survived the Somme by a miracle, and a few new men who had come in drafts. I saw them first in the mist of the morning we started from Estree Cauchie for the line – a column of shuffling, swearing men loaded with sacks ... I saw the Company slowly grow with new recruits and patched up returned men ... Then I saw them in the chalk trenches and the craters round Hulluch where some were killed; later in the cellars and weird places in the village of Calonne where more were killed.
>
> Then, while resting in a little village behind the line, Dymond took charge of the Company and his magic hand turned it into a living thing that became magnificent.[33]

THE JOURNEY'S END BATTALION
THE 9TH EAST SURREY IN THE GREAT WAR

Michael Lucas

Journey's End Battalion tells the remarkable story of 9th battalion East Surrey Regiment and its service in the First World War. More than 850 men lost their lives serving with it. It suffered 50% casualties on its second day at the Front-at the Battle of Loos and won the nickname 'The Gallants' from the enemy. The Battalion went on to serve on the Somme and Ypres and was almost annihilated in a famous last stand in March 1918. Reconstructed, it continued to serve on the Western Front to the Armistice.

Using official and unofficial sources, diaries, letters, and British and German wartime records, he describes the individuals who served in it and the operations they took part in. He identifies the inspiration for Journey's End and considers how Sherriff delved into his experiences and those of his fellow soldiers in order to create his drama.

The narrative covers the battalion's bloody initiation at Loos, its role in the fighting on the Somme at Guillemont and Delville Wood and during the Third Battle of Ypres, then the part it played in the desperate defence against the German 1918 offensives and its contribution to the Allied advance to victory.

Despite the presence of Sherriff and other notable individuals, the 9th East Surrey was in many ways typical of the southern Kitchener battalions, and Michael Lucas's account of its service provides a fascinating contrast with the northern Pals battalions whose story has been more often told. Not only does the book shed new light on the wartime experience of R.C. Sherriff, but it is a valuable record of the operation of a British battalion on the Western Front during the Great War.

9781848845039 • Illustrated • Hardback • RRP £19.99 • 272pages

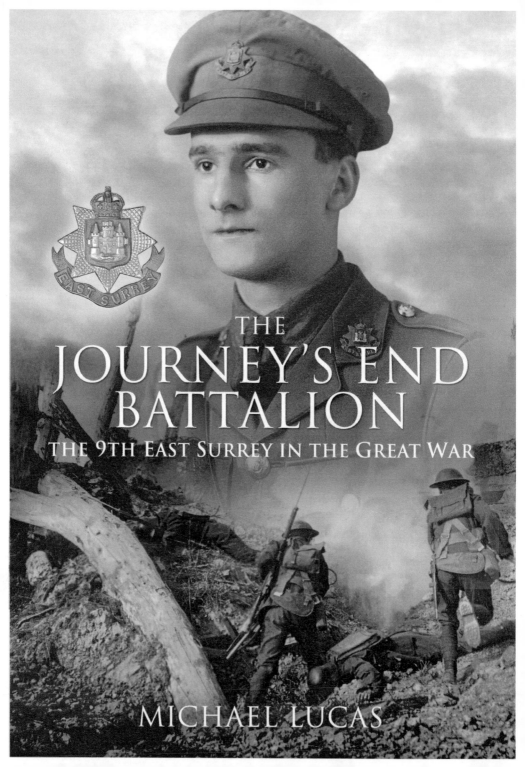

THE
JOURNEY'S END
BATTALION
THE 9TH EAST SURREY IN THE GREAT WAR

MICHAEL LUCAS

Chapter 8

Messines and Pilckem Ridge, April–September 1917

Not only did Nivelle's offensive fail in April, but the enormous casualties and bitterly disappointed expectations were soon followed by a collapse of morale and widespread outbreaks of disorder in the French Army. It became increasingly clear that no further significant offensive by the French would be possible in 1917.

Nivelle's failure meant that Haig could revive his plans for a British offensive in Flanders. This seemed necessary not only to tie down the Germans, but also because of the unrestricted submarine campaign. This was already proving a very serious threat to Britain's supply lines. The Admiralty believed the Army must seize the Belgian ports used by the U-boats, or Britain would face starvation. Whilst the submarine campaign, along with German intrigues in Mexico, had finally persuaded the USA to enter the war on the side of the Allies, it would clearly be a long time before the USA could fully mobilise. As for Russia, revolution had broken out in March and whilst the new government pledged to continue the war, Russia's ability to do this was becoming increasingly questionable. Moreover, Bucharest had been captured and Rumania virtually knocked out of the war.

It had long been clear that a successful British offensive at Ypres would first require seizure of Messines Ridge which dominated so much of the Salient. General Plumer, commanding Second Army at Ypres, had been long preparing such an operation, including by extensive tunnelling under the German positions. He advised Haig early in May that he would be ready to attack Messines in a month's time.

Since 24th Division had come out of the line on 19 April, 9/East Surrey had been in training at Coyecques, near St Omer. As well as weapons handling and such like, this had included exercises to attack trenches under a creeping barrage. For recreation there was much sport, including inter-company football and tug-of-war matches. The men were very sorry to leave Coyecques on 9 May, especially as their next destination appeared to be Ypres.

By a series of hard marches, in unseasonably hot weather, the battalion moved to the Ypres Salient. On 14 May it went forward, for six days in the front line, to Hooge where it had previously served in early 1916, taking over the left sub-sector. The three companies in the line had their HQs in Wellington Crescent, Leinster Street and Birr Crossroads. Pirie was pleased to note that although the Germans had pushed forward, the trenches were in better condition and things were quieter than the year before.[1] After a tranquil start, however, there were a number of casualties to shelling.

Then nine days were spent in Brigade Support, before relief and training, including 'platoons in the offensive'. The Army's manual 'Instructions for the Training of Platoons in the Offensive', issued in February 1917, had formally introduced a much-improved tactical organisation for the infantry. Instead of riflemen supported by a few specialists detached from the company or higher formations, the platoon was to be a self-contained unit of four specialist sections. These were riflemen, Lewis gunners, bombers and rifle grenadiers. The riflemen and bombers would advance under covering fire from the other sections. This along with the improvement in the quantity of artillery, the quality of its ammunition and continued refinement in its tactics made the British Army of 1917 much more formidable in the attack than its predecessor.

There were also working parties, as Billman recorded, 'Work, work, work, night and day; sometimes laying light railways, sometimes digging, sometimes laying water pipes, and a thousand and one jobs that have to be seen to before a battle.' Billman's work took him into 'Ypres, the city of the dead, the one place above all dreaded by soldiers, was being pounded by continual bombardments.'[2] Casualties in May, however, had been mercifully light at sixteen.

Facing 9/East Surrey at Hooge was 195 Division, the infantry mostly jägers, recently arrived from the Eastern Front. A deserter went over to the British on 24 May from RJägB 24, in JägR 8, which held outposts in Jackdaw Trench. He had been 'weeded out' for front-line service from transport. His division had made two unsuccessful raids around this time. The second, forty-four-men strong, on 23 May, was frustrated by British artillery fire and inability to find British infantry to take prisoner in their forward positions.[3]

Major General Capper was recalled to Britain and left 24th Division in mid-May. 8/R West Kent recalled his last speech to them, 'complimenting us on what we had done in the past, and saying that even greater things would be required of us in future, finishing up with blood and hatred in his very best style'.[4] He was soon appointed Director-General of the new Tank Corps, and was to play an important part in its development. His successor as divisional commander was Major General L.J. Bols, son of a Belgian diplomat. Formerly Major General General Staff of Third Army, 1915–1917, he had been 'effectively downgraded' during the Battle of Arras and moved to command a division.[5]

June commenced with the provision of working parties, but late on 6 June, the battalion marched to Mic Mac Camp, of huts and tents, near Ouderdam, ready to take part in the battle, due the following day. The Battle of Messines commenced just before dawn on 7 June, with the explosion of nineteen huge mines. These blew apart the German defences on Messines Ridge. The British artillery then opened a crushing barrage. During the morning, many of the surviving Germans were taken prisoner and British casualties were light. German attempts to counterattack failed under terrible artillery fire and simply added to their already heavy losses.

24th Division was one of three divisions that had been held back as a reserve, to exploit success and take the advance further forward. Guns and tanks were moved forward through the devastated ground, to support the infantry. 24th Division, advancing on the left, was able to reach and seize its objective – the Oosttaverne Line behind the ridge, with 17 and 73 Brigades. 72 Brigade was in reserve at Château Ségard. The British artillery fire had been overwhelming: the lessons of the Somme had been well learned. The division took large numbers of prisoners and suffered negligible casualties. The tanks provided to support the attack of 73 Brigade were not needed. Whilst Australian troops on the right had met stiffer resistance, the Germans were unable to stop the advance. The reserve was not required.

Not until 10 June was 9/East Surrey moved up to Mount Sorrel and Rudkin House, in Brigade Support. Pirie described the move up,

> Last night we left Chateau Segard at 8p.m. and marched via Swan Chateau, Shrapnel Corner, to Transport Farm where we picked up our guides. Fritz was shelling the road but we came up B route, a cross country path through Zillabeck village and all went well till we reached Valley Cottages when he began to whiz bang us. When that stopped on we went up the road to Stafford Trench on which Rudken House stands and just as I reached the trench an S.O.S. rocket went up on the right and then he poured shells into that area around Valley Cottage and Rudken House. Simmons, the O.C.'s servant and Bish, the Adjutant's servant were killed and one of the transport men wounded, otherwise we had no casualties. I can't understand how we escaped so lightly considering the whole Batt. was out in the open with all that shelling. They have been shelling the life out of us in Rudken House with 5.9s and 8inch armour-piercing and put one of the latter clean through into our deep dugout and killed two men so we are shifting up to the big tunnel dugouts in Winnipeg St. to-morrow. This is a poisonous place!

Following this move, 'B' company had the misfortune to have many men buried when a tunnel in which they were sheltering collapsed – eleven killed and twenty-eight wounded, crushed and shaken. One of these, who died of internal injuries on 18 June, was Corporal Richard Cattell, an Oxfordshire gamekeeper, out with the battalion since October 1915.[6]

From 13 to 17 June, the battalion took over the front line on the western edge of Shrewsbury Forest. The trenches were in a bad state following the recent fighting and gave little cover. In Sergeant Billman's opinion, 'Any soldier would much rather attack than hold the ground afterwards.' As well as enemy artillery fire to contend with, there was also a strafing attack one day, by five aeroplanes. Pirie recorded,

> It was an awful job getting the wounded out as the whole country was shell-swept. My bearers carried from the front line to me at Hedge St. and then the R.A.M.C. bearers from me down through Armagh Wood to Fosse Wood and

thence by light railway to Zillebeck village; Armagh Wood was an awful place, nothing but stumps of trees and shellholes and the bearers could be seen the whole way. The R.A.M.C. bearers were simply splendid.

From 23–26 June, the battalion returned to the front line. This time it was about 1 mile south east of Verbrandenmolen, from, on the left, the Ypres–Menin railway, and then near the southern edge of Battle Wood to the Ypres–Comines canal. After three days in Brigade Support, the battalion returned to camp and then set off for the rest area around Coulomby, near St Omer. Total casualties in June (159) had been heavy. Billman noted sadly, 'I lost lots of real good pals, fellows that had gone through the Battles of Loos and Somme with me.' Amongst the dead was Private John Hybart, a company runner, aged 21, adopted son of a Swansea timber merchant, killed by a shell on 17 June. His commander wrote,

> He was selected for this duty because of his intelligence and the keen way in which he had been doing his work in the trenches, and for eight months he was my faithful follower and friend. I say 'friend' because many were the talks we had as we went round on our rounds on current events of the day, and sometimes on politics, political economy, etc. As a runner he was always reliable, and showed a keen intelligence, and never once during the whole period he was with me had I occasion to find fault with him.[7]

Also amongst the casualties was Captain Tetley, wounded for a third time, losing a foot.

Sherriff seems to have recovered well from his crisis in April. Whilst some men, like Pirie, found solace in religion, Sherriff found his in the stoic philosophers. These emphasised endurance rather than hope, the importance of living a virtuous life and of dying nobly. On 13 May, he wrote to his father, 'I am trying to take everything quite calmly a la Marcus Aurelius.' He had 'Marcus Aurelius in one pocket and Epictetus in the other which are unfailing comforts.'[8] On 2 June he refers to walking and talking with his schoolmaster friend, Percy High. He was on a Sniping and Intelligence course from 9 June. He felt very positive at this time, although impatient for his first home leave. He had been buoyed up by the success of the Messines attack: a great victory with light casualties. He found the course stimulating, writing at the end, on 21 June to his father, 'I have had one of the happiest of times in the last 12 days – in beautiful country and pleasant companions – and a lot of interesting work to do.' Shortly after his return to the battalion he received his long-awaited leave, from 24 June to 4 July.

Sherriff's happiest memory of his 'C' Company was,

> when I returned from leave to the village where 'C' Company was doing duty as a model Company to a Training School. I never saw a finer sight than 'C' Company lined up on the white road in the morning – a straight line of men with brown faces and clear eyes – clean uniforms with bright green and red slashes on their arms that appeared with a vivid splash as they turned together. When they presented arms a line of glittering bayonets set a flash of

light across the fields. A line of bronzed knees below the khaki shorts and a line of jet black boots on the chalky road: the rare sight of a perfectly trained, perfectly equipped and perfectly happy company of men.[9]

Indeed, the war diary proudly recorded, 'The Commandant of the Training School ... expressed to the X Corps commander his extreme satisfaction on the performance of C. Coy at the school'.[10]

The battalion stayed at rest around Coulomby, for the first half of July, receiving some replacements to make good recent losses. Pirie wrote, 'This is a very beautiful part of the country and very peaceful.' A Battalion Sports was held on 11 July, with 'refreshments on a large scale for both officers and men', as the war diary noted. The events included, amongst less usual ones, 'wrestling on mules'.

However, the men well knew what was in store for them. As Billman wrote, 'While here we recovered from our hard times, but of course we were only getting fit to go into action again. This we knew well, for we practised attacks almost every day. All the same, we enjoyed our "rest" for the weather was grand.' From 16 to 21 July, the battalion was on the march, returning to Mic Mac Camp and Ypres. 'All this marching was supposed to get us fit,' wrote Billman, 'but that was not our view of it.' Sherriff sympathised with the men, seeing lengthy periods of trench duty as rendering them unfit for long marches. Moreover, most new men were conscripts 'often around forty years of age'. After describing the horrible state of the feet of some of them after a day's march, he adds,

> The men marched like beasts of burden with heavy packs on their backs, rifles and bandoliers of ammunition slung across their shoulders.
>
> Sometimes they would break into a marching song to ease the misery, but now and then, as I marched at the head of my platoon, I would hear a clatter behind me and turn to see a man lying prostrate in the road.
>
> The sergeants were instructed to prod them and order them to get up. There was always the possibility that the man had decided that he had taken as much as he could bear and had staged his collapse to get out of it. But most of them were genuine – down and out.[11]

During this period the men were put through gas-helmet drill by Pirie. The Germans had just started using a new gas – mustard gas. Masks, however, could only protect the lungs and eyes: there was no fully effective protection from other parts of the body being burned.

The British High Command had, unfortunately, been unable to follow up promptly the success at Messines during the good weather. But Haig was intent on continuing the offensive at Ypres. He had passed the leading role to General Gough and was looking for a more ambitious advance than Plumer had achieved at Messines. The offensive was to begin on 25 July.

During 21/22 July, the battalion moved up to the front line. 'C' and 'D' companies manned Image Crescent, just north of Klein Zillebeke, with the other two supporting in old German trenches around Zwarteleen, by Hill 60. Pirie had written, 'I am not looking forward to going into the line to-morrow night. It's a beast of an area.' With the Germans expecting a British offensive, there was much shelling. Five officers were amongst the twenty-seven casualties suffered over the three days.

Amongst the dead was Captain George Pirie, killed by a shell on 24 July, his 29th birthday. Typically of him, the last words in his diary are concern for a comrade, 'I hear Lt. Royal has been invalided out of the army with consumption. Jolly rotten luck.' We have already seen much of Pirie's courage and dedication whilst serving with the battalion. His previous service in Gallipoli was also recognised by one who had known him there, 'Of all brave men who throughout this period deserve most generous gratitude there is Pirie, the surgeon. He was apparently untiring. To realize the casualties is to know his task, fulfilled with sympathy, fine skill, and unruffled nerve. He ignored danger.'[12] Pirie was mentioned in dispatches twice – for his work on both fronts.

After a day in brigade support, the battalion moved to camp for the rest of the month. Amongst awards made that month there was an MC to Lieutenant James Picton, for rescuing buried men, under heavy shellfire, when a tunnel collapsed. Sadly, he had been killed since. Total casualties for July were thirty.

Gough set ambitious objectives for the new offensive. There was to be a 6,000yd advance on the first day through three lines of German defences. After some delay, the Battle of Pilckem Ridge began on 31 July, with Fifth Army attacking on a 7-mile front. The power of the artillery was awesome, especially to its victims. General von Kuhl, writing after the war recalled,

> In the early hours of 31st July a hurricane of fire, completely beyond anyone's experience, broke out. The entire earth of Flanders rocked and seemed to be on fire. This was not just drum fire; it was as though Hell itself had slipped its bonds. What were the raw terrors of Verdun and the Somme compared to this grotesquely huge outpouring of raw power?[13]

British hopes were high, 'If all goes well, there will be no Ypres Salient by this time tomorrow', Hamilton, the artilleryman, had written on 30 July.[14]

However, such optimistic expectations were to be cruelly disappointed. At best, the German first line and part of the second line were captured, and at heavy cost. 24th Division was in Jacob's II Corps, on the right flank of Gough's Fifth Army. It was advancing towards the Gheluvelt Plateau, a critical position that gave the Germans good artillery observation over the British lines and lighter batteries and shelter behind for their own guns. II Corps had a particularly difficult task, with especially strong German defences here partly concealed by, and strengthened by, the remains of a number of woods, impassable to tanks. The Germans were also well supported by artillery. 24th Division, facing Shrewsbury Forest, had some initial success. But 73 Brigade, in the centre, was held up by a group of pillboxes on the far edge of Shrewsbury Forest, at Lower Star Post. This forced the flanking brigades, 17 and 72, into a partial retreat, 72 Brigade being enfiladed from Dumbarton Wood. Tower, 72 Brigade's Brigade Major, who had prepared the

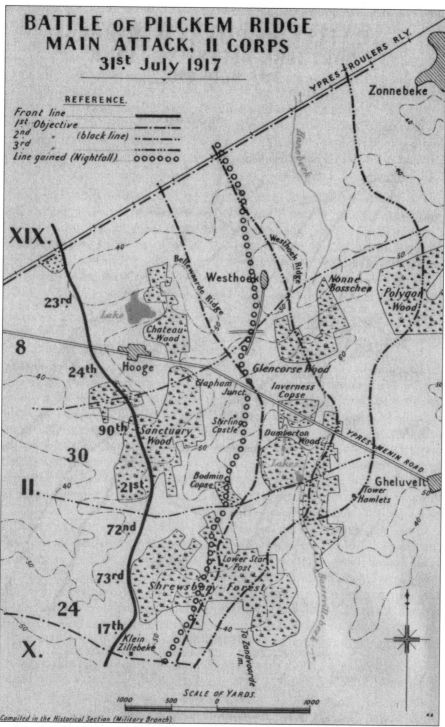

Figure 13. Pilckem Ridge, 31 July 1917.

plans for the whole division, blamed Duggan, 73 Brigade's commander, for ignoring his advice to attack from no-man's-land, instead keeping his men well back in cover.[15] To make matters worse, heavy rain began to fall that afternoon.

However, the Germans opposite were under heavy pressure. Bavarian RIR 8 in 10 Bavarian Division had been hard hit by the British bombardment, which had not only caused casualties and damage to its positions, but had all but destroyed communications, preventing effective support. The commander of the adjoining Bavarian RIR 6, whose casualties, facing the right of 24th Division, were extremely high, recorded,

> The front line established in the crater field was gradually yielded after an obstinate defence. In fact it had to be, because the British were enfilading it from the right flank, where they had pushed on deep into the sector of the neighbouring Prussian regiment [RIR 82, 22nd Reserve Division]. The line there was in any case too weakly held. The many dead British soldiers lying scattered around the blockhouses on our extreme right flank near the Prussian Front line bore silent witness to how determined our defence of it had been.[16]

The Germans withdrew from Lower Star Post early on 1 August and 73 Brigade occupied it.

On the evening of 1 August, 9/East Surrey's battalion HQ and 'C' and 'D' companies moved to Old French Trench, 2 miles south-west of Ypres. The following evening the battalion relieved 1/North Staffordshire and 8/Queen's of its own brigade, both heavily engaged the previous day. It took over captured positions about half a mile north east of Klein Zillebeke, with 'C' and 'D' companies in the front line. Conditions were very bad after continued heavy rain. The communication trenches were over waist-deep in water and liquid mud, forcing the troops to move forward in the open. Warre-Dymond's 'C' company lost around twenty killed and wounded to shelling, whilst moving up. The war diary, written at this period by Second Lieutenant Webb, observes, however, 'The men were not to be discouraged, and they went on cheerfully.'

It was on 2 August, in the line with his beloved 'C' company, that Sherriff's front-line service came to an end. Writing about it fifty years later, in the essay 'The English Public Schools in the War', he expresses, in retrospect, bitter disillusionment and hostility to the generals. His account, although very vivid, is confusing in some respects, both with respect to time and also by describing the action as an attack, when, from other sources, including the orders in the brigade war diary[17] it was a relief, and late on the second day of the battle. However, there is no doubt that conditions were truly horrible. Sherriff recalled,

> The whole thing became a drawn-out nightmare. There were no tree stumps or ruined buildings ahead to help you keep direction. The shelling had destroyed everything. As far as you could see, it was like an ocean of thick, brown porridge. The wire entanglements had sunk into the mud, and, frequently, when you went in up to your knees, your legs would come out with

strands of barbed wire clinging to them, and your hands were torn and bleeding through the struggle to drag them off.

The enemy began to send over heavy shells called coalboxes. Fired from away behind the German lines, they came down almost perpendicularly and exploded with a thunderous crash and a huge cloud of black smoke.

All of this area had been desperately fought over in the earlier battles of Ypres. Many of the dead had been buried where they fell and the shells were unearthing and tossing up the decayed bodies ... It was a warm, humid day, and the stench was horrible ...

After meeting up with 'the survivors of the first wave',

We found an old German shelter and brought in all our wounded that we could find ... You did what you could, but it was mainly a matter of watching them slowly bleed to death. Even if there had been stretcher-bearers, it would have been impossible to carry them to safety ...

Our company commander had made his headquarters under a few sheets of twisted corrugated iron.

'I want you to explore along this trench,' he said to me, 'and see whether you can find B Company [actually 'D'] ... If you can find them, we can link up together and get some sort of order into things.'

So I set off with my runner. It was like exploring the mountains of the moon. We followed the old trench as best we could but had to crawl across the blown in gaps. There were small concrete blockhouses here and there called pillboxes that the Germans built when the swampy ground prevented dugouts.

The Germans were now shelling us with whizbangs ... We heard the report of it being fired, and we heard the thin whistle of its approach, rising to a shriek. It landed on top of a concrete pillbox that we were passing, barely five yards away ... The crash was deafening. My runner let out a yell of pain. I didn't yell so far as I know because I was half stunned. I remember putting my hand to the right side of my face and feeling nothing: to my horror I thought the whole side had been blown away.

Afterwards, with time to think in hospital, I pieced the whole thing together. The light shell, hitting the solid concrete top of the pillbox had sent its splinters upward, mercifully above our heads; but it had sent a ferocious spatter of pulverized concrete in all directions, and that was what we'd got.

How badly we were wounded we didn't know. We were covered with blood and mud ... The company commander took one look at us and said 'Get back as best you can, and find a dressing station.'

We began the long trek back, floundering through the mud, through the stench and black smoke of the coalboxes that were still coming over. Here and there were other walking wounded, mainly in pairs, supporting themselves pitifully with arms around each other's shoulders. Many were so badly wounded they could barely drag themselves along, but to save themselves was their only hope ...

> It seemed hours before we reached a dressing station ... The doctor
> swabbed the wounds on our hands and faces ... 'You don't seem to have got
> anything very deep,' he said. 'Can you go on?'[18]

Sherriff and his orderly then walked another mile or so to the nearest field hospital.
Back at the base hospital, he wrote a card to his father that was meant to reassure
him

> Dear Pips,
> Am writing this left handed as my right is 'hors de combat' at present.
> I was hit by several small splinters also on the right side of my face – the
> shell was so close that the big pieces went over my head – it burst about 5 feet
> away; lucky for me my wounds are none worse and the shell no bigger.
> I feel quite fit no pain – hope to get to England.
> Am very much bound up & look worse than I feel.
> Hoping to see you soon.
> From your loving son
> Bob

Sherriff records a doctor took fifty-two pieces of concrete out of him, all about the
size of beans or peas. These were from his face, hand and leg. All the same, he was
perhaps lucky to be evacuated to Britain.

9/East Surrey remained in the front line until 7 August, with its companies
relieving each other in turn. Conditions were terrible, the rain continued and there
was heavy shellfire. Billman wrote,

> Altho' it was the first week in August, it was as cold and dreary as November.
> The battlefield was turned into one huge quagmire, into which were sucked
> men, horses, guns, it being an impossibility to extricate them when once in
> the grip of this terrible mud. During this time, we lost lots of brave men of my
> battalion, and the rest suffered terribly from the cold and wet, besides being
> heavily bombarded.

According to the war diary, 'Great credit is due to almost every individual man in
the battalion for the energetic way in which he worked. No matter whether they
carried rations, water, wounded, or anything else they stuck to their jobs in the
terrible conditions, and always won through with a smile.' Captain Warre-
Dymond particularly distinguished himself in these appalling circumstances,
including by reinforcing and temporarily taking over 'A' Company after it had
suffered particularly severely from shellfire.

The Germans were suffering similarly. 12 Division had been fed in to support
and then replace the badly battered 22 Reserve Division. 12 Division was a Silesian
division with a good reputation. After a terrible ordeal on the Somme, where it had
served three tours, it had been sent to the Eastern Front to recover. Returning to
the West in May, it had been designated an *Eingreifdivision* to counterattack
and/or reinforce as needed, in the anticipated British offensive. It was now in the

front line east of Klein Zillebeke, with IR 23 to the right and IR 62 to the left of the crossroads south of Groenenburg Farm. A company commander of IR 62 wrote to his parents after relief on 4 August about his experiences since 31 July,

> Suddenly a dreadful artillery concentration hammered down on the front edge of the wood ... It was awful! My company was being shot to pieces in front of my eyes and there was not a thing which I could do to help. The firing went on for one and a half hours. There was then a short pause and a further thirty minute bombardment from 9.15 pm. The fire died away then and we could rally the survivors. The company had suffered nine killed, thirty five wounded and fifteen missing.
>
> I led the remainder forward; there were about thirty of them ... and moved up eighty metres beyond the house to the so-called front line, which was simply a line of craters full of water and it was still raining heavily ... That night we re-occupied the craters. I simply cannot find words to describe our appearance or the conditions. Suffice it to say that two men of 11th Company drowned that night in the craters, because they could not free themselves from the clinging mud.[19]

The Germans were encouraged to launch a counterattack at this time, to improve their poor positions, which were on lower ground than the British. They understood, from an intercepted carrier-pigeon message and prisoner interrogation, that the British 41st Division on 24th Division's right had been so badly hit that it was in urgent need of relief. They planned to attack immediately, on the night of 4/5 August, with the operation coded *Sommernacht* (Summer Night), using men from 12 Division on the right and 207 Division on the left. Whilst the main attack was further south, on Hollebeke, three attacks were made on 9/East Surrey, from 6.00am on 5 August. These were made under cover of thick mist, on advanced posts in the vicinity of Jordan Trench, near Groenenburg Farm. The four posts were held, with two Lewis guns, by Second Lieutenant Taylor and around thirty men, who put up a good resistance, but the third attack took the posts and around half the men were lost. Lieutenant Colonel de la Fontaine, concerned as ever for his men, went forward to the front line to make a personal reconnaissance. Observing over the parapet, he was shot in the head by a sniper. Second Lieutenant Webb, who had accompanied him, later led a party forward, under heavy shellfire, which re-established the line, winning an MC. A DCM was awarded to Private C.W. Shere for his gallantry in holding an advanced post that day, although wounded in both legs, and Private A. Gates was awarded an MM for his bravery on the same occasion.

De la Fontaine's death was a sad blow to his battalion. Its war diary describes him as 'A personal friend of, and beloved by, every man in the battalion.' Billman calls him 'a very brave officer'. Condolences were sent by Brigadier General Sweny who referred to the great loss the brigade had suffered with his death and, 'It was, I fear, due to his great personal courage that he met his end, and not only his courage, but his continual self-sacrifice and untiring zeal to ensure the success of his Battalion and the Brigade.' He then praised the battalion, 'I again wish to tell the 9th East Surrey Regt how essential their tenacity in holding this very exposed position was to the main operations. Their sacrifices were just as important as any that were made during the actual attack, and have added to their reputation for steadiness and discipline under shell fire.'[20]

It seems that it was men from IR 23 who had attacked the 9/East Surrey outposts, although their account does not go into detail about what was merely part of a bigger operation. This regiment had found conditions gruelling in the extreme. In addition to the horrors described above by the company commander of IR 62, IR 23 recorded that it had been suffering from repeated British gas attacks, apparently by Livens Projectors. These were accompanied by conventional artillery fire, to try to prevent the massive flashes of the Livens discharges being seen before it was too late to don gasmasks. As part of *Sommernacht*, according to IR 23's regimental history,

> this opportunity was used to push our line forward a few hundred metres in the sector of the 9 and 12 Companies south of Groenenburg at dawn on the 5 [August]. With the support of our artillery the stormtroops went forward at 4.50am, followed by 9 and 12 Companies. Wholly unhindered by the enemy the designated line was reached, where the companies deployed, echeloned in depth. Thick fog, which began to lift about 9am, assisted the whole operation. At about 6.00am the enemy artillery fire became more intense, but dropped off again over the course of the day. The aerial activity on both sides, however, was all the more vigorous.[21]

Major Swanton returned to command the battalion, but was wounded early on 7 August, leaving Captain Clark, the adjutant, to take command. The battalion was relieved late on 7 August, moving to Divisional Reserve at Mic Mac Camp.

Casualties in this first week of August had been heavy, at 151, including 38 dead. Amongst them was CSM John Tanner, who died of wounds on 6 August, leaving a widow and six children. The eldest, Ellen, then aged 9, recalled,

> Good neighbours would come round and offer their sympathy, feeling sorry for us, bringing us sweets and biscuits to cheer us up. But that was all. In no time at all Mother had made black-and-white check dresses with a black belt for all the girls, and I can see us now, all walking down the street together and people looking at us because Father was well known in the community. I never cried in front of other people. You are too proud to let people see that things reach you, you are taught that. I wanted to cry, inwardly, but you didn't want anybody to see it, especially being the eldest. I kept everything inside because I daren't let the other children see me break down because they looked up to me, so I waited until I got to bed then had a good cry, just as I'm sure Mum did when she was on her own.

Ellen also recalled that for a long time her mother could not bear to see her husband's photograph in the dining room and turned it to the wall.[22]

Lieutenant Colonel L.J. Le Fleming took command on 8 August. Born in 1879, like de la Fontaine he was a regular officer of the regiment, who had served with it in the Boer War. He was an instructor at the Royal Military College in 1914, but was with the BEF by October 1914. He was then severely wounded twice but sought to return to the Front.[23]

The battalion remained in reserve for a week, with training in the mornings and recreation and rest in the afternoons. There was fairly frequent bombing of the vicinity by German aeroplanes.

From 15 to 19 August the battalion was back in the line, at Mount Sorrel, just north of its previous position, probably facing 12 Division, again. Hamilton, spotting for his battery, visited the position on 21 August and, used to trenches, found 'A most extraordinary situation, neither side has any sign of a trench – both are sitting in shell-holes a few yards apart, with no wire in between, and separated by nothing but a few yards of open ground.'[24] Fortunately for the battalion, enemy shellfire had been less heavy than the previous tour. There also seems to have been 'live and let live' between the opposing infantry, who were suffering the same conditions, although the battalion sustained twenty-four casualties. With the Battle of Langemarck from 16–18 August, Gough sought to renew the offensive, replacing some worn-out units, but with limited success. 24th Division made some contribution. However, the Gheluvelt Plateau remained in German hands.

Periods in rest and Divisional Support followed for 9/East Surrey, before another period in the Mount Sorrel trenches, during which five more casualties were sustained. Total casualties for August were almost 200. With the particularly heavy losses of officers in recent weeks, thirteen second lieutenants joined the battalion in August, and forty-nine ORs.

For the first week of September, the battalion was in Divisional Reserve or Support. Bols, the divisional commander, visited and was very complimentary about the battalion. It then served four days in Brigade Reserve in dugouts in the Ypres–Menin railway embankment, behind the Front at Stirling Castle. Whilst marching there, one man was killed and one wounded by an aeroplane bomb.

Haig, having lost confidence in Gough, had handed the renewal of the offensive back to Plumer, who, after careful preparation and drier conditions, launched a successful attack on 20 September –the Battle of Menin Road Ridge. However, 9/East Surrey had already finished with Ypres. It had left the Salient on 14 September, never to return.

Chapter 9

Before the Storm,
September 1917–February 1918

Following heavy losses at Ypres, as after Loos and the Somme, 24th Division was sent to a quiet sector to recover and rebuild its strength. It joined III Corps of Third Army on the Somme Front. The line was well in advance of the previous year, because of the German withdrawal to the Hindenburg Line early in 1917. However, as it retired, the German Army had taken considerable pains to devastate the abandoned territory.

The division had received a new commander, Major General A.C. Daly, on 15 September. Bols, his predecessor, became Chief of Staff to Allenby's Egyptian Expeditionary Force, proving a great success in that capacity. Daly, aged 46, a general's son, had been commissioned into the West Yorkshire Regiment in 1890. He had served in the Boer War. After Staff College, he had held several staff positions with the BEF, before being given command of a brigade. He was to command the division for the rest of the war.

9/East Surrey travelled by train to Miraumont on 18 September and then marched to Beaulencourt, where it rested. Whilst there, many visited nearby Delville Wood, Guillemont and other scenes of the desperate fighting of the year before.

Moving on, on 28 September the battalion took over the front line 1,500yd east of Hargicourt, 10 miles north-west of St Quentin. Casualties in September totalled thirteen. Approximate strength at the end of the month was 25 officers and 650 ORs.

The battalion remained in the front line until 3 October, when it moved to Brigade Support at Cote Wood, just south-west of Hargicourt. From then until mid-December, the battalion held the same trenches alternately with 8/R West Kent, with reliefs every five to seven days. When not in the front-line trenches, the battalion was in Brigade Support, or in Reserve. This latter position was initially by Montigny Farm, a ruined sugar factory, then in the ruined village of Hancourt and finally at Vendelles.

72 Brigade held the centre of the division's front. 8/R West Kent recalled,

> Our front section consisted of a front line – tumbling to pieces – called Railway Trench on the right, and Pond Trench and Bait Trench on the left, a support line just being dug about 200 yards behind, and reserve positions

with Battalion Headquarters in a chalk quarry, known as the Egg, just outside the ruined villages of Hargicourt and Villaret. There were good communication trenches, Club Trench and Onion Lane.

From the front line at Bait Trench we had a splendid view of the Hindenburg line and the village of Bellicourt. The ground sloped down steeply from this part of our positions, and we could see almost the whole of the valley called Buckshot Ravine, across which the Hindenburg front line and switches in front of Bellicourt had been dug. The country behind our lines was undulating and splendidly open. All villages had been totally destroyed by the enemy on his retirement in the spring.

The position of the support battalion at Cote Wood was quite comfortable. Protected from view, the trenches were well dug on the reverse slope of a ridge.[1]

October was a quiet month with only thirteen casualties. Whilst there was some mortar fire, the little artillery fire was generally directed at rear areas. Work was carried out to improve the defences. The lines here were relatively far apart – between 1 and 1.8km according to German sources. Patrols sent out at night had no encounters with the enemy. A score of Germans, advancing early on 11 October, were driven off by Lewis guns.

The British were not, however, planning to leave the Germans in complete tranquillity. The Germans of RIR 440 were alarmed on 24 October when aerial reconnaissance identified the installation of the much-feared Livens Projectors. An imminent gas or smoke attack appeared to be confirmed from an intercepted telephone call. It was not, however, until early on 26 October that there was a sudden British heavy artillery and mortar bombardment and 1/North Staffordshire, on 9/East Surrey's right, mounted a raid. 9/East Surrey assisted with a feint, directed by Major Clark, with signal rockets and smoke bombs. This proved useful in distracting the enemy, at the cost of one man wounded in the resulting shelling. The raiding battalion was grateful for the assistance and succeeded in capturing a prisoner from RIR 440, 183 Division.

183 Division had a brief, but good record, but had suffered severe losses on the Chemin des Dames in April 1917 and then had been heavily engaged at Langemarck, Ypres, in August 1917, transferring to Hargicourt in early September. Those of its regiments apparently opposite 72 Brigade, were IR 418 from Hesse and RIR 440 from the Grand Duchy of Oldenburg. Although the Hindenburg Line was impressive, RIR 440 did not think much of their positions in front of it, 'a trench system which was in an incomplete and neglected state throughout, and which absolutely failed to meet the requirements of a fighting position. The men were poorly accommodated; many of the dugouts lay underwater.'[2] The regiment had a policy of aggressive patrolling, each battalion using, in particular its established *Jagdkommando* (a hunting/raiding party) routinely active at night. However, the regiment was also a target, admitting to two dead and five wounded in the 1/North Staffordshire raid on 26 October. The British attempted

another (small–scale) raid two nights later, but this was easily repelled. It was, however, 183 Division's third infantry regiment, IR 184, that had perhaps the greatest success. This launched a big raid on 4/Loyal North Lancashire of 55th Division at Gillemont Farm on 18 November. It sustained and inflicted heavy casualties, taking forty prisoners.

9/East Surrey was holding the front line when the British surprise attack at Cambrai began in the early morning of 20 November, on a 6-mile front extending northwards from near Gonnelieu, 7 miles north of the battalion. Demonstrations were held at many places along the line, in the hope of confusing the Germans. 9/East Surrey's contribution took the form of a raid, for which training had commenced a month before. An area had been taped out and dug to represent an area of no-man's-land and adjoining British and German trenches, so each volunteer could practise his role.

The object of the raid was to capture or kill Germans and blow in any dugouts. There were five raiding parties, with Lieutenant Cowper in overall charge – two fighting and blocking parties; one party to deal with dugouts; one covering party; and one party to facilitate withdrawal. Each party consisted of an officer or NCO and six men, with the fifth, under Cowper himself, to cover the retreat of the others. Two of the men were engineers with explosive charges.

The raid began at 6.20am. Although the enemy trench was lightly held, its sentries, probably from IR 418, were on the alert. Two threw grenades at the first two parties, which killed one man and wounded Second Lieutenant Carter, Sergeant Bell and another man. Two men were sent back with the badly wounded officer. Bell, though wounded, pursued and killed two Germans. Second Lieutenant Luty, with No. 3 Party was wounded, along with three of his men, as they neared the enemy trench. Sergeant Medlock took over and there was further action with casualties on both sides. The wounded were successfully evacuated. The action lasted for 20 to 25 minutes, supervised by Cowper, although wounded. Covering fire was provided by mortars and Vickers guns. Unfortunately, it had not been possible to bring back a prisoner for identification. It had been necessary to kill all those Germans encountered at close quarters, five or more, and their uniforms did not appear to have the usual shoulder straps with regimental numbers. Nor had it been possible to blow up any dugouts. Casualties amongst the raiders were quite heavy, with three dead and eleven wounded. Decorations were awarded to Lieutenant Cowper and Second Lieutenant Carter (MCs), Sergeants Bell and Medlock (DCMs) and Privates Bell and Mortimer (MMs). Mortimer and Bell had brought back Second Lieutenant Carter. Carter, although completely crippled by his wounds after cutting the wire, had cheered on his men. He died of wounds on 28 November.

The battalion returned to the front line on 25 November. As it was anticipated the Germans might retire because of the British advance at Cambrai, orders were issued to patrol no-man's-land and keep in touch with the enemy in case he withdrew. The battalion was already routinely patrolling and Second Lieutenant

Grantham was killed on this duty late on 27 November. Casualties for November totalled twenty-nine.

A German deserter came over at Fish Lane on 30 November. He identified IR 20 as opposite, from 5 Guard Reserve Division. This was correct, except it was 5 Guard Division, which had a formidable reputation. This division had only relieved 183 Division on 24/25 November. IR 20 was not a Guard unit, but a very solid Brandenburg regiment.

A German attack was expected in the light of the deserter's report, but nothing occurred on 24th Division's front. 5 Guard Division was a fine formation, but seems to have been content to spend its time opposite 24th Division in recovering from its recent hardships at Craonne, rather than showing aggression. On 5 December 9/East Surrey, less one company, was relieved by dismounted cavalry, and moved back to Vendelles.

Training for a second raid was conducted, as the first had failed to secure a prisoner for identification and the British may have suspected the deserter of giving false information. The raid was then carried out, successfully, on the evening of 9 December, the day after the battalion's return to the front line. It was led by Lieutenant Thomas, with two other officers and twenty-four ORs. A German sentry was quickly seized and the raiders withdrew without loss. The prisoner was from IR 20 and besides this identification provided other useful information. The identification was considered particularly valuable, with the Corps commander sending his congratulations. Thomas was awarded a bar to his MC.

In December, Brigadier General R.W. Morgan took over 72 Brigade and was to command it for the rest of the war. Born in 1879, he was, like Daly, an Army officer's son and a Boer War veteran.

On 14 December, with the battalion out of the line, there was a heavy fall of snow, and the weather turned very cold. Training continued, nonetheless, with afternoon sports. On 19 December there was a move to a new camp at Hancourt. Unfortunately, this proved to be unfinished and the battalion had to put in much work to complete it.

Christmas was duly celebrated in camp. According to the war diary, the men sat down to 'the best and largest Xmas dinner that even the oldest soldier amongst them could ever remember'. This was followed by a regimental concert with the signallers' humorous sketch being the highlight. This 'merry Xmas Day was unanimously agreed the happiest spent by this battalion in France'.[3] Sporting events were held in the days after Christmas. Casualties in December were very light, at three wounded. Strength at the end of the year was 36 officers and 850 ORs.

Regarding the officers of 1917, Lindsay had written from the battalion to Sherriff on 11 September, 'My dear boy we have 11 new subalterns but as to seduce [*sic*] them as you say they are awful people. They have hardly an aitch between them, and are very terrible people, I can't stick em at any price.'[4] Fewer officers being appointed to the battalion may have been to public school, but they were generally clerks from a lower middle-class background, although they had usually served previously in the ranks (as Lindsay himself, a meat broker, had in

Figure 14. 9/East Surrey Christmas card, 1917.

the Rifle Brigade). More of these than before had front-line experience. Previously, Sherriff, and many others, had enlisted into units like the Artists' Rifles, which were acting essentially as officer training units, and had been commissioned without front-line service.

Amongst these new arrivals Ernest Grantham, for instance, was a clerk, who had served a year in France as a trooper in the Life Guards. Albert Nilson, educated at King's College, was an architect's clerk. He had served six months in France in the ranks of the Queen's Westminster Rifles. Felix Seel was a Stock Exchange clerk, who had served in the ranks of the very prestigious Honourable Artillery Company. William Corley was a bank clerk with OTC experience who had, nevertheless, served for more than two years in the ranks of the Hertfordshire Regiment in France.

George Carter was most unusual in being working class, a gardener by profession. He had enlisted in the Bedfordshire Regiment aged 16 in September 1914, saying he was 19. Transferred to the East Surrey Regiment, he served with 8/East Surrey in France from August 1915 to the following January. He had then served for some months in Salonika with 2/East Surrey. After a Cadet Battalion and being commissioned, he had served with 9/East Surrey from August 1917. Both Grantham and Carter were killed in autumn 1917.[5]

It is possible that some new officers (particularly with so many arriving together – nine on 26 August, including the four above) did not feel they needed to conform to public-school values, or to the behaviour expected of junior officers. These values were generally held by the battalion's existing officers, whether or not they had been to public school, and the cadet battalions endeavoured to inculcate them into their cadets.

Lieutenant Colonel Le Fleming, the new CO, seems to have been well received. Writing to Sherriff on 20 September, Lindsay described his new commander as, 'A ripping chap – you'd like him', even though he was frustrated by his own lack of promotion. 'I am still <u>asst.</u> adjutant. I saw the C.O. about it and asked him why I wasn't made adj he said I was young and junior but he was keeping me up his sleeve it's a bit of a b-g-r isn't it I said fuck with venom. All the 2nd Lieuts over 18 months service are full Lieuts now.' Now aged around 23, he had first served in the ranks in France from February 1915. He had won an MC for his part in the January 1917 raid. Clark considered him both very efficient and very brave. Le Fleming clearly recognised Lindsay's qualities and made him adjutant in late October, without promotion, but by the end of November, it was Captain Lindsay!

The battalion's other ranks in 1917 included a good number of conscripts as more of the old volunteers became casualties. Although somewhat more diverse, it was still, however, very much a Surrey and London unit.

Waits for leave for the other ranks seem to have become longer. Woodbury and Billman, who had both had leave in spring 1916 after six or seven months at the Front and had then been wounded in June and August 1916 respectively, had to wait until autumn 1917 for their second spells of ordinary home leave. In November 1917, after unfavourable comparisons were made with French practice, leave for other ranks was extended from ten to fourteen days. Officially, it was to be granted every fifteen months, although some had to wait longer.[6]

From early August, Sherriff was in Britain. Writing to his father on 8 August, six days after his wounding, he recognised that without serious wounds he had been 'lucky enough to get home at all. My wounds are now practically better.' He anticipated two or three weeks' sick leave, only, after perhaps ten more days in hospital,

> After that you return to duty with the reserve Battalion of your regiment – I would probably go to Dover again, and then you are not very long in England unless you can 'work' anything to keep you back – I should certainly not hurry my return, for 10 months have been quite enough for me although I can hardly see any loophole (save a sudden peace) by which to remain in England permanently.[7]

Warre-Dymond, his company commander, sent Sherriff a somewhat ambiguous letter on 15 August, as he prepared to go back into the line,

> You lucky young beggar getting back home. I do hope you are getting along really well but just not well enough to come out again this summer.
> As I daresay Homewood has told you we had to go up again & had a good many more wounded. Poor old Sadler died of wounds from I imagine the

same shell that caught you. I & all the others are awfully upset about it & so sorry for his poor young wife.

As regards what you say about yourself, all I can say is don't be a boob & we all are awfully sorry to lose you. However, the thing is to rejoin the Battalion the day before peace is declared & we hope we'll all be there.

Lindsay wrote from the battalion on 11 September, 'Dear Sheriffa, was awfully pleased to hear from you, you have got well quickly what a pity you couldn't have stayed in hospital a month or so longer. You saw dear old Tetley didn't you did he tell you any stories worth repeating if so lets have em.' Sherriff had been in touch with Captain Tetley, who had lost a leg. Tetley replied on 17 September, 'I was saddened at hearing you were once more in Hospital, but glad your return to the Front was thus postponed.'

Sherriff was also in correspondence with 'Jimbo' Webb, congratulating him on his MC and saying, 'My great hope is that I get back to the dear old 9th again when I return to France.' Webb wrote from the battalion on 7 October, addressing Sherriff, it seems, as 'Billy', 'It was good to get your letter of 13th ult., and to know that at that time there was still some prospect of you remaining at home for another few weeks (not much of a compliment is it?)'

Like other officers who had been hospitalised, Sherriff faced medical boards every few weeks. These repeatedly passed him as fit for Home Service, but not front-line service abroad. Sherriff wrote on 14 November to his father from the Grand Shaft Barracks at Dover, where he had arrived a few days before to serve with 3/Reserve Battalion of his regiment. He was clearly enjoying life and finding tasks like taking a working party out into the countryside pleasantly undemanding. He never did return to the Front, but served as a musketry instructor to recruits and then battalion gas officer. Promoted to lieutenant in March 1918 and captain in January 1919, he was demobilised two months later.[8]

For Germany 1918 had to be the year of decision. Peace terms acceptable to its rulers were not on offer from the Allies. The Americans were gradually building up their forces and transporting them to France. The U-boat campaign had, after initial success, failed to bring decisive results, whilst the British blockade was starving Germany of food and many strategic raw materials. The collapse of the Eastern Front, however, gave Germany one last opportunity for victory in the West. Russia was in chaos following two revolutions, and its new masters, the Bolsheviks, wanted peace with the Central Powers at any price, in order to defeat their internal enemies. An armistice was negotiated at Brest Litovsk in December. Ludendorff set about planning a great offensive to break the Western Allies.

As for the Allies, whilst the French Army had recovered from the disorders of the 1917 mutinies, the British and French had been obliged to shore up Italy with eleven of their own divisions after the rout of Caporetto in October 1917. The Allies were well aware that the Germans were gradually transferring divisions from the East to the West, but Haig, initially, underestimated the danger. Lloyd George

1. Private 'Teddy' Cutt, kia September 1915.
(© *Surrey History Centre, ref. ESR/25/CUTT*)

2. Captain J.L. Vaughan, kia August 1916.
(© *Surrey History Centre, ref. ESR/25/LYNDH*)

3. Captain G.S. Pirie, RAMC, kia July 1917.
(© *Family of the late Captain G.S. Pirie*)

4. Second Lieutenant R.C. Sherriff, about 1916.
(© *Kingston Grammar School, and courtesy of Surrey
History Centre, ref. 2332/Box 12/Part I*)

5. 9/East Surrey regimental police. (© *Surrey History Centre, ref. ESR/19/2/1*)

6. 9/East Surrey officers, March 1917. Front row: first left, Lieutenant G.W. Warre-Dymond; third from right, Lieutenant Colonel H.V.M. de la Fontaine, kia August 1917; second from right, Lieutenant C.A. Clark. Middle row: centre, Second Lieutenant R.C. Sherriff. Third row: first left, Second Lieutenant A.H. Douglass, dow April 1918. (© *Surrey History Centre, ref. ESR/25/CLARK/7*)

7. Officers of 'C' Company, March/April 1917. Seated, left to right: Second Lieutenant A.H. Douglass, dow April 1918; Captain G.W. Warre-Dymond, POW March 1918; probably Second Lieutenant R.J. Homewood; Second Lieutenant C.W. Trenchard, wounded April 1917. Standing, left to right: Second Lieutenant H.W. Kiver, kia April 1917; Second Lieutenant R.C. Sherriff, wounded August 1917; probably Second Lieutenant A.A.H. Toplis, to RFC April 1917. (It is difficult to tell Homewood and Toplis apart.)
(© *Kingston Grammar School, and courtesy of Surrey History Centre, ref. 2332/Box12/Part I*)

8. Sergeant F.W. Billman and his wife, 1918. (*Imperial War Museum, ref. 76/210/1*)

9. Lieutenant Colonel L.J. Le Fleming, kia March 1918. (© *Surrey History Centre, ref. ESR/LEFL/1*)

10. A 'minnie', a 25cm heavy *minenwerfer*, with Prussian *Pionier* crew and visiting Saxon artillerymen, 1915.
(© *Mrs M.A. Hemmings*)

11. (*Right*) Second Lieutenant D.W. Keep, kia October 1918. (© *Surrey History Centre, ref. ESR/25/KEEP/1*)

12. (*Below*) Corporal J. McNamara VC, kia October 1918. (© *Surrey History Centre, ref. ESR/25/MCNAJ/3*)

13. Saxon Jägers of RJägB 26 in the Bellewaarde area, 1915. Here they opposed 9/East Surrey in January 1916. Note pouches for early pad-type gas protection, as used at Loos. (© J. Schmieschek)

14. Prussian and Saxon heavy gunners with a 150mm long-range naval gun. Range directions for the current rear-area target are painted on the shield. (© J. Schmieschek)

15. German infantry about to go into action, spring 1918. These are members of 1 Company, *Schutzen* Regiment 108, 23 Division. (© *A.R. Lucas*)

16. Germans in the ruins of Lens, about 1917. (© *A.R. Lucas*)

7. 9/East Surrey on Armistice Day. Lieutenant Colonel Cameron calls for three cheers for the King.
© *Imperial War Museum, ref. Q.3362)*

8. Men of 9/East Surrey turn to face the camera on Armistice Day. Note the bandsmen.
© *Imperial War Museum, ref. Q.3363)*

19. 9/East Surrey officers, around New Year 1919. With identifications from other photographs and internal evidence it has been possible to name some of those seen here. Front row, from the left: third (probably) Captain E.L. Whiteman; sixth Major J.C. Brown; seventh Lieutenant Colonel E.A. Cameron; tenth Captain R.W.L. Wallace, RAMC; extreme right Captain E.H.B. Nobbs. Middle row: ninth from left Second Lieutenant H.R. Tucker; extreme right Lieutenant and Quarter Master E.F. James. Back row: seventh from left Second Lieutenant F.J. Wood. (© Surrey History Centre, ref ESR/25/WOODFI/3)

had been shocked by the losses of the Passchendaele campaign and sought to hold back men in Britain. He had no confidence in Haig, but did not see it as practical to replace him. However, he still also believed that the war could be won elsewhere than on the Western Front. He seemed blind to the danger that this was the front where the war could be most easily lost. His government addressed the BEF's manpower issue by forcing a reorganisation of divisions on Haig – each brigade was to lose one of its four battalions. At this time, there were approaching a million troops employed in secondary theatres of war and there were 1½ million troops in Britain.

At the Front, the men of 9/East Surrey were concerned with the day-to-day issues of survival. On 5 January, the battalion took over trenches at Ronssoy, 1½ miles north-west of Hargicourt. These were on high ground with good observation. After frost and snow, the weather moderated on 7 January but, with the thaw, the trenches flooded. Relieved on 13 January, the battalion was then nominally at 'rest', but had to provide numerous working parties, digging trenches in back areas. It also devoted much labour to improving its camp, leaving little time for training. It returned to the Ronssoy trenches on 30 January. At least the Germans had been quiet, with the battalion losing just six wounded in January. The Prussian Guards had been replaced at the end of December by the considerably less formidable 9 Bavarian Reserve Division, which had been badly hit at Chemin des Dames and Langemarck. Bavarian RIR 11 or 14 now faced 9/East Surrey at Ronssoy.

The reorganisation of divisions was underway at this time, but the disruption to 24th Division was not as bad as some. During February 8/Queen's was moved from 72 Brigade, to 17 Brigade in the same division. 8/Buffs and 12/R Fusiliers were disbanded and 2/Leinster moved to 16th (Irish) Division. 7/East Surrey in 12th Division had been disbanded and, as its share, 9/East Surrey received 9 officers and around 100 other ranks on 7 February. Any surplus infantrymen from the reorganisation were put into 'entrenching battalions', to be used for work on defences until required to replace casualties. Around the same time, each division's machine-gun companies were brought together, formally, into a battalion.

Things continued quiet, with 9/East Surrey serving in Reserve, Support and then the Line near Hargicourt. Patrols had had no encounters with the enemy and casualties remained light, with simply three wounded that month. Following the reinforcements, the battalion was well up to strength at the end of February with 1,009 ORs and liberally supplied with 49 officers. The Army, however, measured the strength of a unit in many different ways. 'Effective Strength' could include sick and wounded men, as well as those detached to other units; 'Fighting Strength' would exclude these men; and 'Trench Strength' would exclude as well as transport men, those left out of the line as a nucleus for reconstitution and some base details.[9] On 26 February, the battalion had been relieved and moved to Neuville, 8 miles east of Amiens. Although conditions in the Hargicourt sector had been less onerous than most, the men were no doubt looking forward to a reasonable period of rest. It was not to be.

Chapter 10

Kaiserschlacht,
March 1918

Principally by transferring soldiers from Russia, in anticipation of early peace with the Bolsheviks (finally signed on 3 March), and from Italy following the victory of Caporetto, Ludendorff built up German forces in the West. He prepared for a great series of attacks to begin in late March. The focus of the initial attack, 'Michael', was to be from Arras to La Fère. This was a relatively weakly held section of the Allied Front, had no significant terrain obstacles and an attack there was less weather dependent than Flanders. Ludendorff aimed to achieve a decisive breakthrough and, whilst holding off the French to the south, to roll up the British line northwards. This was to be followed by a further offensive, 'Georgette', against the British in Flanders. There would then be further attacks, elsewhere, if necessary. He hoped a decisive defeat would force the Allies to seek peace on terms very favourable to Germany.

The measures to achieve this breakthrough were to include great superiority in men and guns at critical points. Whilst, like the British attack at Cambrai in late 1917, the Germans aimed for surprise by dispensing with a long preliminary bombardment, they placed no great reliance on tanks, of which they had very few. (The nine only available on the day would be used south of St Quentin). Instead, there would be a short, but extremely intensive bombardment by 10,000 guns and heavy mortars. This would be followed by an assault led by stormtroopers, specifically trained and equipped for infiltration, with light machine guns, light trench mortars and flamethrowers. These might be in special 'storm battalions' (used for critical missions and to inculcate stormtrooper tactics in others), or in detachments from ordinary regiments trained by the 'storm battalions'. They were to penetrate the enemy's lines as deeply as possible, bypassing centres of resistance, leaving these for following waves. Such tactics had already been used successfully, on a smaller scale, in the counterattack at Cambrai. Hindenburg issued the final orders for the offensive on 10 March. It was to begin on 21 March. Most German soldiers were optimistic – this was to be the decisive, war-winning attack – *Kaiserschlacht* – the Kaiser's Battle.

The Germans did their best not to alarm the Allies, but it was obvious that the Germans were busy transferring units from Russia to the Western Front for an offensive. The uncertainties were when precisely the attack would begin, how heavy it would be and where precisely it would fall. By early February, however,

Gough, commanding the British Fifth Army, had correctly ascertained German intentions. The focus of the German attack would be his own army and the British Third Army on his left. German rail and road movements, which could not be completely concealed, seemed to confirm Gough's conclusions. However, German machinations deceived the French into thinking they would be the main target.

As for 9/East Surrey, the heightened tension brought its period of rest to an abrupt end. On 1 March, it had to leave La Neuville and set off for the Péronne area. Here at Devise, it remained until 11 March, training.

24th Division was under XIX Corps, commanded by Lieutenant General H.E. Watts. It took over the front line near Villecholles, just north-west of St Quentin, from men of 2nd Dismounted Cavalry Division. This was a little south of the line it had held over the winter.

The British, after long being on the offensive, had been obliged to plan for a defensive battle. Aiming to learn from German experience, particularly, defence was intended to be in depth. The Forward Zone was to be based on the existing front-line system. Behind it was to be the Battle Zone, usually 1 to 2 miles to the rear and at least 2,000 to 3,000yd in depth. Finally, there was to be the Rear Zone, 4 to 8 miles behind the Battle Zone. Whilst the Forward Zone depended for its siting on the existing defences, the defences of the Battle Zone were intended to be as favourably located as possible, with respect to fields of fire, etc. The Forward Zone was to be held in reasonable strength, so that if the enemy could not be stopped, he could be delayed and punished severely before reaching the Battle Zone. Rather than simply relying on a passive defence, the defenders were to launch counterattacks to force the enemy back. If all else failed, the enemy was to be stopped by the Rear Zone (Green Line). Each zone was intended to have successive lines within it of trenches and/or strongpoints. Unfortunately, there had not been adequate labour and time available to make these defence lines sufficiently strong. In particular, the Rear Zone, especially behind Fifth Army, amounted to little more than lines marked out on the ground.

72 Brigade was on the right of 24th Division's front and held around 3,000yd of front in rolling countryside. 8/R West Kent, which put up a fine defence on the brigade's left when the Germans attacked, recalled that there was a very wide no-man's-land and the outpost zone was about 800yd deep. Behind these were trenches. There was also a redoubt at Vadencourt. Most of the positions were moderately well wired and had good fields of fire. The River Omignon, part of which formed a swamp, ran between the two front-line battalions. The positions south of the river, held by 1/North Staffordshire, 72 Brigade's right-hand battalion, and only recently taken over from the French, were not so satisfactory. They were heavily dependent on interlocking machine-gun fire, for which good visibility was necessary.

During 9/East Surrey's first front-line tour here according to the war diary, written some time later as the original was soon to be lost in action, 'There was a marked lack of Artillery fire on the part of the enemy, it seemed as if he were waiting and saving his ammunition for some definite purpose … It was a most uneventful tour.'[1]

Quite apart from the weaknesses of the British defences, there were simply insufficient men to hold them against the weight of the attack to come. XIX Corps was part of Gough's Fifth Army, which had twelve infantry and three (much smaller) cavalry divisions to hold 42 miles of front. It had far fewer men per mile than Third Army to the north. Moreover, the defences, some recently taken over from the French, were generally unimpressive. However, Haig's reasoning was that Gough's front, being furthest from the coast, was the least critical. He could afford loss of ground on the Somme Front, but not near the Channel ports.

Haig underestimated the ferocity of the German attack that was to come. Fifth Army was to be attacked by forty-three German divisions. 8/R West Kent recalled, 'In spite of the seeming uncertainty of things, leave was never better in the whole war. When the great enemy offensive commenced on March 21, about 200 officers and other ranks of the Battalion were on leave in England.'[2] Presumably because of this, 9/East Surrey's 'B' Company could only field 5 officers and 120 men at this time. This would be consistent with the battalion having a combat strength of only around 500, which seems to have been average then. The brigade commander, Morgan, was also on leave, only managing to rejoin late on 24 March.

For what happened to 9/East Surrey in the great German offensive, there is the problem already mentioned. The battalion war diary was lost, and what had happened had to be pieced together later, from the few survivors. Also record keeping, at such a difficult time, could not be a priority. There is, therefore, more than usual conflict between different sources for late March 1918. As for personal accounts, Billman's finishes with the end of December 1917. It seems quite possible he lost any 1918 diary in the retreat. Some official records, however, like 72 Brigade's war diary, do survive. Part of this was clearly written down as events unfolded and has the immediacy of a running commentary. There are also reports by some returned officer POWs.

24th Division had 66th Division of its own Corps on its left and 61st Division of XVIII Corps on its right. Of 24th Division's three brigades, 17 Brigade was on the left and 72 Brigade on the right. 73 Brigade was in Corps reserve. The River Omignon was the boundary between two of the attacking German armies – Von der Marwitz's Second Army north of the river and von Hutier's Eighteenth Army, to the south. North of the Omignon, 24th Division's left would be attacked by 208 Division of LI Corps. South of the Omignon, 113 Division of III Corps would lead the attack. Moreover, 4 Guard Division from XIV Corps turned south during the course of the day to join in the attack on 24th Division's left. Each of these divisions had further divisions in second and third lines. Behind the British XIX Corps was only 1st Cavalry Division.

113 Division had fought with distinction on the Chemin des Dames as late as November 1917. Since then, it had been fully rebuilt and recuperated for its role as a first-line attack division on 'Tag X', the opening of the great offensive. Its

infantry were FR 36 and IR 66, both from Prussian Saxony, and RIR 32 from Thuringia.

9/East Surrey spent the last few days before the offensive in Reserve at Vermand, a village 3 miles behind Maissemy. On 20 March, 'B' Company was sent to reinforce 1/North Staffordshire east of Maissemy. 8/R West Kent, on the brigade's left around Vadencourt, received a report in the evening that, according to information provided by a German prisoner, an attack might be expected on 20 or 21 March. Night patrolling found no unusual activity. A clear night turned to mist just before dawn. This became so thick that 'It was impossible to see more than fifteen yards.'[3] The divisional artillery was ordered to fire periodically to harass the Germans.

At 4.40am on 21 March the German offensive suddenly began with a bombardment of crushing intensity and remarkable precision. Under *Oberst* Bruchmüller's carefully orchestrated plans for Eighteenth Army, the first 2 hours were devoted mostly to known enemy batteries, trench mortars, command posts and billets, with mixed high explosive and gas. The next 3 hours were devoted largely to the British infantry and their defences. At 9.40am the German infantry moved forward under a creeping barrage. The British response was severely handicapped, not only by the destruction of men and guns in the bombardment, but also by loss of telephone communications, whether cables were buried or not, and the dense mist. The surviving artillery could only fire on pre-arranged target areas. Communications had to be maintained by runners. Some of these became casualties and others were seriously delayed. It took 3½ hours for a 10.00am message from 8/R West Kent to reach 72 Brigade HQ.[4]

Private Nurse of 8/Queen's, with a companion, was sent with a message to 72 Brigade HQ, witnessing some strange sights on the way,

The guns of a 9.2 battery were in the process of being dismantled in readiness for withdrawal. One of the battery crew ... presented us with a large tot of rum, remarking that the forward observation officer was still passing back information, although his observation post had been overrun by the Germans.

We hurried on our way to where the railway began to run on level ground, where we spoke to a lone artilleryman firing an 18pdr gun. As we continued on our way we noted a number of riderless horses running wild along the railway and in the fields beside the line.[5]

Lechmere Thomas had been working at 72 Brigade HQ as Intelligence Officer. With communications lost, he had set off, through the bombardment, to find out what was happening in front. By the time he found the two battalions concerned, the Germans had overrun the front trenches. He returned, reported and asked to rejoin 9/East Surrey.[6]

Covered by the mist, which did not lift until 11.00am or later, the German infantry of 113 Division had soon overcome the troops from 1/North Staffordshire in the Forward Zone. Essling Redoubt held out for some time longer. IR 66 then pressed on to attack the North Staffordshire HQ near Maissemy, in the Battle

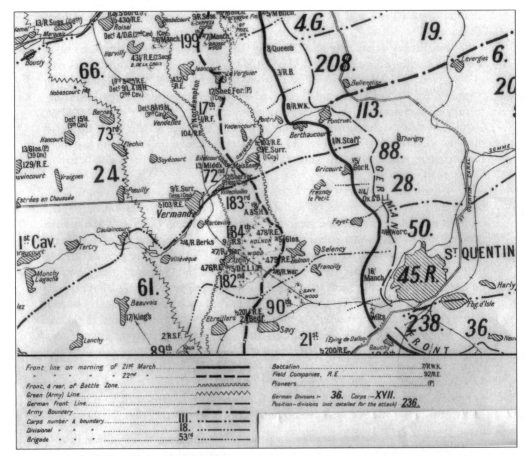

Figure 15. Kaiserschlacht, *21 March 1918.*

Zone. By 12.45pm it had seized the village and remnants of the North Stafford-shire battalion withdrew to join 9/East Surrey. 8/R West Kent on the left, however, was able to put up a more effective defence. Its two forward companies were overwhelmed and the remaining companies around Vadencourt found they were under fire from the right, but Vadencourt held. They were assisted by 17 Brigade and 24th Machine Gun Battalion on their left putting up a ferocious resistance around Le Verguier, holding the Germans back from the Battle Zone. On the right the Germans could not get across the swampy River Omignon. In its dramatic 10.00am report, 8/R West Kent advised 72 Brigade, as recorded in the latter's war diary,

> Enemy broken through on right and advancing on Essling Redoubt. VADENCOURT bridge blown up in face of enemy. PONTRU trench has been occupied by enemy from right flank and remains of 2 forward coys.

holding on in Cookers Quarry and trenches on Watling St. facing South. Enemy advancing from river. We are inflicting heavy casualties. Mounted men are coming over the sky line by Lone Tree Post. Several Battalions advancing against us.

'B' Company of 9/East Surrey was behind 1/North Staffordshire. It suffered several casualties in the German bombardment, including its commander, Second Lieutenant Pratt, killed. However, there was no sign of the enemy in the dense mist. Second Lieutenant Seaton set off with his orderly for 1/North Stafford-shire's HQ south of Maissemy to seek information. Both were captured as they entered the village.[7] A little after 11.00am, Germans were sighted by 'B' Company and fire opened. The company inflicted and sustained heavy casualties. Around noon, with the defenders reduced and ammunition running low, the Germans rushed the trench and captured those left. Only around thirty managed to get back to the battalion.

By 11.00am, Fifth Army, except for some isolated posts, had lost its Forward Zone, with many of the defenders. Except opposite Le Verguier, the Germans were up close to the Battle Zone. This was the more serious because the Forward Zone had the best developed defences. Whilst German losses had not been light, these could be afforded, with their big local numerical superiority.

Meanwhile, the main body of 9/East Surrey had been in reserve at Vermand when the shelling began early that morning. Private J. Crimmins later recalled,

We were literally caught with our trousers down. It was pitch black and, if you can picture sixteen men with full equipment packed into a bell tent with heavy shells falling all around, you can imagine the chaos which existed. We awoke to grab at our trousers only to find often enough that we had one leg in our own and the other in someone else's. Eventually someone found matches and when a couple of candles had been lit a little order came out of the confusion.

Considering the intensity of the bombardment the casualties were very light. A bell tent does not offer a lot of protection against flying shrapnel.[8]

About 10.00am, orders were received for 9/East Surrey to move forward and occupy high ground east of Villecholles, to counter the German advance. 1/8 Argyll and Sutherland Highlanders from 61st Division had taken position behind 1/North Staffordshire and was to throw back a number of German attacks. As the Surrey men advanced they encountered some artillerymen withdrawing with breechblocks from their abandoned guns. They said the Germans were on the road not far behind them. At Villecholles, one platoon was positioned to hold the road, whilst the rest of the battalion advanced to the high ground to the east. Contact was made with neighbouring units, but these knew little of the enemy's whereabouts. Lieutenant Colonel Le Fleming and Major Clark went forward to observe. Clark suddenly saw what he suspected were enemies, but it was too late. They were fired on and Le Fleming was killed instantly.

Clark managed to crawl to safety and took charge, withdrawing Warre-Dymond's 'C' Company which, crawling forward in extended order, had come under machine-gun fire from a flank when it topped the ridge. Instead, he chose a position 200yd in the rear of the crest in broken ground. Thomas late recalled taking a machine gun out to enfilade the attackers, perhaps around this time, or possibly the following morning. Unfortunately,

> I ran over some Germans in a shell hole and they opened fire and I got wounded and I managed to hobble back about 50 yards or so to a shell hole and from there the stretcher bearers eventually got me in . . . they had already taken my revolver and ammunition because they said the Germans would probably bayonet one if they found that on one because they didn't like these lead bullets we had in the old revolver.[9]

Heroic efforts were made to evacuate the wounded. 73rd Field Ambulance's war diary records that Captain Webster went up through a heavy barrage with extra stretcher bearers and cleared the collecting post at Maissemy of wounded. Driver Griffiths, ASC 'showed great devotion to duty and courage in driving his car whose body was mostly blown away leaving a skeleton frame and the radiator was penetrated, in spite of which he brought back 8 sitting wounded 4 of whom were unable to walk'. A total of thirteen RAMC men from this unit were amongst the missing that day.[10] As for 9/East Surrey's stretcher bearers, Lance Corporal A. Trish was subsequently awarded the MM for his work on 21 and 22 March. He saved at least twenty to thirty seriously wounded from being captured, working under heavy shellfire until wounded himself.

The artillery made a report to division at 3.45pm that the Germans were massing in Maissemy and 'every available gun was being turned on to them there'.[11] Where the artillery had survived German bombardment, it fought hard to hit the Germans and defend its infantry, on this day and the following days, often firing over open sights and under attack by low-flying aircraft. There were 2 batteries of Canadian horse artillery and 108th Battery RFA supporting the division's right, and they fired 750 rounds per gun on 21 March, before withdrawing to the Brown Line, from which they then fired another 76 rounds per gun that same day.[12]

At 4.00pm 9/East Surrey's line was reported to 72 Brigade as running from Villecholles east and then south, joining with the Argylls. Half an hour later the enemy was stated to be massing on the battalion's left. During the course of the afternoon and evening, the Germans (IR 66 with extensive support from its division's mortars and artillery) made repeated attempts to seize the high ground south of Maissemy and outflank the strong Holnon forest position, stubbornly held by 61st Division. With 9/East Surrey were two companies of the divisional pioneers, 12/Sherwood Foresters, and some 18pdr guns. It seems likely that fighting here that day, however, was essentially between the Germans and 61st Division, with IR 66 seeing that it had to clear Hill 119.6 before advancing further from Maissemy.

72 Brigade recorded it was ordered to prepare a counterattack on Maissemy for 7.30pm, using two companies of 9/East Surrey and the dismounted 11th Hussars of 1st Cavalry Division, with Lieutenant Colonel Anderson of the Hussars commanding. But the counterattack was cancelled because of the late arrival of the cavalry and since 61st Division on the right was no longer able to assist. Instead, 9/East Surrey was to hold its positions, reinforced by the cavalry. The Hussars' war diary records this as 'just E of a small wood 1,000 yards S.E. of VILLECHOLLES (R.28.c.Sheet 62.c.1/4000)'.[13] This would appear to be Mount Huette Wood with, on the right, Spooner Redoubt.[14] During the night the defences were improved with digging and wiring, and supplies were brought up.

Elsewhere on 24th Division's front, the Germans had at last succeeded in capturing Cooker Quarry that evening, which had stopped their advance along the Vadencourt–Bellenglise road all day. This led to 8/RWest Kent evacuating Vadencourt. Taking Fifth Army as a whole, much of the Battle Zone had been lost by nightfall and no substantial reinforcements could be expected soon. Gough saw no alternative to further withdrawal if his army was to avoid destruction.

Nevertheless, the Germans were disappointed with the first day of their offensive. Many objectives had not been achieved and casualties were not light. After their easy advance through the front line under cover of fog, the Germans had encountered strong resistance. Initially, facing 66th Division, 4 Guard Division was drawn into the fight for Le Verguier, because of the fierce resistance there of 8/Queen's of 24th Division.

> Major von Kriegsheim [RIR 93] turned his 1st and 2nd battalions southwards against the heavily fortified Le Verguier, which the neighbouring division had been unable to take. Slowly, in harsh and bloody hand-to-hand fighting, the trenches of the artillery defence line were rolled up to the south; only the forces and time available could not stretch far enough to take Le Verguier from the north on this day (the sun was already at the western horizon). IR 185 of the Division Groddek [208 Division] drove in vain from the front against this position, which was worked upon by the shells of FAR 267 [208 Division] and Fussart.Batl.157 [attached to 208 Division] from their advanced posts by Ascension Farm. Only IR 25 from Aachen [208 Division] had succeeded by evening in gaining a foothold in the south western portion of the strongly fortified town.[15]

However, the German unit which had suffered the most casualties that day (761) was IR 66 of 113 Division, which had overrun 24th Division's 1/North Staffordshire and 'B' Company, 9/East Surrey and then endeavoured to push on.[16] It seems to have been very roughly handled trying to capture the high ground south of Maissemy.

> Right behind the creeping barrage, [III] Battalion Trenk of the 66th from Magdeburg descended upon Maissemy and had it secure in their hands by

12.45. The Fifth Battery of the 225th [FAR 225 of 113 Division] came forward and harried the disintegrating enemy with their shells. Feldwebel Ackermann had already brought his heavy machine guns into the first line and 10 Company [IR 66] had stormed forward [to the high ground] above Maissemy, clearing out extensive British battery positions – but then a British counterattack [presumably by men of 61st Division] pushed the company back almost beyond the town. The resistance of the enemy was awakened. It seemed that the town itself, lying in the valley of the Omignon, was less important to the enemy than Hill 119.6 immediately to its [the British] right. The savage struggle for this position stretched out from the midday hours to the early evening. Battalions Niemeyer and Rochlitz [also of IR 66] were both drawn in. Kreidmer's company stormed well forward – however sacrificing many good men including their leader in the process, they were obliged to fall back before the scything machine gun fire.[17]

It seems it was almost certainly IR 66's 12 Company that had clashed with the main body of 9/East Surrey. It tried to probe forward along the road from Maissemy to Villecholles, but was halted from fire from the front, from the far bank of the Omignon and from Hill 119.6, overlooking Maissemy from the south. A local counterattack forced it to fall back to a defensive crater line 200m west of Maissemy.

On the British side, XIX Corps, whilst it had committed nearly all its troops, including the cavalry, and had sustained heavy casualties, now at least had reinforcements in hand – two Entrenching Battalions, a tank battalion and more heavy artillery. Finally, 50th Division was in the process of arriving.

The next morning, 22 March, opened with a thick fog. 9/East Surrey took the opportunity to recover Le Fleming's body, with a small party led by Private Turner (who was himself killed later that month). An artillery officer reported several abandoned field guns in front and nine were recovered, chiefly by the Hussars. They also brought back some gramophones from abandoned dugouts and these were distributed to the troops and played during the following enemy attack!

The Germans opened their assault that morning by shelling the crest, apparently missing the battalion's positions. German infantry from III/IR 66, in conjunction with a wider attack by their division, advanced after half an hour, but were cut down at the British wire by rifles and Lewis guns. A further attack an hour later was similarly stopped. The men were elated with their success. The Germans then made a third assault, bringing machine guns to bear on the left. Whilst a portion of the line was driven in, the position was quickly restored with the help of Major Clark with some HQ staff. The ground was now thickly strewn with German bodies.

Unfortunately, whilst 9/East Surrey's line above Villecholles was holding, supported by the dismounted cavalry, the Germans were making progress elsewhere. 17 Brigade, on the left, was finally pushed out of Le Verguier, after holding up the

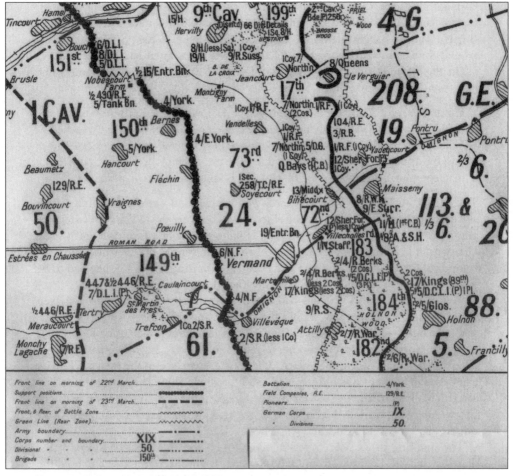

Figure 16. Kaiserschlacht, *22 March 1918.*

enemy advance for almost a day and inflicting enormous losses on the attackers. The Germans were also starting to outflank 12/Sherwood Foresters on 9/East Surrey's left.[18] As Major Clark recalled ten years later for the Official Historian, 'About 1.0 p.m. a message was received from the 72nd Infantry Brigade for the Battalion and the 11th Hussars to withdraw to the Cross Roads, half mile east of ESTREES-EN-CHAUSSEE. This order was not popular, as everyone was in the highest spirits and quite confident of beating back any attack of the enemy.'[19] The withdrawal was achieved with some difficulty, with the enemy close by. According to the Hussars, 'At this time some 2,000 Germans could be seen advancing down the hill towards VERMAND. A detachment of signallers, runners & etc from various units was organised to cover the flank, and the retirement was successfully conducted under cover of 2 Coys, 10th Dublin Fusiliers [from 19th Entrenching

Battalion].' There were a number of East Surrey casualties, including Captain Lester, commanding 'D' Company, who was mortally wounded and captured. Brigade warmly congratulated the battalion on its fight. 9/East Surrey withdrew around 5 miles to near Estrées-en-Chaussée, where the men had a brief rest.

On the German side, IR 66 had continued the attack on 22 March and must have been engaged by 9/East Surrey.

> Up on the right wing, the Magdeburger 66th slowly gained ground; Trenk's battalion, which had already distinguished itself on the previous day, reached Villecholles on the edge of the Omignon valley; Oberst von Stoecklern had rapidly driven a bold, pointed wedge into the enemy's left flank. But the machine gun 'hedgehog' west of Hill 119.6 still resisted as if possessed.[20]

The assault on Hill 119.6 on 22 March was heavier and more concentrated than any of the previous attacks, with the objectives of clearing the hill and the machine-gun nests beyond it and outflanking the Holnon Forest line from the north. The Germans of 113 Division probably used two assault groups, one of which certainly comprised three battalions, plus a machine-gun company. Even so, they had to be reinforced with a battalion of IR 24 from their Corps reserve.

Both 24th and 66th Divisions had withdrawn, covered by the recently arrived 50th Division. It was hoped to hold the Germans on the Green Line, but as this was only dug a foot deep, with little wire, this looked impossible for long.

9/East Surrey moved on another 2 miles to Monchy Lagache that evening, taking up positions east of the village. The cookers arrived and the men were given a hot meal. The night was bitterly cold and lit up by burning hangars at the nearby aerodrome. During the night, General Watts heard that XVIII Corps on his right was withdrawing behind the Somme. However, German planes bombing his HQ caused many casualties and delayed orders.

The morning of 23 March was another foggy one. With XVIII Corps withdrawing, and 8th Division, from GHQ Reserve, having arrived too late to hold the gap between the two corps, 24th and 50th Divisions, with their supporting cavalry, had to retreat and cross the River Somme, if they were not to be cut off. 9/East Surrey set out for Falvy, 5 miles away. 'D' Company, under Second Lieutenant Crabb, was detached to 17 Brigade. Unfortunately, the division had made a late start and the fog lifted, so that the withdrawal had to be made under a hail of shellfire. 72 Brigade, covering the withdrawal of the rest of the division, deployed on the high ground east of Falvy and sighted the Germans advancing. The brigade, with its infantry much depleted, had been reinforced by 24th Divisional Depot Battalion, 19th Entrenching Battalion, and two companies of 12/Sherwood Foresters. After an hour 9/East Surrey was ordered to withdraw across the Somme from Falvy to Pargny, which it did, around mid-afternoon, under fire and in some danger of being cut off. The battalion then halted at Licourt, 4 miles west of Falvy, leaving the line of the Somme to be held by fresher troops. It was to spend the night in the open, under a hard frost.

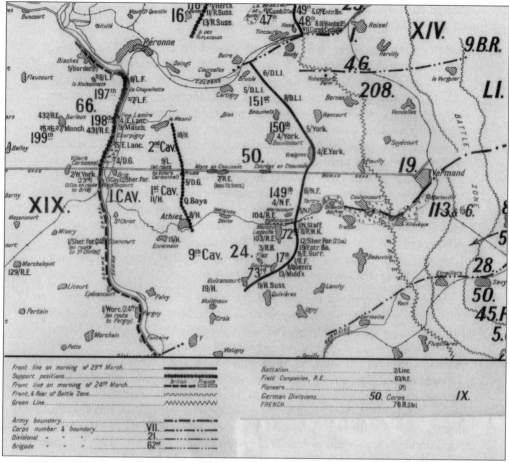

Figure 17. Kaiserschlacht, *23 March 1918.*

The River Somme here does not flow in a single channel, but in many narrow channels through broad marshes. With the river useless for navigation, a canal 58ft wide and 6ft 6in deep had been cut alongside it. There were, thus, a number of separate bridges to be crossed before safety could be reached behind the canal. All these then had to be blown by the engineers before the Germans arrived. It is difficult to destroy a bridge completely and the German infantry were later to take advantage of where sufficient material remained for them to cross. Whilst many troops crossed at Falvy, much of the cavalry and the horsed transport of 24th Division had crossed a little further north at St Christ.

'D' Company had been attached earlier to 17 Brigade, as rearguard to 3/Rifle Brigade. According to the Official History,[21] the company was cut off south of Falvy and put up 'a good fight which delayed the enemy'. However, Second Lieutenant Orchard, on his return from captivity, gave a less heroic account and indicated the company had been further north. He wrote that the company was unable to make contact with 3/Rifle Brigade and,

> had to retire to the river owing to the advance of the Germans. The Compy. remained some time about ¼ mile east of the river and a short distance south of St Christ in the hope of still getting in touch with the Rifle Brigade, although by this time all other troops had made for the river crossings which were in danger of being cut off by the enemy. Information then came to us that the Germans were nearing St Christ, so, to avoid being cut off the Company was marched to the river bank and endeavour made to find a bridge. A disused bridge of planks was found near St Christ but it was found that there was a gap of 20 yards or so on the other side which a few of our people swam across. The bridge at St Christ was now heard to be occupied by the enemy so we decided to try along the river bank in an opposite direction. However, at this time we were seen by Germans from a hill near by and an officer and some men came forward to demand our surrender. As our Company by this time was only about 20 it was considered useless to put up a fight and we surrendered to the German officer.

He later added, 'Nearly all the coy had got across by swimming the river. The 20 men remaining with us could not swim. 2 Lt. Crabb thought it right to stick to the men and especially as we hoped to find a crossing further along [?].'[22] A total of twenty-five men had escaped to the battalion by swimming.

Second Lieutenant Bishop, captured with Crabb and Orchard, makes clear in his statement that the company lost touch with 3/Rifle Brigade only after 4 miles of retreat, that three runners were sent to make contact and that the enemy were pressing closely. 'We then came to the Somme after fighting all the way back.' Being then left with the men who couldn't swim and some of them wounded, the officers decided they should all hide in the rushes by the river until dark. However, they were discovered about 7.00pm and with a large number of Germans nearby, obliged to surrender.[23]

By the evening of 23 March, therefore, there was little left of either 'B' or 'D' companies of the battalion and the other companies had also taken heavy losses. Second Lieutenant Austin, returning from leave that day, took command of 'A' Company from its one remaining officer.

On 23 March the German 5 Division, a first-class assault division from Brandenburg, originally in reserve, was now leading the advance towards 24th Division. Its IR 52 moved off at 8.00am after a breakfast of British rations, advancing towards Falvy.

> Only isolated enemy MG nests and weak detachments caused any delay [to our advance]. On the high ground covering the Somme crossings at Falvy and Pargny, due east of these villages, the enemy seems to have first decided to make a stand – and even advanced against the right flank of the regiment, which was hanging entirely 'in the air' . . . Nevertheless . . . the heights east of

Falvy were taken by about 3pm, [and] the Somme crossings lay under our fire. But the English tenaciously defended the villages and the bridges themselves, whilst at the same time their artillery [fire] increased in strength. Nevertheless elements of I Battalion finally succeeded in taking the village of Falvy, and in reaching the bridges at the same time as the fleeing garrison – so that the bridges fell into our hands in an only partially demolished state. In the evening I and II Battalions stood west and south west of Falvy on the canal, and III Battalion in the Bois de Croix.[24]

Following up the British retreat with the Saxon 23 Division in the third line of III Corps, was I/FsAR 19, with its eight 15cm howitzers and four 10cm guns. On its route to Beauvois-en-Vermandois it recorded,

At every step along the route of the advance the battalion encountered the traces and the wreckage of the rearguard fighting and the hasty English retreat. The fallen, lying alone or together in groups (the majority English, with here and there also a German comrade), abandoned enemy guns and wagons, most of them with shot-up teams still in harness, weapons and ammunition, pieces of clothing and equipment and military apparatus of every kind which had been cast aside by the enemy in the interests of faster movement – littered the sides of the road.[25]

The Germans were delighted with their successes on 23 March. However, Ludendorff now fell into the temptation of dispersing his strength with a variety of objectives, which he did not have the strength to achieve and so eventually compromised the success of his offensive. Yet Fifth Army, particularly, was in a very precarious position. After three days of heavy and continuous fighting, many of its units were sorely depleted, dispersed and exhausted, and short of supplies; there were few reinforcements yet to hand; and there was too long a line to defend with the troops available. With the men so stretched it was all too easy for the Germans to infiltrate between units. Once the Germans had broken through, the British, all too often, did not have the men available to counterattack them. As a result, units would feel forced to withdraw to avoid being surrounded. In such a fluid situation, it was difficult to maintain communications, issue orders based on up-to-date information and get orders through to the front-line units.

The Germans attacked the line of the Somme during the night, hoping to secure bridgeheads, but were repulsed with substantial losses. For example, 'A daring attack on Pargny by Schmidt's Thuringian battalion [RIR 32, 113 Division] cost them 102 of their best men. The name "Somme" was already linked with bloody memories from the year 1916, which came to mind again for many when they heard the dark waters of the river rushing darkly in the moonlit night.'[26] (Other units of 113 Division were suffering similarly, trying to establish a bridgehead at St Christ.) During the following day, most of the British XIX Corps' line along the Somme was to be held by its freshest formation – 8th Division, 24th Division was to be in reserve.

At around 4.30am on 24 March, 9/East Surrey was ordered to withdraw the 3 miles to Chaulnes in 3 hours time. In spite of their fatigue, 72 Brigade's war diary proudly noted that the men 'marched out splendidly'. It was hoped rest could be given at Chaulnes, but instead there were orders to march 4 miles south to Hattencourt and take up a defensive position. At Hattencourt, there was a belt of wire, but trenches had to be dug behind it. By midnight, these had been completed.

Not all troops were in good order. Captain Westmacott, Assistant Provost Marshal 24th Division, who had been busy in the retreat rounding up stragglers, recorded scenes of disorder in Rosières amongst a battery, transport and labour units, who believed the Uhlans were right behind them. (This was highly unlikely as the Germans made very little use of cavalry for *Kaiserschlacht*.) This panicked

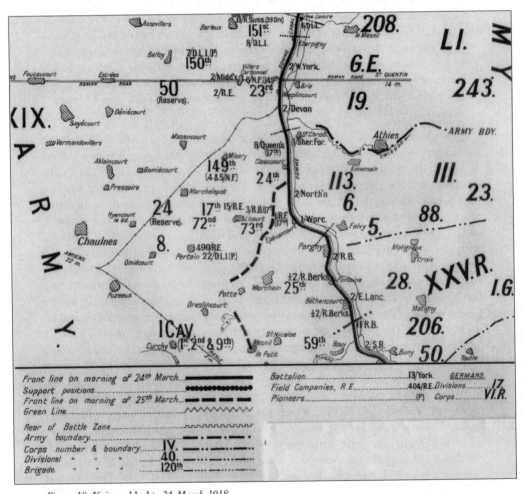

Figure 18. Kaiserschlacht, *24 March 1918.*

the local civilians. Westmacott restored order and traced the rumours to a mysterious officer on a motorcycle, whom he believed to be a German in disguise. 'In the end this thing had a good result, as people were so ashamed of themselves, that they did not stampede later on when they would have had plenty of excuse.'[27]

Meanwhile, XIX Corps had endeavoured to hold the line of the Somme. Whilst the Germans were bloodily repulsed at St Christ and elsewhere, to the south they were able to seize a bridgehead at Béthencourt. This eventually forced the British to the north to withdraw partially. However, with the arrival of French reinforcements, Gough hoped that a successful counterattack could be launched. 24th Division was ordered to assist, but the French counterattack was postponed to the following day.

On the morning of 25 March, 9/East Surrey set off to support the attack. But the Germans attacked first and 24th Division found itself under fire from the south-east. The battalion was ordered to cover Fonches, with 8/R West Kent on its left and 19/Entrenching Battalion on its right, towards Hattencourt. 9/East Surrey was reinforced with around 150 men from other units. The battalion was heavily shelled, but in the following attack the German infantry was beaten off with substantial losses. The Germans then subjected the battalion to heavy shelling, causing it many casualties. Captain Warre-Dymond, with Lieutenant Blower and an NCO, attempting to contact 8/R West Kent on the left, came across a party of Germans building a trench barricade and drove them off.

It would appear 24th Division was now being engaged principally by 28 Division, of III Corps, supported by 1 Guard Division, whilst 206 Division on the left became engaged with the French. 28 Division was a first-class formation. Its infantry were the Grand Duke of Baden's lifeguard regiment LGR 109, GR 110 also from Baden and FR 40 from the little principality of Hohenzollern. In the afternoon III/LGR 109 was moving towards 72 Brigade, 'approaching Fonches from the east along the [Ingon] valley. At the Fonchette–Liancourt road they encountered strong resistance supported by artillery. Nevertheless by about 7.00pm they had approached very close to the road and had secured a favourable jumping off point for the assault on the following day.'[28] On LGR 109's left was FR 40.

Fonches was occupied in strength and II Battalion would have to take it by storm. 2 and 3 Companies were attached to the battalion. However the assault was cancelled because of the approach of darkness. Under heavy machine-gun and artillery fire II Battalion dug in around the periphery of Fonches. I and II Battalions reached the Liancourt–Fonches road and secured both flanks, since both places were occupied by the enemy.[29]

GR 110 came up on the German right. The Badeners had only advanced this far after a day of heavy fighting and were concerned they were overextended on the right, where the neighbouring division was struggling to keep up.

Whilst the Germans were held by 72 Brigade, elsewhere the situation was deteriorating. The Germans were attacking along the line of the Somme, with

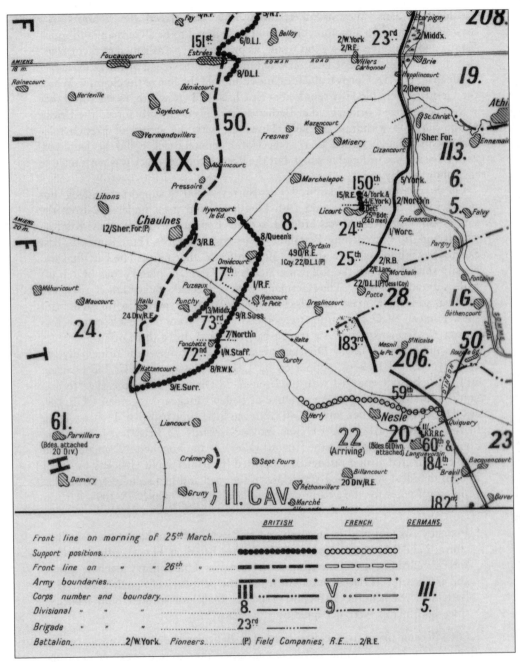

Figure 19. Kaiserschlacht, *25 March 1918.*

some success, and the French had not only failed to counterattack, but also to close up to the British line, leaving a dangerous gap. General Watts realised he would have to withdraw XIX Corps, ideally under cover of darkness, if it was not to be isolated. He ordered a retreat to the Hattencourt–Frise Line. Even so, this was less than secure with weakly held gaps between XIX Corps and Third Army on the left and the French on the right. A further withdrawal to the line Rouvroy–Froissy, 5 miles back, had, therefore to be planned.

9/East Surrey withdrew, around 1.00am on 26 March, to the line from Hattencourt to Hallu. This was the old 1916 German front line, 5 miles south-east of Rosières, which gave its name to the battle. 8/RWest Kent was on the left and an Entrenching Battalion on the right. Around 8.00am, the enemy attacked Austin's 'A' Company through the wood on its right. Major Clark ordered Austin to hold on, promising assistance, if required. However, at about 9.00am, Austin reported, after repatriation,

> the Germans made a bayonet attack and I was shot through the Right Shoulder and Lungs by a Point Blank Rifle Bullet. When I saw it was useless to resist further at this point I ordered the Company to retire to the Communication Trench 50 yards in rear. This was done in a very orderly manner and in two minutes from the time of my order the company was in action again in the new position.[30]

Clark was then warned by 72 Brigade that the enemy had turned the flank of the Entrenching Battalion on his right. He sent the Signals Officer, Lieutenant Blower, with thirty to forty men, principally signallers and HQ staff to secure his right flank. He then tried to warn 8/R West Kent that he would have to withdraw, but found it had already retreated.

The Germans then made a heavy attack. The battalion was now, apparently, reduced to around 300 men, holding a front of around 1,000yd, largely in the open. Nevertheless, it managed to hold off repeated assaults. During a lull, Clark withdrew his men successfully, although the Germans were very close. However, he then found that several lines of the enemy were in front as well as behind. Writing from a POW camp in April, Clark recalled,

> I split the company into two and took advantage of some old communication trenches and a sunken road to try to escape detection, but we were seen and the enemy began to surround us, so I decided to fight it out. We took up position in an old communication trench and used our rifles with great effect. [Lieutenant] Grant was doing excellent work until shot through the head, and Warre-Dymond behaved admirably. It was a fine fight and we held them up until the ammunition gave out: they then charged in and mopped up the remainder. They were infuriated with us.[31]

The survivors (only around sixty of them unwounded) were taken prisoner. Clark, hit in the face by shellfire, was amongst the wounded. He described himself as 'a

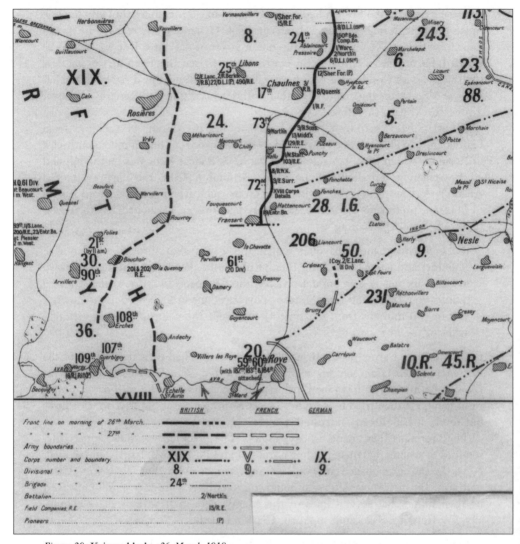

Figure 20. Kaiserschlacht, *26 March 1918.*

curious looking object – my clothing had been riddled with shrapnel, my nose fractured and my face and clothing smothered with blood'.

Blower later reported his part,

My C.O. instructed me to take up a position on our right flank in charge of H.Q. Coy. This position I found and held for over 2 hours during which time I lost over half my party, this left me with 15 men chiefly youthful signallers and runners ... After keeping up a steady fire under these desperate conditions in a position where retreat was impossible our ammunition was finally exhausted. When we were ultimately taken we had an opportunity of seeing the damage we had done which was considerable.[32]

Clark regretted the casualties and paid tribute to his men, 'It was a great fight and the men were simply splendid – I have the greatest admiration for them. It was a glorious end, but it is sad to be parted when there is still so much to be done.' Clark's popularity and powers of leadership were later recalled by former Private F.T. Eatwell,

> He said 'We have nothing on our flanks and there are no supports behind. You will either be killed or captured before the morning is out. Stick it out for the honour of the Regiment.' A very brave man, and loved by every man in the Battalion. I am very pleased he received the decoration [the DSO] he so richly deserved.[33]

The same indomitable spirit was shown by Fred Billman, who had been wounded and evacuated earlier in the Retreat. Writing to his future wife from hospital in London on 27 March, 'I got wounded Sat. night [23 March] and landed here last night. Am hit in left foot, right leg and right arm but not serious ... Well darling, I guess you are wondering why you have not heard from me, but it's been a bit busy over there just lately.'[34]

This last stand at Rosières had inflicted considerable casualties on the Germans, held up their advance and won fame for the battalion, although it left it virtually annihilated. Some criticism was made at the time in 72 Brigade war diary, 9/East Surrey 'holding on too long & lost heavily', although a later entry that day notes that the brigade 'was very fortunate to have got back from Hallu as enemy were right round flank on right'. Lieutenant Blower, on his return from captivity, reported, 'Owing to a misunderstanding with the West Kents on our left, they retired before we were aware of this leaving our left flank in the air. On our right the Composite battalion were supposed to be in position. Of this unit we saw nothing.'[35]

The Germans acknowledged they had had a hard fight. For GR 110,

> At 6am on 26 March, after a ten minute bombardment, the attack was resumed against the Hallu–Hattencourt line. The regiment was on the right flank of the division ...
>
> The regiment was approaching the main combat zone of the Battle of the Somme. The countless trenches aided the tough resistance of the English. Everywhere there were opportunities to deploy machine guns where they would be well hidden from the attackers.
>
> Thus the advancing companies soon came under strong machine-gun fire from the old German trenches along and east of the Hallu–Hattencourt road, which the Kaiser Grenadiers [GR 110] were able to overcome ...
>
> Heavy friendly artillery fire on the trenches southwest of Hallu, already reached by I Battalion, inflicted some very unfortunate losses and forced them to make use of some parts of these trenches [as cover].

The small woods to our front were defended tenaciously by the enemy. Slowly, individual assault groups from the battalions worked their way closer to them ...

In a reckless surge forwards into the first line, these [three] companies cleared out the enemy machine gun nests ...

After the enemy resistance at Hallu and Hattencourt had been broken by these companies, the advance of the whole regiment resumed at 11.30am. II Battalion and 12 Company pursued close upon the heels of the enemy as they fled back towards Chilly ... In an inexorable advance the general line Méharicourt–Rouvroy was reached.[36]

In spite of its heavy losses in many days of fighting in retreat, the morale of most men in 24th Division seems to have held up remarkably well. Westmacott recorded that at Warvillers on 26 March, 'The morale of the troops was fine; they found some old clothes in the village & dressed up in them, dancing and singing & laughing. No one would have thought that they had been fighting for their lives for 6 days and nights.'

9/East Surrey was now reduced to a remnant of around thirty men under Lieutenant Mann. Captain Whiteman, Transport Officer, took command. It was attached to 8/RWest Kent, as were the survivors of 1/North Staffordshire. 72 Brigade, reinforced with various details, fought on 27 March to defend Rouvroy. Although the Germans were by now tiring, they continued to attack, and their progress elsewhere obliged the much weakened and exhausted 24th Division to retire. By the evening of 29 March, the division was at Thézy, just 8 miles south of Amiens. However, as Westmacott recounts, it was on 29 March that 'I saw battery after battery of French guns, and columns of French infantry coming up the road in support. It meant we were saved for the time being, and unless you have been retreating for 9 days, and are at your last gasp, you can't realise what that means.' On 31 March, the East Surrey company was just three officers and thirty ORs strong.

On 3 April, the East Surrey company was put into forward posts. 72 Brigade was in support for the Battle of the Avre on 4 April. The following day it was used to dig a line of posts. At last, on the following night, the company was withdrawn. On 4 April, the combined battalion had received a number of visitors. 'They were all surprised to find us still in the line. Numbers of our visitors told us they had heard of the 24th Division on all sides, and had imagined that we were all killed long ago.'[37] The division had been the first to be mentioned in Haig's dispatch on the fighting of 21 March and Gough had commended 8/R West Kent and 9/East Surrey in his first dispatch on the day. Stopping the Germans advancing along the Omignon valley was seen as having been critical. At a terrible cost, the division had lost the last traces of the bad reputation it had gained unfairly at Loos.

Many awards were made to the battalion. Of the officers, Clark received a DSO for his gallantry and skill; and Warre-Dymond, whose 'coolness and steadying influence' were particularly mentioned, an MC; Captain Whiteman, Transport

Officer, also received an MC for recovering valuable stores and other property under heavy fire and keeping the battalion supplied with ammunition and rations through the difficult days of the retreat. Captain Walker, the battalion's US Army medical officer, was awarded an MC for his brave work under shellfire with the wounded Brigade. Chaplain George Poole was also given an MC,

> for conspicuous gallantry and devotion to duty during seven days of intense fighting, when by his cheerfulness and fine example of courage under heavy shell and machine gun fire he did much to cheer and keep up the morale of the men. He also performed splendid work in organising stretcher bearers and on two occasions assisted in the removal of the wounded under the most intense fire. It was mainly through his initiative that many badly wounded men escaped from falling into the hands of the enemy.

Acting RSM G. Hyde received a DCM. On 21 March, he had fought on with a Lewis gun, causing many casualties and checking the enemy's advance, when the front-line garrison had all become casualties (presumably he was with 'B' Company'). On the following day, he ensured, when the battalion was in a critical position, that ammunition was carried up. A number of MMs were also awarded to men of the battalion for conspicuous gallantry and devotion to duty. There were relatively few, but so many of the officers who would have made recommendations were dead or prisoners. There would have been even more men lost if it had not been for those like Private Wilson, who had taken charge on 26 March and, although wounded, had continued to direct the evacuation of the wounded on the day of the battalion's last stand. He was awarded an MM.[38]

By early April, the 'Michael' offensive had been halted. Ludendorff had attempted to extend it with his 'Mars' attack on Arras on 28 March, but with no fog cover and stronger British defences, it had been a costly failure. To the south the Germans had now advanced almost to Amiens and had inflicted heavy casualties, particularly on Fifth Army, but had taken even heavier casualties themselves. Moreover, the land captured was a desert, being the old Somme battlefield and what the Germans themselves had deliberately ruined before their withdrawal in 1917. However, Ludendorff still had reserves in hand for further throws of the dice, before the Americans arrived in force.

Chapter 11

Holding the Line,
April–September 1918

When 9/East Surrey was finally taken out of the line on 5/6 April, it had been, ostensibly, all but annihilated. The fighting company had only 3 officers and 30 men at the end of March, to which most of the transport section (establishment 50 plus) and some of the medical section should be added. Certainly, the battalion's losses, like the division's as a whole, had been heavy. 24th Division in its war diary[1] calculated it had lost, including in 2 attached entrenching battalions, 255 officers and 4,371 men killed, wounded and missing from 21 March to 5 April. The infantry, as one would expect, had been hit particularly hard and especially 72 Brigade. Within that brigade 1/North Staffordshire, all but destroyed on 21 March, had lost 566 and 8/Royal West Kent had lost 325. According to the same figures, 9/East Surrey had lost 455. However, the battalion's war diary[2] shows a few more killed and wounded and considerably fewer missing, totalling 418. As there seem to have been few casualties before the German offensive, it seems possible that the battalion's own figures are later and allow for the return of some missing men to the unit. All the same, these casualty figures were very heavy:

	Killed/Mortally Wounded	Wounded	Missing
Officers	6 (including later amendments)	9	11
ORs	23	154	215

With regard to the officers, for whom there are the best records, it would appear, in actuality, that 9 had been killed in action or died of wounds (at least 1 in enemy hands); 8 had been wounded, but escaped capture; and 9 were POWs (at least 3 of whom were wounded). It is much more difficult to account for the men. Some of those listed as wounded were dead, or died of wounds. Whilst more than a score of the 'missing' were dead, most had been captured. According to Anon., *Soldiers Died in the Great War 1914–19 Part 36 The East Surrey Regiment* (London, 1920), sixty-nine ORs were killed or died of wounds from 21 to 31 March and three more died, presumably of March wounds, in April. Some of those named as dead in the war diary lists are in neither *Soldiers Died* for the battalion, nor the Commonwealth War Graves Commission (CWGC) lists. Many of the dead were buried by the

Germans or British POWs and most have no known grave, being commemorated on such memorials as the Pozières Memorial.

In spite of these very heavy losses, the battalion was to be reconstituted. The remnants were moved on 6 April to near the coast at St Valery, and the battalion resumed its separate existence on 8 April at Franleu. On the following day, 10th Loyal (North Lancashire) (10/Loyals) was amalgamated with the battalion, under Lieutenant Colonel Ewen Cameron of the Loyals. The Lancashire battalion had been a victim of the reorganisation earlier in the year, which had seen it reduced to an Entrenching Battalion (15th). It had laboured and fought under XIX Corps for the whole retreat. Cameron brought 10 officers and 120 men to his new unit, the rest going to 1/North Staffordshire. Brigadier General Morgan inspected the survivors on 10 April and spoke of the great sacrifice made in Clark's last stand.

Whilst drafts of young soldiers were sent to 9/East Surrey (112 with 11 officers on 11 April), it would seem rather more men of the original battalion than the casualty figures would suggest were soon back with it. After all, the battalion had had 49 officers and 1,009 other ranks on 28 February. Some returned men could be stragglers, taken in by other units, and some recovered sick or wounded. By 14 April the battalion was already 580 strong. As usual, it is only the officers about whom it is possible to be reasonably precise. In March, forty-three are listed as serving with the battalion, to which Douglass and Austin, as known casualties, should be added. Of these men 26 had become casualties, but all but 1 of the remaining 19 (plus the wounded Whiteman) are listed as serving with the battalion in April, although supposedly only 3 officers had been with the battalion at the end of March. They brought important experience and continuity to the battalion, as did Captain Hilton who rejoined now. Few of these officers could have been with the battalion, however, at the end of March. Some would have been detached on other duties, or sick. Others could have been on leave or courses and been unable to rejoin the battalion in time.

Cameron, the new CO, had had a chequered career. Born in 1877, he was the son of an Assistant Inspector General of the Royal Irish Constabulary and Hereditary Clan Chief. After Sandhurst, Cameron had served with the Royal Warwickshire Regiment, being severely wounded in the Boer War. He had later served in West Africa, where he was wounded again, before transferring to the Cameron Highlanders. In 1906, whilst in West Africa and sick, a deficit of £65 was found in funds for which he was responsible. This was only made good by borrowing money from fellow officers. His CO recommended he should be required to resign. However, he was given another chance. Unfortunately, whilst serving in India in 1911, his cheque to repay a loan bounced. His Brigadier General described him as 'more fool than knave' and 'a good officer, but he is likely to bring discredit on the Service through his money affairs'. It was decided he should be allowed to resign, but his request to be included in the Special Reserve was denied. He seems to have remained in India, as a tea planter. Following the outbreak of war, he was commissioned again, in the Bedfordshire Regiment in November 1915, as a lieutenant. Transferred to the Lincolnshire Regiment as captain in February 1916, he was lieutenant colonel by December 1916 and then the same in 10/Loyals in April 1917, with whom he won a DSO. Writing in late 1918, Major General Daly was to describe Cameron as 'A fine type of fighting c.o. and has commanded his battalion with great success', and referred to his 'great powers of organisation'.[3]

For the first time in its life, the battalion was under an officer who had no connection with the regiment. Moreover, the second in command, Major Brown, was also from the Loyals. Of the captains, however, most had served previously for a considerable time with 9/East Surrey – men like High, Hilton, Lindsay, O'Connor and Whiteman.

Bringing the battalion up to strength was not enough. Officers and men had to be adequately trained as individuals and in sub-units and *esprit de corps* fostered. The draft of 11 April was described in the war diary as 'mostly young energetic soldiers, who had not been out before, and should be good material to build up the Bn'. Training began the following day and the history of the regiment was told to all the newcomers.

Following a move to Diéval, north-east of St Pol, intensive training was resumed for the remainder of the month. As well as musketry, etc. small tactical schemes were practised. The war diary commented, 'The tactical use of the Lewis gun is brought very much into play in these schemes, and they form a sound basis on which to train inexperienced teams in open warfare.' (Around this time, probably, the battalion's complement of Lewis guns was increased to twenty-four.) The battalion also marched to Pernes, to obtain the services of specialist instructors and facilities at the Canadian School there, including for gas warfare. On 19 April twenty-two officer reinforcements arrived. The war diary noted a total of 38 officers and 651 OR reinforcements received in April and that the battalion was 908 strong on 1 May.

Whilst 9/East Surrey was being reconstituted, the Germans launched the most dangerous of their offensives for the British. On 9 April, the Germans attacked on the Lys Front, south of Ypres, routing the opposing Portuguese and tearing a hole in the Allied line. The British gains of 1917 in the Ypres Salient, won at such terrible cost, were lost and, for a time, it seemed the Germans might force the British out of Ypres altogether. Only after bitter fighting and heavy casualties was the Front stabilised.

Meanwhile, as on previous occasions when it had suffered heavy losses, 24th Division was sent to a relatively quiet sector to hold the line. On 1 May, 9/East Surrey found itself back at Bully-Grenay, where it had served a year before. On 2 May it went into the line, taking over the right sector at St Emile, north-west of Lens, from the Canadians. This had been a densely populated mining district, and had trenches running through ruined houses.

Facing 24th Division was 42 Division, recruited from the Rhineland and Alsace-Lorraine. With men from the latter area regarded as potentially disloyal, it had spent most of the war fighting the Russians, with some distinction. However, it had been brought west in early 1918. On the Lys, it had, initially, great success, especially against the Portuguese, but had then taken massive losses against the British and Australians. Its senior infantry regiment, IR 17, which was to face 9/East Surrey at Lens, had taken 1,650 casualties. Out of the line for a few days only, and with few replacements, this battered division was sent, in late April, to recover, hopefully, in the 'Lens salient'. Here the German line bulged out around the outskirts of the dead city. Since the Germans had fallen back here in spring 1917 (at which time the last civilians had been evacuated), Lens had been squarely in the front line and subjected to systematic devastation by the British artillery.

The landscape that greeted the new arrivals was thus even bleaker than in previous years. 'The whole region with its totally demolished coal-pits, factories and workers' suburbs made a cheerless impression. To our men of IR 17, going back to the front again from the spring idyll of their rest villages, it seemed that in no other place had the war worn such a dark and ominous aspect.'[4] The deep accommodation galleries in the Lens sector, often 8m or more below the surface, as protection from heavy British shells, were also unfamiliar and even disturbing to the troops, who only had a few months experience of the Western Front. However, the British artillery was clearly dominant, with better observation positions and copious ammunition. In addition, to venture out of these claustrophobic, lice-infested underground dens by daylight was, the German infantry found, to invite the immediate attentions of snipers and machine-gunners. Thus, the men were forced into a depressing, troglodytic existence whilst in the forward areas.

To make matters worse, 42 Division was also subjected to the malign attentions of British gas engineers. By this point in the war, the British clearly had the upper hand and the Germans were reaping the consequences of their introduction of poison gas three years earlier. British cylinder release had been entirely superseded by the Livens Projector – unquestionably the most effective chemical weapons delivery system of the war. Electrically fired in huge numbers in tightly emplaced, roughly pre-targeted batteries, these brutally simple heavy mortars were capable of saturating a large area with lethal concentrations of gas almost instantaneously; the victims of Captain Livens' terrible 'judgements' would have almost no time at all in which to don their masks. In addition to the attacks themselves, the use of Livens Projectors on this front meant frequent gas alarms and a heightened state of gas readiness which further increased the misery of the trench garrison – simply to wear gasmasks for extended periods in warm weather was an ordeal. 'The companies had to wear gasmasks in the trenches for many hours, every day and every night. This was more than just a disruption and a nuisance. It was a torture.'[5] Even worse, one company of IR 17 was to lose fifty men in a single artillery and gas-projector attack on 8/9 May.

Patrols from 24th Division went out nightly into no-man's-land and to enter the German trenches if possible, but the enemy was generally quiet, with 42 Division having to maintain an extensive line with insufficient men. 9/East Surrey then went into Brigade Support at Cité St Pierre from 8 to 16 May. This was followed by another six days in the front line. During this time, intelligence from a prisoner taken elsewhere indicated a big German attack on 9/10 May. However, nothing occurred.

At 1.00am on 17 May, a raid was carried out, at 6 hours notice. It was conducted by three officers and thirty-eight men. Contrary to prisoners' reports, the wire in front of the objective was found impassable, although strenuous attempts were made to break through it, under fire, and the raiders were out until 3.20am. Fortunately, there were no casualties and the divisional commander was complimentary. In view of uncertainty over German intentions, 8/R West Kent tried to seize prisoners in conjunction with a gas-projector attack on the night of 24/25 May. Initially unsuccessful, the raid was repeated later that night and three prisoners taken.

Later in the month, the arrangement of having two battalions in the front line was altered to one, on a reduced front, with one each in Brigade Reserve and Brigade Support. Battalions took turns in each. Total 9/East Surrey casualties for the month were twenty-six.

24th Division was lucky to be sent to a quiet front at Lens. Not all were so fortunate. 25th Division, for one, had come to the assistance of Fifth Army in March. It had then been hit by the German Lys offensive in April. One of five exhausted British divisions sent to recover on a supposedly quiet front, the Chemin des Dames, it was overwhelmed in the next great German offensive beginning on 27 May.

June at Lens remained relatively quiet, with the usual occasional artillery and trench-mortar fire and sniping. The battalion continued taking its turn in the front line, Brigade Support and Brigade Reserve. As usual, it was providing working parties when not in the front line, but also carrying out training. Battalion HQ when in the front line was at the old Mine Office, dubbed Cameron Castle. As well as frequent patrols, of no-man's-land at night, observers were sent out to hide out in an old boiler, only 100yd from the enemy, to overlook a section of his line that was in dead ground.

In the early morning of 6 June, 19 Germans from IR 17 raided 2 of the battalion's front-line posts, under cover of artillery and mortar fire, which wounded 6 of the 13-strong garrison. However, the posts were on the alert and the enemy driven off leaving three dead and a prisoner, for the loss of two wounded, only. Second Lieutenant Wood, who had gone forward with his orderly and taken charge, won an MC for his leadership in repulsing the raid. According to IR 17, 'Two assault troops which broke into the enemy positions on 6 June encountered extremely heavy resistance there and had to withdraw without accomplishing anything, after the leader of one of the troops, *Vizefeldwebel* Parthier of 7/17, and several men had fallen in hand grenade fighting, and the leader of the other, *Unteroffizier* Brinsa, had been wounded.'[6]

Later on 6 June, one of the battalion's snipers hit a man at 1,350yd range. Two days later a sniper, hiding in no-man's-land, shot a German sniper who was similarly hidden 5 hours after he was first detected.

On the night of 23 June, however, Sergeant Dugdale, DCM, MM, who had distinguished himself on many occasions, was sadly killed, leading a night patrol. A daring patrol three nights later entered the enemy trenches and advanced 200 to 300yd, but found no one. Around this time the battalion was suffering severely from pandemic influenza, 'Spanish Flu'. This was to take many lives in 1918–1919, but this was an earlier, less-lethal strain, from which recovery was relatively rapid. The battalion's strength on 30 June was 47 officers and 858 other ranks, but its 'fighting strength' was only 17 and 635 respectively. Casualties in June totalled 43.

Opposite, the Germans had replaced 42 Division with 36 Reserve Division. IR 17 had been 'heartily glad' to leave 'the dreadful hell of Lens', where it had sustained almost 200 casualties in 2 months, but had managed to maintain its morale and its front, in spite of its weakness. 36 Reserve Division was a predominantly Pomeranian and West Prussian formation. It, too, had suffered severely in the Lys offensive. The Pomeranian IR 54 replaced IR 17 facing 9/East Surrey. (Unfortunately, IR 54's history ends in 1916, so there is a lack of German material for the rest of this chapter.)

July seems to have fairly uneventful, with the battalion rotating, as before between front line, Brigade Support and Brigade Reserve. In the front line, the garrison was now reduced to a single company and the remainder placed in supporting positions, for defence in depth. There was much patrolling of no-man's-land at night. However, on the night of 24/25 July, Lieutenant Birtles, another officer and 58 men of 'A' Company, plus 3 sappers, carried out a raid under cover of a bombardment. There were 8 sections: 2 blocking parties, 2 covering parties, each with a Lewis gun and 4 sections to enter the enemy trenches. The password was 'Gallants'. (The orders for this raid are included in Appendix VII.) Two sections were held up by machine-gun fire, but the other two entered the German first line. They shot two Germans and seized a machine gun, without loss to themselves, but failed to secure a prisoner. However, Birtles repeated the raid on 31 July with fifty-nine men. At the cost of a man killed and two wounded, a prisoner was secured. Although opposition was met, the casualties seem to have been from enemy artillery fire. Initially, this was fooled by Very lights into shooting in the wrong area. In a manner reminiscent of 8/East Surrey on 1 July 1916, one party dribbled a football across. Birtles received an MC and the Corps Commander congratulated the CO on his unit's morale. Total casualties for the month were thirteen. The Effective Strength of the battalion on 31 July was now 40 officers and 958 ORs, of whom 27 and 858 respectively were with the battalion.

By this time, the tide was turning for the Allies. Ludendorff had launched fresh offensives in June on the Matz and in July on the Marne. However, the Marne offensive was to be his last. Not only was it a failure, but it was followed by a massive French counterattack. The British attack at Amiens on 8 August was to prove what Ludendorff later called 'The Black Day of the German Army'. It was becoming clear now to the Germans that the war was lost. This was not always apparent to the Allied leadership. Haig was now looking to finish the war in 1918, through a series of Allied offensives, giving the Germans no respite. The British government, however, believed the war would long continue. As late as 5 September, Winston Churchill, Minister of Munitions, was assuming the war would last into 1920.

Regarding raiding at this time, the battalion would no doubt have been heartened if it had been able to see the views of von Below, commanding German Seventeenth Army, in a paper dated 2 August.

> During July the Army has lost 233 men missing and only captured 47 prisoners. [Desertion probably had much to do with this disparity, but His Excellency would not wish to acknowledge this, openly!] This shows that the English have at the present time a fighting superiority in 'no man's land'. Such superiority can only result in the fighting spirit of our infantry being impaired. It is also of the highest importance that the higher command should be kept constantly informed as to the enemy's dispositions and intentions. This is best done by means of patrol enterprises. If these are carefully planned and well carried through good results are accomplished and casualties are light.
>
> It is my impression that the infantry are in need of more practical training in this form of fighting, and I request that Corps and Divisional Commanders will devote particular attention to this.[7]

9/East Surrey continued at Lens, taking its turn on the usual rotation. Once out of the line on 2 August, there was cleaning up and training, but also entertainment from the new brigade concert party 'The Dragonflies'. The following month, the brigadier gave a recitation and the chaplain sang! Horse shows were also organised and very popular.

As well as the usual bombardments, there was increased night bombing by aircraft, but mostly of back areas and without injury to the battalion. Back in the line, a night patrol on 14 August encountered a large German working party and directed artillery on to it. On 19 August, in the afternoon, a small party of the enemy tried to 'snaffle' one of the battalion's posts, but without success. The line held by the brigade was now to be extended, requiring battalions to be in the front line for six days and six days at Bully-Grenay, in rotation.

Great events were happening to the south in late August, where the Canadians at Arras now joined in the Allied offensives. By early September, Ludendorff was forced to accept a withdrawal that would abandon the hard-won gains of his spring offensives.

On 24th Division's front, by 31 August it was believed the enemy was withdrawing from Lens. Night patrols, however, ran into opposition. There had been fourteen casualties in August. The following day there was a further report, from a prisoner taken elsewhere, that suggested the Germans were evacuating Lens. Again, patrols were sent out, including in daylight, but encountered strong resistance. Attempts were made that night to establish posts in the enemy front line, although half had to be abandoned in the day. The battalion continued to try to push forward.

On 3 September, after a heavy bombardment with artillery and trench mortars, the enemy made three morning attacks to try to drive out men of 'A' company from their posts. The two officers present became casualties almost immediately. However, Private John McNamara, who was operating a telephone in a trench, seized the initiative. He rushed to the nearest post and used a revolver from a wounded officer against the enemy. He then seized a Lewis gun and continued to fire it until it jammed. By this time, he was alone. He then 'joined the nearest post and again displayed great courage and initiative in maintaining Lewis gun fire until reinforcements arrived. It was undoubtedly due to the magnificent courage and determination of Pte McNamara that the other posts were enabled to hold on and his fine example of devotion is worthy of the highest praise.' McNamara was promoted to Corporal and awarded the VC.[8] The Divisional Special Order adds that he was 'the spirit of the defence throughout ... He moved about freely, urging everyone to "stick it", which they did.'[9] Captain Lindsay MC, the adjutant, was killed in the action 'standing up to overwhelming odds in a manner to increase even his reputation for courage and devotion to duty'.[10] Lieutenant Churcher received multiple wounds. The left-hand posts were lost, but later, according to Pearse and Sloman, recovered by a party led by Colonel Cameron. The war diary seems to suggest otherwise. Cameron and McNamara recovered Lindsay's body. Neither the war diary nor Pearse and Sloman give total casualties for this action, separately, but it seems at least four ORs were killed and possibly then, too, that a number of the eight men listed as 'missing' that month were captured.

Again, two days later, the Germans attacked one of the East Surrey posts, under cover of a bombardment, but failed to capture it. Private Hammond was missing but returned that night. He had been chased by the Germans but had managed to hide in a shell hole and brought back useful intelligence.

Once out of the line, a funeral was held for Lindsay and the four men killed with him. The brigadier, his staff and the whole battalion attended. Time was then spent in training for open warfare, including a tactical exercise with artillery, trench mortars and Vickers guns.

The battalion returned to the front line on 12 September and proceeded to explore the new line, St Emile, by daylight. A party of Germans was successfully attacked at Gibraltar Chateau, a large house reinforced with concrete. Early the following morning, the Germans attempted to raid 1/North Staffordshire on the left of 9/East Surrey. The British infantry and artillery repulsed the attack. A wounded German gave himself up to an East Surrey post. He was a sergeant of the 2nd Guard *Ersatz Pionier* Battalion, seemingly attached to IR 54. He seems to have identified himself as an expert in making tank traps.[11] What he would have been less happy to reveal was that his unit was the replacement element for a specialist flamethrower unit, popularly known as the *Totenkopfpioniere*. Flamethrower troops were particularly unpopular with opposing infantry.

The battalion moved to the left sector on 18 September and two days later around thirty Germans attacked posts in Happy and Cosy trenches, but were driven off. The battalion sent out frequent patrols to reconnoitre the enemy lines. One left propaganda leaflets. Periodic shelling continued, catching seven men on 23 September returning from a working party. The battalion was finally relieved the following day. As the war diary proudly records, Daly, the divisional commander, commended the battalion's 'initiative and enterprise ... All this patrol – work spirit of adventure, which appears now to be second nature in all ranks of the Battalion, is excellent for *morale*.' Casualties in September, at sixty, had been quite heavy.

At the end of the month, the battalion moved out of the Lens sector, to Beaudricourt, north-east of Doullens. Here it remained until 6 October, training, for open warfare, which it would soon face. A tactical scheme was enacted by the whole brigade. As each objective was gained, a halt was made so that each stage could be critically assessed and explained to the men.

Chapter 12

Advance to Victory, October–11 November 1918

During September, whilst 24th Division had been at Lens, a series of Allied offensives had pushed the Germans back. At the end of September the Hindenburg Line was stormed and the Allies also broke out of the Ypres Salient. Bulgaria was asking for an armistice. Ludendorff conceded that Germany must seek one, too. However, whilst the Germans were in retreat from much of their line on the Western Front, most of their units were still ready to fight on and set out to devastate the occupied territories as they retreated, in the hope of slowing the Allied advance. Ludendorff saw an armistice not as an opportunity to make peace as soon as possible, but rather as a breathing space for his armies. Many more men would die before the Armistice came into force.

24th Division was moved up to join Byng's Third Army, as part of XVII Corps, in the attack on Cambrai, reaching Graincourt on 6 October. There was a general attack on the German positions at Cambrai two days later. 72 Brigade was in support. The battalion was moving from Rumilly that afternoon, to relieve a unit of 63rd Division a little forward of the captured village of Niergnies, when the enemy counterattacked, forcing a partial withdrawal by the battalion awaiting relief. The attackers were RIR 65 from 208 Division, led by six captured and refurbished British tanks from *Sturmpanzerkraftwagen-Abteilungen* 11 and 15. Cameron went forward with 'D' Company, leaving the others to follow. The German tanks encountered four British ones and quickly destroyed three and damaged the other. The British then destroyed two of the enemy tanks, using captured German field guns, partially manned by surviving tank crewmen. The remaining German tanks, all damaged to some extent, shot up opposing infantry and then withdrew to their start positions, with only one still fit for use. Their infantry was unable to get far enough forward to support their tanks effectively and take advantage of their success. The German attack was, therefore, stopped from reaching Niergnies. The German tank men and infantry each blamed the others for the failure, but bearing in mind their lack of experience in this sort of operation, the lack of success is readily explicable. Although the battalion war diary credits the battalion with halting the German advance on Niergnies, a lack of fatalities for 8 October would seem to indicate 9/East Surrey was relatively lightly engaged. 72 Brigade, in and behind the village, was then shelled heavily during the night. The following day the battalion advanced with the division and helped seize Awoingt village,

2 miles south-east of Cambrai. Little opposition, apart from heavy shelling, was encountered and five field guns and a machine gun were captured. Patrols were sent forward to support the cavalry and round up enemy stragglers in Cambrai, whilst one company filled in shell holes in the roads to assist the advance.

From 10 October, the battalion advanced eastwards, by stages, to St Aubert. 17 Brigade, in the lead, took heavy casualties from German rearguards, as enemy resistance stiffened. By 13 October, 72 Brigade's forward units had reached the line of the River Selle, 10 miles east of Cambrai. Here the Germans had decided they must make a stand. Patrols found all the bridges demolished and the Germans holding the line of the railway behind, in considerable strength. However, patrols from 8/R West Kent managed to get into Haussy, although the village was strongly held. Presumably encouraged by recent progress, it was decided that 72 Brigade should attack early on 16 October, to seize a bridgehead in readiness for a further advance.

The right flank of 72 Brigade was facing the village of Haussy, which lay on both sides of the river, with the larger part on the eastern, German, side. High ground lay either side of the village, with that on the German side being somewhat higher and steeper, with some sunken roads. The original plans for the attack, as set out in the brigade war diary,[1] were very modest, using only 8/R West Kent on the right and 1/North Staffordshire on the left, with each to deploy no more than two companies. They were to be supported chiefly by five brigades of field artillery, providing a creeping barrage. The infantry was to seize positions to the north of Haussy and not to attack Haussy. 9/East Surrey was to take over the positions to be vacated by the reserve companies of the two attacking battalions.

Lieutenant Colonel Cameron, however, had made a reconnaissance at Haussy early on 15 October, with his Intelligence and Signalling Officers. He found a good position to bridge the river where it was narrow and screened from view by overhanging trees. He reported this to brigade and division. The divisional commander decided, that evening, after the orders had been prepared, to extend the scope of the attack. 9/East Surrey was to seize Haussy on the right flank of the planned attack, early the following day. It was agreed that 'B' and 'D' companies should attack, with 'C' to 'mop up'. 'A' would be lent to 1/North Staffordshire to form a defensive flank. The Guards Division was on the right and this was to support the attack with artillery and some infantry. That same evening, civilians from the west side of the village were evacuated and the Germans bombarded the whole British forward area with gas shells.

9/East Surrey now prepared to attack. A party of REs arrived with a small plank bridge, which proved too short. However, with the addition of a handcart, ladder and planks, the bridge sufficed. The two leading company commanders, Captains Whiteman and Maingot, crossed over and reconnoitred the ground directly in front. They ran into an enemy machine-gun team, but escaped unhurt. The British artillery discouraged enemy posts near the river by harassing fire during the night. 9/E Surrey had all three attacking companies across the river in time for zero hour. 8/R West Kent had similarly advanced its two attacking companies.

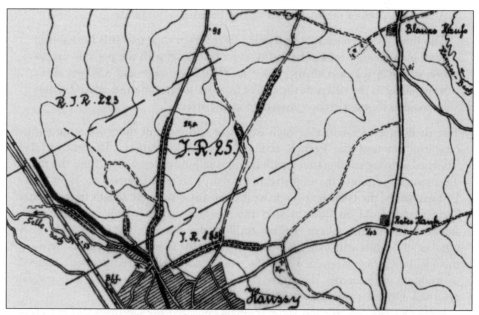

Figure 21. Haussy: the northern part of the field, with German unit boundaries shown, 16 October 1918. Scale: 1in equals approximately 1,100yd.

The attack opened at 5.15am on a wet and misty morning. Unfortunately, 1/North Staffordshire had been badly hit by the gas bombardment and advised it could only send one company forward. As soon as the British bombardment opened the Germans retaliated with their own heavy barrage on the line of the river. However, the attack by 9/East Surrey and 8/R West Kent went very well, initially. The former's 'B' and 'D' companies were to press rapidly forward to the sunken road along the ridge just beyond the village, leaving 'C' to mop up in Haussy. The roads were barricaded and there was some stiff fighting. Nevertheless, the battalion's objective had been seized by around 7.00am, apparently for the loss of only nine British lives. Second Lieutenant Kerckhove had earlier recovered a wounded man under heavy machine-gun fire. He had then taken ten men and surrounded an enemy position in a sunken road, which was holding up the advance, capturing sixty. Private Johnson attacked a machine-gun nest and captured ten men. By noon, 285 prisoners were counted at Battalion HQ, including 9 officers. In addition, two *minenwerfen* had been captured along with various machine guns and anti-tank rifles. It was reckoned around eighty enemy had been killed. Close support had been provided by Second Lieutenant Nilson, with his mortars, which had suppressed a number of machine-gun nests. French civilians were discovered sheltering in cellars. North of Haussy, 8/R West Kent had suffered significant casualties, but had captured over 200 prisoners. It was obliged to form a defensive flank to the north because of 1/North Staffordshire's misadventure. The Kentish battalion had its HQ and dressing station, only, in Haussy.

At around 2.00pm German artillery fire became very intense.

> The fury of this concentrated bombardment from then onwards beat almost anything we could remember in the way of shelling, with the possible exception of the attack on Delville Wood in 1916. Eight-inch and 5.9 inch shells were falling in the village at the rate of from six to ten a minute, and it became impossible to move troops anywhere in the streets.[2]

The shells were a mixture of high explosive and gas and there were numerous casualties amongst the French civilians trapped in Haussy. The enemy also launched a strong counterattack with infantry in nine or ten waves, from the right. This passed in front of the Coldstream Guards, who were to guard the right flank. Unfortunately, the Guards, a single weak company only, were caught in the enemy barrage and could do little to stop the German attack, which broke into the southern end of the village. British artillery did not halt the attack, either. A number of officers and men of 9/East Surrey now found the Germans between them and their line of retreat across the river. Under heavy fire, they were obliged to wade or swim across the river. A number of men were killed and several drowned. Others were taken prisoner.

Cameron with his HQ and some remnants ensured the Germans did not cross the river, the Quartermaster, Lieutenant James, organising all stray men and stragglers. But the battalion was much depleted by the end of that day, having lost, the war diary[3] estimated at the time, three-quarters of its fighting strength. It was relieved that night by 7/Northamptonshire from 73 Brigade and returned to its billets at St Aubert. Patrols from the relieving battalion, with East Surrey guides, sought for missing men in Haussy that night, but without success.

8/R West Kent had come under the same heavy barrage, but German infantry did not attack it. However, shortly after midnight, a German counterattack forced back 7/Northamptonshire, so that the British were forced to fall back to the ridge above the west bank of the Selle.

An attack that had started with such promise had ended up costing the battalion heavily. Casualties are not recorded separately for Haussy in the war diary, but the following listed at the end of October, when some missing men had returned, must have almost all been incurred there. They amount to 3 officers and 40 ORs dead; 3 officers and 100 ORs wounded; 1 officer and 12 men gassed; and 2 officers and 121 men missing. Of the missing, around 7 appear to have died. Amongst the dead was Corporal John McNamara VC, who had died without knowing of the award for his bravery in September. Cameron wrote to his wife,

> It is with the deepest sympathy I write to condole you on the death of your husband. He was one of the most gallant fellows I have ever seen and he richly deserved the V.C. which has just been awarded him. It is particularly sad that he didn't live long enough to hear of it, the highest and most coveted award any soldier can get.

Your husband has been buried near to where he fell in the village called Haussy; a cross has been put over his grave. The regiment greatly distinguished itself in capturing this village and your splendid husband was as usual distinguishing himself when he fell. The whole Regt, Brigade and Division are thoroughly and immensely proud of him, whilst I myself feel it a distinct honour to have had him serving under me. We have been together for a long time now, and my one wish was that we both should be spared to come home together.

I will esteem it an honour if when the time comes, and it can be arranged, you allow me to take you personally to his Majesty the King to receive the V.C.[4]

Second Lieutenants Walter Baber and Albert Nilson were amongst those taken prisoner and made statements on repatriation. Baber reported,

My Coy was detailed to mop up ... After clearing the village of enemy, I proceeded to establish a post S[outh] of the village with my remaining men having sent supports to the two front Coys. Being held up by an enemy M.G. I ordered my men to take cover in a house owing to heavy enemy artillery fire, whilst endeavouring to locate M.G. position. Whilst writing a message to HQ a direct hit demolished the house followed simultaneously by a gas shell which burst in the debris from which we were trying to extricate ourselves. Several men had to go back to the Aid Post being slightly gassed ... Before the [Guards] Division on our right came up the enemy counterattacked. I was joined by seven or eight of our own M/Gunners who were compelled to fall back owing to enemy's superior numbers. We endeavoured to make a stand but the enemy by this time had worked round the flank and got behind us, killing or wounding the whole party. I tried to crawl and get assistance for one or two wounded but my own wound compelled me to give up and I fell into enemy's hands, who had by then practically retaken the village. My mask, gun and personal belongings were taken from me and I lay for nearly an hour during which time a gas shell burst near by and my improvised mask offered little or no proof. I was eventually taken behind enemy's lines and sent to Hospital.[5]

Nilson, attached to 72nd Trench Mortar Battery, made a brief report only, saying, essentially, that he had been cut off in Haussy by the German counterattack and the bridges behind had been destroyed. On being questioned he added, 'I couldn't see what happened on my right owing to houses in the village ... I heard rifle shots behind me and suddenly found the village full of the enemy. I had only 4 men with me. I could do nothing'. No blame was attached to either officer, and, indeed, a year later his CO described Nilson as 'an excellent officer'.[6]

Amongst the ORs missing was Private Woodbury, who had served with the battalion since October 1915. He had previously escaped the Germans by swimming in March 1918.[7] He was now wounded, for the third time, this time in the head, and captured.

Following the action at Haussy, 9/East Surrey withdrew to Cambrai on 17 October. Lieutenant Williams, missing at Haussy, who had been sheltered by a Frenchwoman at great risk of reprisal, turned up safe.[8]

A number of awards recognised the gallant effort made by the battalion – a Bar to his DSO for Cameron; MCs for Captains Maingot, Taylor and Wallace (the Medical Officer), Lieutenant James, Second Lieutenant Kerckhove and Sergeant Major Hyde; and DCMs to Privates Attew and Johnson. Other decorations were awarded to men for service in the final weeks of the war, which may have included for Haussy, but the details have not survived.

Let us now look back from the German perspective. Facing 72 Brigade across the Selle had been 208 Division, its old adversary from 21 March 1918 and also Niergnies earlier in October. After two months retreating, however, it had become seriously under strength. Nevertheless, British Intelligence rated it a strong defensive division with above average morale. In the centre of its line, IR 185, from Baden, reduced to two battalions and supported by a divisional *Pionier* company, held Haussy and its immediate vicinity. On its left was RIR 65 and on its right IR 25, both from the Rhineland. To the division's right was the Hessian 48 Reserve Division.

By late 1918, whilst each German infantry regiment retained a 3-battalion establishment, each of 4 rifle companies, a battalion was now only around 650 all ranks at full strength. Weak units combined battalions and/or reduced the number of companies. On the other hand, each battalion now had its own heavy machine-gun company with twelve guns, in addition to six lighter guns with each rifle company. Each regiment also had a *minenwerfer* company with twelve mortars and each rifle company had two *granatenwerfen*. (British practice, by contrast, was to hold heavy machine guns in a divisional machine-gun battalion, with mortars at brigade level and Lewis guns with each platoon.)

The Germans were not comfortable with the position at Haussy. The British had occupied the western part of the village, across the Selle, which was not a major barrier, and IR 185 was weak. There was also considerable embarrassment on 14 October, when men of 8/R West Kent were able, in broad daylight, to break into the village unobserved and penetrate the main defensive line. Indeed, they caught a squad from I/IR 185 engaged in their laundry! They were able to withdraw with three prisoners. Although there were recriminations, a proposed rearrangement of German positions was left too late.

Two days later there was something of a rerun of 21 March 1918, but with the positions reversed: now the Germans were overextended and the British were infiltrating under cover of fog. IR 185's history records for 16 October,

> After a quarter of an hour's artillery preparation, the enemy launched a strong attack on Haussy at 6.15am. I/IR 185 was overrun and the majority of them, including the staff, went into captivity. The composite II and III/185, outflanked from the north, made a fighting withdrawal across the neighbouring regimental sector to the left [RIR 65]. *Pionier* Company 252 was

committed to an immediate counterattack, without success. The battalion staffs of II and II/185 made a fighting withdrawal to the line 'Red House'– 'White House', occupied this line and brought the [surviving, composite] companies of II and III/185 there. In the afternoon after artillery preparation, Haussy was stormed from the south by *Radfahrer* Regiment 26. The composite II and III/IR 185 together with the subordinated II and III/RIR 65 supported the attack from the east, and IR 25 likewise from the north. Numerous prisoners were taken.

The remnants of the regiment were reassembled as *Bataillon von Mucke . . . Radfahrer* Regt.26 (subordinated to the regimental staff of IR 185) continued to hold Haussy.[9]

The men of 9/East Surrey had seen the *Radfahrer* Brigade attacking from the south. The war diary described them as appearing to be 'fresh reinforcements as they were all dressed in entirely new uniforms & looked like picked "Storm troops"'. It was natural to describe those who had defeated them as elite troops, but they were perhaps correct. The *Radfahrer* Brigade was an independent formation, perhaps eight battalions strong by this time, made up of cyclist companies from the jäger battalions. It was in excellent order when it arrived on the Western Front early in 1918. Since then, unlike the jäger battalions, it seems not to have been ground down by constant fighting and diluted with indifferent replacements. Certainly IR 25, who had met them some days previously, noted their much bigger company strengths, although they considered them inexperienced in Western Front fighting.[10] The brigade seems at this time to have been kept as a mobile counterattack reserve. Compared with the infantry regiments, because of its specialist role, it had relatively few heavy weapons. The men wore 'mountain trousers' and puttees and only light equipment, so closely resembled stormtroopers.

Even though it appears that only part of the *Radfahrer* Brigade was deployed at Haussy, it is clear that 9/East Surrey and 8/Royal West Kent, with very limited support from 1/North Staffordshire and one weak company of the Coldstream Guards, were seriously outnumbered when the Germans counterattacked. All the same, the Germans took heavy punishment at Haussy, in the initial British attack. IR 25 reported 'extraordinarily heavy losses' when attacked in the flank from Haussy. There was also disruption, with the 1st Battalion staff being cut off, taking casualties and only narrowly escaping capture. After Haussy IR 25 was reformed as a single composite battalion with a fighting strength of a mere 180 ORs.[11]

In addition to the men of 208 Division and the *Radfahrer* unit, RIR 221 and RIR 223 of 48 Reserve Division (immediately to the north of 208 Division) had also been drawn into the battle. From Haussy the British had inflicted heavy losses on I and II/RIR 223 with flanking machine-gun fire. Poor visibility added to the confusion. Leutnant Blümel, with the second of RIR 223's machine-gun companies recalled,

In front of our position shapes now appeared in the fog in the sunken road, which we at first took for Germans going to the rear. Despite observation with our binoculars, it was only at a distance of about 60 metres that we realised we had an English machine gun squad in front of us. There was no time to deploy. A few infantrymen shot from their holes. Both machine guns were brought into position on the road. Meanwhile the Tommies had nestled themselves in a shell hole and were shooting apparently with a Lewis gun and carbines [*sic*]. A few of our men fell or were wounded.

Both of our machine guns, which had stood in the rain ready to fire since the beginning of the drum fire, were jammed [the fabric ammunition belts had swelled in the wet].[12]

The single British squad withdrew back into the fog when Blümel managed to get one of his machine guns working.

When the counterattack was ordered RIRs 221 and 223 also participated, attacking from the north-east, although some of their elements were held up by British artillery fire. Notwithstanding their heavy losses, it seems the Germans were heartened by their local success in recapturing Haussy, after 'weeks of bloody fights and hard privations'.[13]

The days following were spent by 9/East Surrey in recovery, getting billets to order and training. The Germans had trashed the houses in Cambrai and left delayed action mines. There was some light relief from 'The Dragonflies' concert party. On 23 October forty-eight reinforcements arrived to fill some of the gaps. A brigade tactical exercise, with contact aeroplanes, was held on 25 October. Next day, the battalion moved forward to Avesnes les Aubert. On 28 October, Cameron visited Haussy, now clear of Germans, who had been driven well beyond the Selle in the battle of that name. Four missing men were found alive, along with the bodies of several others.

By the beginning of November Ludendorff had been obliged to resign and the Allies were poised to make a further advance to prevent the Germans holding the line of the Meuse. On 2 November, the battalion returned to Haussy and went into billets there. A large number of civilians were returning and were fed by the British. The battalion assisted by giving here and elsewhere 10 per cent of its rations.

Preparations were underway for a big attack by Fourth, Third and First Armies, which was to last from 4 to 11 November – the Battle of the Sambre. On 4 November 9/East Surrey moved off to Sepmeries, 6 miles south of Valenciennes. The battalion came under the temporary command of Major Hilton, who had served with the battalion, except for six months in Britain, since December 1915. 72 Brigade was Reserve Brigade for the division, which was itself in reserve for the attack. The battalion marched on in heavy rain, but with billets at night, through scenes of recent fighting. A single unlucky shell on 6 November fell on 'D' Company at La Bois Crette, killing 7 and wounding 9 others, of whom 2 subsequently died.

The battalion was set to attack Bavai early on 7 November with 8/R West Kent. Bavai is just 13 miles south-west of Mons, where the British Army had fought its first action in 1914. There was little opposition, except from heavy artillery. The Germans had abandoned the town a few hours before and the troops were given a great reception by the local inhabitants. The battalion pushed on towards its final objective, mopping up stragglers and taking slight casualties from shelling. As darkness was falling, 2 miles on, an advanced patrol encountered the German rearguard at L'Hogneau rivulet. At some time during the day, contact had been lost with the flanking units. Major Hilton made 'several fearless reconnaissances well in advance of our forward patrols and even behind the enemy's isolated machine guns and it was entirely due to his magnificent example that touch was regained and further advance rendered possible'. He was awarded an MC.[14] The following day 1/North Staffordshire took over the advance, 9/East Surrey following, through Longueville and Le Gros Chêne. The Surrey battalion relieved 8/R West Kent in the line on 9 November and advanced to the Mons–Maubeuge road.

> On clearing the village [Feignies] we reformed and got into touch with the Staffords on our right. We then again advanced, the weather being perfect. It was here that I saw a thing that I never expected to see – open warfare exactly as it appears in the textbooks. We were advancing in beautiful extended order at five paces; our right was correctly aligned on our objective, the Fort de Leveau. We were in touch with the Staffords on our right and with the West Kents on the left; while, looking back, the country for miles was covered with perfectly aligned lines of men advancing. The weather was gorgeous, and there was no opposition except for one easily silenced machine gun on the left.[15]

Westmacott, 24th Division's APM, stopped at Feignies, 'Except that the railway had been blown up there were no signs of battle. The Maire said that the Bosche infantry were 3 days march ahead of us with no fight in them, but that the Machine Gunners and artillery were covering the retreat.' Relieved by men of 20th Division on 10 November, the battalion marched back to billets at Feignies.

By now, all Germany's allies had collapsed, its High Seas Fleet had mutinied, and its army had no more reserves. The country was on the verge of revolution and the Kaiser now abdicated. Germany had no choice but to agree to an armistice, however harsh the terms appeared. Signing was completed at 5.10am on 11 November, with the armistice to come into force at 11.00am.

The battalion's war diary recorded the last day of the war,

> The march was continued. The Battn. moved off at 5.30a.m. & on the way news was received that the enemy had accepted the terms of our armistice. The men hardly credited the news. The march was continued to LE PISSOTIAU [a mile west of Bavai] & the Battn. was billeted there. In the afternoon the C.O. [Cameron] had the Battn. paraded & addressed a few words to them. One of the official photographers (Lt. Brooks) took some

photos of the Battn. gathered round the C.O. who thanked them for their splendid work. The C.O. resumed command of the Battn.

So, one of the iconic photographs of the war was taken, although catalogued as being taken the following day and at St Waast. (The war diary makes no mention of photographs being taken on 12 November.) Both this and a further photograph taken at the time in which the men turn to face the photographer are reproduced in this book (see plates 17 and 18).

There seems to have been little celebration of the Armistice at Le Pissotiau. Westmacott recalled, 'There were no great demonstrations by the troops, I think because it was hard to realize that the war was really over ... Shortly before 11 A.M. our Divisional Artillery let the Hun have it with every available gun. I never heard such a roar. A great contrast to the deathly silence, which followed at 11 A.M.'

8/R West Kent also marched to Le Pissotiau,

On the route the news of the signing of the Armistice was read by a D.A.P.M. [Deputy Assistant Provost Marshal] Passing Bavai Station a group of A.S.C. men asked what the cheering was about, and were told by one of our men that the infantry in the line were tired out and were being relieved by the A.S.C. [!]

The billets at Pissotiau were very bad and overcrowded, and it is small wonder that the news of the cessation of hostilities, which arrived about 1p.m., evoked no great enthusiasm. To make matters worse, there was no beer or other suitable beverage with which to celebrate it.[16]

9/East Surrey's war diary records casualties for November as nine dead and twenty-two wounded. Captain Whiteman, who had served with the battalion throughout its service in France, was one of the latter.

Part III
Reflections

Chapter 13

9th Battalion East Surrey Regiment in Review

In his study of the Buffs, Mark Connelly provides an analysis of four battalions of that regiment. He endeavours to answer questions including ones relating to the social complexion of both officers and men and the combat effectiveness of the battalions concerned, and changes in both during the course of the war. These matters have been touched on in passing, in this work on a single battalion of the East Surrey Regiment. With the Armistice it seems an appropriate time to look back briefly over the history of 9/East Surrey and consider some general conclusions.

9/East Surrey had not been a particularly fortunate unit. It had been thrown into a hopeless attack at Loos only the day after its arrival at the Front. Its second attack had been at Guillemont on the Somme in August 1916, where it had again taken heavy losses for no success. It had then suffered heavily at Delville Wood. It was satisfying to have even a minor role in the Messines victory, but the battalion had then endured the misery of August 1917 at Ypres. After a quiet few months, the battalion found itself facing the great German offensive of March 1918, but went out in a blaze of glory. Reconstituted once again, and left to hold the line, it had then taken a mauling in the Advance to Victory at Haussy, only a month before the Armistice. It had lost more than 50 officers and 750 men, dead as the result of combat, in a little over 3 years, and more than 50 to disease and accidents. This may be compared with the 1914 establishment of 1,007, 30 of whom were officers, although the battalion's level of loss was not exceptional for that length of service on the Western Front.

With the Buffs, Connelly highlights the way that the regiment maintained its influence through the service battalions by transferring regular officers, especially as COs, to them.[1] A rather similar set of arrangements existed in the East Surrey Regiment, if the experience of 9/East Surrey is typical.

Looking first at the command of the battalion, Loos had exposed the risks of relying on ageing former Militia officers. The situation was taken in hand very firmly with the appointment of H.M.V. de la Fontaine to replace the sacked Lieutenant Colonel Sanders. De la Fontaine was not only a long-serving regular officer, but also had active service experience in South Africa and the present war. He was to prove a singularly happy choice. Not only was he extremely able and experienced, but he had a winning personality and a sympathetic approach to volunteer soldiers: something that many regulars did not share. Under his careful and inspirational leadership, the battalion recovered and became a very much more effective unit than before. Unfortunately, he was very badly wounded on the Somme and was unable to return to the battalion for many months. But the regiment provided another very experienced regular officer, H.S. Tew. He seems to have been thoroughly effective, although of a more reserved disposition. However, he had to depart after only six weeks, because of a riding accident.

Tew's replacement was T.W.S. Swanton, another regular officer of the regiment. However, Swanton had only joined the regiment in 1910, aged 22, through the 'backdoor' – the Special Reserve. He seems to have had command of the battalion on an acting basis. Although apparently effective, and of comparable age to other COs at the time, he may have had a difficult personality. Certainly, Pirie, the MO, said so and fell foul of him. De la Fontaine returned in March 1917, but, always prepared to take the same risks as his men, was killed by a sniper in August 1917, aged 44. Fortunately, the regiment found a good replacement for him in L.J. Le Fleming. He again, aged 38, was a regular of long service and much experience. He seems to have been well received and respected by the battalion.

The regiment only lost its 'control' of 9/East Surrey, through finding its CO, in April 1918. Le Fleming had been killed in much the same circumstances as de la Fontaine and his battalion had subsequently been all but wiped out. The amalgamation with 10/Loyals brought a new CO, E.A. Cameron, from outside the regiment. Cameron, aged 40, had served in a number of different units and was not popular with the War Office. He seems, however, to have been a good leader and sound commander. He led the battalion through to the Armistice and to eventual disbandment.

Besides the CO, few other experienced officers were provided from the regiment's regulars. The position of second in command seems often to have been difficult to fill. Major Bretell had left for the Suffolks, just before Loos. Major Welch died of wounds received at Loos. Until Swanton stepped down to major in March 1917, the battalion had long periods without a formal second in command. Sometimes a captain would be appointed on a relatively short-term basis. At others, an officer from another regiment might be brought in. W.H. Anderson, for instance, served with the battalion for three months from November 1916, leaving through sickness. He then distinguished himself in command of 12/Highland Light Infantry on 25 March 1918, winning a posthumous VC for two brilliant counterattacks.

Swanton's time with 9/East Surrey ended in November 1917. As an acting lieutenant colonel he commanded 4/Lincolnshire from December 1917 to January 1918. He was then given command of a North Staffordshire battalion from April to June 1918. He seems to have fallen out of favour, being called to the War Office and given a post of Chief Instructor in an officers' convalescent hospital as acting major.[2]

C.A. Clark, a former regular RSM and commissioned in January 1916, had proved an outstanding officer. After lengthy service as adjutant with 9/East

Surrey, he was promoted to major and acted as Le Fleming's second in command. He took command when Le Fleming was killed and distinguished himself through the terrible days of March 1918. With Clark a POW, Cameron had an ex-Loyals officer and not a regular, J.C. Brown, as his second in command. When Brown was away C. Hilton, who had first joined 9/East Surrey in December 1915, now a major, took over. Brown then continued with the battalion to its disbandment.

Whilst there was initial lack of continuity in the second in command's post, a number of the captains, in particular, served for long periods with the battalion, helping to foster *esprit de corps*, although not all were as noteworthy as Warre-Dymond and Lindsay. D.P. O'Connor was promoted captain as early as February 1915 and played an important role as, by the time of Loos, where he won an MC, he was probably the only officer in the battalion who had been trained as a regular officer and had served as such, albeit briefly. Although he was with the battalion until mid-1918, he spent a good deal of time in hospital, being wounded twice, and suffering long periods of sickness. Indeed, illness forced his final departure.

A slower, but steadier, rise was that of E.L. Whiteman. He was with the battalion at Loos and was still with it in November 1918. Perhaps because he had been a trooper in the Surrey Yeomanry, he was given the role of Transport Officer for the battalion. This was unglamorous but required a good knowledge of equine matters. Wounded and winning an MC in March 1918, as the most senior officer left he took command of the battalion's composite company. He seems to have given up the transport thereafter and commanded a fighting company.

Apart from those who made captain, there were a number of more junior officers who served for eighteen months or more with the battalion in France, including the outstanding L.C. Thomas.

Much has been made of the short lives of officers, especially subalterns on the Western Front. With respect to 9/East Surrey, a handwritten list of officers who served abroad with the battalion survives.[3] It includes the ex-Loyals officers, but excludes a few others who served with it who were not of the East Surrey Regiment. It indicates high officer turnover, but not simply through combat casualties. It lists 232 names of those who arrived and served with the battalion before the Armistice. These are listed alphabetically in Appendix IV of this book. Of these 194 appear to have left by the Armistice. Adding additional information, especially regarding the 'missing', we have the following reasons for departure:

Dead, including some dying in enemy hands, one accidental death and one pneumonia	55
Wounded	41
POWs	12
Sick, including those sent to Medical Boards	47
Transfers	35
To senior officers' course (Brown)	1
Cashiered (Abrams)	1
Sacked (Sanders)	1

No details   1
Total   194

The dead included two lieutenant colonels, one major and nine captains. (They exclude at least three more officers killed whilst attached to the battalion – Captain Pirie RAMC, Major Ottley, Royal Fusiliers, killed at Delville Wood, September 1916 and Captain Badcock, Gloucestershire Regiment, killed in the March 1918 Retreat. They also exclude at least two officers killed whilst attached to other units.)

A total of fifty-three combat fatalities comprises around 23 per cent of those who served. This may be compared with a regular battalion, 2nd Royal Irish Rifles, which was also virtually annihilated in March 1918, for which readily comparable statistics exist. From August 1914 to October 1918, this lost 87 officers dead, around 26 per cent, of the 326 who served. Deducting those fatalities that occurred before 9/East Surrey arrived in France, the Irish battalion lost sixty-two in the same period in which the Surrey battalion lost fifty-three: not a great difference.[4]

Sickness could include neurasthenia as well as accidental injury, trench fever, haemorrhoids, etc. Yet many wounded and sick officers did return to the battalion and of those who left it permanently, a number went on to serve with other units, on the Western or other fronts. These included men diagnosed as neurasthenic.

Of the 35 officers recorded as transferring directly from the battalion to other units, quite often soon after arrival, 7 went to other East Surrey battalions; 5 to other infantry regiments; 7 to the RFC/RAF; 5 to the MGC (including to tanks); 2 to trench mortar batteries; 2 to the signals service; 1 to 72 Brigade staff as Intelligence Officer; 1 to the ASC; 1 for duty in West Africa; and 4 to miscellaneous rear-area duties. A number seem to have transferred in search of adventure, although some perhaps got more than they bargained for. A.A.D. Toplis served nine months at the Front as an RFC observer in RE8s. He survived four air crashes, but his nerves did not.[5] H.H. Puttock was gassed and W.A. Wyatt wounded, serving in tanks.[6] Of the others, some may have been found unsuitable or unfit as infantry officers, including on medical grounds. For an instance of the latter, W.A.V. Waldron, after a year with the battalion, was medically downgraded to Bii in mid-1918 and put to run a POW camp.

As for those killed serving with the battalion, some had a very brief active service – those dying at Loos had only arrived at the Front the previous day. The nine subalterns killed in 1917 provide a contrast. Whilst both N. Le Poer Trench and H.W. Kiver had been only seven weeks with the battalion, J.A. Picton had served with it for nineteen months. The average over the nine is around thirty weeks.

The above analyses give results not far from those for 10/West Yorkshire's subalterns discussed by Martin Middlebrook: 21.3 per cent leaving killed, 27.6 per cent through wounds, 3.4 per cent as POWs, 47.7 per cent for other reasons and, after allowances for temporary absence, an average service of 6.17 months of front-line service with the unit before departure. This battalion had much the same BEF service history as 9/East Surrey.[7]

As for the social origins, education and military experience of the battalion's officers, at various times these have been discussed earlier in this work. The most senior officers had been found, initially, primarily from the Militia, and the rest largely from upper middle-class men who had attended public school and had OTC experience. Later, regulars had been put into the most senior posts and middle-class men from the ranks of other units commissioned. By 1918, there was overwhelming reliance, for new officers, on lower middle-class men, often clerks, who had served in the ranks and had then trained in Officer Cadet units. They might also have had extensive front-line service as rankers. W.H. Baber, son of a clothier, attended elementary and technical schools, entered glass manufacture and then enlisted in the Artists' Rifles. D.W. Keep had attended a grammar school and served in its OTC, before becoming a bank clerk and enlisting in the Surrey Yeomanry. W.S. Kelly was a butcher who had served three years in the ranks of the Royal West Kents before being commissioned. However, except for the lieutenant quartermasters, traditionally found, like W.P. Sheffield, from long-standing regular NCOs, there were always very few officers in the battalion who had been regular ORs, like C.A. Clark or T.H. Yalden (who had been a squadron sergeant major in the 6th Dragoons in 1914) or working class wartime ORs, like G.S. Carter, a gardener.

Whilst it is possible to find a good deal of information about individual officers, through the survival of War Office files for most of them,[8] and arrive at some conclusions about them, this is much more difficult for the other ranks.[9] Officers, particularly the younger and less experienced, had to lean heavily on good NCOs. Some of the most outstanding can be identified. RSM W. Ladd was a Boer War veteran killed in spring 1916. Sergeants A. Bell, G.W. Medlock and W.G.T. Summers won distinction as raiders. CSM G. Hyde was particularly distinguished in the desperate days of March 1918. Some NCOs may have been pre-war regulars, but these seem to have been comparatively few and apparently promising men were promoted on limited knowledge of them at first. There was also some cross posting of NCOs between battalions, in part, presumably, to spread experience. Edwin Myall, presumably a regular of some service, had served in France from January 1915, as a private with 2/East Surrey, when it had arrived from India. At some stage he was transferred to 9/East Surrey and was killed in September at Loos as a lance sergeant. Acting Sergeant Henry Hollins had previously served in the Reserve. Sent to 1/East Surrey in February 1917, he was transferred to 9/East Surrey in March and killed in April 1917. From problems that manifested themselves around the time the battalion first went to France, it would appear that there were some unsatisfactory NCOs, whatever their origins, who had to be weeded out. Later, many NCOs distinguished themselves and a few, like Summers, E.C. Ericson, L.A. Knight and F.G. Oakey, were commissioned. Summers was sent to another battalion of the East Surrey Regiment, where he won an MC, whilst Ericson was commissioned into the Royal Sussex and Knight was commissioned into the Labour Corps, running a POW camp for a time. Unlike, for instance, the Royal Irish Rifles, it seems to have been regimental policy not to send officers to battalions where they had previously served in the ranks.

As for the ordinary soldiers, these had originally been predominantly working class men from the London area and Surrey. There had been little change in this, although conscription had been introduced in 1916, until April 1918. An analysis of the first fifty fatalities in 1918 from Anon., *Soldiers Died in the Great War 1914–19 Part 36 The East Surrey Regiment* (London, 1920) indicates 72 per cent had lived in Surrey, London and Middlesex, 10 per cent in East Anglia, 6 per cent in other Home Counties, 6 per cent in the Midlands and 6 per cent in the North. Transfers into the battalion from other regiments in late 1916 and during 1917, for those in *Soldiers Died*, seem to have been predominantly from the Royal Fusiliers (nine) and the Middlesex Regiment (three), both of which recruited from the London area. However, there were also six from the Durham Light Infantry.

A significant number of northerners were added in spring 1918, primarily as the result of the amalgamation with the former 10/Loyals. There are also a number of 1918 deaths in *Soldiers Died* recorded as having served in other Lancashire regiments. An analysis of the battalion's last 100 fatalities in the ranks (from August 1918 to early 1919) gives the following results, from place of residence/place of enlistment in *Soldiers Died*. (The figures for 1915 fatalities are as Chapter 1 above):

County etc.	% 1918–1919	% 1915
Lancashire	29	nil
London	21	29
Surrey	18	53
Essex	9	1
Kent	3	1
Sussex	3	nil
Middlesex	2	10
Norfolk	2	nil
Shropshire	2	nil
Bedfordshire	1	nil
Cambridgeshire	1	nil
Cumberland	1	nil
Hertfordshire	1	nil
Staffordshire	1	nil
Suffolk	1	nil
Warwickshire	1	nil
Other English counties	nil	6
Wales	2	nil
Ireland	1	nil
Unknown	1	nil
Total	100	100

Assuming these fatalities are reasonably typical of the battalion in later 1918, it is clear that it had become much more diverse. Whilst most men in 1918 still came from London and the Home Counties, they were only a small majority now and there was a very substantial Lancashire contingent.

Unfortunately, there is not the information available to measure turnover in the ranks as there is with the officers. Sickness, however, is likely to have been a major factor. As some indication, 8/Buffs, also in 24th Division, had 666 sickness cases during 1917, compared with 699 other casualties.[10] In that same period 9/East Surrey had, according to Pearse and Sloman and the war diary, 152 fatalities and 422 wounded.[11] One would guess its sickness level was not far off that of the Buffs. Another factor influencing turnover, from later 1916, was that it could be difficult for a man to return to his battalion if absent through such as sickness. The Army no longer respected unit cohesion and, all too often, sent men to where they were most required, regardless of their regiment. A rather extreme example is John Claughton, an apprentice grocer from Oldham, Lancashire. Born in 1899, he had enlisted in 1915 in the Border Regiment, but had been discharged four months later as underage. After six months he enlisted again, expressing a preference for the Seaforth Highlanders. Initially enlisted in the South Lancashire Regiment, he was passed to the Manchester Regiment. Arrived in France in April 1918, he was almost immediately transferred to 9/East Surrey. A POW at Haussy, he survived the war.

As for initiative, this was not expected of junior NCOs and privates, but when they showed it, as with various private soldiers under bombardment at Hooge in 1916, and most notably with McNamara VC in 1918, it was proudly commended. This was something in which the German Army had a lead for most of the war. A number of 9/East Surrey officers were killed undertaking duties that the Germans would have left to NCOs, only partly because the Germans had a smaller proportion of officers.

With regard to combat effectiveness, this was substantially improved after Loos, with training and front-line experience. This, however, took time. Captain Johnston, a regular with 9 Brigade had fairly recognised, regarding 21st and 24th Divisions at Loos, that 'The people who are really to blame are those who decided to employ absolutely untried troops in a big show like this; it is not really giving them a fair chance.' However, visiting 72 Brigade on 20 November 1915, in trenches his brigade was taking over, he was very critical.

> I am afraid these New Army troops still have much to learn. One saw things that would never be tolerated amongst regular troops, numerous men in the trenches with their equipment off, actually an officer without his respirator on! no gongs or arrangements for meeting a sudden gas attack, men who did not know where their officers or their dugouts were, the guides given to us were supposed to know their way about but did not in reality etc. etc.: however good work has been done in places: the men are all right but lack experience and have no officers to teach them.

The unit visited was not 9/East Surrey, which was out of the line at this time, but one wonders how much de la Fontaine had managed to achieve with it in just a month.[12] The casualties sustained whilst patrolling during January 1916 seem to indicate continued inexperience.

9/East Surrey, like others, pursued different levels of aggression in the trenches at different times. It is, however often difficult to measure this.[13] Even the combative regulars of 2/Leinster were happy to accept 'live and let live' against the Saxons in the flooded trenches at St Eloi. A typical 'let sleeping dogs lie' attitude is expressed by Trotter in the novelised version of *Journey's End*, as he explains to Raleigh, 'If we was to throw a bomb you can bet yer boots the old Boche would chuck one back, and Mr. Digby and Mr. 'Arris, lying there, are both married men with kids. Wouldn't be – be cricket, would it?'[14]

Against such aggressive opponents as those at Wulverghem in 1916, 9/East Surrey sought to give markedly more back in exchange for any aggression received. Moreover, apparently friendly overtures by the Germans were not necessarily welcomed and at Hooge in February 1916 were sharply rebuffed. Looking at casualty rates, in particular, there appears to have been a very low level of aggression around Hargicourt in the winter of 1917–1918, although for some time the battalion was facing a Prussian Guard Division. Both sides seem to have decided they had little to gain here from active hostilities and the troops do not seem to have been pressed to be aggressive by their respective high commands, once things had settled down after Cambrai. There was, however, to be a higher tempo of operations in the summer of 1918 around Lens, with 24th Division wishing to give its newly rebuilt units combat experience and tie down the enemy as far as possible.

The battalion went through the same changes in provision of improved weapons and tactics as the rest of the BEF's infantry. However, every time the battalion had to be reconstructed after heavy casualties, many new officers and men had to be trained, not only in front-line tactics, but also to fight in their respective sub-units. The danger of incorporating large numbers of new men during active operations was graphically demonstrated by the collapse of 13/Middlesex at Delville Wood. However, training at the Front was always hampered by the demand to provide working parties from battalions in support or reserve.

Support from the artillery, in particular, was much improved after the dismal performance at Loos and the less than satisfactory results on the Somme. The British artillery became truly formidable. Gas warfare, too, was transformed, from reliance on the ineffective cylinders used at Loos to the fearsome Livens Projectors from late 1916.

Following virtual annihilation in March 1918, the reconstituted battalion showed its abilities in trench warfare at Lens. It participated in sophisticated training for open warfare and then displayed such skills in the last weeks of the war. Haussy was initially a great success. It was unfortunate that the strength of the Germans had been underestimated, that 1/North Staffordshire could not participate to the extent planned and that the Guards were unable to protect the battalion's right flank. All this led to many East Surrey men being cut off by the

German counterattack. As to the degree of initiative that the battalion and its commanders could show, this was much circumscribed in the early days, like Loos and the Somme. By early 1917, however, the battalion seems to have been allowed to work out for itself such matters as detailed plans for raids, with a <u>daylight</u> attack in January 1917. The battalion's incorporation in the Haussy attack was made at a very late stage, as a result of its CO's initiative.

9/East Surrey seem to have been competent raiders. The objectives were modest, but plans were thorough and casualties light. The battalion made a late start, with no raids until January 1917. Connelly[15] suggests the battalion only ever raided once, but it made five other raids – in November and December 1917, May 1918 (at 6 hours' notice) and two in July 1918. Of these, three of the raids were successful in securing prisoners. The strength of a raiding party varied from 27 to 63 (in total 283, including some engineers). Their casualties were relatively light – 6 killed, 1 missing, 17 wounded (of whom at least 1 died later). The only 'leader' to be lost in a raid was the intrepid Second Lieutenant Carter in the November 1917 raid, during which most of the above casualties were incurred.

In 9/East Surrey, raids seem to have been conducted by second lieutenants and directed by a second lieutenant or lieutenant, rather than more senior officers directly participating. There may have been a number of reasons for this, including that the more junior may have been the keenest to volunteer; they may have been chosen because they had the most up-to-date experience of no–man's–land; and they were more expendable. Experienced NCOs might lead small parties on raids, instead of officers – men like Sergeant Summers for the January 1917 raid, who had repeatedly proved their ability and daring on patrols in no–man's–land. Such NCOs were certainly not expendable.

Night patrolling of no–man's–land was occasionally made more aggressive, as by Sergeant Summers. Indeed, more 'leaders' were lost on patrols than raids: including Second Lieutenants Marchant and Handford in January 1916, Second Lieutenant Grantham in November 1917 and the very experienced Sergeant Dugdale in June 1918. Day patrolling was undertaken extensively at Lens in later 1918 which, with the raids undertaken then, must have helped develop competence and confidence, which was then to be used so effectively to infiltrate Haussy in October.

Esprit de corps in 9/East Surrey could not rely on locality or class solidarity to the extent that the original' 'Pals' battalions or the middle-class London Territorial units could. It had to be founded more on shared hardships and dangers and fostered by good leadership by officers of the quality of de la Fontaine, Clark, Warre-Dymond and Cameron. Such spirit came to the fore on many occasions, especially in August 1917 at Ypres and in the desperate struggles of March 1918, as well as in the strength of the post-war old comrades' gatherings.

Chapter 14

After the Armistice

Under the terms of the Armistice, Germany was required, in particular, to: cease all hostilities; evacuate all occupied territory within fifteen days; evacuate all German territory west of the Rhine and three Rhine bridgeheads within a month; surrender such quantities of war material as to prevent any resumption by it of serious hostilities; and to release all POWs without reciprocity. The Armistice was to run, initially for thirty-six days, but could be (and was) renewed, pending a peace treaty.

Each of the Allies selected the troops required to advance and occupy the Rhineland: those from the BEF were to occupy the British sector, around Cologne. The rest, including 24th Division, were to stand fast in France and Belgium. The Germans returned to the east of the Rhine, in general, as disciplined units. However, the officers were unable to prevent most men then returning to their homes.

On a lighter note, British GHQ issued guidance to Army commanders that, whilst emphasising the need to maintain firm discipline, said that irritating restrictions should be avoided; recreational facilities should be made available; and amusements organised for the men, who should be given time and transport to visit places of interest; and censorship and restrictions on use of cameras should be relaxed.[1]

Life with the battalion after the Armistice was something of an anticlimax. The German collapse had seemed very sudden. Brigadier General Morgan held a parade on 13 November to thank his men. Time was given over to training and organised games. (An 'OC Sports' had been appointed for each battalion on 14 November). News of Corporal John McNamara's VC arrived on 16 November, but sadly he had been killed a month earlier. On 22 November, four lorries were allocated to the battalion, so that those who had served at Lens and Bully-Grenay could visit the old battlefield. After withdrawal to the Douai area, reached on 19 November, a move to Tournai in Belgium was commenced on 25 November. All 72 Brigade's men were quartered in Tournai Infantry Barracks, with officers billeted in the town, from 18 December. The first Christmas of Peace was celebrated.

With the Armistice all Allied POWs were to be immediately released. It was believed these included 140,000 British. Whilst officer POWs were listed by unit, by the military agents Cox and Co., I have not found a list of the ORs POWs from the battalion and it is difficult to estimate accurately how many there were. Quite a large number, almost all wounded, had been captured at Loos – probably nearer

With all

Good Wishes

. for .

Christmas

and the

New Year

from

9th Battalion

East Surrey Regiment.

'A HOPELESS DAWN!'

Figure 22. 9/East Surrey Christmas card, 1918.

200 than 100. Again, a good number must have gone 'into the bag' in March 1918, with the battalion's last stand, and events leading up to it. At that time, 215 were initially reported missing, in addition to those known to be dead, but around two dozen of these 'missing' had been killed. Some 'missing' could, however, have turned up later. More were captured at Haussy in October, cut off by the German counterattack. Of the 121 missing then, only a few had been killed. In addition to these three periods, a few more would have been lost along the way, in other actions. There were perhaps, therefore, in total around 500 other ranks taken prisoner. As for the officers, who were held in separate camps, the records are precise. Leaving aside those who were captured severely wounded and died very soon after being captured, there were fourteen. They included three captured at Loos, of whom only one survived the war. In March 1918 nine were captured, most either taken prisoner when 'D' company was cut off, or in the battalion's last stand. In October 1918 two more were captured at Haussy.

Being taken prisoner in any conflict is a risky business. Both sides on the Western Front took large numbers of prisoners. However, in the heat of battle, men who left it late to surrender, for example, by holding out to the end and causing heavy casualties to the attackers, might well be refused mercy. Similarly, particularly hated opponents like snipers, machine-gunners and trench-mortar men might be killed out of hand. Moreover, whilst on the field of battle, prisoners remained as vulnerable as other troops to gunfire sweeping the field. Once passions had cooled, prisoners were generally well treated by front-line troops, who saw they had much in common. Similar consideration from rear-area troops and civilians was, however, unlikely.

Reports from returned prisoners from Loos have been used to examine their initial experiences (in Chapter 2). They also throw interesting light on their later experiences. They are not, however, typical, as their physical condition generally prevented them from being obliged to work for the Germans. Under the Geneva Convention, it was permissible for OR POWs to undertake certain kinds of work for their captors, for which they were to be paid.

Lance Corporal David Ballantyne, captured wounded at Loos, gave an extremely detailed account of his experiences, in May 1916, after his exchange. He was very positive about his treatment in hospital: 'I was treated the same way as the German wounded were treated ... The doctors were very good to me.' He was transferred to Giessen Camp in January 1916. After receiving good food in hospital, the camp's came as an unpleasant shock, 'it was detestable, consisting of chestnut soup, cabbage soup, swedes boiled up, and sometimes a piece of meat with it. One loaf was supplied as a day's rations for 5 men. If it had not been for the packets of food from home, I should have been very badly nourished.'

Lance Corporal Herbert Marten had much the same experiences to report. After hospital he was transferred to Stendal Camp, where he found the food very bad. Private C. Morrissey, after having a foot amputated, ended up in the Camp Hospital at Friedrichsfeld, which he said was supposed to be the best camp in Germany. He even describes the commandant, married to an Englishwoman, as 'a nice man'. Even so, the food was 'very bad' and he received no letters or parcels for five months. When the American Ambassador's representative visited, 'They gave an extra ration for dinner, and gave a new pair of crutches or shoes to anyone who had old ones, but took them back after he left. We only saw him in the presence of Germans, and it was no good making complaints.'

Private Williams had a rougher time. Whilst in hospital he saw the American Ambassador alone, but had no complaints. However, he was sent to Mannheim Camp for two and a half months before being exchanged.

Accommodation was very bad. A dirty straw mattress and one blanket ... I had two baths in three months ... French and Russian prisoners had to work in mines, etc. British prisoners were all badly wounded and unable to work, so refused. We were paraded and punished by being made to stand at attention for two hours at a time in hot August sun ... The food in this camp was so bad that no one could possibly exist on it. I did not receive parcels from home for about eight weeks after arriving in camp, and was so weak for want of proper nourishment that I could not walk. I received no clothes. We were too weak to take exercise ... Most of the men in camp suffered from dysentery owing to bad food. They were taken to hospital.

There was considerable anger in Britain about German treatment of POWs and there were undoubtedly many instances of cruelty and neglect. However, not all of the claims made were entirely reliable. Those officials interviewing returned POWs, whilst keen to hear of bad behaviour by the Germans, were also concerned to make notes about the reliability of their informants. Ballantyne's interviewer considered him 'honest and reliable, and I believe his statement to be true. He appears, however, to be very grateful to the camp doctor for recommending him for exchange after the French doctor had ordered him "back to duty" (work) and to be of such a happy and cheerful nature as to minimise hardships and difficulties.' However, Private H.A. Pledge has two very short interview notes. His interviewer considered him 'rather too garrulous in the absence of corroboration. I should be chary of accepting all his statements.'[2] Pledge's claims of ill treatment, were, however, eagerly published by the *Daily Sketch* under the headline 'Germans' fiendish treatment of wounded.' Pledge claimed the Germans had picked him up at Loos, with a smashed arm and deliberately left him, with many others, exposed to gunfire on a trench parapet for 10 hours. Captain Birt, also a POW from 9/East Surrey, according to a German report, wrote to his CO indignantly repudiating the accusations. When Birt died, in a German hospital, in April 1916, there was a remarkable and lengthy tribute in a Cologne newspaper. 'He was loved and respected by everyone with whom he came into contact, whether friend or foe – from the highest to the lowest. He was truly one of the best; his mere presence was an example for good. The world is the poorer for the loss of such a man.'[3]

Conditions worsened as the war lengthened. Food shortages, partly due to the Allied blockade, but also to the dislocation of food distribution, hit German civilians hard, so there was little food left over for prisoners. Parcels of food and other comforts were sent to POWs through the Red Cross, from individual relatives or well-wishers and local and regimental associations. A newspaper appeal in late 1917, soliciting support for POWs, was frank,

It is a melancholy fact that the British prisoner of war in Germany fares badly; yet his ration is nearly, if not quite as much as that of the ordinary German or Austrian civilian not engaged on particularly laborious work ... Our men, with the Briton's preference for solid 'tack' cannot tolerate the dreadful messes provided, and many prefer partial starvation, to the extreme detriment of their health. Nor can it be denied that the calorific value of the food supplied is very low and of itself barely enough to sustain life. It is, therefore, essential constantly to supplement our men's food by parcels.

It goes on to report that, in spite of pilfering by hungry Germans, at least 70 per cent of parcels sent were received practically intact and 'afford profound satisfaction to the recipients'. The central committee in Britain claimed that 95 per cent of parcels sent to the larger camps were received.[4]

Some prisoners taken in spring 1918, rather than being sent to POW camps, were used to clear up the battlefields. Apart from the traumatic task of clearing away the dead, they were used for the often potentially dangerous task of salvage.[5]

Some prisoners died in captivity. They are included in Anon., *Soldiers Died in the Great War 1914–19 Part 36 The East Surrey Regiment* (London, 1920), but their place of death is given as the theatre in which they were captured. It is difficult to be precise with those buried in France and Flanders, but around twenty-five other ranks of those listed as 'died ', rather than 'died of wounds', appear to have died in captivity, or on their way home from it. Most are buried in Germany or behind the German lines in France. Lance Corporal Allan Horlock was a 23-year-old Sussex man, married and a manager in the wine and spirits trade when he attested in December 1915. Mobilised in April 1916, he had first been posted to the Queen's Regiment. Speedily transferred to the East Surrey Regiment, he was posted to the BEF in June 1917 and soon found himself with 9/East Surrey. He was reported missing on 27 March 1918. He died, cause unknown, 14 August 1918 and was buried by the Germans near Ham.[6] Far from his birthplace in Nottinghamshire, in the Nikolai cemetery at Jelgava in Latvia, then occupied by Germany, is Private Samuel Argyle. He died 13 September 1917.

Unfortunately, the terms of the Armistice regarding Allied prisoners were insufficiently specific and the Germans were not minded to co-operate. Repatriation of POWs was, accordingly, disorganised. Many held in areas like Alsace that were being evacuated by the Germans were simply turned loose by their guards and told to find their own way home. For men weakened by privation and without rations, this was not easy. Nevertheless, around 75,000 reached Allied lines within a month of the Armistice. With the Germans making inadequate arrangements, medical parties and ambulance trains were sent into Germany. Roughly equal numbers of POWs were repatriated through German ports, Dutch ports and Calais/Boulogne.[7]

The Germans had no central management of POWs and this made it difficult to establish numbers of men due. On 9 January 1919, according to British records, there were still about 36,000 to be released. The Germans said there were only 13,579. It seems this discrepancy was never properly resolved, and owed much to German laxity in reporting POWs deaths to the Red Cross.[8]

Some 9/East Surrey POWs, weakened by privation, sadly did not quite reach home after their release. Private James Watford had been captured at Loos, wounded in both legs. He was returning home from a South German camp when he fell ill with influenza on 26 November 1918. He died of pneumonia on 3 December, being buried at Vevey, Switzerland.[9] Private William Dennison was captured in March 1918. He died on 31 December and is buried at Sangatte, on the French coast. Private Joseph Wrigley, captured in October 1918, died on 30 November 1918 and was buried in Nijmegen, Holland.[10]

Not all surviving POWs made a full recovery from their experiences, whether from wounds or otherwise. Private Charles Woodbury had been captured at Haussy, in October 1918, wounded in the head and was no longer the man he had been. Discharged from the Army on 1 April 1919, he turned to alcohol for relief. Fortunately for his family, he was comfortably off. He was dead within three years. Second Lieutenant Walter Baber, also captured wounded at Haussy, was repatriated on 11 December. He was later awarded a 20 per cent disability pension for life, in relation to neurasthenia, a gunshot wound and gassing.[11]

With the Armistice signed, the Rhineland occupied and Germany handing over much of the armaments necessary for her to resist, the Allies could turn their attention to reducing the huge forces they had raised. The vast majority of British servicemen had joined for the duration of the war and wanted to get home as soon as possible. The government was anxious to reduce the size of the Armed Forces as quickly as was safe, but also with the minimum disruption to the economy. According to the terms announced in late November, discharged servicemen were to be given twenty-eight days' paid leave, a gratuity based on rank and length of service, a clothing allowance, a rail warrant and up to twenty weeks' unemployment benefit, if required. These terms were not contentious, but the system for discharge was. This gave priority to men's skills, e.g. as coal miners, or the availability of their employment, rather than length of service. As a result, young conscripts with very little service were to be discharged before volunteers who might have served three years or more at the Front. This led to disturbances amongst servicemen in Britain. Of around 3,500,000 officers and men serving at the Armistice, rather more than 750,000 were discharged in the first two months. A new system was then announced by Winston Churchill, War Minister, on 29 January 1919. This allowed for the discharge of all men who wished to be, who had enlisted before 1 January 1916 (i.e. before conscription was introduced); or were aged 37 or more; or had three or more wound stripes. This was to be part of a first stage reduction of the Army to 900,000 men.

With demobilisation already in hand, many group photographs were taken as souvenirs at Tournai around New Year 1919. These included the battalion's officers, the senior NCOs and individual companies. The war diary[12] was already noting by mid-January that demobilisation was proceeding faster and the band could not march with the battalion as so many players had now left. Training and educational activities continued, along with sport and the occasional half holiday. Increasing manpower shortages, however, interrupted these when working parties were required.

A parade was held on 21 February, to present colours to the Kitchener battalions of 72 Brigade. (Unlike the regulars, they had never received any.) Lieutenant General Holland, representing General Horne, the Army commander, paid tribute to the battalions. As recorded in the war diary, he made particular mention of the brigade's services in March 1918, in which it 'played a glorious part, holding up many overwhelming attacks, and by its courage and fighting spirit saving the situation on many occasions'.

9/East Surrey left Tournai, and 72 Brigade, on 4 March, to join the British Army of the Rhine. It replaced the disbanded 12/East Surrey in 122 Brigade, 41st Division, under Major General Sir Sydney Lawford. (These units were soon to be renamed 1 London Brigade and the London Division.) It brought 21 officers and 385 other ranks with it and took over around 300 officers and men from the disbanded battalion. The battalion went into billets at Hoffnungsthal, near Volberg, 10 miles east of Cologne, in brigade reserve. Companies were short of men, with so many granted leave. More officers and men were taken over from 8/East Surrey. On 22 March, the battalion took over positions in the outpost line for a three-week tour, but the situation remained quiet, with time devoted to working parties and training. A Divisional Race Meeting over two days at the end of April proved very popular.

The battalion moved to Kalk, an eastern suburb of Cologne on 14 May and two days later was cheering Marshal Foch as he sailed past. The following day, a Guard of Honour of 100 men and the band was provided for him. On 27 May, the battalion took over guarding bridges in Cologne. Civil disturbances were expected and the guards reinforced, but no trouble was forthcoming. A parade was held for the Corps Commander, Sir Aylmer Haldane, on 2 June. Photographs taken show the battalion's band, under Drum Major Levitt, marching through Cologne with sailors and tanks.[13] Later that month 200 men were received from 23/R Fusiliers.

Life on the Rhine was pleasant. There was little friction with the local inhabitants, many of whom were happy to avoid the chaos of revolutionary uprisings elsewhere in Germany. The troops were comfortably housed. Pay was enhanced for service in the Armies of Occupation and the troops also enjoyed a very favourable exchange rate. Duty was not onerous, there was much opportunity for recreation and leave was generous. There were momentary periods of minor excitement, especially in June, when an attempt to sabotage the Rhine bridges was expected and orders were received for a possible advance to put pressure on the German government on 19 June to sign the peace treaty. This was signed by the Germans, with considerable reluctance, on 28 June and was celebrated by the battalion with a holiday.

The British Army of the Rhine was steadily reduced, with the peace treaty signed and the danger from Germany diminished. Down to 6 infantry divisions in August 1919, a reduction to 5 brigades followed that autumn, and then to 7 battalions the following February.

In early November 1919, the battalion was ordered to return to Britain. Reduced to 24 officers and 362 other ranks, it set off on 8 November. On 11 November, the first anniversary of the Armistice, it reached Britain. It was posted to Clipstone Camp, Nottinghamshire. Colonel Cameron, Major Brown and sixty more, travelled to Kingston upon Thames, on 20 November, where the mayoress placed a laurel wreath on the battalion's Colour. The mayor and corporation afterwards gave them lunch.

The battalion then remained at Clipstone, with final demobilisation taking place in March 1920. On 27 March, the battalion officially ceased to exist. By then,

Britain's huge wartime army no longer existed. The British Army was returning to be a wholly regular one, backed by the Territorials, as pre-war.

For the survivors, there were now the challenges of peace. A few stayed on in the Army, or soon rejoined, like Private Frederick Ivey.[14] No doubt, many of the other ranks had difficulty finding work and coping with wounds, both physical and psychological, and died prematurely. Unfortunately, there is little on record about them. One for whom brief records have survived was Private Edward Wigg, a Sussex-born farm labourer, who had joined up in September 1914, aged 19. He had served in France with 9/East Surrey from August 1915, winning an MM for his bravery, but in January 1917 was wounded and lost a leg. He was discharged as unfit. A single man, he was to receive 27s 6d ($£1.37½$) a week for nine weeks, then 16s 6d (82½p) a week for life.[15]

The officer records throw more light on the post-war experiences of individuals. Some officers continued in the Army. 'Nobby' Clark, repatriated from a German POW camp, stayed with the East Surrey Regiment. Lechmere Thomas received a regular commission in the Northumberland Fusiliers after being wounded in Iraq in 1920. Walter Summers, who had distinguished himself as a sergeant with 9/East Surrey, had been commissioned in 1918. He won an MC serving with 12/East Surrey. Not long after demobilisation he was feeling restless, writing to the War Office in October 1920, 'I have been demobilised since January last, but the service and all that campaigning means, has got into my blood, and frankly I want to come back. I want to join one of those minor Field Forces operating in odd corners of the Empire: Persia, West Africa, Russia, or anywhere where men who know their business are needed.' He was accepted for a regular commission, but resigned after six months to return to his first love, the film industry.

Ex-officers had varying fortunes in civilian life. Some ex-officers were men of means or had well-paid jobs to return to. Gerald Tetley, who had lost a leg, resigned his commission in 1918 to return to the Bar. Gilbert Frankau's cigar business had not survived the war, but he became a very successful writer. Some went, or returned, abroad – Eric Nobbs went to a Malayan plantation. Others, however, found themselves in relatively junior and poorly paid jobs. Charles Hilton had been a temporary major, but became a salesman in electrical goods.

Some officers died, or developed serious health problems not long after leaving the Army. Charles Cowper, a subaltern severely wounded in September 1917, left the Army in 1919 and died suddenly a year later. Reg Howship, who had joined the battalion as a subaltern in 1919, after winning an MC with 12/East Surrey, was discharged entirely fit in September 1919. However, by the following spring he was receiving treatment for tuberculosis, apparently contracted in the Army. He died of the same disease in 1927, aged 29.

For former soldiers suffering disablement from wounds, physical or mental, the outlook for them and their families could be grim. Pensions were awarded, but were not overgenerous and were reduced if the man's health was seen as improved. William Spencer, born in 1870, had enlisted in the cavalry, before being commissioned in the mounted infantry in the Boer War. Awarded a Territorial commission in 1914, he was acting major with 9/East Surrey when wounded in November 1916. An exploding shell threw him against a beam, hitting his head. When the Medical Board visited him at home he was found in a confused state, unable to say where he was or name his regiment, and with his gait unsteady. The Board concluded he was 'quite unfit for any service and should be admitted to hospital for nervous diseases'. He was sent to Craiglockart Hospital, but it seems there was little that could be done for him. By 1919, his wife wrote that she had been obliged to give up their home and rent a working man's cottage, as they had no money, except his pension. Her husband was unable to work and required constant attention and she had a young son. William Spencer died in 1937, leaving his wife apparently destitute.[16]

For the families of those who had died in the war, there was grief to live with, often economic hardship with the loss of the breadwinner and the challenges of bringing up children without a father. As well as photographs and letters, medals and commemorative scrolls and plaques were often treasured in memory of the dead. Old Mrs Chappell's daughter-in-law wrote in 1922, seeking assistance in obtaining the medals, scroll and plaque due in respect of Private John Chappell. (Posted as missing after March 1918, it had only been established in February 1919 that he had died of wounds in a German hospital soon after capture.) 'Mother who is 75 years old and very poorly keeps asking me about them she says she don't expect she will see them which is very hard to hear. I have received all mine in respect of her other son who was killed in July 1916.'[17]

Chapter 15

R.C. Sherriff's *Journey's End*

Like many of his comrades, Sherriff found it difficult to settle into civilian life after the war. On leaving school, he had taken a job, without enthusiasm, as a clerk with Sun Insurance, for whom his father and grandfather had worked before him. The war had come as an exciting diversion. Afterwards, he applied for a regular commission in 1919, without success.[1] He returned, reluctantly, to Sun Insurance. The only improvement was that he was no longer tied to an office, but, as a claims adjuster, had the freedom of working outside.

As for recreation, Sherriff had been a keen oarsman at school and joined the Kingston Rowing Club. He began playwriting from putting on entertainments to raise money for the club. After three years, however, he handed over the captaincy of the club and wondered how to spend the extra time. For a while he tried studying for insurance examinations, but gave up. He also wrote more plays, but without professional success.

Sherriff now picked up a novel he had started to write a few years before. (He had previously tried his hand at writing stories in France.) The theme was hero worship, starting at school. The two main characters were Dennis Stanhope and Jimmy Raleigh. Dennis seemed to have all the gifts, whilst Jimmy was a plodder, who worshipped him. Yet after school the positions of the two gradually reversed, with Jimmy becoming a success and Dennis a failure. Jimmy then set out to save his hero, who, however, secretly despised him. But Sherriff found it difficult to write a novel and wondered if the story could be made into a play. He had not considered the war as part of the novel, but realised the younger boy would have 'moved heaven and earth' to join his hero at the Front as soon as he was old enough. He came to the idea of distilling 'the essence of the novel into a few days in a front-line dugout' and 'the story fell naturally into the most dramatic episode on the Western front; the days before the final, desperate attack of the Germans in March 1918'.[2]

Sherriff was soon absorbed in his new project, eventually named *Journey's End*, which, nevertheless, took him a year. 'All the previous plays had been about imaginary people in imaginary situations, and now for the first time I was writing about something real, about men I had lived with and knew so well that every line they spoke came straight from them and not from me.'[3]

The play opens in a company officers' dugout, 50yd from the front line, in France, near St Quentin, three days before the great German offensive there in March 1918. As such, the characters are 'caught in a trap with no hope of escape'.[4]

Young Jimmy Raleigh, aged 18, has hero-worshipped Dennis Stanhope since school. Stanhope is also unofficially engaged to his sister. Raleigh manages to get sent to Stanhope's company, but finds him unwelcoming and dramatically changed by the war. The other main characters are Osborne, Stanhope's right-hand man, Trotter, a cheerful, unimaginative ex-ranker, and Hibbert, a nervous officer. Stanhope, who keeps his shattered nerves going with whisky, resents Raleigh's arrival, as impinging on his privacy and discovering his weaknesses. All know that the great German offensive is imminent and the Germans seem ominously quiet. Light relief is, however, provided, in particular by Mason, the officers' cook. Hibbert demands to be sent away to hospital, pleading neuralgia. Stanhope refuses, seeing this as simply an excuse to avoid danger. When Hibbert confesses his fear, Stanhope reveals his own and urges Hibbert to stand by his comrades. Brigade orders a raid to identify opposing units, although the Germans are on the alert. Osborne and Raleigh are chosen to lead it. Whilst a prisoner is secured, Osborne and most of his men are killed. Raleigh is then mortally wounded in the German bombardment beginning the German offensive. Stanhope, now reconciled with Raleigh, has to leave him dead in the dugout, to face the German attack. The play ends.

The play was well received by Sherriff's agents who were, however, well aware of the then prejudice against plays about the war. It also had the disadvantages, as Sherriff perceived, of little plot, no love interest, no female characters and a predictable, rather than surprise, ending. The Incorporated Stage Society, however, performed *Journey's End*, with the then unknown Laurence Olivier as Stanhope, in December 1928. (Years later, Olivier apparently said that of all the characters he had played, Stanhope was his favourite.) The play was produced by James Whale, another former infantry officer and also then an unknown. Following the play's rapturous reception by the critics, it was taken up by the commercial theatre in January 1929. It proved a sensation and played to packed houses. Whale also produced a film of it and pursued a career in Hollywood.

Sherriff could only conclude this overwhelming success was because it was,

> the first war play that kept its feet in the Flanders mud. All the previous plays had aimed at higher things: they carried 'messages', 'sermons against war', symbolic revelations. The public knew enough about war to take that all for granted. What they had never been shown before on the stage was how men really lived in the trenches, how they talked and how they behaved. Old soldiers recognised themselves, or the friends they had served with. Women recognised their sons, their brothers or their husbands, many of whom had not returned. The play made it possible for them to journey into the trenches and share the lives that their men had led. For all this I could claim no personal credit. I wrote the play in the way it came, and it just happened by chance that the way I wrote it was the way people wanted it.[5]

There was some criticism of the play: from some because it was not overtly anti-war; and from others who saw it as picturing the British officer in an unflattering light. Winston Churchill, then Chancellor of the Exchequer, however, was enthusiastic and invited Sherriff to meet him to discuss the play.

The play was seen by many 9/East Surrey veterans. Sherriff was pictured with Clark, Warre-Dymond, Thomas, Webb and others after a performance in 1930. He also wrote to Clark to say that High and Summers, too, had seen it.[6]

Sherriff does not discuss the models for the characters in *Journey's End* in *No Leading Lady*, although he writes, 'Besides Stanhope and Raleigh, the other characters walked in without invitation. I had known them all so well in the trenches.'[7] He also refers to a discussion in 1939 with a former fellow officer about possible models for the characters.[8] Sherriff had earlier written to 'Nobby' Clark in 1936, 'None of the characters are drawn from life – but you may find in some of them a likeness to men you knew.' Clark went so far as to write, 'I posted Sherriff to "C" (Fortunately, otherwise I fear that there would have been no "Journey's End").'[9]

Whilst Sherriff did not give names for those who inspired his main characters, it is possible to identify some. A clipping at Surrey History Centre, from an unidentified source, reproduces a photograph of 'C' Company officers, which must, from those present, have been taken in late March/early April 1917. The accompanying text includes, 'The prototype of Osborne, Lt. Douglas ... Trotter (2nd Lt. Trenchard ... and ... Captain Godfrey Warre-Dymond, who bore more than a passing resemblance to Stanhope'.[10] This photograph is included as Plate 7 in this book. Furthermore, Warre-Dymond's 1955 obituaries in the *Regimental Journal*, and *The Times*[11] both refer to him 'having some claim to have been the original "Stanhope"'.

Godfrey Warre-Dymond, the apparent inspiration for Stanhope, was born in November 1890. He was educated at Marlborough and then Cambridge, where he was a distinguished sportsman, but left after two years without a degree. Commissioned in early 1915, he arrived in France on 28 August 1916 and joined 9/East Surrey on 1 September. With so many experienced officers lost on the Somme, he was in acting command of 'B' company from mid-September for two months. He was then given acting command of 'C' company from 10 March 1917, whilst Captain Hilton was at the Base. When Hilton returned, Warre-Dymond kept 'C' and Hilton had to go to 'D' as second in command instead!

As a company commander, it seems that Warre-Dymond was not simply effective, but positively inspirational. Sherriff refers to his 'magic'.[12] He rendered conspicuous service in the terrible conditions of early August 1917 at Ypres. He later distinguished himself in the gruelling days of March 1918, ending in the battalion's last stand. He won an MC. His citation says that, 'By his coolness and steadying influence on his men he kept his position intact after three determined enemy attempts to take it. Three days later he reorganised the left of his line under very heavy shell and machine-gun fire. He set a splendid disregard for danger to all ranks.'[13] He survived as a POW.

Warre-Dymond was Sherriff's immediate superior for much of the latter's service with the battalion. As an inspiring leader, a 'varsity man', and an athlete, he was just the sort of man to inspire hero-worship – including, quite possibly, in Sherriff himself.

The similarities between Warre-Dymond and Stanhope do not simply extend to the play of *Journey's End*. The novel that Sherriff had started to write in the early 1920s around the characters of Stanhope and Raleigh was very possibly inspired, in part, by Warre-Dymond's early post-war life, and also proved curiously prophetic. During the war, Warre-Dymond had been the courageous and inspirational leader, who had made a great reputation for himself. Sherriff had been the diligent, plodding officer, who had found it difficult to overcome his fear, and had done nothing to distinguish himself. Soon after the war, Warre-Dymond's wife divorced him. Through guaranteeing a loan for a friend who defaulted and through his own extravagance, he fell into the hands of moneylenders. His father then sacked him from the family auctioneering business. He was fined for being drunk in charge of a motor car. He was declared bankrupt in 1923, although he was able later to make composition with his creditors and have the order against him lifted.[14] By the time of his second divorce, in 1931, he was a commercial traveller.[15] Sherriff, on the other hand, after an initial return to frugal obscurity in insurance, in 1929 suddenly became an international celebrity and a man of means. The relative positions of Sherriff and Warre-Dymond were completely changed. The latter even used Sherriff as a referee in 1939 when seeking acceptance for the Officers Emergency Reserve. Whether or not Warre-Dymond resented the change in any way, as his fictional character did in Sherriff's unfinished novel, it is not known.

Archibald Douglass seems to have been the model for 'Uncle' Osborne in *Journey's End*. His nickname in the battalion was 'Father'. He was a clergyman's son and appears from the 1911 census to have been in electrical engineering. Enlisting in the Middlesex Regiment in December 1914, he was commissioned in July 1915. He arrived in France on 5 June 1916 and joined 9/East Surrey on 18 June, initially as signals officer. He was one of its few officers to survive the Somme. Sherriff recalled him as,

> a tall, dark man . . . one of the finest men I have ever known. He was a man of few words. He hated affectation and he hated vulgarity. He would sit for an hour or more at a Mess table, without saying a word, smoking cigarettes that dangled from his upper lip – leaning forward and occasionally chuckling to himself at something that amused him. He was also about the coolest man I ever saw in the trenches. Nothing seemed to make the slightest impression on him, and he did his job as if he were trying to make a silly game seem as if it were sensible in order to encourage the others.[16]

He was badly wounded, as a captain, with the battalion, in March 1918. He died of wounds on 8 April, aged 30 and is buried in Hanwell Cemetery, Middlesex.[17] Sherriff made some changes with his Osborne, who is older, more talkative, married with children and a schoolmaster. Percy High, born 1879, an officer in 'D' Company, was a friend to Sherriff and wrote to him as 'Youngster'. He was a schoolmaster and would seem to have contributed to the Osborne character. Sherriff described him as,

> a sturdy little man-about thirty five, I should think, although he was one of those whose age is difficult to judge. He had a deep, hoarse voice, a deep-lined, brown face, with two keen grey eyes peeping through the wrinkles.
>
> But, despite a certain abruptness of manner, I liked him instinctively from the first. He inspired confidence and his supply of shrewd common-sense was enormous. He was a good companion.[18]

Cecil Trenchard, the supposed model for Trotter, according to the SHC clipping, certainly looks in the photograph as Trotter is described! He was a stock agent, born in 1881, who had been living in Australia. He was commissioned in August 1915. (There is no indication that he had served first in the ranks.) His departure for France was delayed by an accident: he fell and broke his leg badly leaving the officers' mess. He arrived with 9/East Surrey on 16 March 1917. After four weeks, only, of active service, he was wounded on 12 April by a shell. He lost an eye, but served on in Britain. He and Sherriff served together again at Dover.[19]

As for Mason, the droll officers' cook, it would seem Sherriff based him on his own soldier servant, Morris (first name unknown) from Molesey. Sherriff mentions him and his sayings in his letters home. For example, writing to his father on 11 November 1916, 'My servant has just been reading the instructions of a box of veal which came up in Rations last night "Cut very thin an' place between sloices of noo bread with a lit'le tender lettuce & mayonnaise dressing' it'l be a bit hawkward about the lettuce." '[20]

There are good reasons, as discussed above, for accepting that certain men were models for specific characters in *Journey's End*. At the same time, the differences should be recognised, with Sherriff altering ages and marital status, in particular. Most notably he makes Stanhope much younger than Warre-Dymond and unmarried. It is Stanhope, not Osborne, who is the son of a clergyman.

For the characters of Raleigh and Hibbert, perhaps one should look first at aspects of Sherriff's own personality. I have previously referred to Sherriff's profound admiration for Warre-Dymond as his company commander. As for Hibbert, he is a man who finds it difficult to control his fear and suffers from neuralgia, although other aspects of his character are dissimilar to Sherriff's.

Whilst Sherriff was in Britain in March 1918 when the German offensive broke, his old battalion was near St Quentin, as in *Journey's End*. One company was near the front line – not Warre-Dymond's – with the rest in Reserve. Sherriff advised Clark that the raid in *Journey's End* was based on the battalion's raid in January 1917, at Hulluch, although he had not participated in it. That raid, moreover, was carefully planned and much more successful than the one in the play. The fictional raid is clearly futile, with the German offensive immediately imminent and the Germans expecting a raid.

There are a number of little features in *Journey's End* which were clearly drawn from Sherriff's experience with the battalion. For instance, he recalls when he first met Douglass he was drying a sock over a candle[21] – a scene he gave to Hardy in the play.

Following the success of his play, Sherriff produced a novel of the same name, with Vernon Bartlett, published in 1930. This opens with Stanhope and Raleigh becoming friends as boys, although three years apart in age. As the narrative moves on, it incorporates dialogue from the play. Like the play, it ends with Raleigh's death in the dugout and Stanhope going to face the German attack. The novel is interesting, has some good descriptive passages and clarifies some points in the play, but inevitably lacks the economy and dramatic impact of the play. From the novel it seems clear that the colonel is not based on any of 9/East Surrey's COs whom Sherriff served under. He is a country squire and Territorial officer, who finds it difficult to contest the orders for the raid with his regular Army superiors.[22]

Journey's End, the play, continues to be successfully revived, more than eighty years after it first appeared. It is not a simplistic anti-war play, as might be expected from its time, when unqualified disillusion with the First World War was coming into vogue. Instead, I think it has subtlety. It is about many things, including comradeship, fear, and duty. It also has its moments of humour. Sherriff's experience of what he wrote about and his fine ear for dialogue, shine through. Long may it continue to be performed.

Chapter 16

The Last of the 'Gallants'

With the extraordinary success of *Journey's End*, Sherriff had suddenly become the most famous veteran of 9/East Surrey. Now able to afford a university education at Oxford, he decided to become a schoolmaster, but found success instead as a scriptwriter, for Hollywood then Alexander Korda. He wrote scripts for *The Invisible Man* and many other films. Men from the East Surrey Regiment, then serving in the Sudan, participated in the filming of Korda's *Four Feathers*, scripted by Sherriff.

Walter Summers had also made his name in the film industry. He produced a series of films on battles of the First World War, including *Ypres* and *Mons*, as well as others films like *Bolibar* and *The Lost Patrol*, before moving on to more obviously commercial thrillers and 'whodunnits'.

Gilbert Frankau had gained celebrity as a writer, being one of the most widely read novelists in Britain between the wars. He also had political ambitions, with leanings towards the extreme right. He gained some notoriety for a 1933 article, 'As a Jew, I am not against Hitler' – a position he later repudiated.

Leonard Knight, who, like Summers, had served in the ranks of 9/East Surrey before being commissioned, became known as the writer of numerous novels of mystery and adventure.

Those officers who had stayed in the peacetime Army found promotion slow. However, 'Nobby' Clark reached brevet lieutenant colonel before his retirement in 1933 and Lechmere Thomas commanded 2/King's African Rifles from 1934.

Many men had endeavoured to stay in touch with comrades, dead and alive. Sherriff had made a trip to the battlefields in 1921. Clark was a member of the Ypres League, dedicated to remembrance of the sacrifices made in defence of Ypres, 1914–1918.

However, Hilton, Swanton, Tetley, all young men in 1914, and no doubt many others, had already died within fifteen years of the end of the war. In many cases, one assumes, their lives were shortened by their war service.

There was a thriving old comrades association. It was open to all ranks, although not all such bodies were. Annual reunion dinners were held from 1927 and well attended. For the 1937 reunion, the accounts show that of the £70 cost, nearly £20 was met by subscriptions, in order to keep the cost down to 5 shillings per head. Amongst the subscribers, donating from a shilling to a guinea, were many familiar names, including Sherriff, Clark, Frankau, High, Tew and Fenwick, former Lance Corporal Bertram Allam, MM, Pirie's medical orderly and former Private Edward

Wigg, MM. (The largest contribution was from former Private Allan Lopez). Even 5 shillings a head was clearly beyond some in 1937, and fifteen free tickets were provided, as were grants to assist men to join their old comrades. A total of 132 men attended, of the 350 'on the books', a number of whom lived overseas. Popular wartime music was played whilst the veterans ate, drank and reminisced. Amongst the messages read was one from General Gough, giving unstinted praise of the battalion's record when serving under him in March 1918. The final toast was to 'The Gallants' and 'When we drink to the "Gallants" let us remember with gratitude those very many and very gallant gentlemen of our old Battalion, both the dead and the living, who cannot be with us tonight.' The reunion dinners came to an end with the outbreak of a new war in 1939.[1]

Some veterans served in the Armed Forces in the Second World War. Lechmere Thomas fought at Dunkirk and rose to command brigades in Burma, being awarded a DSO and bar and a CBE, and becoming a major general. Godfrey Warre-Dymond served, as a major, in the Royal Army Ordnance Corps, which dealt with the supply and maintenance of munitions. Gilbert Frankau served in the RAF. Ewen Cameron did work on displaced persons for the United Nations Relief and Rehabilitation Administration at the end of the war.

On the Home Front, no doubt a good number of veterans joined the Home Guard. Too old for the Army, Clark went into Air Raid Precautions, becoming Chief Warden for Folkestone. Sherriff was discouraged when offering his services to his old regiment. During 1940–1941 he was in Hollywood, working on pro-British films like Korda's on Nelson and Lady Hamilton, a particular favourite of Winston Churchill's.

As the years passed, a steady stream of old soldiers went to join their dead comrades – Frankau in 1952, Warre-Dymond in 1955, Cameron in 1958. Billman died in 1967, in Foulden, Norfolk, his birth place. Clark passed on in 1971, aged 92 and Summers followed him in 1973.

After the war, Sherriff regained success as a playwright, as well as continued success as a scriptwriter for such productions as *The Dambusters*. His career was only ended by the changes of theatrical fashion brought by the 'Angry Young Men' of the late 1950s. In 1968 he had seen both his autobiography, *No Leading Lady* and his essay, 'The English Public Schools in the Great War', touching on his experiences at Passchendaele, published. Fifty years after the Armistice, he reflected on his service with 9/East Surrey with inevitably mixed feelings. 'There had been bad times in France but all in all it had been a magnificent, memorable experience.'[2] He had never married and when he died in 1975, he left considerable benefactions to charity.

Amongst the last survivors were Lechmere Thomas dying in 1981, aged 83, five years after being interviewed by Peter Liddle about his First World War experiences, and the former underage Private 'Syd' Hannan. 'Syd' joined with veterans from other units, as his old comrades passed on, and revisited the battlefields. He contributed some reminiscences to the regimental magazine in 1981 and died in 1993, aged 93, possibly the last of 'The Gallants'.

The East Surrey Regiment's memorial is at All Saints Church, Kingston upon Thames. The memorial to 24th Division is a striking one of three soldier figures in stone, in a modernist style. It is a 1924 work by Eric Kennington, soldier and official war artist. Rather than in France or Belgium, it is in Battersea Park, London. However, the division is commemorated in France by the 'Rue de la 24eme Division Britannique' at Le Verguier, where it fought so hard in March 1918, and it is also remembered on that village's war memorial.

If the dead could see their battlefields today, they would find most quite unrecognisable. The poisoned wilderness of the Ypres Salient has been replaced by a quiet landscape of green fields and woods, whilst Ypres itself was rebuilt to look as much as possible as it was in 1914. Lens has been rebuilt in a modern style and spread. The 'field of corpses' at Loos is crossed by a very busy road, and the nearby villages have been rebuilt, although many slag heaps remain. The battlefields of March 1918, already devastated in the German Retreat of 1917, were fought over again later in the year as the Allies advanced. The hamlet of Falvy, on the Somme, now a quiet and picturesque spot is, however, still worth a visit. Perhaps the least changed battlefield is Haussy, which had seen relatively little destruction when 9/East Surrey first saw it October 1918.

Many hundreds of men who died serving with 9/East Surrey lie in France and Belgium, and some both nearer and further afield, often in the beautifully maintained cemeteries of the Commonwealth War Graves Commission. Many, however, especially those of Loos, of Ypres and of March 1918, still have no known grave. May they all be remembered.

Roll of Honour

Surname	Christian Names	Rank	Serial No.	Fate	Date of Death
Ainge	William	Pte	9154	kia	26/9/15
Allcroft	Victor Harry	Pte	4132	kia	26/9/15
Allum	Edward James	Pte	2590	kia	26/9/15
Arnall	Percy	L/Cpl	2595	kia	26/9/15
Atkinson	William	Pte	6244	kia	26/9/15
Baker	George Arthur	Pte	2544	kia	26/9/15
Ballard	Ernest	Pte	2579	kia	26/9/15
Barham	Charles	Pte	2482	kia	26/9/15
Barnett	Arthur	Sgt	6008	kia	26/9/15
Barnett	Thomas George	L/Sgt	2181	kia	26/9/15
Barrett	Richard	Pte	676	kia	26/9/15
Barron	George Henry	Pte	6310	kia	26/9/15
Bartlett	Thomas Ernest	Pte	5806	kia	26/9/15
Batch	Clarence Cecil	Pte	8897	kia	26/9/15
Bate	Eric Raoul Hender	2/Lt	n/a	kia	26/9/15
Berry	Thomas Arthur	Pte	1708	kia	26/9/15
Blackett	Henry	Pte	8812	kia	26/9/15
Blair	Bert	Pte	1696	dow	26/9/15
Bourne	George	Pte	1310	kia	26/9/15
Brench	George William	L/Cpl	2562	kia	26/9/15
Buckenham	William John	Cpl	2512	kia	26/9/15
Bullock	Walter	Pte	6269	kia	26/9/15
Bundle	Frederick	Pte	2543	kia	26/9/15
Burch	Percy Harry	Pte	4206	kia	26/9/15
Burt	Thomas Jesse	L/Sgt	1637	kia	26/9/15
Callow	Leonard James	L/Cpl	4128	kia	26/9/15
Campbell	Alexander Charles Penn	Lt	n/a	kia	26/9/15
Chalcraft	Frank	Pte	2598	kia	26/9/15
Chapman	Henry	L/Cpl	4403	kia	26/9/15
Church	Thomas Stanley	Pte	1639	kia	26/9/15
Collean	Frederick Charles	Pte	6597	kia	26/9/15
Collinson	Arthur Amery	Capt	n/a	kia	26/9/15
Cook	Arthur George	Pte	1089	kia	26/9/15
Cooper	Frederick William	L/Cpl	2381	kia	26/9/15
Cooper	Harold Charles	L/Cpl	4299	kia	26/9/15
Courtnell	William George	Pte	2172	kia	26/9/15
Coutts	Norman Vawdrey	2/Lt	n/a	dow	26/9/15
Cullender	Henry	Pte	1501	kia	26/9/15
Culverhouse	Albert	Pte	2466	kia	26/9/15

Surname	Christian Names	Rank	Serial No.	Fate	Date of Death
Cunningham	Andrew	Pte	1722	kia	26/9/15
Curd	George Henry	Sgt	1193	kia	26/9/15
Curtis	Lionel Jack	Pte	2430	kia	26/9/15
Cutt	Edward	Pte	5765	kia	26/9/15
Davey	Arthur Ernest	L/Cpl	1472	kia	26/9/15
Dealtry	Herbert Arthur Berkeley	Capt	n/a	kia	26/9/15
Dean	Henry Douglas	Pte	4389	kia	26/9/15
Dickman	William	Pte	6609	kia	26/9/15
Dockrell	Robert Edward	Pte	8707	kia	26/9/15
Driscoll	John Patrick	Pte	8696	kia	26/9/15
Dudman	William John	Pte	1504	kia	26/9/15
Ellis	Samuel	Cpl	8843	d	26/9/15
Elverson	Ronald Whidborne	Lt	n/a	kia	26/9/15
Ely	Frank	Pte	2478	kia	26/9/15
Eyre	Henry	Sgt	1164	kia	26/9/15
Felton	Alfred William	L/Sgt	685	kia	26/9/15
Field	John	Pte	1773	kia	26/9/15
Fletcher	Edgar James	Pte	4163	kia	26/9/15
Fletcher	Percy George	Pte	4162	kia	26/9/15
Foster	Arthur Frederick	Pte	2507	kia	26/9/15
Fundell	Francis Theopplus (*sic*)	Pte	2535	kia	26/9/15
Gapper	William James	Pte	6844	kia	26/9/15
Gascoigne	Albert	Pte	1533	kia	26/9/15
Godley	Leonard	Pte	8940	kia	26/9/15
Goode	Alfred George	Pte	4281	kia	26/9/15
Gore	Albert Charles	L/Cpl	1429	kia	26/9/15
Gould	Percy John	Sgt	2493	kia	26/9/15
Govier	George	Pte	1425	kia	26/9/15
Gray	George James	Pte	6532	kia	26/9/15
Gray	Walter Edwin	Pte	2365	kia	26/9/15
Grayland	James	Pte	8832	kia	26/9/15
Greaney	Archibald	Pte	2290	kia	26/9/15
Guy	Harry	Pte	1163	kia	26/9/15
Harris	John Charles	Sgt	1854	kia	26/9/15
Hatcher	John Thomas	Sgt	785	kia	26/9/15
Hawker	Samuel	Pte	4173	kia	26/9/15
Haysom	Arthur Henry	Pte	8856	kia	26/9/15
Hitchcock	William George	L/Sgt	1791	kia	26/9/15
Hodges	Frederick	Pte	1441	kia	26/9/15
Holbey	George Henry	Pte	2326	kia	26/9/15
Holman	Herbert Robert	Pte	1790	kia	26/9/15
Ingarfill	Frank	Pte	8822	kia	26/9/15
Ingram	Albert	Pte	2358	kia	26/9/15
Jackson	Henry	CSM	957	kia	26/9/15
Jackson	Henry James	L/Cpl	819	kia	26/9/15
Jeal	Richard Albert Joseph	Cpl	1431	kia	26/9/15
Johnson	Frederick	Cpl	654	kia	26/9/15
Joiner	Charles William Edgerton	CSM	663	kia	26/9/15
Jones	William Douglas	Pte	9211	kia	26/9/15
King	Ernest	Pte	2068	kia	26/9/15

Surname	Christian Names	Rank	Serial No.	Fate	Date of Death
Lancaster	William Joseph	Pte	2267	kia	26/9/15
Lawson	Herbert	Cpl	2027	kia	26/9/15
Lewis	Henry George John	Pte	798	kia	26/9/15
Lewis	Victor Herbert	Pte	4365	kia	26/9/15
Lilver	Alfred	Pte	1603	kia	26/9/15
Lindsay	Leslie	Pte	2488	kia	26/9/15
Lloyd	Frank	Pte	8903	kia	26/9/15
McDonald	Patrick	Pte	4419	kia	26/9/15
Mackinney	George	Pte	2476	kia	26/9/15
Matthews	Frederick William	Pte	2541	kia	26/9/15
Mayrick	Reginald Thomas	Pte	6556	kia	26/9/15
Meadows	Ernest	Pte	2258	kia	26/9/15
Meek	Ernest John	Pte	1029	kia	26/9/15
Moorcock	William Albert	Pte	1823	kia	26/9/15
Moorey	Fred	Pte	2130	kia	26/9/15
Morton	Reginald	L/Cpl	2087	kia	26/9/15
Murphy	William Barry	Pte	893	kia	26/9/15
Murray	Kenneth Desmond	2/Lt	n/a	kia	26/9/15
Myall	Edwin	L/Sgt	10057	kia	26/9/15
New	William Alfred	Pte	8872	kia	26/9/15
Nightingale	Charles Albert	Pte	2473	kia	26/9/15
Noles	Henry Cattin	Pte	1596	kia	26/9/15
Norris	Walter	Pte	6009	kia	26/9/15
North	Ercildowne Wilton	Pte	6551	kia	26/9/15
Odgers	George William	Pte	820	kia	26/9/15
Osman	Ernest Edwin	Pte	4318	kia	26/9/15
Page	Alfred Edward	Pte	2584	kia	26/9/15
Peach	Reginald Bertie Jeremiah	Pte	1570	kia	26/9/15
Pescud	Percy	Pte	1779	kia	26/9/15
Peters	Alfred Bernard	L/Cpl	4298	kia	26/9/15
Pike	George	Pte	6585	kia	26/9/15
Plowman	Samuel	Sgt	4354	kia	26/9/15
Price	Alfed (*sic*) John	Pte	1552	kia	26/9/15
Ralph	Herbert Daniel	Pte	6314	kia	26/9/15
Randell	Harry Richard	Pte	4438	kia	26/9/15
Rice	Harold	Pte	6300	kia	26/9/15
Rich	Sidney	Pte	2269	kia	26/9/15
Risby	Charles Frederick	Pte	2529	kia	26/9/15
Russell	Edward	L/Cpl	6302	kia	26/9/15
Sales	Leonard	Pte	2026	kia	26/9/15
Sallabanks	William Frederick	Pte	6235	kia	26/9/15
Sanderson	Charles William	Sgt	1789	kia	26/9/15
Scoones	Alfred Walter	L/Cpl	4424	kia	26/9/15
Scott	Sydney	Pte	1550	kia	26/9/15
Selwood	William	Pte	2566	kia	26/9/15
Skiggs	Harry	Pte	6607	kia	26/9/15
Sleep	Harold Ernest	Pte	6252	kia	26/9/15
Slinger	Thomas	Pte	8825	kia	26/9/15
Smith	Charles	A/Sgt	1057	kia	26/9/15
Smith	Charles	Sgt	1705	kia	26/9/15

Surname	Christian Names	Rank	Serial No.	Fate	Date of Death
Smith	Herbert	Pte	6253	kia	26/9/15
Smith	Percy Frederick	Pte	9115	kia	26/9/15
Smith	William James	Pte	1471	kia	26/9/15
Spicer	James	Cpl	6557	kia	26/9/15
Stafford	Henry	Pte	1538	kia	26/9/15
Stanbridge	Henry Charles	Pte	2517	kia	26/9/15
Stevens	Walter Sydney	Pte	2316	kia	26/9/15
Stockdale	Frank	Pte	1678	kia	26/9/15
Sullivan	Ernest	Pte	4320	kia	26/9/15
Taylor	George Francis	Pte	2490	kia	26/9/15
Tester	Francis Joseph	Pte	9210	kia	26/9/15
Thompson	George	Pte	4242	kia	26/9/15
Tidey	Frank Edwin	Pte	2142	kia	26/9/15
Tinson	George Victor	Pte	2377	kia	26/9/15
Toft	Mark	Pte	1517	kia	26/9/15
Vidler	Herbert	Pte	496	kia	26/9/15
Walsh	Thomas	Pte	1315	kia	26/9/15
Weatherley	Frederick	Pte	1677	kia	26/9/15
Westbury	Frederick	Pte	6598	kia	26/9/15
Wickens	Henry Percy	Pte	4334	kia	26/9/15
Wilson	Archibald	L/Cpl	2483	kia	26/9/15
Wingrove	George Arthur	Pte	8827	kia	26/9/15
York	John Arthur	Pte	8834	kia	26/9/15
Downer	Frederick Charles	Pte	800	d	28/9/15
Comment: Prob. POW, buried Douai					
Light	Charles Richard	Pte	6538	d	30/9/15
Comment: Prob. POW, buried Carvin					
Barnett	Charles Edward	Capt	n/a	dow	1/10/15
Moore	George Ernest	Pte	4208	dow	3/10/15
Welch	Howard Vyse	Major	n/a	d	4/10/15
Comment: POW, buried Carvin					
Young	Frederick Joseph	Pte	4127	dow	4/10/15
Taylor	Harry James	Pte	6545	kia	7/10/15
Jolly	William John	Pte	6547	dow	9/10/15
Vear	James Victor	L/Cpl	805	d	9/10/15
Comment: POW, buried Cologne					
Richards	Arthur Joseph	L/Cpl	1428	d	20/10/15
Comment: POW, buried Douai					
Barnett	Harold Thornton	Lt	n/a	dow	21/10/15
Hoare	Eric	Pte	4159	dow	21/10/15
Plumb	Albert Victor	Pte	8057	kia	21/10/15
Goby	Horace	L/Cpl	2449	dow	22/10/15
Cooper	Herbert	Pte	2620	kia	2/11/15
Langford	Alfred	Pte	824	d	5/11/15
Britts	Charles William Gordon	2/Lt	n/a	d	6/11/15
Comment: Killed in accident					
Childs	William Frederick	Sgt	655	d	6/11/15
Comment: Killed in accident					
Baker	Charles	Pte	1721	kia	7/11/15
Morgan	Ernest	Pte	2680	dow	10/11/15

Surname	Christian Names	Rank	Serial No.	Fate	Date of Death
Seager	Albert Henry	Pte	5817	dow	20/11/15
Hernage	Harold Edward	Pte	8901	kia	7/1/16
Hill	Thomas	L/Sgt	4494	kia	7/1/16
Burch	Albert	Pte	1505	kia	9/1/16
Humphrey	William Joseph	Sgt	529	dow	10/1/16
Ingram	Arthur	Pte	4729	kia	11/1/16
Smith	Harold Arthur	Pte	8394	kia	11/1/16
Dalliday	George	Pte	8294	kia	12/1/16
Snook	Walter	Pte	4032	dow	13/1/16
McDonald	James	A/Cpl	1305	kia	20/1/16
Carter	Walter Thomas	Pte	8139	kia	26/1/16
Marchant	Richard Henry	2/Lt	n/a	kia	26/1/16
Handford	Frederick Stanley	2/Lt	n/a	kia	27/1/16
Masters	Leonard	Sgt	8339	kia	27/1/16
England	William George	Pte	2120	kia	28/1/16
Stevens	Thomas	L/Cpl	8383	kia	28/1/16
Vinall	Albert	Pte	8045	d	3/2/16
Pettifer	Arthur	Pte	6299	kia	5/2/16
Townsend	Joseph	Pte	1966	dow	7/2/16
Butler	Charles	Pte	2271	kia	22/2/16
Chimes	Douglas Percy	Pte	3137	kia	22/2/16
Jennings	Charles	Pte	7133	kia	25/2/16
Lovegrove	Bert	Pte	3012	kia	25/2/16
Hibbins	Fred	Pte	3109	dow	26/2/16
Brian	Ernest James	Pte	7165	dow	1/3/16
Bassett	James George	L/Cpl	6291	kia	2/3/16
Green	Henry Thomas	Pte	4395	kia	2/3/16
Judd	Henry Richard	Pte	4731	dow	2/3/16
King	Frederick Henry	Pte	3611	kia	2/3/16
Spiers	John	Sgt	2503	kia	2/3/16
Wareham	Charles Henry	Pte	4536	kia	2/3/16
Wells	Horace	Pte	3025	dow	2/3/16
Hutchison	George	Pte	8320	dow	5/3/16
Owen	John Edward	Pte	2427	d	9/3/16
Handley	George	L/Sgt	2657	dow	11/3/16
Brown	Henry William	Pte	3095	dow	16/3/16
Hawkins	Roland Arthur	Pte	4519	kia	17/3/16
Hancock	George Thomas	Pte	8194	d	23/3/16
Schooling	Peter Holt	2/Lt	n/a	dow	30/3/16
Aveling	John William	Pte	8248	dow	31/3/16
Gibson	Joseph	Pte	4407	kia	31/3/16
Broad	Alfred	Pte	6270	kia	1/4/16
Evans	Albert	Pte	2774	kia	1/4/16
Rushbridge	Charles	Pte	1785	kia	1/4/16
Desmond	Frank	Pte	8192	dow	2/4/16
Rabey	Henry	Sgt	749	d	3/4/16
Proudman	William Charles	Pte	2705	kia	11/4/16
Willats	Frederick Claude	Pte	4558	kia	12/4/16
Payne	John	Pte	395	kia	13/4/16

Surname	Christian Names	Rank	Serial No.	Fate	Date of Death
Birt	Wilfred Beckett	Capt	n/a	d	18/4/16
Comment: POW, buried Cologne					
Edwards	George Henry Arthur	Pte	2452	kia	21/4/16
Howell	Wilfred Symonds	2/Lt	n/a	kia	25/4/16
Puttock	Leonard	Pte	2134	d	25/4/16
Garton	Nelson Leonard	Pte	4562	kia	30/4/16
Hall	Ernest Richard	Cpl	2047	kia	2/5/16
Page	William Henry	Pte	8167	kia	2/5/16
Groves	Ernest Sidney	Pte	6401	kia	10/5/16
Hall	Ernest William	Pte	4412	kia	14/5/16
Daley	Patrick	Pte	9206	dow	16/5/16
Day	Edgar	Pte	2402	kia	16/5/16
Huck	Thomas	Pte	14697	kia	17/5/16
Legood	Albert	Pte	3568	dow	17/5/16
Tremeer	William	Pte	8560	kia	27/5/16
Wyatt	Clifford Charles	Pte	964	kia	27/5/16
Stait	Albert	Pte	707	d	13/6/16
Prestage	Alfed (*sic*) Thomas	Pte	5498	dow	14/6/16
Pescud	Albert Charles	Pte	16205	dow	16/6/16
Ling	Jacob	Pte	5254	kia	17/6/16
Luckett	Reuben	Pte	17343	dow	17/6/16
Pursey	William John	Pte	15910	kia	19/6/16
Tromans	Captain	Pte	1185	kia	21/6/16
Hall	Charles	Pte	14476	dow	22/6/16
Browning	William	Pte	9035	kia	23/6/16
Gresty	William	Pte	6412	kia	23/6/16
Ladd	William	RSM	963	kia	23/6/16
Youngman	John Marshall	Lt	n/a	kia	23/6/16
Comment: MC					
Sims	William	L/Cpl	4748	dow	25/6/16
Vincent	Henry Victor	Pte	794	kia	28/6/16
Harding	Thomas	Pte	8422	dow	30/6/16
Crawford	William	Pte	3136	kia	1/7/16
Cheatle	George Ernest	Pte	8280	dow	3/7/16
Claydon	Stanley Alan	Pte	2114	dow	3/7/16
Doughty	John	Pte	17755	kia	14/7/16
Goodwin	Horace William	L/Cpl	2651	kia	14/7/16
Stanley	Frederick Edward	Pte	4392	kia	14/7/16
Steele	Rollo Peter	Pte	17657	kia	14/7/16
Wadds	William James	Pte	17774	kia	14/7/16
Hadenham	Lawrence George	2/Lt	n/a	dow	18/7/16
Barnett	William	Pte	17776	dow	31/7/16
Clarke	Albert Harry	Pte	15867	dow	6/8/16
McAuliffe	William	Pte	6464	kia	6/8/16
Porter	Harry	Pte	19162	kia	7/8/16
Dowling	Henry	Pte	8241	kia	11/8/16
Noble	George	Pte	1686	kia	11/8/16
Smith	George	Pte	11828	kia	11/8/16
Varnham	Sinclair Arthur	Pte	18263	kia	11/8/16
Martin	Albert	Pte	1514	kia	12/8/16

Surname	Christian Names	Rank	Serial No.	Fate	Date of Death
Potts	Horace Henry	Pte	1602	kia	12/8/16
Stainer	Alfred Ernest	Pte	17371	dow	13/8/16
Tanner	Robert William	Pte	17369	kia	13/8/16
Barrett	Walter Edwin	Sgt	642	dow	15/8/16
Anning	Joseph	Pte	8916	kia	16/8/16
Ardouin	George	Pte	8193	kia	16/8/16
Baker	Reginald William	Sgt	2140	kia	16/8/16
Ball	Frank Granville	2/Lt	n/a	kia	16/8/16
Beadle	William	Pte	4125	kia	16/8/16
Berry	John	Pte	4175	kia	16/8/16
Bolton	Nicholas	Pte	15975	kia	16/8/16
Breewood	Thomas	Pte	8866	kia	16/8/16
Brewer	Herbert Alfred	L/Cpl	4359	kia	16/8/16
Brigden	William	Pte	2919	kia	16/8/16
Came	Bertram Claude	Pte	16236	kia	16/8/16
Caseley	John Thomas	Cpl	6648	kia	16/8/16
Cassidy	Herbert Sidney	L/Cpl	2763	kia	16/8/16
Clarke	Herbert	Pte	13817	kia	16/8/16
Collins	Charles William	Pte	1939	kia	16/8/16
Cumbers	Arthur	Cpl	8137	kia	16/8/16
Currier	Samuel Charles	Pte	2289	dow	16/8/16
Dale	Samuel	Pte	9558	kia	16/8/16
Dalton	Thomas Edmund Patrick	Pte	4567	kia	16/8/16
Dickason	Edward	Pte	7187	kia	16/8/16
Dowding	Lionel	Pte	8208	kia	16/8/16
Frost	John Albert William	Pte	1296	kia	16/8/16
Game	Herbert Charles	Pte	1040	kia	16/8/16
Gerrish	Thomas Charles	Sgt	8303	kia	16/8/16
Gill	Francis William	L/Cpl	2793	kia	16/8/16
Graves	David Herbert	Cpl	4007	kia	16/8/16
Halliday	Francis	Cpl	2487	dow	16/8/16
Comment: MM					
Hawkins	Albert	Pte	3524	kia	16/8/16
Hill	Frederick	Pte	1816	kia	16/8/16
Hooper	Edward Ernest	Pte	1484	kia	16/8/16
Horton	James	Pte	1748	kia	16/8/16
Jenner	George Ivan	Pte	4192	kia	16/8/16
Jewson	Frederick	Pte	8324	kia	16/8/16
Comment: DCM					
Lawrence	Joseph Reginald Mark	2/Lt	n/a	kia	16/8/16
Matheson	Homer Lindsay	2/Lt	n/a	kia	16/8/16
Newman	Albert Victor	L/Cpl	8855	kia	16/8/16
Nowland	Arthur	Pte	8851	kia	16/8/16
O'Brien	Francis Pat	2/Lt	n/a	kia	16/8/16
Parker	James	Pte	1833	kia	16/8/16
Pease	Percy Henry	Pte	2486	kia	16/8/16
Pocknee	Frederick	Pte	4741	kia	16/8/16
Porter	Frederick Charles	L/Cpl	2446	kia	16/8/16
Priddy	Victor Herbert	Pte	18121	kia	16/8/16
Rapley	Walter	Pte	6674	kia	16/8/16

Surname	Christian Names	Rank	Serial No.	Fate	Date of Death
Sadler	Walter Alfred	Pte	7266	kia	16/8/16
Scott	Walter Frederick	Pte	4030	kia	16/8/16
Smith	Alfred	Pte	8571	kia	16/8/16
Solly	Ernest	Pte	4423	kia	16/8/16
Southgate	James	Pte	953	kia	16/8/16
Stone	Alfred Ernest	Sgt	4589	kia	16/8/16
Tanner	William Ernest	Pte	4751	kia	16/8/16
Taylor	Frank Edwin	Pte	2237	kia	16/8/16
Thomas	James	Pte	9053	kia	16/8/16
Vaughan	John Lindhurst	Capt	n/a	kia	16/8/16
Viner	Albert Victor George	Pte	4154	kia	16/8/16
Warner	Thomas Henry	Pte	17470	kia	16/8/16
Wiggins	William Thomas	Pte	5800	kia	16/8/16
Williamson	Harold Angus	Pte	18163	kia	16/8/16
Willis	Frederick	L/Cpl	3127	kia	16/8/16
Yeoman	Roland Sounes	L/Cpl	18118	kia	16/8/16
Bowler	Leonard	Pte	17346	kia	17/8/16
Martin	Alfred William	Pte	6230	dow	17/8/16
Walker	William Thomas	Pte	17372	kia	17/8/16
Cuthbert	Charles Louttit	2/Lt	n/a	dow	18/8/16
Sharp	Albert Victor	Pte	23434	d	18/8/16
Metcalfe	Wilfred Charles	Lt	n/a	dow	19/8/16
Page	Arthur	Pte	5751	kia	19/8/16
Barnes	Charles Henry	Pte	4700	kia	21/8/16
Bennison	Victor Humphrey	L/Cpl	4439	kia	21/8/16
Lloyd	Charles Edward	Pte	9308	kia	21/8/16
Mayland	Victor James	Pte	1895	kia	21/8/16
Rivers	George Claude	2/Lt	n/a	kia	21/8/16
Spurling	Henry Stephen	2/Lt	n/a	dow	21/8/16
Wernham	George	L/Cpl	784	dow	21/8/16
Govier	Ben Ernest	Pte	1424	kia	22/8/16
Winfield	Frederick Alfred	Pte	4758	dow	22/8/16
Arbourne	Arthur Frederick	Pte	18045	dow	23/8/16
Francis	Albert Edward	Pte	16234	dow	23/8/16
Brooks	Walter	Pte	20630	kia	24/8/16
Haley	Arthur	Cpl	1858	dow	25/8/16
O'Connell	Frank	Pte	985	dow	25/8/16
Comment: DCM					
Baines	Edward Henry	Pte	690	kia	26/8/16
Howes	Frank Harold	Pte	8686	dow	28/8/16
Fewell	George Lynn	Pte	9032	dow	29/8/16
Potter	Alfred John	Pte	18112	dow	30/8/16
Boston	Henry Frederick	Pte	7135	kia	1/9/16
Clipson	Leonard Drage	Pte	22940	kia	1/9/16
Coles	Percy James	Pte	4445	kia	1/9/16
Ward	Frederick	Pte	17692	kia	1/9/16
Budgen	William	Pte	2515	kia	2/9/16
Gregory	Herbert	Pte	8058	dow	2/9/16
Shaw	William Alfred	L/Cpl	5531	kia	2/9/16
South	George	Pte	8395	kia	2/9/16

Surname	Christian Names	Rank	Serial No.	Fate	Date of Death
Stevens	Herbert	L/Cpl	15992	kia	2/9/16
Bailey	George	Pte	7081	kia	3/9/16
Beasley	William James Henry	Pte	6537	kia	3/9/16
Boston	Charles	Cpl	2922	kia	3/9/16
Burke	Augustin	Pte	6703	dow	3/9/16
Clarke	Frank	Pte	2526	kia	3/9/16
Coombes	Harry	A/Cpl	8197	kia	3/9/16
Copus	William Henry	Pte	2764	kia	3/9/16
Coxhill	William Henry	Pte	9152	kia	3/9/16
Elsey	Alfred William	Pte	1084	kia	3/9/16
Faulkner	William Ernest	Pte	9078	kia	3/9/16
Friday	Edward	Cpl	2043	kia	3/9/16
Haines	Ernest Andrade	2/Lt	n/a	kia	3/9/16
Hammond	Charles Nathan	Pte	1017	kia	3/9/16
Hartley	Richard	Pte	1901	kia	3/9/16
Hayes	John	Pte	4156	kia	3/9/16
Hine	Frederick	L/Cpl	2014	kia	3/9/16
Hornett	William Robert	Pte	6086	kia	3/9/16
Hull	Albert Edward	Pte	1433	kia	3/9/16
Ingrams	Frank Ridley	2/Lt	n/a	kia	3/9/16
Joyce	William	Pte	2166	kia	3/9/16
Kelly	James	Pte	11761	kia	3/9/16
Kirk	John Richard	Pte	6733	kia	3/9/16
Lange	Reginald Stuart	L/Cpl	17505	kia	3/9/16
Ling	Charles	Pte	961	kia	3/9/16
Macro	William James	Pte	17963	kia	3/9/16
Pearce	Frank	Cpl	1900	kia	3/9/16
Pitman	Alfred James	Pte	16208	kia	3/9/16
Price	Thomas Frederick	Pte	6671	kia	3/9/16
Radford	Tom	Pte	8813	kia	3/9/16
Robinson	George William	Pte	18175	kia	3/9/16
Robinson	Jacob	Sgt	28104	kia	3/9/16
Rogers	Charles Ellis	Pte	8144	kia	3/9/16
Saunders	William	Pte	2293	kia	3/9/16
Smith	Henry	Pte	8225	kia	3/9/16
Speed	James	Pte	4425	kia	3/9/16
Stannard	Arthur George	Pte	14829	kia	3/9/16
Stannard	William	Pte	2031	kia	3/9/16
Urban	Oscar Arthur	2/Lt	n/a	kia	3/9/16
Webb	Frederick	Pte	5105	kia	3/9/16
Wheeler	Astley Peregrine	Pte	8667	kia	3/9/16
White	Ernest	Pte	1436	kia	3/9/16
White	Walter William	CSM	812	kia	3/9/16
Comment: MM					
Willis	Walter Henry	Pte	6242	kia	3/9/16
Wood	Leslie	Pte	5557	kia	3/9/16
Wright	William Walter	Pte	1727	kia	3/9/16
Young	George	Pte	1398	dow	3/9/16
Bettell	George	Pte	1413	dow	4/9/16
Bridger	Ernest Edwin	Pte	17342	kia	4/9/16

Surname	Christian Names	Rank	Serial No.	Fate	Date of Death
Coleman	Reginald Herbert	Pte	17314	kia	4/9/16
Manning	Charles James	Pte	5746	dow	4/9/16
Kenward	Arthur	Pte	4200	kia	5/9/16
Nutkins	William Henry Robert	Pte	17780	kia	6/9/16
Spooner	William	Pte	951	dow	7/9/16
Wye	Frederick William	Pte	1262	dow	7/9/16
Wilkinson	Harry Herbert	Pte	3087	dow	9/9/16
Matthews	Alfred Apsley	2/Lt	n/a	dow	12/9/16
Riley	William Benjamin	A/Cpl	8700	kia	16/9/16
Spray	William	L/Cpl	1843	kia	16/9/16
Palmer	Alfred John	Pte	11877	dow	17/9/16
Scott	Henry	Pte	12614	kia	25/9/16
Mutton	Henry William	L/Cpl	865	kia	26/9/16
Jones	Howard Archibald	Pte	25054	dow	6/10/16

Comment: Formerly 23597 Royal Fusiliers

Surname	Christian Names	Rank	Serial No.	Fate	Date of Death
O'Connell	Jeremiah	Pte	9025	kia	6/10/16
Henry	Thomas	Pte	28107	dow	11/10/16
Chapman	John Victor	Pte	17883	kia	14/10/16
Dodson	Albert Edward	L/Cpl	8894	kia	14/10/16
Hunt	John Henry	Pte	5447	dow	14/10/16
Lamb	Ingram Cleasby	Pte	25035	kia	14/10/16
Wells	Eric John	Pte	644	kia	17/10/16
Gilbert	Thomas	Pte	8859	kia	2/11/16
Launder	Henry Newton	Pte	25043	kia	2/11/16
Tyrell	Frank Cecil	Pte	25044	kia	2/11/16

Comment: Formerly 23568 Royal Fusiliers

Surname	Christian Names	Rank	Serial No.	Fate	Date of Death
Nedd	William	Pte	20620	kia	6/11/16
Cark	Alfred	Pte	8281	kia	8/11/16
Lambert	Robert Ernest	Pte	1598	kia	15/11/16
Farrow	Herbert Sands	Cpl	25074	d	21/11/16
Meecham	Joseph	Pte	7197	kia	10/12/16
Mack	William Herbert	Pte	17345	d	15/12/16
Cairns	Robert	Pte	22714	kia	22/12/16
Herhing	Rudolf Fritz	Pte	21534	kia	23/12/16
Clements	Henry Herbert	Pte	18164	kia	24/12/16
Hart	Charles Theodore	Pte	21568	kia	24/12/16
Marks	Patrick Stuart	Pte	20978	kia	24/12/16
Parsons	Stanley James	Sgt	8213	kia	24/12/16
Reynolds	Ernest Frederick	Pte	25046	dow	24/12/16
Murfin	William	Pte	2690	kia	26/12/16
Martin	Charles	Pte	10929	kia	30/12/16
Billings	Ernest	Pte	10817	kia	1/1/17
Chenery	Henry Herbert	L/Sgt	5200	kia	1/1/17
Dutton	Harry Edgar	Pte	25042	dow	1/1/17
Larkinson	Albert Gazeley	Pte	17904	kia	1/1/17
Mortimer	William Francis	Pte	20884	kia	1/1/17
Keeble	Robert	Pte	23498	kia	2/1/17
Searles	William Joseph Seymour	Pte	18168	dow	4/1/17
Elliott	Bertie George	Pte	22773	dow	7/1/17
Williamson	John	Pte	6720	kia	12/1/17

Surname	Christian Names	Rank	Serial No.	Fate	Date of Death
Bear	Joseph Turner	Pte	23896	dow	13/1/17
Russell	Benjamin	Pte	23727	dow	13/1/17
Trench	Nugent Chas. Le Poer	2/Lt	n/a	kia	16/1/17
Dorking	Charles Victor	Cpl	25003	kia	17/1/17
Loveridge	Matthew	Pte	23920	kia	22/1/17
Donnelly	Albert	Pte	8101	kia	25/1/17
Lacey	Frank	Pte	8336	kia	25/1/17
Moore	Alfred	Pte	11078	kia	25/1/17
Brown	Walter Frederick	Pte	16200	dow	2/2/17
Wood	Ernest	Pte	4037	kia	7/2/17
Carter	John	Pte	2616	dow	9/2/17
Foot	William Douglas	Sgt	8301	kia	9/2/17
Wilson	Frederick	Pte	3204	dow	10/2/17
Clements	Ernest	L/Cpl	32282	kia	15/3/17
Comment: Formerly 1485 Royal Fusiliers					
Reynolds	Herbert Lewis	Pte	24891	kia	18/3/17
Smith	Stanley	Pte	30039	kia	18/3/17
Woodall	William John	Pte	2439	kia	18/3/17
Benham	Fred Cyril	Pte	22291	dow	19/3/17
Enever	Thomas	Pte	24892	kia	10/4/17
Rees	William	Pte	21885	kia	10/4/17
Ramsden	Richard Charles	Pte	21898	dow	14/4/17
Harris	Thomas	L/Sgt	830	kia	17/4/17
Comment: MM					
Hollins	Henry James	A/Sgt	319	kia	17/4/17
Kiver	Herbert William	2/Lt	n/a	kia	17/4/17
Starkey	Frederick Henry	Pte	19403	kia	17/4/17
Harris	Charles Frederick	Pte	1853	dow	3/5/17
Miles	Charles	Pte	32346	kia	3/5/17
Comment: Formerly 2475 Middlesex Regt					
Munro	Walter	Pte	18963	kia	3/5/17
Kirby	Harold	Pte	23518	dow	6/5/17
Hardy	William Charles	Pte	25019	kia	8/5/17
Comment: Formerly 2497 Royal Fusiliers					
Callaway	Henry	Pte	10735	dow	19/5/17
Sexton	Thomas William	Pte	4556	dow	20/5/17
Hunt	George Kino	Pte	5785	kia	21/5/17
Scowen	Robert	Pte	25045	dow	23/5/17
Comment: Formerly 23569 Royal Fusiliers					
Dickson	Frank Ernest	L/Cpl	20963	dow	4/6/17
Clarke	Albert	Pte	32317	dow	5/6/17
Comment: Formerly 13192 Queen's Royal Regt					
Bish	Edward	Pte	5762	dow	11/6/17
Hatherall	Albert Edward	Sgt	652	d	11/6/17
Hodges	Charles Francis	L/Cpl	1988	kia	11/6/17
Simmons	Leonard	Pte	7211	dow	11/6/17
Thorpe	Herbert John	Pte	22543	kia	11/6/17
Turner	Edward	L/Cpl	1328	kia	11/6/17
Haddon	John	Pte	32281	kia	12/6/17
Pett	Thomas William	Pte	20865	kia	12/6/17

Surname	Christian Names	Rank	Serial No.	Fate	Date of Death
Adams	William Charles	Pte	8217	kia	13/6/17
Baldwin	John Frederick	Pte	212	kia	13/6/17
Beasley	Charles Peter	L/Cpl	1444	kia	13/6/17
Cook	Ernest	Pte	21793	kia	13/6/17
Evans	Edward	Pte	15990	kia	13/6/17
Finch	Frank	Pte	22377	kia	13/6/17
Fitchett	Sidney James	Pte	17365	kia	13/6/17
Gillman	Richard Joseph	Cpl	8591	kia	13/6/17
Herring	Thomas John	Pte	1767	kia	13/6/17
Holder	Henry	Pte	20597	kia	13/6/17
Hollingshead	Frederick	Pte	30643	kia	13/6/17
Martin	Sydney Robert	L/Cpl	7084	kia	13/6/17
Plested	Fred	Pte	9412	kia	13/6/17
Potton	Herbert Wilson	Pte	33191	kia	13/6/17
Prior	George	Pte	11777	kia	13/6/17
Pursey	Albert Harry	Pte	12807	kia	13/6/17
Rogers	Ernest James	Pte	24931	kia	13/6/17
Wimble	Arthur	Pte	24960	kia	13/6/17
Daniels	Fredrick Herbert	Pte	11521	kia	15/6/17
Daniels	Jesse Walter	Pte	2525	kia	15/6/17
Edwards	George	Pte	14415	kia	15/6/17
Hyland	George	L/Sgt	9518	dow	15/6/17
McCormack	David	Pte	10148	kia	15/6/17
Morgan	John	Cpl	4186	kia	15/6/17
O'Brien	Daniel	Pte	21998	kia	15/6/17
Roper	William	L/Cpl	8178	kia	15/6/17
Taylor	George	Pte	18023	kia	15/6/17
Forster	William Hinton	Sgt	8706	dow	16/6/17
Hybart	John	Pte	25030	kia	16/6/17
Croucher	Albert	Pte	10789	kia	17/6/17
Burton	William Thomas	Pte	2341	dow	18/6/17
Cattell	Richard	Cpl	8074	dow	18/6/17
Weed	James Thomas	Pte	8135	dow	18/6/17
Driver	Percy William	Pte	21533	dow	23/6/17
Acca	Albert Edward	Pte	24072	kia	24/6/17
Barnard	Arthur	Pte	33472	kia	24/6/17
Cruickshank	Alexander	Sgt	7385	kia	24/6/17
Jennings	Charles Henry	Pte	32293	kia	24/6/17
Jennings	Walter Charles	Pte	6409	kia	24/6/17
Knight	Stanley Horace	Pte	17570	kia	24/6/17
Cadenaci	Frederick Charles	Sgt	2327	dow	27/6/17
Newson	John William	Pte	25092	kia	27/6/17
Comment: Formerly 34758 Royal Fusiliers					
Postlethwaite	Harold	L/Cpl	32322	kia	27/6/17
Comment: Formerly 36368 Royal Fusiliers					
Phillips	Edgar Samuel	Pte	33506	d	11/7/17
Bogue	Patrick Yule	2/Lt	n/a	kia	23/7/17
Duck	Fredrick James	Pte	25075	kia	23/7/17
Picton	James Allanson	Lt	n/a	kia	23/7/17
Comment: MC					

Surname	Christian Names	Rank	Serial No.	Fate	Date of Death
Wheeler	Richard	Pte	9590	kia	24/7/17
Buss	William	Pte	24702	dow	25/7/17
Wilkins	Victor John	Cpl	8407	kia	31/7/17
Atkinson	John Ireson	Pte	33043	kia	2/8/17
Barker	Edward James	Sgt	2923	kia	2/8/17
Carter	Charles Sydney	Pte	33601	kia	2/8/17
Ellwood	Raymond Goodman	Pte	17855	dow	2/8/17
Griffiths	Ethelbert George	Pte	30040	kia	2/8/17
Hills	Alfred	Pte	13437	kia	2/8/17
Mead	James Joseph	Pte	8348	kia	2/8/17
Trunfull	Richard Charles	Pte	21540	kia	2/8/17
Ward	William Clement	Pte	204315	kia	2/8/17
Comment: Formerly 4981 Durham Light Infantry					
Wood	William Alfred	Pte	19312	kia	2/8/17
Barber	William Ernest	Cpl	2435	kia	3/8/17
Bassett	Albert Edward	Pte	21108	kia	3/8/17
Bell	Alfred	Pte	3148	dow	3/8/17
Fox	Richard William	Pte	21073	kia	3/8/17
Fry	Henry William George	Pte	31824	kia	3/8/17
Hammond	William Francis	Pte	22976	kia	3/8/17
Hyde	Thomas Frederick Allison	Pte	25086	kia	3/8/17
Comment: Formerly 23585 Royal Fusiliers					
Lines	Ernest	Pte	33651	kia	3/8/17
Rose	Alfred	Pte	204326	kia	3/8/17
Comment: Formerly 276754 Durham Light Infantry					
Sadler	William Douglas	2/Lt	n/a	dow	3/8/17
Smith	James Henry	L/Sgt	9052	kia	3/8/17
Spoor	Thomas William	Sgt	204319	kia	3/8/17
Comment: Formerly 3710 Durham Light Infantry (medal card has Spoors and DLI no. 276015)					
Talman	James	Pte	25064	kia	3/8/17
Whitehorn	George	Pte	204311	kia	3/8/17
Burgess	Leonard Reginald	Pte	24749	dow	4/8/17
Hopkins	John	Pte	24912	kia	4/8/17
Menzal	Carl Frederick	Sgt	1757	dow	4/8/17
Chapman	Edward	Pte	23175	kia	5/8/17
Collins	John William	Pte	33644	kia	5/8/17
Cornwell	George	Pte	4610	kia	5/8/17
de la Fontaine	Henry Victor Mottet	Lt Col	n/a	kia	5/8/17
Comment: DSO					
Garratt	Joseph	Pte	24930	kia	5/8/17
Gibson	William Harold	Pte	20833	kia	5/8/17
Hopkins	Alfred James	Pte	827	kia	5/8/17
Lambert	Philip John	Pte	30654	kia	5/8/17
Martin	Harry Andrew	Pte	21527	kia	5/8/17
Reed	William Henry	Pte	33606	dow	5/8/17
Smith	James Henry	Pte	11783	kia	5/8/17
Sulley	George	Pte	25950	kia	5/8/17
Comment: Formerly 70579 Durham Light Infantry					
Valante	Galato	Pte	30283	kia	5/8/17

Surname	Christian Names	Rank	Serial No.	Fate	Date of Death
Watkins	James Henry	Sgt	10234	kia	5/8/17
Comment: Formerly 18951 Hussars of the Line					
Watkins	Joseph Stanley	Pte	17418	kia	5/8/17
Dean	Robert James	Pte	24368	dow	6/8/17
Tanner	John	CSM	187	dow	6/8/17
Grant	Hubert Brasier	Pte	31810	kia	7/8/17
Glazebrook	Leonard Charles	Pte	2434	dow	8/8/17
Hyder	Sydney Albert	Pte	19209	d	8/8/17
Bramley	Sidney	L/Cpl	32329	dow	9/8/17
Comment: Formerly 12859 Royal W Kent Regt					
Hopkins	Joseph William	Pte	203508	dow	9/8/17
Birch	Charles Richard Eli	Lt and QM	n/a	d	12/8/17
Comment: Pneumonia					
Allsop	Frederick	L/Cpl	8109	kia	15/8/17
Coe	Sidney	Pte	21595	dow	16/8/17
Comment: Formerly 4377 APC					
Downing	William	Pte	19155	dow	16/8/17
Fairbrass	George Thomas	Pte	23429	kia	17/8/17
Godfrey	Herbert Henry	Pte	4761	kia	17/8/17
Lindsay	James	RSM	770	kia	17/8/17
Millard	Alfred George	2/Lt	n/a	dow	17/8/17
Webb	Thomas Henry	Pte	204317	kia	17/8/17
Daysh	William	Pte	30744	kia	18/8/17
Pigden	George Ernest	Pte	7077	kia	18/8/17
Walters	Arthur Herbert	Pte	33658	kia	18/8/17
Ovenden	Arthur	Pte	24321	dow	19/8/17
Chaplin	Cyril	Cpl	2548	dow	20/8/17
Petley	Hubert Steward	Pte	30068	dow	24/8/17
Coppick	Charles George Edward	Pte	8830	kia	28/8/17
Duffell	Jesse	Pte	2530	kia	28/8/17
Lee	Harry	Pte	20981	dow	2/9/17
Watts	Archibald	Pte	33235	kia	7/9/17
Holder	Frederick Thomas	Cpl	15503	kia	9/9/17
Lee	Charles Henry	Pte	24669	dow	9/9/17
Rumbell	Edgar Arthur	Pte	33657	kia	9/9/17
Argyle	Samuel	Pte	6611	d	13/9/17
Comment: POW, buried Latvia					
Sullivan	Alfred	Pte	30056	d	21/9/17
Pike	John Samuel	Pte	16356	kia	30/9/17
Pitt	Percy Douglas	Pte	30011	kia	15/10/17
Comment: Date corrected from war diary and CWGC from 15/9/17					
Hill	William Frank	Pte	24795	kia	2/11/17
Tettmar	Victor Downes	Pte	21030	dow	4/11/17
Bicker	Frederick	Pte	30970	kia	16/11/17
Hunt	James	Pte	4229	kia	20/11/17
Millard	Henry George	L/Cpl	2282	kia	20/11/17
Prested	Frederick William Thomas	Pte	21210	kia	20/11/17
Grantham	Ernest Russell	2/Lt	n/a	kia	27/11/17
Carter	George Sidney	2/Lt	n/a	dow	28/11/17
Comment: MC					

Surname	Christian Names	Rank	Serial No.	Fate	Date of Death
Rowe	Herbert Henry	Pte	1826	kia	30/11/17
Taylor	Henry George	Pte	1972	kia	3/12/17
Williams	Stephen	Cpl	2109	kia	3/12/17
Comment: MM					
Patterson	John Keppel Priuli	Lt	n/a	dow	26/12/17
Usher	James	Pte	24959	d	30/1/18
Brown	George	Pte	12500	dow	5/2/18
Jones	William Robert	Pte	341	d	23/2/18
Baker	Thomas	Pte	32108	kia	21/3/18
Charman	Frederick Ernest	Pte	10832	kia	21/3/18
Crick	Cecil	Pte	32069	kia	21/3/18
Cropp	Albert	Pte	6220	kia	21/3/18
Day	George Herbert	Pte	1653	dow	21/3/18
Dodson	Walter	Pte	23888	kia	21/3/18
Gooch	Walter	Pte	17818	dow	21/3/18
Kime	Austin Fuller	L/Cpl	24101	kia	21/3/18
Le Fleming	Lawrence Julius	Lt Col	n/a	kia	21/3/18
Mathie	Cecil George	Pte	24046	kia	21/3/18
Newland	George William	Pte	20647	kia	21/3/18
Parsons	Sidney Joseph	Pte	6232	kia	21/3/18
Pratt	Arthur Victor	2/Lt	n/a	kia	21/3/18
Rackham	George Robert	Pte	23476	kia	21/3/18
Rycraft	Rayner William	Pte	31843	kia	21/3/18
Sharp	George Benjamin	2/Lt	n/a	kia	21/3/18
Stickland	George Henry	Pte	22751	kia	21/3/18
Stilwell	Henry Ernest	Pte	23445	kia	21/3/18
Thane	Ralph John	Pte	22237	kia	21/3/18
Tibbitts	Walter Alfred	Pte	12800	kia	21/3/18
Webb	Harold Stanley	2/Lt	n/a	kia	21/3/18
Wheatley	Thomas William	Pte	25942	kia	21/3/18
Hayes	John	Sgt	10320	kia	22/3/18
Gibbs	Herbert Charles	Pte	21283	dow	23/3/18
Jenkins	Jesse	Pte	2512	kia	23/3/18
Turner	Albert Edward	Pte	15529	kia	23/3/18
Sweetland	John	Pte	203487	dow	24/3/18
Turner	Arthur	Pte	16104	kia	24/3/18
Lester	Frank	Capt	n/a	dow	25/3/18
Comment: POW, buried Bellicourt					
Bournes	Ernest	Pte	21573	kia	26/3/18
Chappell	John William	Pte	8440	dow	26/3/18
Davies	Sydney Bruce	2/Lt	n/a	kia	26/3/18
Grant	Stanley Kenneth	Lt	n/a	kia	26/3/18
Hillsdon	Thomas	Pte	4411	d	26/3/18
Whiting	Herbert Edward	Pte	6673	kia	26/3/18
Atkinson	Thomas	Pte	35864	kia	27/3/18
Bent	Richard John Woolman	Cpl	25076	kia	27/3/18
Bunn	Frederick George	Pte	204747	kia	27/3/18
Carter	Henry Thomas	Pte	35218	kia	27/3/18
Chalmers	George	Pte	1824	kia	27/3/18
Clevely	Frank	Pte	22825	d	27/3/18

Surname	Christian Names	Rank	Serial No.	Fate	Date of Death
Cooke	Frank	L/Cpl	8203	kia	27/3/18
Cooper	John Joseph	Cpl	9217	kia	27/3/18
Corley	William Raymond	2/Lt	n/a	kia	27/3/18
Cranston	George	L/Sgt	10368	kia	27/3/18
Day	Charles George	Pte	11921	kia	27/3/18
Dean	Henry Fielder	Pte	32140	kia	27/3/18
Dollamore	William Edward	Pte	18167	kia	27/3/18
Duffield	Arthur George Robert	Cpl	2542	kia	27/3/18
Foster	Christman Thomas George	Pte	203016	kia	27/3/18
Franks	Sidney George	Sgt	9532	kia	27/3/18
Fuller	James	L/Cpl	9343	kia	27/3/18
Comment: MM					
Godfrey	Edward Mark	Pte	25961	kia	27/3/18
Comment: Formerly 50978 Sherwood Foresters					
Harvey	Bertie	Pte	204367	kia	27/3/18
Hicks	William Robert	L/Cpl	24098	kia	27/3/18
Higgins	David Henry	L/Cpl	11800	kia	27/3/18
Higgins	Herbert	L/Cpl	4136	kia	27/3/18
Hope	Frank Slaughton	Pte	24923	kia	27/3/18
Knight	Arthur John	Cpl	21363	kia	27/3/18
Lawes	Alfred	Pte	32345	kia	27/3/18
Mace	Sydney Charles	Pte	19223	kia	27/3/18
McLean	Daniel	Pte	37550	kia	27/3/18
Comment: Formerly 300124 RE					
Nash	Ernest	Cpl	5986	kia	27/3/18
Palmer	Reggie William	Pte	35015	kia	27/3/18
Phillips	Jeffrey Blundell	Pte	32273	kia	27/3/18
Rayner	Sidney Joseph	Pte	33623	kia	27/3/18
Rogers	William	Pte	28605	kia	27/3/18
Comment: Formerly 26536 Royal Fusiliers					
Sanders	Leonard William	Pte	5318	kia	27/3/18
Sorge	Percival Linsey Pallant	Pte	18325	kia	27/3/18
Standen	William James	Pte	2034	kia	27/3/18
Sturgeon	Reginald	L/Cpl	5089	kia	27/3/18
Tilbury	William James	Pte	9214	kia	27/3/18
Tyson	William	Pte	8128	kia	27/3/18
Whistle	Benjamin	Pte	1034	kia	27/3/18
Wright	Ernest Percy	Pte	32319	kia	27/3/18
Woolgar	Henry George Charles	L/Cpl	4325	dow	28/3/18
Gough	William	Cpl	1631	dow	31/3/18
Douglass	Archibald Henry	Capt	n/a	dow	8/4/18
Hockin	Albert Victor	Pte	33689	dow	13/4/18
Walters	James	L/Cpl	10017	d	18/4/18
Comment: POW, buried Premont					
Johnson	Nathaniel	Pte	32152	dow	19/4/18
Melia	Michael	Pte	28944	kia	7/5/18
Comment: Formerly 13983 LNL Regt					
Humbles	Bert	Pte	20485	d	14/5/18
McNaughton	Alfred George	Pte	26640	kia	15/5/18

Surname	Christian Names	Rank	Serial No.	Fate	Date of Death
Strong	Benjamin Clarence	Pte	10486	d	17/5/18
Comment: POW, buried Annois, France					
Livingstone	Robert James Andrew	Pte	27271	kia	18/5/18
Faber	Charles	Pte	8746	d	1/6/18
Comment: POW, buried St Souplet, France					
Holland	Edward Arthur	Pte	203018	d	1/6/18
Comment: POW, buried Peronne, France, as Hollands					
Elkin	Percy George Arthur	Pte	10808	d	2/6/18
Horsey	Arthur	Pte	37180	dow	6/6/18
Munns	Frank Arthur	Pte	27285	kia	6/6/18
Webb	Frederick George	Sgt	28782	dow	16/6/18
Comment: Formerly 10083 LNL Regt, MM					
Smith	George	Pte	30955	d	21/6/18
Comment: POW, buried Berlin					
Dugdale	James	Sgt	28787	kia	23/6/18
Comment: Formerly 21629 LNL Regt, DCM, MM					
Haslam	George	Pte	2803	d	23/6/18
Comment: POW, buried Berlin					
Adams	Ernest Frank	Pte	23488	d	25/6/18
Comment: POW, buried Saaralbe, France					
Smith	Percy Sudbury	Pte	23029	d	27/6/18
Comment: POW, buried Berlin					
Smith	Henry	L/Cpl	2232	d	28/6/18
Comment: POW, buried Berlin					
Ring	George	Pte	242637	dow	9/7/18
Holt	John Afred (*sic*)	Pte	35075	kia	16/7/18
Nicholson	Alexander Lester	Pte	31023	kia	16/7/18
Finer	Alfred John	Pte	27232	kia	31/7/18
Pritchard	Albert	Pte	20887	d	1/8/18
Comment: POW, buried Berlin					
Harris	William Levi	Pte	204324	dow	3/8/18
Comment: Formerly 5013 Durham Light Infantry					
Dove	John William	Pte	24906	d	6/8/18
Comment: POW, buried Neuf Brisach, France					
Allen	George Alfred	Pte	25001	dow	7/8/18
Butler	Frank Ernest	Pte	39802	kia	12/8/18
Horlock	Allan	L/Cpl	10936	d	14/8/18
Comment: Formerly 12587 Queen's Royal Regt POW, buried St Souplet, France					
Bottomley	John Willey	Pte	29010	dow	16/8/18
Comment: Formerly 23588 LNL Regt					
Willmott	John Alfred	Pte	9438	kia	16/8/18
Butcher	William	Pte	9885	dow	23/8/18
Richardson	Henry David	Pte	32328	kia	1/9/18
Comment: Formerly 17107 Royal W Kent Regt					
Clements	William Thomas	Pte	27212	kia	3/9/18
Cripps	Reginald	Pte	37558	kia	3/9/18
Davies	Gilbert William	Pte	26713	kia	3/9/18
Comment: Formerly 55989 Manchester Regt					
Heyes	Jesse	L/Cpl	28979	kia	3/9/18
Comment: Formerly 7391 LNL Regt, MM					

Surname	Christian Names	Rank	Serial No.	Fate	Date of Death
Hyman	Samuel	Pte	27262	kia	3/9/18
Lindsay	William Henry	Capt	n/a	kia	3/9/18
Comment: MC					
William	Samuel	Pte	26698	dow	4/9/18
Comment: Formerly 63312 Manchester Regt					
Tribe	George Herbert	Pte	24374	d	13/9/18
Comment: POW, buried Le Cateau, France					
Urmston	Nathan	Pte	28969	kia	13/9/18
Comment: Formerly 36914 LNL Regt					
Smith	Percy Lonsdale	Pte	35956	kia	18/9/18
Anderson	Gilbert	Pte	204596	kia	22/9/18
Helm	James	Pte	28918	kia	22/9/18
Comment: Formerly 31876 LNL Regt					
Wadsworth	Herbert	Pte	29070	kia	22/9/18
Comment: Formerly 24581 LNL Regt					
Blake	George	Pte	35047	dow	23/9/18
Childs	Charles Edward	Pte	30771	kia	23/9/18
Pedder	Charles	Pte	22765	kia	23/9/18
Pritchard	Frank	Pte	28949	dow	23/9/18
Gegan	Cyril Norman	Pte	36676	dow	9/10/18
Malham	Thomas	L/Cpl	19936	kia	9/10/18
Shrubsall	Frank Arthur	Pte	33517	d	10/10/18
Comment: POW, buried Niederzwehren, Germany					
Warren	William	L/Cpl	36247	kia	10/10/18
Lindley	James	Pte	28933	kia	12/10/18
Comment: Formerly 203723 LNL Regt					
Hurwitz	Lionel	Pte	35077	dow	15/10/18
Soanes	Albert Arthur	Pte	33596	dow	15/10/18
Black	Benjamin Rufus	Pte	34348	kia	16/10/18
Bullen	Robert	Pte	28802	kia	16/10/18
Cordery	Arthur	Pte	16227	kia	16/10/18
Cowperthwaite	John	Pte	28810	kia	16/10/18
Coyne	James	Pte	35186	dow	16/10/18
Croger	Reginald Earl	Pte	35163	kia	16/10/18
Crump	James	Pte	26710	kia	16/10/18
Comment: Formerly 55960 Manchester Regt					
Davis	William Edward	Pte	35199	kia	16/10/18
Denoon	Jack George	L/Cpl	27228	kia	16/10/18
Edge	John	Pte	29014	kia	16/10/18
Ellis	William	Pte	29058	kia	16/10/18
Ford	Frank Edward	L/Cpl	22545	kia	16/10/18
Comment: MM					
Franklin	Fred	Pte	28891	kia	16/10/18
Girling	Claude Stanley Charles	Pte	27240	kia	16/10/18
Goddard	Gordon Cecil	2/Lt	n/a	kia	16/10/18
Ingle	Leonard Lanham	L/Cpl	10686	kia	16/10/18
Jones	Frederick William	Pte	26718	kia	16/10/18
Comment: Formerly 55902 Manchester Regt					
Keep	Douglas William	2/Lt	n/a	kia	16/10/18
Kendall	Montague James Hulbert	Pte	35085	dow	16/10/18

Surname	Christian Names	Rank	Serial No.	Fate	Date of Death
Kettle	Alfred	Pte	27268	kia	16/10/18
King	Stanley Frank	Pte	35087	kia	16/10/18
Knott	David	Pte	28931	kia	16/10/18
Le Grice	Ernest Robert	Pte	21380	kia	16/10/18
McNamara	John	Cpl	28939	kia	16/10/18
Comment: Formerly 25097 LNL Regt, VC					
Marston	Charles Ernest	Pte	17413	dow	16/10/18
Martin	Frank William	Pte	37507	kia	16/10/18
Miller	John Benjamin	Sgt	203423	kia	16/10/18
Newnham	Herbert	Pte	204363	kia	16/10/18
Comment: Formerly 203742 Bedfordshire Regt					
Nugent	Charles	Pte	27287	kia	16/10/18
Palmer	Reginald Charles	L/Cpl	29290	kia	16/10/18
Parsons	Frederick James	L/Cpl	19274	d	16/10/18
Comment: According to CWGC he died on 10/6/18					
Prevotal	William Thomas	Pte	26189	dow	16/10/18
Comment: Formerly 6076 Middlesex Regt					
Roskell	Richard	Pte	28955	kia	16/10/18
Comment: Formerly 35323 Royal Lancaster Regt					
Russell	David	Pte	26667	kia	16/10/18
Comment: Formerly 63280 Manchester Regt					
Smith	John	Pte	26125	kia	16/10/18
Sullivan	John	Cpl	1192	kia	16/10/18
Taylor	Forster	2/Lt	n/a	kia	16/10/18
Turner	Arthur	Pte	28965	kia	16/10/18
Comment: Formerly 32195 LNL Regt					
Tustin	William	Cpl	204327	dow	16/10/18
Comment: Formerly 4911 Durham Light Infantry					
Ward	Frank	Pte	26695	kia	16/10/18
Comment: Formerly 63309 Manchester Regt					
Wardell	John	Pte	8053	kia	16/10/18
Ware	Reginald Isaac	Pte	36249	kia	16/10/18
Comment: Formerly 35150 Hussars					
West	William Edmund	Pte	35882	kia	16/10/18
Wheeler	Frederick Archibald	L/Cpl	22092	kia	16/10/18
Wilcock	Benjamin	Pte	25718	kia	16/10/18
Comment: Formerly 25718 LNL Regt					
Wilson	Stuart Wright	Pte	26701	kia	16/10/18
Comment: Formerly 63317 Manchester Regt					
Young	Edward Albert	Pte	35161	kia	16/10/18
FitzJohn	Ernest Arthur	Pte	25290	dow	17/10/18
Comment: Formerly 23932 Middlesex Regt, MM					
Bowen	Albert William	Pte	26707	dow	18/10/18
Comment: Formerly 55956 Manchester Regt					
Hands	Henry Albert	Pte	19167	d	18/10/18
Comment: Not in CWGC					
Holland	Ashton	Pte	205019	dow	23/10/18
Comment: Formerly 4986 LNL Regt					
Dickson	John Irvine	Cpl	38868	dow	26/10/18
Pratt	Charles	Pte	27206	dow	28/10/18

Surname	Christian Names	Rank	Serial No.	Fate	Date of Death
Ford	Joseph James	Pte	27236	kia	5/11/18
Birch	Ernest John	L/Cpl	9414	kia	6/11/18
Chapman	Frederick Charles	Pte	203720	kia	6/11/18
Horner	George Harold	Cpl	19128	kia	6/11/18
Howell	Charles Joseph	L/Cpl	7425	kia	6/11/18
Hudson	Frederick Russell	Pte	36753	kia	6/11/18
Lawrence	George Ernest	Pte	11491	kia	6/11/18
Rodgers	George	Pte	28952	dow	6/11/18
Comment: Formerly 203673 LNL Regt					
Moore	Frank Denham	Pte	21560	dow	11/11/18
Leyshon	Charles Edward	Cpl	26739	dow	12/11/18
Hill	Frederick William	Pte	30072	dow	15/11/18
Egan	Charles	Pte	28887	dow	17/11/18
Bishop	John Frederick	L/Cpl	8084	dow	30/11/18
Wrigley	Joseph	Pte	26693	d	30/11/18
Comment: Formerly 63307 Manchester Regt, Ex POW, buried Nijmegen, Holland					
Watford	James	Pte	8596	d	3/12/18
Comment: Ex POW, buried Vevey, Switzerland					
White	Samuel	Pte	35155	dow	13/12/18
Dennison	William Arthur	Pte	23955	d	31/12/18
Comment: Ex POW, buried Sangatte, France					
Rochell	Arthur Joseph	Pte	35234	d	8/1/19
Comment: Formerly T/4/062111 RASC					
Disbrow	John William Tom	Sgt	1838	d	9/1/19
Blezard	Wilfred	Pte	28801	d	24/1/19
Knight	George Allen	Pte	17669	d	21/2/19
Pittock	William John	Pte	48287	d	8/3/19

Notes

The Roll of Honour in H.W. Pearse and H.S. Sloman's *History of the East Surrey Regiment* (London, 1924) is for the whole regiment, excluding officers, and does not show men by battalion. My Roll of Honour for 9/ East Surrey has been prepared from Anon., *Officers Died in the Great War 1914–19* (London, 1919) and Anon., *Soldiers Died in the Great War 1914–19 Part 36 The East Surrey Regiment* (London, 1920). However, rather than retain the alphabetical order of the originals (which also list Territorial and non-Territorial officers separately) it seemed better to do something different and prepare a single list, of all ranks, in order of death date.

No guarantee can be given that the list is comprehensive. It is probably complete for officer deaths, but excluding those who were attached from other units (e.g. Major Ottley, Captain Pirie and Captain Badcock) and those who were serving with other units when they died. For the men, however, it seems likely, looking at casualty lists, that there are some who died serving with the battalion who are not listed in *Soldiers Died*. They may be listed under other units. On the other hand, some of those listed under 9/East Surrey in that work may have similarly been serving with other units when they died. The situation in March 1918 was especially difficult for accurate record keeping.

There are clearly other errors in these works. These include dates of death. For instance, in reality, it would appear that no one from the battalion died on 25.9.1915. Those listed for that day have, therefore, been listed for the following day here. Other errors may remain, including the spelling of names. Service numbers especially are often difficult to read in the original *Soldiers Died* because of the poor printing, whilst the possibility of transcription errors cannot be ruled out too. There are also some discrepancies of rank, e.g. A.H. Douglass is listed as a lieutenant in *Officers Died*, but other sources identify him as a captain. Not all honours and awards may be listed.

Of the 868 total, 654 are listed as killed in action, 159 died of wounds and 55 'died'. I have looked especially at those simply shown as 'died'. They include men who died of disease or accidents. They also include a number of POWs, whom I have shown as such, where identified, with place of burial added from the CWGC website (http://www.cwgc.org).

The 868 total breaks down as follows by rank: lieutenant colonels 2; major 1; captain 8; lieutenants, including 1 quartermaster 9; second lieutenants 35; RSMs and CSMs 6; acting sergeants, lance sergeants and sergeants 49; acting corporals and corporals 40; lance corporals 71; privates 647.

Appendix II

9/East Surrey Fatalities by Month

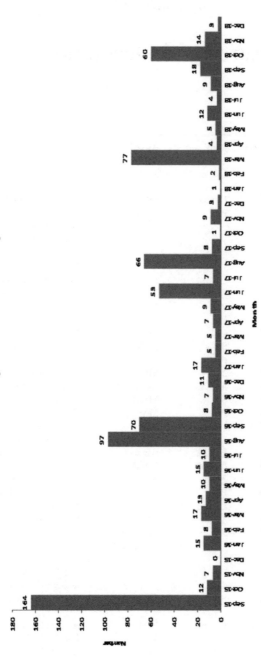

This chart for all ranks, based on Anon., *Officers Died in the Great War 1914–19* (London, 1919) and Anon., *Soldiers Died in the Great War 1914–19 Part 36 The East Surrey Regiment* (London, 1920), includes deaths from disease and accident, as well as enemy action. It excludes the very few who died in 1919. Fatality numbers by month here do not necessarily accord with those mentioned in the body of this book, drawn from H.W. Pearse and H.S. Sloman's *History of the East Surrey Regiment* (London, 1924) or the battalion war diary. This may be because the battalion's records were incorrect: because it was not aware at the time of deaths that took place away from it; or that men are missing or listed incorrectly by unit in *Soldiers Died*. Officer deaths (55) include 9 or 10 at, or following wounds from, Loos; 13 from the Somme and 9 from *Kaiserschlacht*. They were at their lowest level during 1917 (11). It comes as no surprise that the battalion's heavy months for fatalities include September 1915 (Loos), August and September 1916 (Somme), August 1917 (Pilckem Ridge), March 1918 (*Kaiserschlacht*) and October 1918 (Haussy). Less expected is June 1917, when whilst the battalion was in Reserve at Messines, it afterwards suffered heavy losses from shellfire in holding captured ground.

Appendix III

Awards and Decorations

Name	Number	Rank	Award	Remarks
Allam, B.	4338	L/Cpl	MM	For Somme 1916. Medical orderly
Andrews, A.W.	6218	L/Cpl	MM	For Somme 1916
Attew, T.	25071	Pte	DCM	For Haussy. He is not listed in H.W. Pearse and H.S. Sloman's *History of the East Surrey Regiment* (London, 1924), but was, according to his Burnt Records and the *London Gazette*, with 9/East Surrey
Baker, C.A.	?	Pte	MM	For 1/1917 raid
Bashford, J.W.	6272	Pte	MM	For Somme 1916
Batchelor, W.H.	2503	Cpl	MM	For Wulverghem 1916
Bell, A.	8075	Sgt	DCM	For 11/1917 raid
Bell, N.	25947	Pte	MM	For 11/1917 raid
Birtles, E.G.	n/a	2/Lt	MC	For 7/1918 raids
Bishop, J.W.	1459	A/CSM	CdeG (Belg)	Awarded 1/1918
Blackery, D.	8219	Sgt	MSM	For late 1918
Braint, H.E.	6413	Pte	MM	For Wulverghem 1916
Bye, J.T.D.	205011	Pte	MM	For 3/1918
Cameron, E.A.	n/a	Lt Col	CMG	New Year Honours 1919
Cameron, E.A.	n/a	Lt Col	Bar to DSO	For Haussy 10/1918
Carrodus, J.	29055	L/Cpl	MSM	For late 1918
Carter, G.S.	n/a	2/Lt	MC	For 11/1917 raid
Chapman, A.	19406	Pte	MM	Awarded June 1918
Clark, C.A.	n/a	Lt and Adj	MC	For Somme 1916
Clark, C.A.	n/a	Major	DSO	For 3/1918
Clarke, H.N.	14244	Sgt	Médaille Militaire	For late 1918. H.W. Pearse and H.S. Sloman's *History of the East Surrey Regiment* (London, 1924) gives him an MM – this seems to be a confusion
Clarke, H.N.	14244	Sgt	DCM	For ops E of Cambrai October 1918
Collins, J.	200546	L/Cpl	MM	Awarded 6/1918
Cowper, C.R.	n/a	Lt	MC	For 11/1917 raid
Cox, A.	2926	Sgt	MSM	Awarded 6/1918
Crimmins, J.	32269	Pte	MM	For 3/1918
Daniels, J.	1701?	Cpl	MM	For Somme 1916

Name	Number	Rank	Award	Remarks
de la Fontaine, H.V.M.	n/a	Lt Col	DSO	For Somme 1916
Dyke, F.G.	5808	L/Sgt	MM	For Somme 1916
Elliott, R.L.	1597	Cpl	MM	For 3/1918. Transport man
Ellis, R.V.	24389	Pte	MM	Awarded July 1917
Ericson, E.	6392	Sgt	MM	For Wulverghem 1916. Signaller
Evans, J.	1372?	Sgt	MM	For 3/1918
Evans, S.V.	32285	L/Cpl	MM	Probably for 3/1918
Finch, C.	5428	A/CSM	MM	For 3/1918
FitzJohn, E.A.	25290	Pte	MM	For late 1918
Foster, C.B.	2000	Sgt	MM	Awarded 6/1918
Fuller, J.	9343	L/Cpl	MM	Awarded 12/1917
Gates, A.	823?	Pte	MM	For Ypres 8/1917
Gibbs, R.J.	2313?	Pte	MM	For Wulverghem 4/1916. Signaller
Gold, R.C.	n/a	Lt	MC	For Somme 1916
Gowan, A.P.	25409	Pte	C de G (Belg)	Awarded 1/1918
Halliday, F.	2487	Cpl	MM	For Wulverghem 1916. Pirie's corporal
Hammond, A.E.	27248	Pte	MM	For late 1918
Hartley, G.C.	n/a	Lt	MC	For 1/1917 raid. RAMC
Harvey, A.W.	n/a	Lt	MC	Awarded 1/1918
Hastings, H.	8239	L/Cpl	MM	For Wulverghem 1916
Haysom, F.	2457	Sgt	MSM	For late 1918
Hilton, C.	n/a	Capt	MC	For Bavay 11/1918
House, J.	28786	Sgt	Bar to MM	For late 1918
Husk, D.	?	Pte	MM	For Somme 1916
Hyde, G.	4009	CSM	DCM	For 3/1918
Hyde, G.	4009	Sgt Maj	MC	For Haussy 10/1918
Ingrams, F.R.	n/a	2/Lt	MC	For Wulverghem 6/1916
Irons, C.S.	n/a	2/Lt	MC	For patrolling 8/11/1918
James, E.J.	n/a	Lt and QM	MC	For Haussy 10/1918
Jewson, F.	8324	Pte	DCM	For Hooge 3/1916
Johnson, J.	29017	Pte	DCM	For Haussy 10/1918
Kerckhove, H.V.	n/a	2/Lt	MC	For Haussy 10/1918
Kerslake, W.	9997	L/Cpl	MM	For Wulverghem 1916
Kimber, H.	5874?	Pte	MM	For Somme 1916
Kirkum, H.J.	6535	Pte	MM	Probably for 3/1918
Lambert, C.W.	2354	L/Cpl	MM	For Somme 1916
Lee, A.	9038	L/Cpl	MM	For Wulverghem 1916
Lee, H.	698	Sgt	MM	For Wulverghem 1916
Lindsay, W.H.	n/a	2/Lt	MC	For 1/1917 raid
Maingot, P.S.	n/a	Capt	MC	For Haussy 10/1918
Manning, G.E.	n/a	Lt	MC	Awarded July 1917
Matthews, E.S.	1539	Pte	MM	For Wulverghem 1916
McGrath, C.	10075	Cpl	MM	For 3/1918
McNamara, J.	28939	Pte	VC	For defence against German raid 3/9/18. Signaller
Medlock, G.	2682	Sgt	DCM	For 11/1917 raid

Name	Number	Rank	Award	Remarks
Mortimer, W.J.	11790	Pte	MM	For 11/1917 raid
Newman, P.W.	201981	Pte	MM	For 3/1918. Or with Loyals?
Oakey, F.G.	8230	Sgt	MM	For Wulverghem 1916
O'Connell, F.	985	Pte	DCM	For Hooge 3/1916
O'Connor, D.P.	n/a	Capt	MC	For Loos 9/1915
Perrin, G.	27203	Pte	MM	Awarded 6/1918
Perry, J.W.	6642	Cpl	DCM	Awarded 7/1917 – rescue of wounded man in no-man's-land
Picton, J.A.	n/a	Lt	MC	For rescue of men 6/1917 tunnel collapse
Pocock, C.W.	1403	Pte	MM	For Somme 1916
Poole, G.B.D.	n/a	Chaplain	MC	For 3/1918. Brigade Chaplain
Richens, H.J.	8853	Pte	MM	For 3/1918
Robertson, D.O.L.	4422	Sgt	MM	For Somme 1916
Rogers, T.	276	RSM	MSM	For late 1918
Rolls, H.	?	Pte	MM	Awarded 7/1917. Stretcher bearer
Rugg, W.E.	35127	L/Cpl	MM	For late 1918
Shere, C.W.	19363	Pte	DCM	For Ypres 8/1917
Skinner, C.W.	1605	Cpl	MM	For Wulverghem 1916
Summers, W.G.T.	5791	Sgt	DCM	For Wulverghem 6/1916, etc.
Summers, W.G.T.	5791	Sgt	MM	For 1/1917 raid
Taylor, A.J.	2089	Pte	MM	Probably for 3/1918
Taylor, W.M.	n/a	Capt	MC	For Haussy 10/1918
Tetley, G.S.	n/a	2/Lt	MC	For Hooge 3/1916
Thomas, L.C.	n/a	2/Lt	MC	For 1/1917 raid
Thomas, L.C.	n/a	Lt	Bar to MC	For 12/1917 raid
Till, R.A.	31627	Pte	MM	Awarded 6/1918
Tomlinson, G.	30025?	Pte	MSM	Awarded June 1918
Trish, A.	6099	L/Cpl	MM	For 3/1918. Stretcher bearer
Vaughan, J.L.	n/a	Lt	MC	For Hooge 1/1916, etc.
Walker, T.E.	n/a	Capt	MC	For 3/1918 (US Army Med. Services). MO 8/RWKent also
Wallace, R.L.	n/a	Capt	MC	For Haussy 10/1918. RAMC
Warre-Dymond, G.W.	n/a	Capt	MC	For 3/1918
Wearing, J.	35891	L/Cpl	MM	Awarded 6/1918
Webb, G.	8821	L/Cpl	DCM	For Somme 1916. Stretcher bearer
Webb, L.H.	n/a	2/Lt	MC	For Ypres 8/1917
White, W.W.	812	CSM	MM	For Somme 1916
Whiteman, E.L.	n/a	Capt	MC	For 3/1918
Wigg, E.W.	2514	Pte	MM	For Somme 1916
Wilson, A.	8086	Pte	MM	For 3/1918. Stretcher bearer
Wood, E.J.	n/a	2/Lt	MC	For repulse of German raid 6/1918
Wright, J.	?	Pte	MM	For Somme 1916
Youngman, J.M.	n/a	2/Lt	MC	For Wulverghem gas attack 4/1916

Notes

In total the awards and decorations are: 1 Victoria Cross, 1 Commander of the Order of St Michael and St George, 2 Distinguished Service Orders, 1 Bar to DSO, 30 Military Crosses, 1 Bar to MC, 12 Distinguished Conduct Medals, 6 Meritorious Service Medals, 55 Military Medals, 1 Bar to MM, 2 Croixs de Guerre (Belgian), 1 Médaille Militaire (presumably French).

This may well not be a complete list of men who won awards and decorations whilst serving with 9/East Surrey. It includes such as medical officers serving with the unit, although not of the regiment. The names have been assembled, almost entirely, from references in Pearse and Soloman's *History*, but with omission of those who appear to have won their awards before transfer to 9/East Surrey from the Loyals. Serial numbers and other information have been added where possible, principally from medal cards in TNA, citations in the *London Gazette* and the battalion's war diary. Even so, some identifications by serial number are tentative.

Regarding citations, these were usually published, often many months after the award, for the DSO, MC and DCM. The battalion in which the individual served is often not given. With such as the MM the best that survives is the odd reference in Pearse and Sloman or the war diary.

Appendix IV

Officers Serving Abroad with 9/East Surrey, 1915–1918

Rank on Arrival	Name	Disembarkation Date	Date Joining Unit	Leaving Date	Remarks
2/Lt	Abrams, L.E.	28/9/16	1/10/16	12/5/17	Cashiered
2/Lt	Acton, C.	7/10/15	9/10/15	29/11/15	To Britain – sick
2/Lt	Amies, E.L.	20/4/16	23/4/16	6/7/16	To Britain – sick
Capt	Anslow, R.A.	31/8/15	31/8/15	22/2/16	Sick on leave. Returned 3/11/16/, 14/5/17 to Britain – sick
2/Lt	Arding, L.H.	8/9/16	11/9/16	29/1/17	Transferred to ASC
2/Lt	Arundel, E.S.	25/5/16	27/5/16	1/8/16	To Britain – sick
2/Lt	Austin, W.S.	31/12/17	7/2/18	25/3/18	POW 26/3/18 *Kaiserschlacht*
2/Lt	Baber, W.H.	16/4/18	19/4/18	16/10/18	POW Haussy
2/Lt	Ball, F.G.	28/3/16	10/5/16	16/8/16	Kia Somme
Capt	Barfoot, W.M.	5/4/18	9/4/18	19/4/18	Posted to 12/RB
Lt	Barker, L.R.	30/8/15	30/8/15	26/10/17	To General List for service with W. African Frontier Force
Capt	Barnett, C.E.	31/8/15	31/8/15	26/9/15	Kia Loos
Lt	Barnett, H.J.	31/8/15	31/8/15	20/10/15	Dow received at Ypres
2/Lt	Bate, E.R.H.	31.8.15	31.8.15	26.9.15	Kia Loos
2/Lt	Bates, V.C.	16/4/18	19/4/18		Still serving at Armistice
2/Lt	Belham, A.S.	20/1/17	31/1/17	5/10/17	To Britain – sick
Lt	Bennett, W.F.	7/10/15	10/10/15	14/2/16	To Britain – wounded. Returned 1/9/16, 17/9/16 to Britain wounded
2/Lt	Best, M.G.	22/8/17	28/8/17	4/9/17	Posted to 2/1st Bucks
2/Lt	Bingham, H.	31/7/18	7/8/18	6/11/18	To Britain for RAF
Lt and QM	Birch, C.R.E.	25/2/16	26/2/16	12/8/17	Died pneumonia

Rank on Arrival	Name	Disembarkation Date	Date Joining Unit	Leaving Date	Remarks
Lt	Birt, W.B.	31/8/15	31/8/15	26/9/15	POW Loos, died in German hospital 1916
2/Lt	Birtles, E.G.	9/11/17	16/11/17		Still serving at Armistice
2/Lt	Bishop, B.	31/12/17	13/1/18	23/3/18	POW 23/3/18 *Kaiserschlacht*
2/Lt	Blower, M.S.	28/8/16	1/9/16	25/3/18	POW 26/3/18 *Kaiserschlacht*
Lt	Blunden, A.C.	2/11/17	9/11/17	21/11/17	To Britain – sick
2/Lt	Bogue, P.Y.	6/1/17	10/1/17	24/7/17	Kia Ypres
2/Lt	Booker, J.J.	16/4/18	19/4/18		Still serving at Armistice
Maj	Brettell, R.	31/8/15	31/8/15	20/9/15	Posted to 9/Suffolk
Lt	Bridger, J.B.	12/10/15	17/10/15	7/11/15	To Britain – sick
2/Lt	Bridges, G.H.	28/8/16	1/9/16	23/10/17	To Britain – wounded
Lt and QM	Britts, C.W.G.	1/10/15	8/10/15	6/11/15	Died in grenade training accident
2/Lt	Brown, T.G.A.	31/8/15	31/8/15	24/10/15	To Britain – sick
Maj	Brown, A.J.W.	1/10/15	8/10/15	27/10/15	To Britain – sick
2/Lt	Brown, J.C.	30/7/15	9/4/18	28/9/18	Ex Loyals. To senior officers' course
Capt	Buchanan, H.C.	24/8/16	27/8/16	7/2/17	To Britain – sick
Lt Col	Buttle, E.A.	10/5/16	17/5/16	8/7/16	To Britain – sick
Lt	Cameron, E.A.	6/15	9/4/18		Ex Loyals. Still serving at Armistice
2/Lt	Campbell, A.C.P.	31/8/15	31/8/15	26/9/15	Kia Loos
Lt	Carter, G.S.	10/8/17	18/8/17	28/11/17	Dow following trench raid
2/Lt	Cartwright, S.	22/10/17	7/2/18		Still serving at Armistice
2/Lt	Castle, A.B.G.	10/5/16	16/5/16	27/9/16	To Britain – wounded
2/Lt	Churcher, G.L.G.	13/7/16	2/8/16	8/2/18	To Britain for six months' duty. Returned 27/5/18, 15/9/18 to Britain – wounded
2/Lt	Clare, A.E.	22/8/17	27/8/17	21/3/18	POW 21/3/18 *Kaiserschlacht*
2/Lt	Clark, C.A.	23/1/16	29/1/16	25/3/18	POW 26/3/18 *Kaiserschlacht*
Capt	Collinson, A.A.	31/8/15	31/8/15	26/9/15	Kia Loos
2/Lt	Corley, W.R.	22/8/17	27/8/17	27/3/18	Kia *Kaiserschlacht*
2/Lt	Coutts, N.V.	31/8/15	31/8/15	26/9/15	Kia Loos
2/Lt	Cowper, C.R.	24/8/16	27/8/16	24/11/17	To Britain – wounded
2/Lt	Crabb, R.B.	6/11/17	11/11/17	23/3/18	POW 23/3/18 *Kaiserschlacht*
2/Lt	Cuthbert, C.L.	1/12/15	5/12/15	18/8/16	Dow Somme

Rank on Arrival	Name	Disembarkation Date	Date Joining Unit	Leaving Date	Remarks
2/Lt	Cuthbert, W.N.	10/12/15	22/12/15	5/2/16	To Britain – sick
Lt	Daintree, H.S.	7/7/16	18/5/18		Still serving at Armistice
2/Lt	Davies, E.W.	17/7/16	13/8/16	11/4/17	To Britain – sick
2/Lt	Davies, S.W. (sic)	30/11/17	16/12/17	26/3/18	S.B. Davies kia Kaiserschlacht
Lt Col	de la Fontaine, H.V.M.	7/3/15	19/10/15	5/8/17	Kia Ypres
Capt	Dealtry, H.A.B.	31/8/15	31/8/15	26/9/15	Kia Loos
Lt	Dean, C.B.	4/6/16	27/9/17	11/12/17	To Britain – sick
2/Lt	Denny, J.L.B.	20/3/16	27/3/16	20/8/16	To Britain – wounded
2/Lt	Dillon, H.	23/9/17	9/4/18	7/7/18	Ex Loyals. To Base Depot RAF as observer
2/Lt	Douglass, A.H.	5/6/16	18/6/16	25/3/18	To Britain – wounded – dow 4/18
2/Lt	Ellis, H.L.B.	21/9/16	25/9/16	25/7/17	To Britain – wounded
Lt	Elverson, R.W.	31/8/15	31/8/15	26/9/15	Kia Loos
Lt	Embley, W.F.C.	17/4/18	19/4/18	28/4/18	Posted to 8/East Surrey
2/Lt	Faulkner, R.K.	15/10/18	20/10/18		Still serving at Armistice
Capt	Fenwick, B.A.	31/8/15	31/8/15	26/9/15	POW Loos
Capt	Ferrers, E.A.J.	25/5/16	29/5/16	25/7/16	To Britain – sick. Returned 19/4/18, 2/5/18 to Maroc as Area Permanent Base Officer
2/Lt	Fitzpatrick, E.P.	17/4/18	19/4/18	28/4/18	Posted to 8/East Surrey
Capt	Francis, C.C.	18/10/18	22/10/18		Still serving at Armistice
2/Lt	Gabain, E.F.	1/12/15	5/12/15	1/3/16	To Britain – wounded
Lt	Gadsby, H.	9/11/17	16/11/17	21/6/18	To Britain – sick
2/Lt	Goddard, G.C.	16/4/18	19/4/18	16/10/18	Kia Haussy
2/Lt	Gold, R.C.	30/9/15	8/10/15	7/9/16	To Britain – wounded
2/Lt	Gotelee, C. St J.	25/1/17	5/2/17	15/3/18	Attached I Corps Convalescent Camp
2/Lt	Grant, S.K.	24/8/16	27/8/16	16/3/17	To Britain – wounded. Returned 10/17, Kia 3.18 Kaiserschlacht
2/Lt	Grantham, E.R.	22/8/17	27/8/17	27/11/17	Kia patrolling at Hargicourt
2/Lt	Gunning, G.	no entry	30/11/15	8/4/16	To Britain – sick
2/Lt	Hadenham, L.G.	12/3/15	7/12/15	18/7/16	Dow Wulverghem
2/Lt	Haines, E.A.	25/5/16	14/6/16	3/9/16	Kia Somme
2/Lt	Hammond, A.F.	31/12/17	7/2/18	27/3/18	To Britain – wounded

Rank on Arrival	Name	Disembarkation Date	Date Joining Unit	Leaving Date	Remarks
2/Lt	Handford, F.S.	1/10/15	8/10/15	27/1/16	Kia patrolling at Ypres
2/Lt	Harrison, W.G.	no entry	12/10/18	19/10/18	To Britain – wounded
Lt	Harry, G.L.G.	7/7/17	14/7/17	20/9/17	To Britain – wounded
2/Lt	Hart, B.L.	13/9/16	28/9/16	4/12/16	To Britain – sick
2/Lt	Harvey, A.W.	13/7/16	18/7/16	11/10/17	To Britain for six months' duty. Returned 22/4/18. Still serving at Armistice
2/Lt	Hathaway, F.W.	31/12/17	7/2/18	27/3/18	To Britain – wounded
2/Lt	Hatten, D.L.	22/9/16	29/9/16	1/3/18	To Britain for 6 months duty. Returned 26/10/18. Still serving at Armistice.
2/Lt	Hawtin, C.W.	16/4/18	19/4/18		Still serving at Armistice
Capt	Heales, A.G.	13/6/16	18/6/16	15/8/16	To Britain – sick
2/Lt	High, P.	28/9/16	1/10/16		Still serving at Armistice
2/Lt	Hilton, C.	17/3/15	14/12/15	11/10/17	To Britain for six months' duty. Returned 22/4/18. Still serving at Armistice
2/Lt	Hogg, G.A.	30/11/17	16/12/17	29/3/18	To Britain – wounded
Lt	Holmes, C.C.	16/4/18	19/4/18		Still serving at Armistice
2/Lt	Homewood, R.J.	22/2/17	27/2/17	9/9/17	To Britain – sick
Capt	Horsley, S.S.	1/7/17	7/9/17	7/11/17	To Britain – wounded
2/Lt	Howell, W.S.	31/8/15	31/8/15	25/4/16	Kia Wulverghem
2/Lt	Hubbard, P.W.	no date	2/10/15	29/12/15	To Britain – wounded
Lt	Hyslop, W.	7/10/15	8/10/15	5/3/16	To Britain – wounded
2/Lt	Ingrams, F.R.	19/11/15	2/12/15	3/9/16	Kia Somme
2/Lt	Irons, C.S.	15/10/17	9/4/18		Ex Loyals. Still serving at Armistice
Lt	Jackson, R.M.S.	22/9/17	9/4/18	16/6/18	To Grantham – MGC
2/Lt	Jacobs, R.	no date	4/9/15	29/10/15	No info. Returned 9/11/15?
Lt and QM	James, E.F.	8/7/18	27/7/18		Still serving at Armistice
2/Lt	James, J.H.	27/12/15	10/1/16	15/3/16	To Britain – sick
2/Lt	Jamieson, H.S.G.	28/3/16	27/4/16	29/6/16	To Britain – wounded
Capt	Janion, C.W.	31/7/18	7/8/18		Still serving at Armistice
2/Lt	Johnson, J.M.	31/8/15	31/8/15	30/9/15	To Britain – wounded
2/Lt	Jones, C. McL.	31/12/17	13/1/18	29/3/18	To Britain – wounded

Rank on Arrival	Name	Disembarkation Date	Date Joining Unit	Leaving Date	Remarks
Lt	Jones, H.B.	?	9/2/18		Still serving at Armistice
Lt	Jones, H.L.	4/10/16	9/4/18		Ex Loyals. Still serving at Armistice
2/Lt	Keep, D.W.	16/4/18	19/4/18	16/10/18	Kia Haussy
2/Lt	Kelly, W.S.	16/4/18	19/4/18	7/9/18	To Britain – wounded
2/Lt	Kerckhove, H.V.	22/4/18	17/6/18		Still serving at Armistice
2/Lt	Keyes, F.	22/8/17	27/8/17	29/3/18	To Britain – wounded
2/Lt	King, C.	31/12/17	7/2/18	30/3/18	To Britain – sick. Returned 15/9/18. Still serving at Armistice
2/Lt	Kiver, H.W.	21/2/17	27/2/17	17/4/17	Kia Lens
2/Lt	Ladly, O.P.	29/1/17	5/2/17	17/11/17	To Britain – sick
2/Lt	Lancaster, H.J.	22/6/17	9/4/18		Ex Loyals. Still serving at Armistice
2/Lt	Lawrence, J.R.M.	28/3/16	27/4/16	16/8/16	Kia Somme
Lt Col	Le Fleming, L.J.	26/6/17	1/8/17	21/3/18	Kia *Kaiserschlacht*
2/Lt	Lefort, W.J.	10/8/17	18/8/17	15/7/18	To Britain – sick
Capt	Lester, F.	2/10/17	6/10/17	22/3/18	Mortally wounded and POW *Kaiserschlacht*
2/Lt	Lillywhite, G.	24/5/16	28/5/16	27/8/16	To Britain – wounded
2/Lt	Lindsay, W.H.	13/9/16	17/9/16	3/9/18	Kia Lens
2/Lt	Luty, F.	10/8/17	18/8/17	24/11/17	To Britain – wounded
2/Lt	McLaren, D.	30/8/15	30/8/15	1/10/15	To Britain – sick
Capt	Maingot, P.S.	20/4/16	9/4/18		Ex Loyals. Still serving at Armistice
2/Lt	Mann, T.	31/12/17	13/1/18	2/5/18	To Britain – sick. Returned 9/10/18. Still serving at Armistice
2/Lt	Manning, G.E.	13/9/16	17/9/16	15/6/17	To Britain – wounded
2/Lt	Marchant, R.H.	no date	5/12/15	26/1/16	Kia on patrol Ypres
Maj	Marshall, R.B.	21/4/18	26/4/18	26/5/18	Posted to 1/4th London
Lt	Mase, A.O.	24/8/16	27/8/16	7/3/17	To Britain – sick
2/Lt	Matheson, H.L.	25/5/16	27/5/16	16/8/16	Kia Somme
2/Lt	Matthews, A.A.	24/5/16	28/5/16	12/9/16	Dow Somme
Lt	Metcalfe, W.C.	12/5/16	17/5/16	19/8/16	Dow Somme
2/Lt	Mighell, P.	31/8/15	31/8/15	11/11/15	To General List for Signals Service
2/Lt	Millard, A.G.	20/1/17	31/1/17	7/8/17	Dow Ypres

Rank on Arrival	Name	Disembarkation Date	Date Joining Unit	Leaving Date	Remarks
2/Lt	Millis, H.A.	16/4/18	19/4/18	26/9/18	To Britain for RAF
2/Lt	Monro, J.D.	13/7/16	18/7/16	4/9/16	To Britain – wounded
2/Lt	Morphy, N.B.	25/5/16	27/5/16	30/6/16	To Britain – wounded
Lt	Morris, M.C.	15/6/16	24/6/16	6/8/16	To Britain – sick
2/Lt	Morrison, F.W.	no date	19/2/16	16/3/16	Posted to 17th MG Company. Ex-N. Staffs?
2/Lt	Morse, G.E.	10/5/16	17/5/16	22/6/16	Admitted to hospital, Britain, whilst on leave
2/Lt	Murray, K.D.	31/8/15	31/8/15	26/9/15	Kia Loos
Capt	Naunton, H.P.	31/7/18	7/8/18		Still serving at Armistice
Capt	Newington, E.	16/4/18	19/4/18	7/6/18	Posted to 1/East Surrey
2/Lt	Nilson, A.C.	22/8/17	27/8/17	16/10/18	POW Haussy
2/Lt	O'Brien, F.P.	20/4/16	23/4/16	16/8/16	Kia Somme
Capt	O'Connor, D.P.	31/8/15	31/8/15	28/9/15	To Britain – wounded. Returned 17/1/16, 17/8/16 (wounded again) and 1/5/17, 4/6/18 to Britain – sick
2/Lt	Orchard, A.F.	31/12/17	13/1/18	23/3/18	POW *Kaiserschlacht*
2/Lt	Patterson, G.	4/9/18	8/9/18		Still serving at Armistice
2/Lt	Patterson, J.K.P.	24/5/16	28/5/16	31/10/17	To Britain – wounded. Dow December 1917
Lt	Perrett, S.W.	17/4/18	19/4/18	28/4/18	Posted to 8/East Surrey
2/Lt	Petrie, A.H.	19/11/15	30/11/15	10/4/16	To General List for 72nd Trench Mortar Battery
2/Lt	Picton, J.A.	26/12/15	28/12.15	23/7/17	Kia Ypres
2/Lt	Poland, S.C.M.	31/8/15	31/8/15	1/3/16	To Britain – sick
2/Lt	Pope, P.J.	22/4/18	11/5/18		Still serving at Armistice
2/Lt	Pratt, A.V.	10/8/17	18/8/17	21/3/18	Kia *Kaiserschlacht*
2/Lt	Pullan, C.F.	7/10/15	10/10/15	3/11/16	To Britain – wounded
2/Lt	Puttock, H.H.	28/8/16	1/9/16	15/12/16	Transferred to MGC
2/Lt	Rawson, T.E.	31/5/17	7/2/18		Still serving at Armistice
2/Lt	Reading, C.C.T.	31/12/17	13/1/18	1/3/18	To Britain – sick
2/Lt	Reynolds, T.E.S.	5/1/17	10/1/17	2/8/17	To Britain – sick
2/Lt	Richards, J.H.S.	31/8/15	31/8/15	1/10/15	To Britain – wounded
2/Lt	Ridley, G.C.	16/4/18	19/4/18	27/10/18	To Britain – wounded
2/Lt	Rivers, G.C.	31/8/15	31/8/15	21/8/16	Kia Somme

Rank on Arrival	Name	Disembarkation Date	Date Joining Unit	Leaving Date	Remarks
2/Lt	Rivington, H.V.G.	31/8/15	31/8/15	26/6/16	To Britain – sick
2/Lt	Royal, J.H.	21/5/15	7/12/15	22/5/17	To Britain – sick. Returned 19/4/18. 10/8/18 to 72 Brigade as Intelligence Officer
2/Lt	Sadler, W.D.	27/4/17	2/5/17	3/ 8/17	Dow received at Ypres
2/Lt	Sampson, G.M.	16/4/18	19/4/18		Still serving at Armistice
Lt Col	Sanders, F.L.	31/8/15	31/8/15	16/10/15	To report to War Office (removed from command)
2/Lt	Sargant, G.H.	31/12/17	7/2/18	28/4/18	Posted to 8/East Surrey
2/Lt	Schofield, H.N.	25/5/16	27/5/16	20/4/18	Attached to 72nd Trench Mortar Battery
2/Lt	Schooling, P.H.	no date	27/3/16	30/3/16	Dow Wulverghem
2/Lt	Seaton, J.W.S.	19/6/17	7/2/18	21/3/18	POW *Kaiserschlacht*
2/Lt	Seel, F.E.	22/8/17	31/8/17	20/1/18	To Britain – wounded
2/Lt	Service, D.	3/9/17	9/4/18	16/10/18	To Britain for RAF
2/Lt	Sharp, G.B.	22/8./17	27/8/17	21/3/18	Kia *Kaiserschlacht*
Lt and QM	Sheffield, W.P.	8/10/17	11/10/17	6/7/18	To Britain – sick
2/Lt	Sherriff, R.C.	28/9/16	1/10/16	4/8/17	To Britain – wounded
2/Lt	Shipton, W.	22/4/18	17/6/18	8/7/18	To Britain – sick
Lt	Smith, E.C.	7/10/15	10/10/15	2/3/16	To Britain – sick
2/Lt	Smith, H.B.	30/11/17	16/12/17	19/10/18	To Britain – wounded
2/Lt	Smith, L.W.	22/4/18	11/5/18	27/9/18	Medical Board – Britain
2/Lt	Smither, A.W.	17/4/18	19/4/18	28/4/18	Posted to 8/East Surrey
2/Lt	Sparvell, G.E.	31/8/15	31/8/15	9/11/15	To Britain – sick
Capt	Spencer, W. St J.	28/8/16	1/9/16	18/11/16	To Britain – sick
2 /Lt	Spofforth, H.R.M.	26/12/15	29/12/15	27/3/16	To Britain – sick
2/Lt	Spurling, H.S.	26/12/15	29/12/15	21/8/16	To Britain – sick
2/Lt	Squire, J.W.	31/12/17	13/1/18	29/3/18	Dow Somme
2/Lt	Stanley, J.P.	4/9/18	12/10/18		To Britain – wounded
2/Lt	Stevens, E.A.	12/8/17	7/2/18	9/5/18	Still serving at Armistice
2/Lt	Stevens, J.P.	21/9/16	25/9/16	11/10/17	Medical Board – Britain
2/Lt	Stuart, C.	31/12/17	6/1/18	25/3/18	To Britain for six months' duty. Returned 22/4/18, 9/5/18 to Britain – wounded. To Britain – wounded. Returned 9/10/18. Still serving at Armistice

Rank on Arrival	Name	Disembarkation Date	Date Joining Unit	Leaving Date	Remarks
Lt Col	Swanton, T.H.S.	28/4/15	25/10/16	18/8/17	To Britain – wounded. Returned 2/10/17, 24/11/17 to 2/4th Lincolnshire
2/Lt	Taylor, F.F.	16/4/18	19/4/18	16/10/18	Kia Haussy
Captain	Taylor, M.W.	24/8/16	27/8/16	8/2/18	To Britain for six months' duty. Returned 27/5/18. Still serving at Armistice
2/Lt	Taylor, S.W.	24/5/16	28/5/16	29/9/16	To Britain – sick. Returned 21/3/17, 30/10/17 to RAF (*sic*), Britain
2/Lt	Terry, E.P.	9/7/17	14/7/17	30/8/17	To Britain – sick
2/Lt	Tetley, G.S.	7/10/15	10/10/15	23/5/16	To Britain – wounded. Returned 1/9/16, 13/7/17 to Britain – wounded.
2/Lt	Teversham, C.	16/4/18	19/4/18		Still serving at Armistice. Previous service?
Lt Col	Tew, H.S.	3/9/16	5/9/16	22/10/16	To Britain – sick (riding accident)
2/Lt	Thomas, L.C.	28/8/16	1/9/16	26/3/18	To Britain – wounded. Returned 31/7/18 48th Trench Mortar Battery. 21/9/18 to Britain – sick
Capt	Thompson, G.W.	no date	24/11/15	30/12/17	Attached 852 Area Employment Company (Medical Category Bii)
Lt	Thompson, W.	16/12/17	24/2/18	17/4/18	'2nd Entrenching Battalion'. To Britain wounded
2/Lt	Toplis, A.A.D.	14/9/16	17/9/16	19/4/17	To Britain for RFC
2/Lt	Travis, J.B.W.	22/8/17	27/8/17	18/2/18	To Grantham – MGC
2/Lt	Trench, N.C. Le P.	31/10/16	27/11/16	16/1/17	Kia Hulluch
2/Lt	Trenchard, C.W.	7/3/17	16/3/17	15/4/17	To Britain – wounded
Lt	Trim, F.E.	20/11/17	16/12/17	10/2/18	To Britain – sick
2/Lt	Tucker, H.R.	16/4/18	19/4/18		Still serving at Armistice
2/Lt	Turner, A.H.	17/4/18	19/4/18	28/4/18	Posted to 8/East Surrey
2/Lt	Urban, A.	25/5/16	28/5/16	2/9/16	Kia Somme
2/Lt	Vaughan, J.L.	27/8/15	28/9/15	16/8/16	Kia Somme
2/Lt	Waldron, W.A.V.	18/4/17	17/5/17	9/8/18	To 94 POW Company (Medical Category Bii)
Lt	Warre-Dymond, G.W.	28/8/16	1/9/16	26/3/18	POW *Kaiserschlacht*
2/Lt	Webb, H.S.	6/11/17	11/11/17	21/3/18	Kia *Kaiserschlacht*
2/Lt	Webb, L.H.	22/9/16	29/9/16	6/12/17	To Britain – sick

Rank on Arrival	Name	Disembarkation Date	Date Joining Unit	Leaving Date	Remarks
Lt	Webb, W.J.	25/1/17	10/2/17	27/7/17	To Britain – sick. Returned 7/10/18. Still serving at Armistice
Maj	Welch, H.V.	30/8/15	30/8/15	26/9/15	POW Loos. Dow 10/15
Lt	White, G.G.	30/9/15	24/10/15	14/3/16	To Britain – sick
2/Lt	Whiteman, E.L.	31/8/15	31/8/15		Still serving at Armistice
Lt	Wilkinson, H.C.	12/10/15	17/10/15	15/11/15	To Britain – sick. Returned 10/5/16, 22/5/16 to General List for duty with Signals Service
Lt	Williams, A.E.	31/7/18	7/8/18	25/10/18	To Britain – wounded
Capt	Williams, C.T.	no date	16/10/15	24/11/15	To Britain – wounded
2/Lt	Wills, S.W.	31/8/15	31/8/15	2/5/16	To Britain – sick
Lt	Wishart, C.W.E.	7/7/17	22/7/17		Still serving at Armistice, but attached HQ 24th Division
2/Lt	Wood, E.J.	16/4/18	19/4/18		Still serving at Armistice
2/Lt	Wright, C.H.	12/9/16	28/9/16	8/12/16	To Britain – sick
2/Lt	Wyatt, W.A.	28/8/16	1/9/16	15/12/16	Seconded to Heavy Branch MGC (tanks)
2/Lt	Yalden, T.H.	various dates	30/11/15	4/4/16	To Britain – wounded. Returned later?
2/Lt	Young, D.	?	9/4/18	19/4/18	Ex Loyals. To Britain for RAF
2/Lt	Youngman, J.M.	7/10/15	10/10/15	23/6/16	Kia Wulverghem

Main source: lists in Surrey History Centre, 8227/2/6.

Notes

1. This excludes officers like Captain Pirie, RAMC, attached to the battalion.
2. Some of the later 'returns' may be to different battalions of the East Surrey Regiment.
3. An obvious omission is P.M. Yonge who arrived with the battalion as a second lieutenant 27/8/16, was wounded, then sent to Britain sick 22/12/17, but returned 21/10/18.

Appendix V

24th Division Orders of Battle, 1915–1918

I. Loos, September 1915

71 Brigade	9/Norfolk, 9/Suffolk, 8/Bedfordshire, 11/Essex
72 Brigade	8/Queen's, 8/Buffs, 9/East Surrey, 8/R West Kent
73 Brigade	12/R Fusiliers, 9/R Sussex, 7/Northamptonshire, 13/Middlesex
Pioneer battalion	12/Sherwood Foresters

In addition to the infantry, the division's artillery consisted of 48 18pdrs in 3 artillery brigades (106–108), each of 4 batteries of 4 18pdrs; 16 howitzers in 1 brigade (109) of 4 batteries each of 4 howitzers; plus an ammunition column. There were also 3 engineer companies (103, 104 and 129); 3 field ambulances (72–74); 4 transport columns (194–197); a divisional signals company; a cavalry squadron from 1/1 Glasgow Yeomanry; a cyclist company; and a veterinary section.

II. Somme, August 1916

17 Brigade	8/Buffs, 1/R Fusiliers, 12/ R Fusiliers, 3/Rifle Brigade
72 Brigade	8/Queen's, 9/East Surrey, 8/R West Kent, 1/North Staffordshire
73 Brigade	9/R Sussex, 7/Northamptonshire, 13/Middlesex, 2/Leinster
Pioneer battalion	12/Sherwood Foresters

The infantry had been reorganised after Loos, with the exchange of four battalions with a regular division. Each artillery brigade now had three 18pdr batteries and one howitzer battery. The cavalry squadron was removed, but the division by now had trench-mortar batteries and an enhanced number of Vickers machine guns, concentrated in companies.

III. *Kaiserschlacht*, March 1918

17 Brigade	8/Queen's, 1/R Fusiliers, 3/Rifle Brigade
72 Brigade	**9/East Surrey, 8/R West Kent, 1/North Staffordshire**
73 Brigade	9/R Sussex, 7/Northamptonshire, 13/Middlesex
Pioneer battalion	12/Sherwood Foresters

BEF divisional artillery brigades had been reduced in 1917, in order to provide Army Field Brigades as strategic reserves. An infantry division was left with only two artillery brigades. However, field batteries had been increased to 6 18pdrs in 1916 and 6 4.5in howitzers in 1917, so each division had 36 guns and 12 howitzers of its own, as well as numerous mortars. Infantry brigades had been reduced to three battalions each in early 1918. 24th Division's Vickers machine-gun companies were incorporated in 24/Machine Gun Battalion. This form of organisation was maintained to the Armistice.

Sources: R. Westlake, *Kitchener's Army* (Staplehurst, 2003); Sir J.E. Edmonds, *The History of the Great War Military Operations France and Belgium: 1915 Volume II The Battles of Festubert, Aubers Ridge and Loos* (London, 1928), Appendix 3; D. Clarke, *British Artillery 1914–19: Field Army Artillery* (Oxford, 2004).

Orders for a Raid,
24/25 July 1918

Battalion Order No. 156 23rd July, 1918

1. GENERAL. "A" Coy. 9th Bn. East Surrey Regt., will carry out a raid on the night 24th /25th July, 1918. 'ZERO' Hour will be 12.30 a.m., 25th instant.

2. OBJECTIVE. The triangle N.14.a.68.18 – N.14.b.10.70 – N.14.b.30.35
To inflict casualties – blow in dugouts – capture prisoners.

3. STRENGTH. 2 Officers and 8 sections (58 other ranks).

4. POINT OF ASSEMBLY BEFORE RAID Nos. 2 and 4 sections at N.8c.63.05 Nos. 1, 3, 5, 6, 7, and 8 sections at N.14.a.24.70.

5. POINT OF ASSEMBLY AFTER RAID Sections 7, 8, 2, 5, 6, and 4 at dugouts in N.8.c.60.66. Sections 1 and 3 in cellar at N.14.a.05.54.

6. DETAIL
No. 1 section – 1 N.C.O. & 6 men – Right Blocking Party at N.14.a.68.28
No. 2 section – 1 N.C.O. & 6 men – Left Blocking Party at N.14.b.20.68
No. 3 section – 1 N.C.O. & 6 men with Lewis Gun – Right Covering Section at N.14.a.60.30
No. 4 section – 1 N.C.O. & 6 men with Lewis Gun – Left Covering Section at N.14.b.05.85
Nos. 5, 6, 7, and 8 sections – 1 N.C.O. & 6 men for working in enemy trenches, and 3 R.Es.

7. 'Zero' minus 3 to 'Zero' plus 1. Bombardment of front line from N.14.a.65.26 to N.14.b.10.70

8. 'Zero' minus 1. All parties at points of assembly.

9. 'Zero'. (No. 1 Artillery Barrage commences). Sections 2 & 4 move down CONDUCTOR SAP. Sections 1, 3, 5, 6, 7, and 8 move down COMBAT SAP (No. 3 section leading).

10. 'ZERO' plus 3 to 'Zero' plus 7. All artillery on Battalion front silent, after which, barrage No. 2 comes down.

11. POSITIONS
Left Sections. No. 2 Covering Section will take up its position on enemy wire. No. 4 Blocking Section will enter enemy trench and take up position.
Right Sections. No. 3 Covering Section will take up its position.
Sections No. 1, 5, 6, 7, and 8 will enter enemy trenches at N.14.a.65.26
No. 1 Blocking Section will lead and make straight for its position.
2/Lt. TEVERSHAM, Nos. 5 & 6 sections and 3 R.Es. will proceed along enemy front line from N.14.a.65.26 to N.14.b.10.70 inflicting casualties, taking prisoners and destroying dugouts at approximately N.14.a.68.30, N.14.a.75.45, N.14.a.90.60 with mobile charges.
Lieut. BIRTLES and Nos. 7 & 8 sections will move up enemy Support Line from N.14.a.65.26 to N.14.b.30.36, thence to N.14.b.10.70, inflicting casualties and taking prisoners. On arriving at N.14.b.30.36, No. 8 section will establish a block of 1 N.C.O. and 3 men.

12. WITHDRAWAL The O.C., Raid, (Lieut. BIRTLES), is responsible for putting up the withdrawal signal – GREEN over RED over GREEN, fired from a rifle grenade. This he will on no account do unless –
(a) casualties necessitate it.
(b) prisoners have been obtained.
(c) the raiding party has already been in enemy trenches 15 mins., i.e., 'Zero' plus 20 mins.
Provided that prisoners are captured by the time the O.C., Raid (Lieut. BIRTLES), and Nos. 7 & 8 sections have reached the point N.14.b.10.70, he will ascertain if Nos. 5 & 6 sections are all correct, and will put up the withdrawal signal. This signal will be repeated at Advanced Coy. H.Q., N.8.c.60.66.
    Nos. 7, 8, 2, 5, 6, and 4 sections will withdraw along CONDUCTOR SAP, and Nos. 1 and 3 sections along COMBAT SAP.
    Password for Lieut. BIRTLE's party on meeting 2/Lieut. TEVERSHAM'S party, to avoid engaging one another, will be "GALLANTS".

13. AID POST ARRANGEMENTS. The Advanced Aid Post will be at N.8.a.13.00. Two Stretcher Bearers will be at N.14.a.05.54, two at N.14.a.60.32 and two at N.14.b.15.78.

14. ARTILLERY ARRANGEMENTS. Previous to 'Zero' Hour, the following danger points will have been dealt with:-
N.14.a.90.35 and N.14.b.10.92, also wire at enemy end of CONDUCTOR and COMBAT Saps.
'Zero' minus 3 to 'Zero' plus 1. Bombardment of the front line from N.14.a.65.26 to N.14.b.10.70.
BARRAGE No. 1 'Zero' to 'Zero' plus 3 mins.
    Sunken Road in N.14.a.
    Fork Road at N.14.c.44.80
    Sunken Road at N.8.d.40.10 to N.14.b.59.70.
    Sunken Road at N.8.d.80.10 to N.14.b.40.60.
'Zero' plus 3 to 'Zero' plus 7 mins. – SILENCE
BARRAGE No. 2. 'Zero' plus 7 to withdrawal signal plus 5 mins.
At same points as Barrage No. 1 and along Railway from N.14.a.00.90 to N.15.a.44.78.
BARRAGE No. 3. At withdrawal signal plus 5, will creep back on enemy front line and rest there for 5 mins. Silence for 5 mins. Then 5 mins. intense again on enemy front line.
'Zero' to 'Zero' plus 30 mins. Heavy diversion on or about TRIANGLE STACKS. T.Ms. will be included in this. Counter battery work.
ADDITIONAL ARTILLERY. Light T.Ms to fire on LA BASSEE RD (N.14.a.40.15, also N.8.d.50.25 to N.8.d.40.00. Medium T.Ms. firing on N.9.a.35.00, N.9.a.20.80 and N.3.c.30.40 approx.

15. MINOR ATTRACTIONS. At 'Zero' plus 4, various coloured Very Lights will be fired from about N.8.b central.

16. CODE WORDS. Withdrawal signal has gone up – CHEERS
                        Sections all back – BON
                        No casualties – CORRECT
                        KILLED – DULL
                        Wounded – HAPPY
                        Prisoners – RATS

17. Synchronisation of watches at CAMERON CASTLE 10.30p.m., 24th.

18. STRAGGLERS. If necessary, to guide any men who have become detached from their Section and lost direction in "NO MAN'S LAND", Green Very Lights will be fired at intervals from the time withdrawal signal goes up until dawn from N.13.b.90.90
(Sd.) J.C. BROWN, Major, Comdg. 9 th Bn. East Surrey Regt.

Notes

Some sources are quoted from frequently and for these details are given in full in the first instance and subsequent quotations from these sources are not annotated in the main text.

Chapter 1

1. R.C. Sherriff, 'My Diary', *Journal of the East Surrey Regiment, Vol. 1, Nos 1–4 and Vol. II, Nos 1–2 New Series* (May 1937), p. 115.
2. *JESR* (May 1937), p. 145.
3. Sherriff, 'My Diary', *JESR* (May 1939), p. 96.
4. Miller, IWM 11043.
5. I.F.W. Beckett and K. Simpson, *A Nation in Arms: A social study of the British Army in the First World War* (Manchester, 1985), p. 39.
6. The National Archives, files in series WO 339.
7. G. Frankau, *Gilbert Frankau's Self Portrait: A novel of his own life* (London, 1940), pp. 153–154.
8. TNA, WO 339/21442.
9. P. Mealyer and C. Haig, 'Jimmy Carpenter's War Diary', *Stand To!* (January 2005), pp. 15–18.
10. Billman, Imperial War Museum 76/210/1.
11. Letter to the author from Dr E. Webb.
12. Billman, IWM 76/210/1.
13. Mealyer and Hague, 'Jimmy Carpenter's War Diary', p. 16.
14. Ibid.
15. G. Frankau, *Peter Jackson, Cigar Merchant* (London, 1947), pp. 79–80.
16. M. Dierden, 'Nellie's Sad Search for Her "Dear Teddy"', *Surrey Advertiser*, 9 November 2007.
17. Anon., *The History of the Eighth Battalion The Queen's Own Royal West Kent Regiment 1914–19* (London and Aylesbury, 1921), pp. 7–8.
18. Frankau, *Peter Jackson*, pp. 89–90.
19. TNA, WO 95/2215.
20. Surrey History Centre, ESR/25/BIRT.

Chapter 2

1. P. Magnus, *Kitchener: Portrait of an Imperialist* (London, 1961), pp. 331–332.
2. Ibid., p. 333.
3. Stewart to Becke, The National Archives, WO 95/2189.
4. H.W. Pearse and H.S. Sloman, *History of the East Surrey Regiment* (London, 1924), Vol. II, p. 164.
5. Ibid.
6. Billman, Imperial War Museum 76/20/1. He calls his account an 'Abridged diary of my journey to France and my time spent there'. It appears to have been written up as a narrative, at intervals, in loose sheets, and covers his experiences up to the end of 1917. All following references to Billman are from this.
7. Mitford to Edmonds, TNA, CAB 45/121.
8. Ibid.
9. W. von Vormann, *Infanterie-Regiment Fürst Leopold von Anhalt-Dessau (1. Magdeburgisches) Nr. 26* (Oldenburg, 1925), p. 303.

10. G. Herr, *Das Königlich-Preussische Mansfelder Feldartillerie-Regiment Nr. 75 im Weltkrieg 1914/18*, Gräfenhainichen, 1934, pp. 272–273.
11. Stewart to Becke, TNA, WO 95/2189.
12. Capper's report, TNA, WO 158/32. Note particularly that no information was given about the German positions.
13. R.G.A. Hamilton, *The War Diary of the Master of Belhaven* (London, 1924), pp. 75–76.
14. A. Baumgarten-Crusius, *Sachsen in Grosser Zeit* (Leipzig, 1919–1920), Vol. II, pp. 231–232.
15. Mitford to Edmonds, TNA, CAB 45/121.
16. Quoted in A. Rawson, *Battleground Europe Loos–Hill 70* (Barnsley, 2002), p. 123.
17. Pearce and Sloman, *History of the East Surrey Regiment*, Vol. II, p. 166.
18. According to Fenwick, TNA, CAB 45/120.
19. Report in 72 Brigade war diary, TNA, WO 95/2210.
20. TNA, WO 339/18138.
21. E. Schmidt-Osswald, *Das Altenburger Regiment (8. thuringisches Infanterie Regiment Nr. 153) im Weltkrieg* (Oldenburg and Berlin, 1927), p. 188. A list of thirteen different regiments, derived from prisoners' badges follows. It includes the East Surrey, Buffs and Suffolk, from Mitford's attack, along with four from 21st Division and six from 15th Division.
22. Von Vormann, *Infanterie-Regiment Fürst Leopold von Anhalt-Dessau (1. Magdeburgisches) Nr. 26*, p. 304.
23. Quoted in Sir J.E. Edmonds, *History of the Great War Military Operations France and Belgium: 1915 Volume II The Battles of Festubert, Aubers Ridge and Loos* (London, 1928), p. 335.
24. Ibid., p. 342.
25. Pearce and Sloman, *History of the East Surrey Regiment*, Vol. II, p. 168 – Edmonds gives slightly higher figures.
26. *London Gazette*, 18 November 1915, p. 11451.
27. Von Vormann, *Infanterie-Regiment Fürst Leopold von Anhalt-Dessau (1. Magdeburgisches) Nr. 26*. It is tempting to consider that the wounded officer was Major Welch of 9/East Surrey, but IR 26 were a little further to the north. Bertling's task in dealing with so many casualties was made worse by his assistant surgeon being wounded with a shrapnel ball that day.
28. TNA, reports in WO 161/98.
29. TNA, WO 339/18634.
30. TNA, WO 363.
31. M. Dierden, 'Nellie's Sad Search for Her "Dear Teddy"', *Surrey Advertiser*, 9 November 2007. Cutt's body was later identified.
32. *Surrey Comet*, 12 February 1916.
33. TNA, WO 339/13758.
34. TNA, WO 339/18138.
35. TNA, WO 339/11950.
36. R.A. Giesecke, *Erinnnerungsblätter der 178er* (Dresden, 1917), Vol. I, p. 154.
37. R. Graves, *Goodbye to All That* (London, 1963), p. 135.
38. TNA, WO 158/32.
39. Anon., *The History of the Eighth Battalion The Queen's Own Royal West Kent Regiment 1914–19* (London and Aylesbury, 1921), p. 25.
40. IWM 87/3/1. Westmacott later added, after serving with the division, 'In spite of their early bad luck, the 24th Division became a very fine fighting division later on.'
41. R.C. Sherriff, 'My Diary', *Journal of the East Surrey Regiment, Vol. 1, Nos 1–4 and Vol. II, Nos 1–2 New Series* (May 1937), p. 116.
42. Stewart to Becke, TNA, WO 95/2189.

Chapter 3

1. H.W. Pearse and H.S. Sloman, *History of the East Surrey Regiment* (London, 1924), Vol. II, p. 27.
2. *Surrey Comet*, 18 August 1917.

3. F.C. Hitchcock, *Stand To A Diary of the Trenches 1915–18* (London, 1937), p. 106.
4. Lord Moran, *The Anatomy of Courage* (London, 1945), pp. 82–83.
5. Billman, Imperial War Museum 76/20/1. All further references to Billman are from this.
6. P. Mealyer and C. Haig, 'Jimmy Carpenter's War Diary', *Stand To!* (September 2005), pp. 44–45.
7. Pearce and Sloman, *History of the East Surrey Regiment*, Vol. II, p. 169.
8. Hitchcock, *Stand To*, p. 114.
9. Ibid., p. 116.
10. Ibid., p. 119.
11. The National Archives, WO 95/2215. All further references to the battalion war diary are from this.
12. G. Bamberg, *Das Reserve-Infanterie-Regiment Nr. 106 (kgl. sächs.) im Weltkrieg* (Dresden, 1925), pp. 50–51.
13. K. Otto, *Das Kgl. Sächs. Feldartillerie-Regiment Nr. 246* (Dresden, 1928), pp. 55–56.
14. Anon., *The History of the Eighth Battalion The Queen's Own Royal West Kent Regiment 1914–19* (London and Aylesbury, 1921), p. 51.
15. R.G.A. Hamilton, *The War Diary of the Master of Belhaven* (London, 1924), pp. 135 and 184.
16. Ibid., p. 129.
17. TNA, WO 339/50522. Various units could be inserted in this doggerel –especially the A.S.C. (Army Service Corps), most of whose men served well behind the line.
18. L. Orgeldinger, *Das Württembergische Reserve-Infanterie-Regiment Nr. 246* (Stuttgart, 1931), p. 138.
19. Pearce and Sloman, *History of the East Surrey Regiment*, Vol. II, p. 174 and TNA WO 339/50522.
20. H. Lehmann, *Kgl. Sächs Reserve-Jäger-Bataillon Nr. 26* (Dresden, 1923), p. 70.
21. Offiziersverein R.I.R. 214, *Geschichte des Grossherzoglich-Mecklenburgischen-Reserve-Infanterie Regiments Nr. 214* (Dessau, 1933), pp. 54–55.
22. Lambert, IWM 88/18/1. Lambert's diary, for August 1915–November 1916, survives as he wrote it. Unfortunately, the entries are very brief.
23. Pirie, unpublished diary. Pirie wrote this up most days, often at some length. It is a particularly valuable source for the battalion's experiences whilst he was with it.
24. Pearce and Sloman, *History of the East Surrey Regiment*, Vol. II, p. 176.

Chapter 4
1. Anon., *The History of the Eighth Battalion The Queen's Own Royal West Kent Regiment 1914–19* (London and Aylesbury, 1921), p. 38.
2. The National Archives, WO 95/2210.
3. Anon., *The History of the Eighth Battalion*, p. 38.
4. R.G.A. Hamilton, *The War Diary of the Master of Belhaven* (London, 1924), p. 169.
5. Ibid., p. 165.
6. Sir J.E. Edmonds, *The Occupation of the Rhineland 1918–1929* (London, 1987), p. 85.
7. H. Hannan, 'Loos Reflections', *Queen's Royal Surrey Regiment Newsletter*, November 1981, pp. 6–7.
8. Pirie, unpublished diary. All further references to Pirie are from this.
9. E. Makoben, *Geschichte des Reserve-Infanterie-Regiments Nr. 212 im Weltkrieg 1914–1918* (Oldenburg, 1933), p. 208.
10. Billman, Imperial War Museum 76/20/1. All following references to Billman are from this.
11. Sir J.E. Edmonds, *History of the Great War Military Operations France and Belgium: 1916 Volume I Sir Douglas Haig's command to the 1st July: Battle of the Somme* (London, 1932), p. 203 and Divisional War Diary WO 95/2189.
12. Lillywhite, IWM 76/19/1. All following references to Lillywhite are from this.
13. Makoben, *Geschichte des Reserve-Infanterie-Regiments Nr. 212*, p. 220.
14. Lambert, IWM 88/18/1.
15. H.W. Pearse and H.S. Sloman, *History of the East Surrey Regiment* (London, 1924), Vol. II, p. 182. An 'aerial torpedo' was probably a large trench mortar bomb with fins – what the Germans called a *Fluegelmine*.

Chapter 5

1. R. Prior and T. Wilson, *Command on the Western Front The Military Career of Sir Henry Rawlinson 1914–1918* (Barnsley, 2004), pp. 204–207.

2. Billman, Imperial War Museum P76/20/1. All further references to Billman are from this. The temperature on 1 August was recorded as 86 °F.

3. Sir J.E. Edmonds, *History of the Great War Military Operations France and Belgium: 1916 Volume I Sir Douglas Haig's command to the 1st July: Battle of the Somme* (London, 1932), p. 128.

4. F.C. Hitchcock, *Stand To A Diary of the Trenches 1915–18* (London, 1937), p. 134.

5. Ibid., p. 137.

6. Surrey History Centre, ESR19/12.

7. Hitchcock, *Stand To*, p. 133.

8. The National Archives, WO 95/2210. All further references to the brigade war diary are to this.

9. M. Chappell, *British Battle Insignia 1 1914–18* (London, 1991), p. 44, correspondence with Taff Gillingham and SHC, ESR19/1/2 Battalion Orders August 1916.

10. H. Hannan, 'Loos Reflections', *Queen's Royal Surrey Regiment Newsletter*, November 1981, pp. 6–7. Hannan recalls the lines being 80–90yd apart in this case.

11. Pirie, unpublished diary. All further references to Pirie are to this.

12. TNA, officer files in series WO 339 and 374.

13. I.F.W. Beckett and K. Simpson, *A Nation in Arms: A social study of the British Army in the First World War* (Manchester, 1985), pp. 79–80.

14. Lillywhite, IWM 76/19/1. All further references to Lillywhite are from this.

15. TNA, WO 213/9.

16. SHC, ESR/19/12, etc. and TNA, WO 363.

17. S. Rogerson, *Twelve days on the Somme a Memoir of the Trenches, 1916* (London, 2006), pp. 88–89.

18. Lodge Patch, IWM 66/304/1.

19. Abraham, IWM P191.

20. Hannan, 'Loos Reflections', p. 7 with additional information from Dr D. Brooke.

21. Marquis De Ruvigny, The *Marquis De Ruvigny's Roll of Honour: A Biographical Record of His Majesty's Military and Aerial Forces who fell in the Great War 1914–18* (n.p., 1922), Vol. II, p. 17.

22. D. Cohen, 'War Art', *Stand To!* (January 1996), p. 5.

23. R. Bechtle, *Der Ulmer Grenadiere an der Westfront-Geschichte des Grenadier-Regiments König Karl (5. Württ.) Nr. 123 im Weltkrieg 1914–1918* (Stuttgart, 1920), p. 77.

24. Pre-war he had commanded the Army's balloon school. Hitchcock, *Stand To*, p. 137.

25. Lord Moran, *The Anatomy of Courage* (London, 1945), p. 136.

26. B. Martin, *Poor Bloody Infantry: a subaltern on the Western Front 1916–1917* (London, 1987), p. 91.

27. H.W. Pearse and H.S. Sloman, *History of the East Surrey Regiment* (London, 1924), p. 246.

28. Captain W. Miles, *History of the Great War Military Operations France and Belgium 1916 Volume II 2nd July 1916 to the end of the Battles of the Somme* (London, 1938), p. 174.

29. Hitchcock, *Stand To*, p. 169.

30. J. Sheldon, *The German Army on the Somme 1914–1916* (Barnsley, 2005), p. 258.

31. Verein ehemaliger Offizier des Regiments, *Das Füsilier-Regiment Prinz Heinrich von Preussen (Brandenburgisches) Nr. 35 im Weltkrieg* (Berlin, 1929), p. 184.

32. Ibid., p. 185.

33. To clarify what happened, as well as the battalion's war diary, TNA, WO 95/2215, reference has been made to Mitford's copy report to division in it and the division's report in its war diary, TNA, WO 95/2190 and also Pearce and Sloman, *History of the East Surrey Regiment*, Vol. II, p. 247.

34. Verein ehemaliger Offizier des Regiments, *Das Füsilier-Regiment Prinz Heinrich von Preussen (Brandenburgisches) Nr. 35 im Weltkrieg*, pp. 185–186.

35. W. Schmidt, *2.Nassuaisches Infanterie Regiment* (Oldenburg and Berlin, 1922), p. 101.

36. Pirie letter in Lillywhite, IWM 76/19/1. Summers had to perform another exploit before gaining his second medal.
37. TNA, WO 363. Coxhill is commemorated on the Thiepval Memorial.
38. Sheldon, *The German Army on the Somme*, pp. 279–280.
39. Moran, *The Anatomy of Courage*, pp. 83–84.
40. C. Duffy, *Through German Eyes The British and the Somme 1916* (London, 2006), p. 64.
41. Moran, *The Anatomy of Courage*, pp. 11–12.
42. Hitchcock, *Stand To*, pp. 164–168.
43. Divisional history quoted in Edmonds, *History of the Great War Military Operations France and Belgium: 1916 Volume I*, p. 494.
44. E. Jünger (trans. R.H. Mottram) *The Storm of Steel* (London, 1941), pp. 109–110.

Chapter 6

1. Pirie, unpublished diary. All further references to Pirie are from this.
2. Billman, Imperial War Museum 76/20/1. All further references to Billman are from this.
3. R.C. Sherriff, *No Leading Lady: an autobiography* (London, 1968), p. 35.
4. Surrey History Centre, 3813 Box 8 file 2.
5. Letters to his father and mother are in SHC, 2332 Box 44. All further references to Sherriff's letters to his parents are from this.
6. R.C. Sherriff , 'My Diary', *Journal of the East Surrey Regiment, Vol. 1, Nos 1–4 and Vol. II, Nos 1–2 New Series* (May 1937), p. 116.
7. Ibid.
8. Ibid., pp. 117–118.
9. Ibid., p. 189 (November 1937).
10. Ibid., p. 191.
11. Ibid., p. 31 (November 1938).
12. F.C. Hitchcock, *Stand To A Diary of the Trenches 1915–18* (London, 1937), p. 182.
13. Ibid., p. 200.
14. Tower, IWM P472, p. 31.
15. E. Gruson, *Das Königlich Preussische 4. Thüringische Infanterie-Regiment Nr. 72 im Weltkrieg* (Oldenburg, 1930), p. 281.
16. Lambert, IWM 88/18/1.
17. Hitchcock, *Stand To*, p. 206.
18. SHC, ESR/25/ALLE/1.
19. The National Archives, WO 363.
20. TNA, WO 95/2215.

Chapter 7

1. The National Archives, WO 95/2215. All further references to the battalion war diary are to this.
2. Pirie, unpublished diary. All further references to Pirie are from this.
3. Anon., *The History of the Eighth Battalion The Queen's Own Royal West Kent Regiment 1914–19* (London and Aylesbury, 1921), p. 68.
4. F.C. Hitchcock, *Stand To A Diary of the Trenches 1915–18* (London, 1937), pp. 229–230.
5. Ibid., p. 230.
6. M. Connelly, *Steady the Buffs!: a regiment, a region, and the Great War* (Oxford, 2006), p. 133.
7. The raid is described in detail in the battalion's war diary and orders for it are in the brigade's, TNA WO 95/2211.
8. Surrey History Centre, ESR/25/CLARK/19.
9. Liddle Archive, SC Liddle GS 1590.
10. E. Gruson, *Das Königlich Preussische 4. Thüringische Infanterie-Regiment Nr. 72 im Weltkrieg* (Oldenburg, 1930), p. 284.
11. Anon., *The History of the Eighth Battalion*, p. 67.

12. Ibid., p. 69.
13. SHC, 2332/Box 44. All further references to Sherriff's letters home are from this.
14. TNA, WO 339/69081.
15. Billman, Imperial War Museum 76/20/1. All further references to Billman are from this.
16. Tower, IWM P472, p. 31.
17. Anon., *The History of the Eighth Battalion*, p. 73.
18. SHC, 2332/Box 38K.
19. Verein ehemaliger Offizier des Regiments, *Das Füsilier-Regiment Prinz Heinrich von Preussen (Brandenburgisches) Nr. 35 im Weltkrieg* (Berlin, 1929), pp. 226–227.
20. Ibid., p. 229.
21. TNA, WO 339/2048. Spofforth was considered recovered by 1917 and then served at Salonika.
22. Lord Moran, *The Anatomy of Courage* (London, 1945), p. 5.
23. Ibid., p. x.
24. Ibid.
25. Ibid., pp. 19–20.
26. Ibid., p. 117.
27. TNA, WO 339/41728.
28. TNA, WO 339/37035.
29. TNA, WO 339/58568.
30. Sir J.E. Edmonds, *History of the Great War Military Operations France and Belgium: 1916 Volume I Sir Douglas Haig's command to the 1st July: Battle of the Somme* (London, 1932), p. 93.
31. TNA, WO 363.
32. SHC, ESR/25/CLARK/19.
33. Sherriff, 'My Diary', *JESR* (November 1937), p. 190.

Chapter 8

1. Pirie, unpublished diary. All further references to Pirie are from this.
2. Billman, Imperial War Museum 76/20/1. All further references to Billman are from this.
3. WO 95/2211 – brigade war diary and M. von Sinner, *Das 2. Schlesische Jaeger-Bataillon Nr. 6* (Oldenburg and Berlin, 1921), p. 78. Both sides had come to holding front-line positions with fewer men, to save casualties from artillery and mortars.
4. Anon., *The History of the Eighth Battalion The Queen's Own Royal West Kent Regiment 1914–19* (London and Aylesbury, 1921), p. 90.
5. G.D. Sheffield and J. Bourne, *Douglas Haig War Diaries and Letters 1914–1918* (London, 2005), p. 233, note.
6. The National Archives, WO 363.
7. Marquis De Ruvigny, *The Marquis De Ruvigny's Roll of Honour: A Biographical Record of His Majesty's Military and Aerial Forces who fell in the Great War 1914–18* (n.p., 1922), Vol. III, p. 149.
8. Surrey History Centre, 2332 Box 44. All further references to Sherriff's letters home are from this.
9. R.C. Sherriff, 'My Diary', *Journal of the East Surrey Regiment, Vol. 1, Nos 1–4 and Vol. II, Nos 1–2 New Series* (November 1937), p. 190.
10. TNA, WO 95/2215. All further references to the battalion war diary are from this.
11. R.C. Sherriff, 'The English Public Schools in the War', in G. Panichas, *Promise of Greatness: The War of 1914–1918* (Worthing, 1968), pp. 144–145.
12. Major H.M. Farmer in Revd O. Creighton, *With the Twenty-Ninth Division in Gallipoli* (London, 1916), p. 191.
13. Quoted in J. Sheldon, *The German Army at Passchendaele* (Barnsley, 2007), p. 52.
14. R.G.A. Hamilton, *The War Diary of the Master of Belhaven* (London, 1924), p. 356.
15. Tower, IWM P472, pp. 37–38.
16. Sheldon, *The German Army at Passchendaele*, pp. 69–70.
17. TNA, WO 95/2211.

18. Sherriff, 'The English Public Schools in the War', pp. 147–150.
19. Sheldon, *The German Army at Passchendaele*, p. 98.
20. SHC, ESR 19/1/2.
21. P. Fiedel, *Geschichte des Infanterie-Regiments von Winterfeldt (2. Oberschlesisches) Nr. 23: Das Regiment im Weltkrieg* (Berlin, 1929), pp. 184–185.
22. R. Van Emden and S. Humphries, *All Quiet on the Home Front* (London, 2003), pp. 109 and 114.
23. De Ruvigny, *The Marquis De Ruvigny's Roll of Honour*, Vol. 4, p. 108.
24. Hamilton, *The War Diary*, p. 372.

Chapter 9

1. Anon., *The History of the Eighth Battalion The Queen's Own Royal West Kent Regiment 1914–19* (London and Aylesbury, 1921), pp. 134–135.
2. Anon., *Das Reserve Infanterie-Regiment Nr. 440 im Weltkrieg* (Oldenburg, 1933), p. 316.
3. The National Archives, WO 95/2215.
4. This and all following correspondence between Sherriff and his fellow officers is in Surrey History Centre, 2332 Box 33/2.
5. TNA, files from series WO 339 and 374.
6. Sir J.E. Edmonds, *History of the Great War Military Operations France and Belgium: 1918 Volume I The German March offensive and its preliminaries*, London, 1935, with accompanying appendices volume and map case, p. 39.
7. SHC, 2332 Box 44.
8. TNA, WO 339/6908.
9. R. Holmes, *Tommy The British soldier on the Western Front 1914–1918* (London, 2004), p. 187. The Welsh Guards, for instance, are recorded as having a total strength of 715 in October 1918, but only 399 available for battle after the detached, those on courses, leave, sick, details and transport/quarter master's staff, etc. had been deducted. C.H. Dudley Ward, *History of the Welsh Guards* (London, 1920), p. 259.

Chapter 10

1. The National Archives, WO 95/2215. All further references to the battalion war diary are from this.
2. Anon., *The History of the Eighth Battalion The Queen's Own Royal West Kent Regiment 1914–19* (London and Aylesbury, 1921), pp. 157–158. Leave was only stopped on 20 March.
3. Ibid., p. 158.
4. TNA, WO 95/2212. All further references to the brigade war diary are from this.
5. Nurse, Imperial War Museum 81/23/1.
6. Liddle Archives, SC Liddle GS1590.
7. TNA, WO 339/103201.
8. Quoted in M. Middlebrook, *The Kaiser's Battle 21 March 1918, the First Day of the German Spring Offensive* (London, 2000), p. 158. Crimmins received an MM for his bravery on 22 March, acting as a runner between advance Battalion HQ and Battalion HQ under intense machine-gun fire.
9. Liddle Archives, SC Liddle GS1590.
10. TNA, WO 95/2202.
11. TNA, WO 95/2192.
12. TNA, CAB 45/192, narrative sent to Official Historian.
13. TNA, WO 95/1109. All future references to the hussars' war diary are from this.
14. K.W. Mitchinson, *Battleground Europe Riqueval* (Barnsley, 1998), p. 54.
15. G. Goes, *Der Tag X: Die Grosse Schlacht in Frankreich (21.März–15.April 1918)* (Berlin, 1933), p. 48.
16. Middlebrook, *The Kaiser's Battle*, p. 247.
17. Goes, *Der Tag X*, p. 49.
18. TNA, WO 95/2201.

19. Surrey History Centre, ESR/25/CLARK/14. The Hussars' war diary says the message was received by Lieutenant Colonel Anderson at 11.40am.
20. Goes, *Der Tag X*, p. 76.
21. Sir J.E. Edmonds, *History of the Great War Military Operations France and Belgium: 1918 Volume I The German March offensive and its preliminaries*, London, 1935, with accompanying appendices volume and map case, p. 348.
22. TNA, WO 374/51431.
23. TNA, WO 339/97715.
24. M. Reymann, *Das Infanterie-Regiment von Alvensleben (6. Brandenbg.) Nr. 52 im Weltkrieg 1914/1918* (Oldenburg and Berlin, 1923), pp. 190–191.
25. M. Schone, *1. Bataillon des 2. Kgl.sächs Fussartillerie-Regiments Nr. 19* (Dresden, 1925), p. 100.
26. Goes, *Der Tag X*, p. 103.
27. Westmacott, IWM 87/13/1. All future references to Westmacott are from this.
28. R. von Freydorf, *Das 1. Badische Leib-Grenadier-Regiment Nr. 109 im Weltkrieg 1914–1918* (Karlsruhe, 1927), p. 534.
29. F. Führen, *Füsilier-Regiment Fürst Karl Anton von Hohenzollern (Hohenzollernsches) Nr. 40: Die Hohenzollernfüsiliere im Weltkrieg 1914–1918* (Furtwangen, 1930), p. 541.
30. TNA, WO 339/115622.
31. Anon., 'To the Last Man and the Last Round', *Queen's Royal Surrey Regiment Newsletter* (May 1972), pp. 11–12.
32. TNA, WO 339/2036.
33. Anon., 'To the Last Man and the Last Round', pp. 11–12.
34. Billman, IWM 76/210/1.
35. TNA, WO 339/2036.
36. O. von Grüter, H. Lorenz, P. Kirch and W. Schede, *Das 2. Badische Grenadier–Regiment Kaiser Wilhelm I Nr. 110 im Weltkrieg 1914–1918* (Oldenburg, 1927), pp. 299–300.
37. Anon., *The History of the Eighth Battalion*, p. 192.
38. *London Gazette* and battalion war diary. A large number of the decorations listed in H.W. Pearse and H.S. Sloman's *History of the East Surrey Regiment* (London, 1924) were to men for service with the Loyals.

Chapter 11

1. The National Archives, WO 95/2192. All following references to the divisional war diary are from this.
2. TNA, WO 95/2215. All following references to the battalion war diary are from this.
3. TNA, WO 374/11914 and *Who's Who*.
4. K. Held and O. Stobbe, *Das Königl. Preuss. Infanterie-Regt. Graf Barufuss (4. Westf.) Nr. 17* (Berlin, 1934), p. 217.
5. W. Lasch, *Geschichte des 3. Unterelsässischen Infanterie-Regiments Nr. 138, 1887–1919* (Saarbruecken, 1937), p. 296.
6. Held and Stobbe, *Das Königl. Preuss. Infanterie-Regt. Graf Barufuss (4. Westf.) Nr. 17*, p. 20. *Vizefeldwebel* Parthier, who held the Iron Cross 1st Class, was a particularly serious loss to his regiment.
7. Divisional intelligence report 19 September 1918 in WO 95/2192.
8. *London Gazette*, 12 November 1918.
9. H.W. Pearse and H.S. Sloman, *History of the East Surrey Regiment* (London, 1924), Vol. III, p. 207.
10. Ibid.
11. Intelligence reports in the brigade (WO 95/2212) and divisional war diaries.

Chapter 12

1. The National Archives, WO 95/2212.
2. Anon., *The History of the Eighth Battalion The Queen's Own Royal West Kent Regiment 1914–19* (London and Aylesbury, 1921), pp. 242–243.

3. TNA, WO 95/2215. All further references to the battalion war diary are from this.
4. Surrey History Centre, ESR/25/MCNAJ/I.
5. TNA, WO 339/113655.
6. TNA, WO 339/96600.
7. *Surrey Advertiser*, 9 November 1918.
8. Westmacott, Imperial War Museum 87/13/1. Another Frenchwoman had been shot dead trying to rescue a wounded sergeant during the fighting. All further references to Westmacott are to this.
9. C. Mücke, *Das Grossherzoglich Badische Infanterie Regiment Nr. 185* (Oldenburg and Berlin, 1922), p. 100.
10. A. Huttmann and W. Krueger, *Das Infanterie Regiment von Lutzow (1. Rhein.) Nr. 25 im Welt-krieg 1914–18* (Berlin, 1929), p. 209.
11. Ibid., pp. 215–216.
12. F. Bachmann and W. Pfister, *Reserve-Infanterie-Regiment Nr. 223 im Weltkrieg* (Giessen, 1937), pp. 479–480.
13. Huttmann and Krueger, *Das Infanterie Regiment von Lutzow (1. Rhein.) Nr. 25 im Weltkrieg 1914–18*, p. 216.
14. *London Gazette*, 9 December 1919.
15. An anonymous platoon commander quoted in H.W. Pearse and H.S. Sloman, *History of the East Surrey Regiment* (London, 1924), Vol. III, p. 213.
16. Anon., *The History of the Eighth Battalion*, p. 256.

Chapter 13

1. M. Connelly, *Steady the Buffs!: a regiment, a region, and the Great War* (Oxford, 2006), pp. 19–20.
2. *Army List*, January 1928. Serving after 1922, his War Office file has not been released.
3. Surrey History Centre, ESR 8227/2/6.
4. J.W. Taylor, *The 2nd Royal Irish Rifles in the Great War* (Dublin, 2005), p. 134.
5. The National Archives, PIN 26/22607.
6. TNA, WO 339/60424 and WO 339/33782.
7. M. Middlebrook, *The Kaiser's Battle 21 March 1918, the First Day of the German Spring Offensive* (*London*, 2000), pp. 405–406.
8. TNA, files in WO 339 and 374.
9. TNA, records in WO 363 (only a minority survive and most are damaged) and WO 364.
10. Connelly, *Steady the Buffs!*, p. 238.
11. WO 95/2215 and H.W. Pearse and H.S. Sloman, *History of the East Surrey Regiment* (London, 1924), Vol. III.
12. E. Astill, *The Great War Diaries of Brigadier General Alexander Johnston 1914–1917* (Barnsley, 2007), pp. 124 and 126.
13. T. Ashworth, *Trench Warfare 1914–1918: The Live and Let Live System* (London, 2000) is an excellent examination of the phenomenon.
14. R.C. Sherriff and V. Bartlett, *Journey's End*, p. 130, quoted in Ashworth, *Trench Warfare*, p. 30.
15. Connelly, *Steady the Buffs!*, p. 249.

Chapter 14

1. Sir J.E. Edmonds, *The Occupation of the Rhineland 1918–1929* (London, 1987), p. 13.
2. The National Archives, reports from series WO 161.
3. Surrey History Centre, ESR/25/BIRT.
4. SHC, ESR1/12/12.
5. See, e.g. Imperial War Museum, 4229 83/3/1 – memoir of R.A. Backhurst, a March 1918 POW from 8/R West Kent, 24th Division.
6. TNA, WO 363.
7. Edmonds, *The Occupation*, pp. 30–32, 48–52.
8. Ibid., p. 51.

9. TNA, WO 363.

10. Commonwealth War Graves Commission website at: http://www.cwgc.org.

11. TNA, WO 339/113655.

12. TNA, WO 95/2215. All further references to the battalion war diary are from this.

13. IWM, Q.7711 and 7712.

14. TNA, WO 363.

15. TNA, WO 364.

16. TNA, files in series WO 339 and 374 and PIN 26/20016 (Toplis).

17. TNA, WO 363.

Chapter 15

1. The National Archives, WO 339/69081.

2. R.C. Sherriff, *No Leading Lady: an autobiography* (London, 1968), pp. 33–35.

3. Ibid., p. 37.

4. Ibid., p. 38.

5. Ibid., p. 109.

6. Surrey History Centre, ESR/25/CLARK.

7. Sherriff, *No Leading Lady*, p. 35.

8. Ibid., p. 318.

9. SHC, ESR/25/CLARK10. SHC, ESR/19/2/2.

11. *The Times*, 10 February 1955.

12. R.C. Sherriff, 'My Diary', *Journal of the East Surrey Regiment, Vol. 1, Nos 1–4 and Vol. II, Nos 1–2 New Series* (November, 1937), p. 190.

13. *London Gazette*, 20 September 1918.

14. TNA, B 9/998.

15. TNA, J 77/2875.

16. Sherriff, 'My Diary' (May 1938), p. 263.

17. TNA, WO 339/34462.

18. Sherriff, 'My Diary' (May 1937), p. 111.

19. TNA, WO 339/40639.

20. SHC, 2332/Box 44. There is no Morris in the battalion's list in Anon., *Soldiers Died in the Great War 1914–19 Part 36 The East Surrey Regiment* (London, 1920), so I hope he survived the war.

21. Sherriff, 'My Diary' (May 1938), p. 263.

22. R.C. Sherriff and V. Bartlett, *Journey's End* (London, 1969), p. 173.

Chapter 16

1. Surrey History Centre, 3813 Box 8, *Journal of the East Surrey Regiment* (May 1937), p. 145 and Hannan papers.

2. R.C. Sherriff, *No Leading Lady: an autobiography* (London, 1968), p. 317.

Bibliography

Unpublished Sources

Imperial War Museum (IWM)

Memoirs and papers of soldiers of 24th Division, including P191 (Abraham), 83/3/1 (Backhurst), P176/20/1 (Billman), 88/18/1 (Lambert), 76/19/1 (Lillywhite), 66/304/1 (Lodge Patch), 81/23/1 (Nurse), P472 (Tower), 87/13/1 (Westmacott).
Sound recording 11043 (Miller).

University of Leeds

Liddle Collection, SC Liddle GS 1590, L.C. Thomas interview.

Surrey History Centre (SHC)

2332 and 3813 correspondence and papers of R.C. Sherriff.
ESR series, papers of the East Surrey Regiment and its officers and men.

The National Archives (TNA)

B 9, bankruptcy files.
CAB 45, files of correspondence with the Official Historian
J 77, divorce files
PIN 26, pension files
WO 95, series, war diaries
WO 158/132, report on Loos
WO 161, returned POW reports
WO 213/9, courts martial listings
WO 339 and 374 series, files on officers
WO 363, 'Burnt Records' for other ranks
WO 364, 'Pension Records' for other ranks
WO 372, medal cards

Private Collections

Papers relating to H. Hannan
Diary of Captain G.S. Pirie
Woodbury family legal and financial papers

Printed Works

Anon., *The Army List*, London, various dates.
——, *Das Reserve Infanterie-Regiment Nr. 440 im Weltkrieg*, Oldenburg, 1933.
——, *The History of the Eighth Battalion The Queen's Own Royal West Kent Regiment 1914–19*, London and Aylesbury, 1921.
——, *Kgl. Sächs. 13. Infanterie-Regiment Nr. 178*, Kamenz, 1935.
——, *Officers Died in the Great War 1914–19*, London, 1919.
——, *Soldiers Died in the Great War 1914–19 Part 36 The East Surrey Regiment*, London, 1920.

——, 'To the Last Man and the Last Round', *Queen's Royal Surrey Regiment Newsletter*, May 1972.

——, *Who's Who*, London, 1897–2000.

Ashworth, T., *Trench Warfare 1914–1918: The Live and Let Live System*, London, 2000.

Astill, E., *The Great War Diaries of Brigadier General Alexander Johnston 1914–1917*, Barnsley, 2007.

Bachmann, F. and Pfister, W., *Reserve-Infanterie-Regiment Nr. 223 im Weltkrieg*, Giessen, 1937.

Bamberg, G., *Das Reserve-Infanterie-Regiment Nr. 106 (kgl.sächs.) im Weltkrieg*, Dresden, 1925.

Baumgarten-Crusius, A., *Sachsen in Grosser Zeit*, Vols II and III, Leipzig, 1919–1920.

Bechtle, R., *Der Ulmer Grenadiere an der Westfront-Geschichte des Grenadier-Regiments König Karl (5. Württ.) Nr. 123 im Weltkrieg 1914–1918*, Stuttgart, 1920.

Beckett, I.F.W. and Simpson, K., *A Nation in Arms: A social study of the British Army in the First World War*, Manchester, 1985.

Behrmann, F., *Die Osterschlacht bei Arras 1917, 1. Teil: Zwischen Lens und Scarpe*, Oldenburg and Berlin, 1929.

Chappell, M., *British Battle Insignia 1 1914–18*, London, 1991.

Clarke, D., *British Artillery 1914–19: Field Army Artillery*, Oxford, 2004.

Clifton, R., 'What is a Battalion?', *Stand To!*, December 1990.

Cohen, D., 'War Art', *Stand To!*, January 1996.

Connelly, M., *Steady the Buffs!: a regiment, a region, and the Great War*, Oxford, 2006.

Corrigan, G., *Loos 1915 the Unwanted Battle*, Staplehurst, 2006.

Creighton, Revd O., *With the Twenty-Ninth Division in Gallipoli*, London, 1916.

De Ruvigny, Marquis, *The Marquis De Ruvigny's Roll of Honour: A Biographical Record of His Majesty's Military and Aerial Forces who fell in the Great War 1914–18*, n.p., 1922.

Dierden, M., 'Nellie's Sad Search for Her "Dear Teddy"', *Surrey Advertiser*, 9 November 2007.

Doerstling, P., *Kriegsgeschichte des Königlich Preussischen Infanterie-Regiments Graf Tauentzien von Wittenberg (3. Brandenburgisches) Nr. 20*, Zeulenroda, 1933.

Dudley Ward, C.H., *History of the Welsh Guards*, London, 1920.

Duffy, C., *Through German Eyes The British and the Somme 1916*, London, 2006.

Edmonds, Sir J.E., *History of the Great War Military Operations France and Belgium: 1915 Volume II The Battles of Festubert, Aubers Ridge and Loos*, London, 1928.

——, *History of the Great War Military Operations France and Belgium: 1916 Volume I Sir Douglas Haig's command to the 1st July: Battle of the Somme*, London, 1932.

——, *History of the Great War Military Operations France and Belgium: 1917 Volume II 7th June– 10th November: Messines and Third Ypres (Passchendaele)*, London, 1948.

——, *History of the Great War Military Operations France and Belgium: 1918 Volume I The German March offensive and its preliminaries*, London, 1935, with accompanying appendices volume and map case.

——, *History of the Great War Military Operations France and Belgium: 1918 Volume II March–April: continuation of the German offensive*, London, 1937.

——, *The Occupation of the Rhineland 1918–1929*, London, 1987.

Fiedel, P., *Geschichte des Infanterie-Regiments von Winterfeldt (2. Oberschlesisches) Nr. 23: Das Regiment im Weltkrieg*, Berlin, 1929.

Frankau, G., *Gilbert Frankau's Self Portrait: A novel of his own life ...*, London, 1940.

——, *Peter Jackson, Cigar Merchant ...*, London, 1947.

Freund, H., *Geschichte des Infanterie – Regiments Prinz Carl (4.Grossh.Hess.) Nr. 118 im Weltkrieg*, Gross-Gerau, 1930.

Freydorf, R. von., *Das 1. Badische Leib-Grenadier-Regiment Nr. 109 im Weltkrieg 1914–1918*, Karlsruhe, 1927.

Führen, F., *Füsilier-Regiment Fürst Karl Anton von Hohenzollern (Hohenzollernsches) Nr. 40: Die Hohenzollernfüsiliere im Weltkrieg 1914–1918*, Furtwangen, 1930.

Giesecke, R.A., *Erinnnerungsblätter der 178er*, Vol. I, Dresden, 1917.

Gliddon, G., *The Battle of the Somme, A Topographical History*, Stroud, 1994.

Goes, G., *Der Tag X: Die Grosse Schlacht in Frankreich (21.März–15.April 1918)*, Berlin, 1933.

Graves, R., *Goodbye to All That*, London, 1963.

Griffith, P., *Battle Tactics of the Western Front The British Army's Art of Attack 1916–18*, New Haven and London, 1998.

Gruson, E., *Das Königlich Preussische 4. Thüringische Infanterie-Regiment Nr. 72 im Weltkrieg*, Oldenburg, 1930.

Grüter, O. von, Lorenz, H., Kirch, P. and Schede, W., *Das 2. Badische Grenadier – Regiment Kaiser Wilhelm I Nr. 110 im Weltkrieg 1914–1918*, Oldenburg, 1927.

Hamilton, R.G.A., *The War Diary of the Master of Belhaven*, London, 1924.

Hannan, H., 'Loos Reflections', *Queen's Royal Surrey Regiment Newsletter*, November 1981.

Held, K. and Stobbe, O., *Das Königl. Preuss. Infanterie-Regt. Graf Barufuss (4. Westf.) Nr. 17*, Berlin, 1934.

Herr, G., *Das Königlich-Preussische Mansfelder Feldartillerie-Regiment Nr. 75 im Weltkrieg 1914/18*, Gräfenhainichen, 1934.

Hitchcock, F.C., *Stand To A Diary of the Trenches 1915–18*, London, 1937.

Holmes, R., *The Little Field Marshal: Sir John French*, London, 2004.

——, *Tommy, The British Soldier on the Western Front 1914–1918*, London, 2004.

Huttmann, A. and Krueger, W., *Das Infanterie Regiment von Lutzow (1. Rhein.) Nr. 25 im Weltkrieg 1914–18*, Berlin, 1929.

Jünger, E. (trans. Mottram, R.H.), *The Storm of Steel*, London, 1941.

Kastner, H., *Geschichte des Königlich Sächsischen Reserve-Infanterie-Regiments 242*, Zittau, 1924.

Kitchen, M., *The German Offensives of 1918*, Stroud, 2005.

Klitsch, J., *Kgl. Sächs. Reserve-Infanterie-Regiment Nr. 101*, Dresden, 1934.

Lasch, W., *Geschichte des 3. Unterelsässischen Infanterie-Regiments Nr. 138, 1887–1919*, Saarbruecken, 1937.

Lehmann, H., *Kgl. Sächs Reserve-Jäger-Bataillon Nr. 26*, Dresden, 1923.

Lloyd, N., *Loos 1915*, Stroud, 2006.

Lucas, M.J., 'Their "Journey's End" – the 9th Battalion, East Surrey Regiment in the Great War', *Stand To!*, August 2008.

——, 'From "Extra-Cushy" to Klein Zillebeke – R.C. Sherriff, *Journey's End* and the 9th East Surreys', *Stand To!*, December 2009.

——, 'Great War British Army Officer Records as a Research Source', *Stand To!*, December 2010.

McPhail, H. and Guest, P., *Battleground Europe St Quentin 1914–18*, Barnsley, 2000.

Magnus, P., *Kitchener: Portrait of an Imperialist*, London, 1961.

Makoben, E., *Geschichte des Reserve-Infanterie-Regiments Nr. 212 im Weltkrieg 1914–1918*, Oldenburg, 1933.

Martin, B., *Poor Bloody Infantry: a subaltern on the Western Front 1916–1917*, London, 1987.

Mealyer, P. and Haig, C., 'Jimmy Carpenter's War Diary', *Stand To!*, January 2005–January 2006.

Messenger, C., *Call to Arms, the British Army 1914–18*, London, 2005.

Middlebrook, M., *The Kaiser's Battle 21 March 1918, the First Day of the German Spring Offensive*, London, 2000.

Miles, Captain W., *History of the Great War Military Operations France and Belgium 1916 Volume II 2nd July 1916 to the end of the Battles of the Somme*, London, 1938.

Mitchinson, K.W., *Gentlemen and Officers The Impact and Experience of War on a Territorial Regiment 1914–1918*, London, 1995.

——, *Battleground Europe Epehy*, Barnsley, 1998.

——, *Battleground Europe Riqueval*, Barnsley, 1998.

Moran, Lord, *The Anatomy of Courage*, London, 1945.

Mücke, C., *Das Grossherzoglich Badische Infanterie Regiment Nr. 185*, Oldenburg and Berlin, 1922.

Nausch, P., *Geschichte des Reserve-Infanterie-Regiments Nr. 10*, Zeulenroda, 1930.

Offiziersverein R.I.R. 214, *Geschichte des Grossherzoglich-Mecklenburgischen-Reserve-Infanterie Regiments Nr. 214*, Dessau, 1933..

Orgeldinger, L., *Das Württembergische Reserve-Infanterie-Regiment Nr. 246*, Stuttgart, 1931.

Otto, K., *Das Kgl. Sächs. Feldartillerie-Regiment Nr. 246*, Dresden, 1928.

Panichas, G., *Promise of Greatness: The War of 1914–1918*, Worthing, 1968.

Pearse, H.W. and Sloman, H.S., *History of the East Surrey Regiment*, Vols II and III, London, 1924.
Powell, G., *Plumer the Soldiers' General*, Barnsley, 2004.
Prior, R. and Wilson, T., *Command on the Western Front The Military Career of Sir Henry Rawlinson 1914–1918*, Barnsley, 2004.
Rawson, A., *Battleground Europe Loos–Hill 70*, Barnsley, 2002.
Reymann, H., *Das 3. Oberschlesische Infanterie-Regiment Nr. 62 im Kriege 1914–1918*, Zeulenroda, 1930.
Reymann, M., *Das Infanterie-Regiment von Alvensleben (6. Brandenbg.) Nr. 52 im Weltkrieg 1914/1918*, Oldenburg and Berlin, 1923.
Rogerson, S., *Twelve days on the Somme a Memoir of the trenches, 1916*, London, 2006.
Ross of Bladensburg, *History of the Coldstream Guards 1914–18 Vol. II*, London, 1928.
Schmidt, W., *2. Nassuaisches Infanterie Regiment*, Oldenburg and Berlin, 1922.
Schmidt-Osswald, E., *Das Altenburger Regiment (8. Thüringisches Infanterie Regiment Nr. 153) im Weltkrieg*, Oldenburg and Berlin, 1927.
Schone, M., *1. Bataillon des 2. Kgl. Sächs Fussartillerie-Regiments Nr. 19*, Dresden, 1925.
Schulenberg, Graf. A. von der., *Das Infanterie-Regiment Keith (1. Oberschlesisches) Nr. 22 im Kriege 1914–1918*, Berlin, 1932.
Schultz, Kissler and Schultze, *Geschichte des Reserve-Infanterie-Regiments Nr. 209 im Weltkrieg 1914–1918*, Oldenburg, 1930.
Sheffield, G.D., *Leadership in the Trenches: officer and man relations, morale and discipline in the British Army in the era of the First World War*, Basingstoke, 2000.
Sheffield, G.D. and Bourne, J., *Douglas Haig War Diaries and Letters 1914–1918*, London, 2005.
Sheldon, J., *The German Army on the Somme 1914–1916*, Barnsley, 2005.
——, *The German Army at Passchendaele*, Barnsley, 2007.
Sherriff, R.C., 'My Diary', *Journal of the East Surrey Regiment Vol. 1 No. 1–4 and Vol. II No. 1–2 New Series*, 1936–1939.
——, *No Leading Lady: an autobiography*, London, 1968.
——, *Journey's End*, London, 2000.
Sherriff, R.C. and Bartlett, V., *Journey's End* (the novel), London, 1969.
Simkins, P., *Kitchener's Army*, Manchester, 1985.
Sinner, M. von., *Das 2. Schlesische Jaeger-Bataillon Nr. 6*, Oldenburg and Berlin, 1921.
Stedman, M., *Battleground Europe Guillemont*, Barnsley, 1998.
Taylor, J.W., *The 2nd Royal Irish Rifles in the Great War*, Dublin, 2005.
Van Emden, R. and Humphries, S., *All Quiet on the Home Front*, London, 2003.
Van Emden, R. and Piuk, V. *Famous 1914–1918*, Barnsley, 2008.
Verein ehemaliger Offizier des Regiments, *Das Füsilier-Regiment Prinz Heinrich von Preussen (Brandenburgisches) Nr. 35 im Weltkrieg*, Berlin, 1929.
Vormann, W. von., *Infanterie-Regiment Fürst Leopold von Anhalt-Dessau (1. Magdeburgisches) Nr. 26*, Oldenburg, 1925.
Westlake, R., *Kitchener's Army*, Staplehurst, 2003.

Newspapers and Periodicals

Daily Sketch
London Gazette
Surrey Advertiser
Surrey Comet
The Times

Websites

Commonwealth War Graves Commission at: http://www.cwgc.org/ (for casualties)
Great War Forum at: http://1914-1918.invisionzone.com/forums/index.php (for miscellaneous discussion)
Queen's Royal Surrey Regiment Museum at: http://www.queensroyalsurreys.org.uk/index.shtml (for 9/East Surrey war diary online)

Index

Ranks and titles given are generally those held by individuals when last mentioned. In some cases ordinal numbers for units have been used to avoid confusion with page numbers

Abrams, 2/Lt L.E.   72, 95, 165
Ackermann, *Feldwebel*   128
Ainge, Pte W.   21
Allam, Cpl B.   187
Allenby, Gen Sir E.H.H.   112
American Ambassador   174
Anderson, Lt Col R.J.P.   127
Anderson, Lt Col W.H.   164
Argyle, Pte S.   176
Attew, Pte T.   156
Austin, 2/Lt W.S.   132, 137, 143
Australian Army   101, 145
Avre, Battle of the   140

Baber, 2/Lt W.H.   155, 167, 177
Badcock, Capt M.F.   166
Baden, Grand Duke of   135
Baldwin, Lt Col R.H.   4, 6, 9
Ball, 2/Lt F.G.   57
Ballantyne, L/Cpl D.   20, 174, 175
Barnett, Capt C.E.   6, 19, 28
Barnett, Lt H.T.   28
Bartlett, V.   186
Bate, 2/Lt E.R.H.   19
Bell, Sgt A.   114, 167
Bell, Pte N.   114
Below, Gen O. von   148
Bertling, Dr   19, 20
Billman, Sgt F.W.   7, 12, 15, 19, 28, 42, 43, 44, 49, 50, 54, 56, 71, 73, 78, 86, 96, 97, 100, 101, 102, 103, 108, 109, 117, 122, 139, 188
Birt, Capt W.B.   6, 9, 19, 175
Birtles, Lt E.G.   147
Bish, Pte E.   101
Bishop, 2/Lt B.   132
Blower, Lt M.S.   135, 137, 138, 139
Blümel, Lt   157–158
Bols, Maj Gen L.J.   100, 111, 112
Brauer, Pte   21
Bretell, Maj R.   6, 164
Brinsa, *Unteroffizier*   146
British Army
   General: GHQ 9, 23, 49, 130, 172; War Office 6, 21, 22, 23, 52, 95, 164, 167, 179

Armies: First 10, 11, 12; Second 32, 99; Third 26, 100, 112, 121, 122, 137, 151; Fifth 104, 121, 122, 125, 127, 133, 141, 146; of the Rhine 178
Corps: II 104; III 112; X 103; XI 11, 12, 23; XIV 53; XVII 151; XVIII 122, 130; XIX 121, 122, 128, 133, 135, 137, 143
Divisions: 1st Cavalry 122, 127; 2nd Dismounted 121; Guards 11, 12, 19, 23, 29, 152, 154, 155, 157, 170; 1st 14, 15; 2nd 23; 3rd 54; 6th 26, 53; 7th 63; 8th 130, 133; 12th 119; 16th 59; 20th 59, 159; 21st 13, 14, 15, 16, 17, 19; 24th *passim*; 25th 146; 41st 109, 178; 42nd 86; 50th 128, 130; 55th 114; 61st 122, 125, 126, 127, 128; 63rd 151; 66th 122, 127, 130; London 178
Brigades: 9th 169; 17th 26, 28, 36, 119, 122, 124, 128, 130, 131, 152; 63rd 17; 71st 14, 26; 72nd *passim*; 73rd 29, 59, 101, 104, 106, 122, 154; 122nd 178; 1st London 178
Cavalry and Yeomanry: 6th Dragoons 167; 11th Hussars 127, 129; Life Guards 116; Surrey Yeomanry 6, 165, 167
Artillery: 108th Battery RFA 126
Engineers: Royal Engineers 26, 28, 79, 80, 95, 96, 152
Infantry: 1/8 Argyll & Sutherland Highlanders 125, 126; Artists' Rifles 6, 52, 72, 116, 167; Bedfordshire Regt 116, 143; Border Regt 169; Buffs 4, 7, 9, 163; 8/Buffs 7, 9, 17, 19, 21, 26, 28, 46, 61, 64, 66, 83, 85, 119, 169; Cameron Highlanders 143; Civil Service Rifles 51, 95; Coldstream Guards 154, 157; Durham Light Infantry 168; 15/Durham 15; East Surrey Regt 4, 5, 6, 25, 36, 57, 71, 75, 95, 116, 163, 179, 187, 189; 1/East Surrey 4, 6, 71, 75, 167; 2/East Surrey 116, 167; 7/East Surrey 9, 119; 8/East Surrey 52, 116, 147, 178; 9/East Surrey *passim*; 10/East Surrey 6, 25; 12/East Surrey 96, 178, 179; 11/Essex 17; Gloucestershire Regt 166; Hertfordshire Regt 116; 12/Highland Light Infantry 164; Honourable Artillery Company 116; 2/Leinster 26, 29, 49, 59, 66, 74, 75, 77, 83, 90, 119, 170; Lincolnshire Regt 144; 4/Lincolnshire 164; London Rifle Brigade 5;

London Scottish 51; 4/Loyals 114; 10/Loyals 143, 144, 164, 168; Manchester Regt 169; Middlesex Regt 168, 184; 13/Middlesex 65, 66, 170; 7/Northamptonshire 83, 154; North Staffordshire Regt 164; 1/North Staffordshire 26, 28, 44, 46, 59, 64, 106, 113, 121, 123, 124, 125, 127, 140, 142, 143, 149, 152, 153, 157, 159, 170; Northumberland Fusiliers 179; 'Public Schools Battalion' 57; Queen's R Regt 4; 8/Queen's 7, 46, 53, 59, 66, 72, 74, 83, 106, 119, 123, 127; Queen's Westminster Rifles 116; 3/Rifle Brigade 26, 59, 61, 66, 131, 132; 10/R Dublin Fusiliers 129; R Scots 51; R Fusiliers 52, 63, 166, 168; 1/R Fusiliers 26, 59, 93; 12/R Fusiliers 66, 85, 119; 23/R Fusiliers 178; R Irish Rifles 168; 2/R Irish Rifles 166; R Sussex Regt 167; 9/R Sussex 36, 66, 90; R Warwickshire Regt 143; 8/R West Kent 7, 8, 31, 53, 85, 100, 112, 121, 122, 123, 124, 135, 137, 140, 142, 146, 152, 153, 154, 156, 157, 158, 159, 160; Seaforth Highlanders 169; 12/Sherwood Foresters 126, 129, 130; South Lancashire Regt 169; 2/Welch 15, 17, 23; West Yorkshire Regt 52, 112; 10/West Yorkshire 166–167

Corps and other formations: ASC 96, 126, 160, 166; 24th Divisional Depot Battalion 130; 15/Entrenching Battalion 143; 19/Entrenching Battalion 129, 130, 135; 73rd Field Ambulance 126; 74th Field Ambulance 82; Inns of Court OTC 52; MGC 166; 24th Machine Gun Battalion 124; RAMC 33, 95, 126, 166; RAOC 188; RFC 97, 166; Tank Corps 100, 166; 72nd Trench Mortar Battery 155

Brooks, Lt 159
Brown, Maj J.C. 144, 165, 178
Brüchmuller, *Oberst* G. 123
Brunt, Pte 75
Budd, Pte 22
Budgeon 53

Cambrai, Battles of 114, 120, 151, 152, 170
Cameron, Lt Col E.A. 143–144, 149, 151, 152, 154–155, 156, 158, 159, 164, 165, 171, 178, 188
Campbell, Lt A.C.P. 19
Canadian Army 33, 37, 39, 40, 46, 53, 87, 88, 90, 126, 144, 148
Cape Mounted Rifles 6
Caporetto, Battle of 118, 120
Capper family 26
Capper, Maj Gen J.E. 23, 26, 32, 49, 57, 59, 65, 83, 100
Carpenter, L/Cpl J. 7, 8, 28
Carter, 2/Lt G.S. 114, 116, 167, 171
Castle, 2/Lt A.B.G. 64
Cattell, Cpl R. 25, 101
Chappell, Pte J.W. 180

Chemin des Dames, Battles of 81, 113, 119, 122, 146
Childs, L/Sgt W.F. 32
Churcher, Lt G.L.G. 149
Churchill, W.L.S. 93, 148, 177, 183, 188
Clark, Lt Col C.A. 36, 51, 64, 66, 71, 72, 78, 79, 82, 83, 97, 110, 113, 117, 125–126, 128, 129, 137, 139, 140, 143, 164, 165, 167, 171, 179, 183, 185, 187, 188
Claughton, J. 169
Cole, Pte 79
Collinson, Capt A.A. 19
Connelly, Prof M. 163, 171
Corley, 2/Lt W.R. 116
Coutts, 2/Lt N.V. 19
Cowper, Lt C.R. 114, 179
Coxhill, Pte W.H. 65
Crabb, 2/Lt R.B. 130, 132
Cutt, Pte E. 8, 21

Dabbs, Nellie 8, 21
Daly, Maj Gen A.C. 112, 115, 144, 150
Davies, 2/Lt E.W. 83
Dealtry, Capt H.A.B. 19
Deininger, *Musketier* G. 35
de la Fontaine, Lt Col H.V.M. 25, 31, 50, 51, 52, 54, 57, 63, 66, 86, 95, 109, 111, 163, 164, 170, 171
Dennison, Pte W. 176
Denny, 2/Lt J.L.B. 64
Dorsett, Pte H. 21
Douglass, Capt A.H. 143, 184, 186
Dugdale, Sgt. J. 147, 171
Duggan, Brig Gen 106

Eatwell, Pte F.T. 139
Elverson, Lt R.W. 6, 17, 19, 22
Epictetus 102
Ericson, 2/Lt E.C. 167

Fenwick, Capt B.A. 6, 17, 19, 21, 187
Fletcher brothers 21
Foch, *Maréchal* F. 178
Foot, Sgt W.D. 78
Frankau, Capt G. 5, 6–7, 8, 9, 179, 187, 188
Franz Ferdinand, Archduke 3
French Army 9, 10, 11, 13, 14, 15, 24, 29, 33, 39, 40, 48, 53, 54, 73, 74, 99, 117, 118, 120, 121, 122, 135, 137, 140, 147
French, FM Sir J.D.P. 10, 11, 12, 22, 23

Gallipoli campaign 11, 32, 37, 94, 104
Gates, Pte A. 109
German Army
  Armies: Second 122; Seventeenth 148; Eighteenth 122, 123
  Corps: III 122, 133, 135; IV 14; XIV 122; LI 122; XXII Reserve 35

Divisions: 1 Guard 135; 4 Guard 122, 127; 5
Guard 115, 119, 170; 5th 132; 7th 13, 14, 15;
8th 13, 14, 15, 77; 12th 108, 109, 111; 23rd 133;
26th 33; 27th 57, 67; 28th 135; 42nd 144–145,
147; 56th 61, 65, 89, 90; 111th 59; 113th 122,
123, 127, 128, 130, 133; 117th 13, 14, 15, 40;
123rd 13, 15, 29, 31; 183rd 113, 114, 115;
195th 100; 206th 135; 207th 109; 208th 122,
127, 151, 156, 157; 4 Bavarian 61; 10 Bavarian
106; 11 Reserve 88, 89; 22 Reserve 106, 108; 23
Reserve 74; 36 Reserve 147; 45 Reserve 40, 42,
46, 47; 46 Reserve 35; 48 Reserve 156, 157;
54 Reserve 35; 79 Reserve 88; 9 Bavarian
Reserve 119
Artillery: FAR 75 13, 15; FAR 225 128; FAR
246 31; FAR 267 127; Fs AR19 15, 133; Fs AR
Batt 157 127
Infantry: IR 17 145, 146, 147; IR 20 115; IR 23
109, 110; IR 24 130; IR 25 127, 156, 157; IR 26
13, 14, 15, 16, 19, 20; FR 35 61, 62, 63, 89;
FR 36 123; FR 40 135; IR 52 132–133; IR 54
147, 149; IR 62 109, 110; IR 66 123, 126,
127–128, 130; IR 72 77, 78, 83, 84, 85; FR 73
59; IR 88 61, 63, 65; LGR 109 135; GR 110
135, 139–140; IR 118 61, 62, 89; IR 120 58;
IR 121 33; GR 123 57, 58; IR 127 58; IR 153
14, 15, 17, 19; IR 157 14, 16; IR 165 15, 18;
IR 178 15, 17, 29; IR 182 13; IR 184 114; IR 185
127, 156, 157; IR 418 113, 114; Bavarian IR 5
66; Jäg R8 100; RIR 10 88; RIR 32 123, 133;
RIR 65 151, 156, 157; RIR 82 106; RIR 93 127;
RIR 101 74; RIR 106 14, 17, 29; RIR 209 40,
44, 45; RIR 210 44; RIR 211 47; RIR 212 40,
42, 44, 45, 46; RIR 214 35, 36; RIR 221 157;
RIR 223 157–158; RIR 242 40; RIR 246 35, 36;
RIR 440 113; Bavarian RIR 8 106; RJäg B24
100; RJäg B26 35–36; *Radfahrer* Brigade/
Radfahrer R 26 157
Other formations: 2nd Guard *Ersatz Pionier*
Batt 149; *Pionier* Company 252 156; *Pionier* R
36 43; *Sturmpanzerkraftwagen-Abteilungen* 11
and 15 151
Gibbs, Pte R.J.   43
Gold, 2/Lt R.C.   64, 66
Gough, Gen Sir H. de la P.   103, 104, 111, 121,
122, 127, 135, 140, 188
Grant, Lt S.K.   78, 137
Graves, Capt R. von R.   23
Griffiths, Dvr   126

Hadenham, 2/Lt L.G.   52
Haig, FM Sir D.   10, 11, 12, 13, 14, 22, 23, 48,
49, 81, 99, 103, 111, 118, 119, 122, 140, 147
Haines, 2/Lt E.A.   64
Haking, Lt Gen R.C.B.   11, 12, 19, 23
Haldane, Maj Gen Sir J.A.L.   178
Halliday, Corp F.   57
Hamilton, Lt Col R.G.A.H.   32, 33, 40, 104, 111

Hammond, Pte A.E.   149
Handford, 2/Lt F.S.   35, 171
Hannan, Pte H.   25, 50–51, 52, 56, 188
Hardiker   64
Hartley, Lt G.C.   82
High, Capt P.   72, 102, 144, 183, 184, 187
Hill, Pte W.   52
Hilton, Maj C.   51, 54, 59, 71, 73, 74, 79, 82, 95,
97–98, 143, 144, 158, 159, 165, 179, 183, 187
Hindenburg, *Generalfeldmarschall* P. von   81, 120
Hitchcock, Capt F.C.   26, 29, 49, 50, 59, 61, 66,
75, 77, 82–83
Hitler, A.   187
Holland, Lt Gen A.E.H.   177
Hollins, A/Sgt H.J.   167
Homewood, 2/Lt R.J.   117
Horlock, L/Cpl A.   176
Horne, Gen Sir H.S.   84, 177
Howell, Lt W.S.   43
Howship, Lt R.F.   179
Husk, L/Cpl D.   75
Hyde, CSM G.   141, 156, 167

Indian Army   7, 23, 25
Ingrams, Capt F.R.   63, 64
Ivey, Pte F.   25, 179

Jacob, Lt Gen C.W.   104
James, Lt and QM E.F.   154, 156
Jewson, Pte F.   37
Joffre, *Maréchal* J.J.C.   10, 81
Johnson, 2/Lt J.M.   12
Johnson, Maj   15
Johnson, Pte J.   153, 156
Johnston, Capt A.C.   169
Jünger, Lt. E.   59, 67

Kaiserschlacht   95, 120–141
Kay, Maj Sir W.A.I.   14
Keep, 2/Lt D.W.   167
Kelly, 2/Lt W.S.   167
Kennington, E.   189
Kerckhove, 2/Lt H.V.   153, 156
King's African Rifles   187
Kirk, Pte J.   25
Kitchener, FM Earl   3, 9, 10, 11, 26
Kiver, 2/Lt H.   92, 166
Knight, Capt L.A.   167, 187
Korda, A.   187
Kreidmer   128
Kriegsheim, Maj von   127
Kuhl, *Gen der Infanterie* H. von   104

Ladd, RSM W.   167
Lambert, Pte R.E.   37, 42, 46, 77
Lawford, Maj Gen Sir S.   178
Le Fleming, Lt Col L.J.   111, 117, 125, 128, 164,
165

Lehnert, *Jäger* 36
Lester, Capt F. 130
Levitt, Drum Maj 178
Liddle, P. 188
Lillywhite, 2/Lt G. 45, 46, 52, 56, 57, 59
Lindsay, Capt W.H. 79, 83, 84, 92, 115, 117, 118, 144, 149, 165
Lloyd George, D. 81, 118–119
Loos, Battle of 10–24, 25, 26, 28, 29, 32, 33, 37, 40, 46, 48, 50, 51, 53, 65, 73, 75, 77, 102, 112, 140, 163, 164, 165, 166, 167, 169, 170, 171, 172, 173, 174, 175, 176, 189
Lopez, Pte A. 188
Ludendorff, First QMG E. 81, 118, 120, 133, 141, 147, 148, 151, 158
Luty, 2/Lt F. 114
Lys, Battle of the 144, 146, 147

McNamara, Corp J. 149, 154–155, 169, 172
Maingot, Capt P.S. 152, 156
Mann, Lt T. 140
Marchant, 2/Lt R.H. 33–34, 35, 171
Marcus Aurelius 102
Marne (German 1918 offensive) 147
'Mars' offensive 141
Marshallsay, Pte 22
Marten, L/Cpl H. 20, 174
Martin, 2/Lt B. 59, 61
Marwitz, Gen G. von der 122
Mase, Lt A.O. 79
Masters, Sgt L. 35
Matz offensive 147
Maxwell, Corp 78
Mead 64
Medlock, Sgt G.W. 114, 167
Menin Road Ridge, Battle of 111
Messines, Battle of 44, 100–101, 102, 103, 163
Middlebrook, M. 166
Mitford, Maj Gen B.R. 7, 12, 14, 15, 17, 22, 23, 75, 86
Monro, Lt J.D. 64
Mons, Battle of 71, 158, 188
Moran, Lord 26, 59, 65, 66, 93–94, 95, 96
Morgan, Brig Gen R.W. 115, 122, 143, 172
Morris 185
Morrissey, Pte C. 20, 174
Mortimer, Pte W.J. 114
Murray, 2/Lt K.D. 19
Myall, L/Sgt E. 167

Niemeyer 128
Nilson, 2/Lt A.C. 116, 153, 155
Nivelle, Gen R.G. 81, 99
Nobbs, Capt E. 179
Nurse, Pte 123

Oakey, Lt F.G. 167
O'Connell, Pte F. 37

O'Connor, Capt D.P. 6, 19, 51, 144, 165
Olivier, L. 182
Orchard, 2/Lt A.F. 131–132
Ottley, Maj G.G. 63, 64, 166
Oyston 64

Parthier, *Vizefeldwebel* 146
Passchendaele campaign 103–111, 112, 119, 163, 171, 183, 188
Patch, Capt C.J.L. 53
Pearse, Col H.W. and Sloman, Brig Gen H.S. 29, 38, 149, 169
Peter, *Feldwebel* 18
Picton, Lt J.A. 52, 104, 166
Pilckem Ridge, Battle of 104–111 *see also* Passchendaele
Pirie, Capt G.S. 32, 37, 40, 43, 46, 47, 49, 51, 52, 53, 57, 64, 71, 74, 75, 78, 79, 82, 86, 92, 94, 95, 99, 101, 102, 103, 104, 164, 166
Pledge, Pte H.A. 175
Plested, Pte F. 25
Plumer, Gen Sir H.C.O. 32, 99, 103, 111
Poole, Revd G.D.P. 53, 141
Portuguese Army 144, 145
Pratt, 2/Lt A.V. 125
Price, Lt Col 26
Prior, R. and Wilson T. 49
Pugh, Sgt 9
Puttock, 2/Lt H.H. 166

RAF 166, 188
Ramsay, Maj Gen Sir J.G. 7, 22, 23, 26
Rivers, 2/Lt G.C. 52
Rochell, Pte A.J. 96
Rogerson, S. 52
Romer, Col 21
Rosières, Battle of 137–140
Royal, 2/Lt J.H. 104
Russian Army 10, 24, 37, 48, 144

Sadler, 2/Lt W.D. 117
Sambre, Battle of 158
Sanders, Lt Col F.L. 6, 9, 22, 23, 25, 163, 165
Saville-Farr, Maj A.J.M. 6–7
Schofield, Capt H.N. 51
Schooling, 2/Lt P.H. 40
Seaton, 2/Lt J.W.S. 125
Seel, Lt F.E. 95, 116
Sheffield, Lt and QM W.P. 167
Shere, Pte C.W. 109
Sherriff, Capt R.C. 4, 5, 23, 72–73, 74, 79–80, 85–86, 89, 92–93, 95, 97–98, 102–103, 106–108, 115, 116, 117–118, 181–188
Simmons 101
Skinner, Corp C.W. 77–78
Somme, Battle of (1916) 24, 26, 47–67, 71, 72, 74, 77, 81, 86, 88, 94, 95, 96, 97, 98, 101, 102,

104, 108, 112, 133, 139, 141, 164, 170, 171, 183, 184
Spencer, Maj W. St J.   179–180
Spofforth, 2/Lt H.R.M.   93
Spurling, 2/Lt H.S.   51
Staehle, *Ersatzreservist*   35
Stanbury, L/Corp G.   17, 22, 96
Steidle, *Unteroffizier*   35
Stewart, Col C.G.   11, 14, 23–24
Stoecklern, *Oberst* von   130
Summers, Capt W.G.T.   25, 46, 64, 75, 83, 84, 94, 167, 171, 179, 183, 187, 188
Swanton, Lt Col T.W.S.   75, 80, 82, 86, 110, 164, 187
Sweny, Brig Gen W.F.   86, 109

Tanner, CSM J. and family   110–111
Taylor, 2/Lt F.F.   109
Taylor, Capt M.W.   156
Tetley, Capt G.S.   6, 37, 51, 63, 64, 73, 79, 82, 85, 86, 94, 97, 102, 118, 179, 187
Tew, Lt Col H.S   71, 73, 75, 164, 187
Thomas, Maj Gen L.C.   75, 83–84, 94, 115, 123, 126, 165, 179, 183, 187, 188
Toplis, Lt A.A.D.   166
Tower, Maj K.F.B.   75, 86, 104, 106
Trench, 2/Lt N.C. Le P.   166
Trenchard, Lt C.W.   92, 183, 185
Trinidad Mounted Infantry   95
Trish, L/Cpl A.   64, 126
Turner, Pte   128

Urban, 2/Lt A.   64

Vaughan, Capt J.L.   35, 51, 53, 56, 57
Verdun, Battle of   33, 39, 48, 61, 81, 88, 104
Vimy Ridge, Battle of   90–91

Waldron, Capt W.A.V.   166
Walker, Capt T.E.   141

Wallace, Capt R.L.   156
Warre-Dymond, Maj G.W.   97–98, 106, 107, 108, 117–118, 126, 135, 137, 140, 165, 171, 183–184, 185, 188
Watford, Pte J.   176
Watmore, Pte   43
Watts, Lt Gen Sir H.H.   121, 130, 137
Webb, L/Cpl G.   66
Webb, 2/Lt L.H.   106, 110, 118, 183
Webster, Capt   126
Welch, Maj H.V.   6, 19, 21–22, 164
Westmacott, Maj T.H.   23, 134, 135, 140, 159, 160
Whale, J.   182
Whiteman, Capt E.L.   6, 47, 82, 140–141, 143, 144, 152, 160, 165
Wigg, Pte E.W.   179, 187–188
Wilhelm II, Kaiser   34, 35, 79, 120, 159
Williams, Lt A.E.   156
Williams, Pte M.J.   174
Wills, Lt S.W.   53
Wilson, Pte A.   141
Wishart, Lt C.W.E.   95
Wood, 2/Lt E.J.   146
Woodbury, Pte C.   25, 42, 96, 117, 155, 177
Wrigley, Pte J.   176
Wyatt, 2/Lt W.A.   166

Yalden, 2/Lt T.H.   167
Youngman, Lt J.M.   46
Ypres
    First Battle of   11, 26, 28, 35
    Second Battle of   26, 28
    Third Battle of *see* Passchendaele

Zimmer, *Vizefeldwebel*   35